TOM BALDWIN is a political writer who worked in Westminster and Washington for *The Times* before becoming director of communications for the Labour Party. He is the author of several books and is the biographer of Keir Starmer.

MARC STEARS is the inaugural Director of the UCL Policy Lab. He was previously Director of the Sydney Policy Lab, a Professor of Political Theory at the University of Oxford and chief speechwriter to the Labour Party.

England

Seven Myths That Changed a Country – and How to Set Them Straight

Tom Baldwin and **Marc Stears**

BLOOMSBURY PUBLISHING

LONDON · OXFORD · NEW YORK · NEW DELHI · SYDNEY

BLOOMSBURY PUBLISHING
Bloomsbury Publishing Plc
50 Bedford Square, London, WC1B 3DP, UK
Bloomsbury Publishing Ireland Limited,
29 Earlsfort Terrace, Dublin 2, D02 AY28, Ireland

BLOOMSBURY, BLOOMSBURY PUBLISHING and the Diana logo are trademarks of
Bloomsbury Publishing Plc

First published in Great Britain 2024
This edition published 2025

A catalogue record for this book is available from the British Library

ISBN: HB: 978-1-5266-4623-1; PB: 978-1-5266-4624-8
EBOOK: 978-1-5266-4627-9; EPDF: 978-1-5266-4628-6

2 4 6 8 10 9 7 5 3 1

Typeset by Newgen KnowledgeWorks Pvt. Ltd., Chennai, India
Printed and bound in Great Britain by Clays Ltd, Elcograf S.p.A.

To find out more about our authors and books visit www.bloomsbury.com
and sign up for our newsletters
For product safety related questions contact productsafety@bloomsbury.com

To Rebecca, Frankie and Arthur, and Lizzy and Freya

Contents

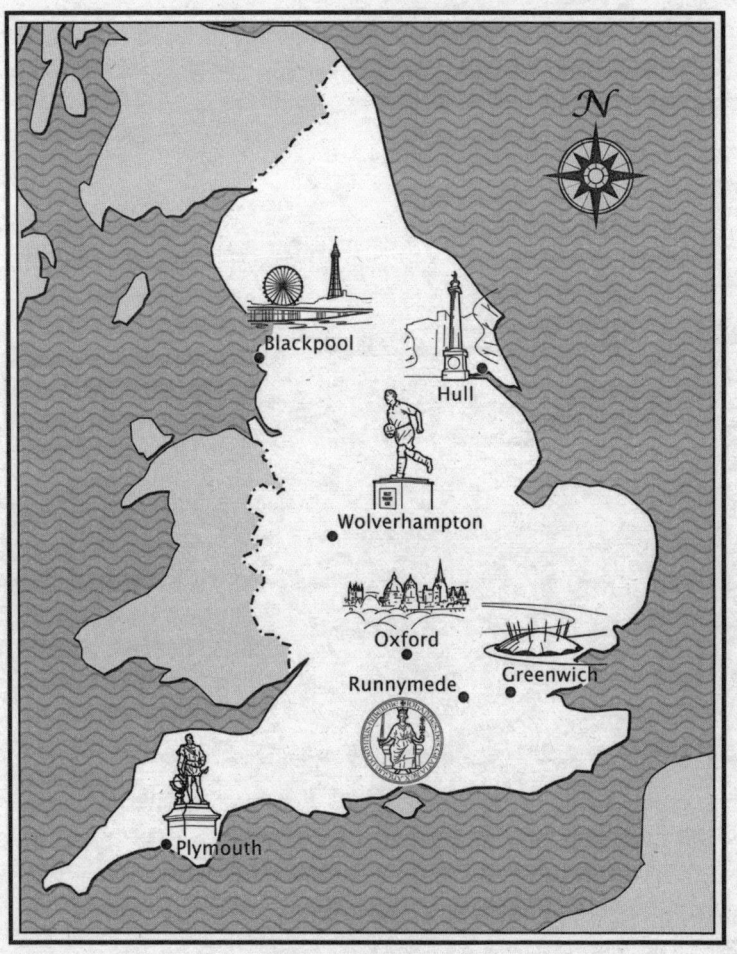

N

Blackpool

Hull

Wolverhampton

Oxford

Runnymede

Greenwich

Plymouth

Introduction

This book is about seven ordinary places where people live, seven extraordinary stories that are not really true and one famous old country that does not properly exist. It is a book about England.

We have travelled from muddy fields in the Home Counties, to the naval port of Plymouth and then on to a commercial one in Hull. We have visited Wolverhampton in the old industrial heart of this country and a soulless new district on the edge of London. We have spent weekends away in the worn-down resort of Blackpool, as well as the well-upholstered seat of learning that is Oxford. While we have been roaming around England's towns and cities, the focus of national attention has swung around from Brexit to Covid, from culture wars on Twitter to real wars in Ukraine and Gaza, from noisy public drama in Westminster to the quiet crisis experienced behind front doors over the cost of living.

Many people have been asking who they should blame, how will they get by, where do they go from here? But the answers proffered are not rooted in real lives. Instead, they are myths – a mixture of fairy tales, exaggerations, omissions or sometimes outright lies – that are boomingly grandiose by design and invariably blown up out of all proportion.

There are those who talk of restoring an English birthright of liberty. Others say England needs to regain the confidence to ride, if not rule, the waves. Still more yearn for some old-fashioned morality with which, they claim, England once civilised a savage world. Then there is an inward-looking story of an enchanted island that only needs more barb-wired sovereignty and fewer foreigners to carry on, alone. On occasions, a pick 'n' mix of nostalgia is just flung in the face of global modernity. Sometimes, a patriotic working class is portrayed as fighting an existential battle against an uncaring cosmopolitan elite. And, sitting on top of all this, there is an English Establishment that supposedly keeps the nation's show on the road while changing nothing too much about anything at all.

Together, these over-inflated myths have resembled the barrage balloons once sent up high above England's skies to protect against the wartime Blitz. So tangled up are they, that they can never help us make sense of the present. And, as they cast their bloated shadows, they stop the people below from seeing a way forward towards a more hopeful future.

Our key purpose is to let some of the air out of these puffed-up versions of England. Such a process should not, though, be confused with being unpatriotic or erasing parts of the country's history. Instead, letting the myths shrink a little is a precondition for coming to terms with its past, dealing with problems now and plotting a path towards a better future.

We are conscious this moderation makes us outliers in an era when so many have sought to use these myths to diagnose simple causes of decline and even more simplistic cures that will make this country 'great again'. But, far from being great or even the greatest, England is not even a country in an official sense. It has neither sovereignty nor passports, embassies nor armed forces. Unlike other bits of the United Kingdom, England does not have its own parliament or elected leader. For most of the last century, England only had formal representation in some of the sports like football or cricket that the English invented – and at which their national teams so often disappoint – or in the public relations outpourings from the heritage, arts and tourism quangos that bear this nation's name.

For a long time that was enough because a vibrant, brilliant England has always clearly been there, existing – as it still can – in people's imaginations. Generations of poets and painters, novelists and musicians, have tried to give shape to this nation. Some have been pompous, grandiloquent and overblown. But not all. In fact, many of the best-loved and longest-lasting have been based around England's ordinary people and their lives.

They have described a know-it-when-you-feel-it 'Englishness' that spreads like love-it-or-hate-it Marmite across the generations. In the 1930s the writer J. B. Priestley went on an *English Journey*, exploring a mundane and newly democratic nation of bypasses, filling stations and 'bungalows with tiny garages'. During the Second World War, George Orwell described how England was held together by 'solid breakfasts and gloomy Sundays, smoky towns and winding roads'. A little later T. S. Eliot included 'the dart board, Wensleydale cheese, boiled cabbage cut into sections, beetroot in vinegar', along with his more predictable '19th-century Gothic churches and the music of Elgar'. In the 1970s, Ian Dury sang about 'Winkles, Woodbines, Walnut Whips, Vera Lynn and Stafford Cripps'. More recently, the self-described anarcho-Communist journalist Ash Sarkar grudgingly came up with her own list of ephemera, albeit one comprised of a single item. 'Crisp sandwiches,' she said, 'you don't get them in other cultures.'

England becomes more problematic, however, when it is a political concept. Many subjugated and enslaved people recognised England as the heart and chief beneficiary of a global empire sustained by brute power. Resentment has flowed too among those who share these Isles with an English people who have so often casually conflated their identity with 'Britain'. When English politicians boasted about how their nation had successfully repelled invasion for 1,000 years, they usually ignored how Scotland, Wales and Ireland were all invaded by the English. Coins used across the UK still bear the face of Queen Elizabeth II, even though Scotland never had an Elizabeth I. 'God Save the King' is played at the start of England's football matches despite that anthem and king supposedly representing the whole of the UK. Such elisions reflect how England, which represents 85 per cent of the UK population, dominates Britain. Even during the mid-2000s when there was briefly a Scottish prime minister at Number 10 Downing Street and a Scottish chancellor of the exchequer next door at Number 11, the imbalance of economic and political power meant England's interests were always paramount.

These sharper, political conceptions of England once nestled beneath the blanket of Britain, with further layers of insulation provided until recently by still bigger political identities. There was a post-imperial Commonwealth, a 'special' relationship with the United States and membership of the European Union. All of these ensured the question of England was muffled in politics to the point where it appeared harmless or obscure.

These covers have slipped recently – as businesses are said to do into bankruptcy – gradually, then suddenly. In the first decade of this century, devolution and growing inequality steadily loosened the ties that once bound Britain together. At the same time any lingering relevance of the Commonwealth unravelled into a globalised economy, while Britain's tightly bound strategic relationship to America frayed in the heat of an unpopular war in Iraq. Then the decision by the UK in 2016 to throw off its membership of the EU exposed the Union's cracks and some of England's least attractive features.

All of these changes are still being worked through. It meant that this bare-faced England was feeling uncomfortably exposed with itself when its old queen, whose long life had served as an enduring symbol of unity, died in 2022. In the final years of her reign, constitutional shifts had taken place at the very same time that tensions between people grew. Ugly old scars over social class or immigration were reopened. Divides have widened between north and south, towns and cities, young and old. Multiplying global problems – the so-called 'polycrisis' of pandemics, mass migration, war and climate change – have pushed voters this way and that with many of them losing faith in politics to make any difference.

It was in this context that England became fertile territory for myth-makers of all kinds and particularly for an angry kind of politics. And, while some of that heat might seem to have dissipated with the departure of polarising figureheads like Boris Johnson or Jeremy Corbyn, there is little reason to suppose it has gone away entirely – and plenty to suggest it will come back soon. Even the remarkable success of the 2024 TV drama, *Mr Bates vs The Post Office*, can be seen as once again demonstrating the potency of a particular idea of England – the opening episode shows Jo Hamilton running into her Hampshire village sub-post office with a tray of fresh baked scones – which has been betrayed by a remote politics and unfeeling globalised institutions. Whatever happens in the years ahead, different conceptions of England and Englishness will matter hugely – whether we like it or not. And there are many English people who wish this wasn't so. There is a noteworthy minority, especially among those with university degrees, who will say that they've never much liked England. Sometimes this is justified as high-minded principle. They object to being dragged into a debate that, to them at least, seems like an overheated old people's home with distinct savoury smells and where all the residents are trapped in the past. These people devour bestselling books which denounce England's history of slave-trading. The youthful among them spend their summers trying to pull down statues or railing against the iniquity of the universities educating them. Such loathing sometimes descends into the unintentionally hilarious. We have friends who refuse to go walking in the English countryside because they cannot stomach its pastoral connotations – 'all those fields and thatched cottages' – or who say they consciously avoid the places where people put 'those little flags up' during events like a royal jubilee or a coronation.

This is as much of a dead end as the myths they so despise. Some English people would now doubtless prefer to source their identity elsewhere, maybe as citizens of Europe or of the world. But the former is no longer an option and the latter has never been available other than rhetorically. No one living in England has much of a choice over whether England matters; it just does. Anyone disdaining anything for long enough stops paying attention to how it's doing or trying to improve it. And there is a real risk of leaving to others the task of defining what this country means.

Our book argues that today's England needs neither the disdain of those who care for it least, nor the weird restoration projects from those who profess to love it most. Instead, our purpose is to set out a different account of a country which people need not love nor loathe.

Whatever their view of England, some readers will still be sceptical that much can be achieved. As authors, they will say, we come from fairly predictable backgrounds and our insights are shaped by them as a result. And it is true that our opportunities have neither been held back by discrimination nor been subject to the 'soft bigotry of low expectations'. Much of our working lives has been spent in some of the most Establishment institutions in the land: the University of Oxford, *The Times* newspaper and the Houses of Parliament. We have worked for think tanks and for various high-profile politicians. There is no point trying to conceal any of this, nor to try to hide our own left-of-centre politics. Indeed, the origins of this book lie in the dimly lit office we shared when we worked for Ed Miliband and helped him with a speech about England which, as is so often the case in politics, was better than it was protrayed. The challenges it presented are no longer overlooked: what is England? Why does it matter? How can we all live with each other?

Lots of people will disagree with our answers. In fact, we have also often disagreed between ourselves. To try to deal with all of this we have sought to build the following chapters not on our own experiences or prejudices, but around the stories of seven different and apparently quite ordinary places in this country. Each has a relationship to one of seven oversized myths about England's past and offers an account of who the English are now, as well as a glimpse of what this country could be. In what follows, we explain how these seven places provide context to the myths associated with them. We pick away at the fabric of each story. And, as we follow the threads of history into current debates, we show how these myths are now being deployed, often in reckless and polarising fashion, by today's politicians.

Of course, we had to make a selection. Other writers might have chosen to make more of myths around Stonehenge and druids, Glastonbury and King Arthur or Lindisfarne and its Venerable Bede. There is no chapter here devoted to the Cotswold-kind of village that so many imagine when they hear the word England. Maybe we could have done more in the east of the country or with one of the big regional cities that have their own identity, or written about an old mining community and a new digital hub. Maybe we should have devoted more space to cricket, or lawn tennis or jam-making or cheese-rolling or gardening. But our book is already long enough.

Our purpose was not to immerse ourselves like an anthropologist, but to look at the face these places present to the world. We have read the histories, then sought out statues, monuments or memorials – or sometimes noticed the lack of them – because what is chosen as worthy of commemoration says so much about how a place sees itself. Similarly, when we spoke to people living in or visiting our seven places, we were neither pretending to be professional ethnographers nor conducting that low form of journalism known as vox pop. We were just trying to get a better sense of how they respond to the myths that are spun in their name.

In addition to these journeys, we have drawn on the culture surrounding them, from great art and literature to television and sport. We have studied those recrafting England's cultural identity like Steve McQueen and Michaela Coel. We have talked directly to some of those, like James Graham, who best understand how that culture interacts with politics, as well as to politicians like Pat McFadden and David Lammy, Michael Gove and Nigel Farage, who have interacted so sharply with that culture. We have spoken, too, to campaigners like Chrisann Jarrett trying to make England's creaking old institutions work for marginalised people, and the vaccine scientist Dame Sarah Gilbert, who used one of them to help save millions of lives.

The chapters follow a sequential path through England's history. Chapter 1 examines the legacy of Magna Carta and the idea the English have a special claim on liberty. Chapter 2 explores England's identity as a race of buccaneering adventurers like Sir Francis Drake and its impact on a post-Brexit nation today. Chapter 3 looks at the way that William Wilberforce's campaign against the slave trade both symbolised and sustained misplaced notions of moral superiority. By Chapter 4, we emerge into the middle of the twentieth century and the myth-making of Enoch Powell who, exploiting the two world wars' worth of insularity, sought to turn England away from the last vestiges of empire and people he deemed too different to be English. Chapter 5 chronicles how an effort to forge a 'New Britain' characterised by global interdependence and a new millennium was ultimately confounded by 'Old England'. Chapter 6 analyses the parody of white and working-class English culture that has emerged in very recent years. Chapter 7 delves into an Establishment that once helped absorb shocks to the system but has been lifted off its moorings and lost its essential connection to the English people.

None of this is meant to lead to despair. Each chapter is deliberately located in the everyday clutter of a real place because that is what really characterises this nation. Once the myths are brought gently back to earth they are not dispensed with entirely because, in the last section of each chapter, we suggest how their deflated form can still help tackle the problems of today.

At a time of accelerating change in everything from genetic mapping and artificial intelligence to the climate itself, we argue there is a grounded hope in the dissonance and chaos of everyday life. Some of this seems particularly relevant given that its publication coincides with the election of a new government led by Keir Starmer who, in his loose-ended ambiguities and disavowal of simple answers, has the potential to resemble England better than any of his predecessors. That is because the most hopeful aspect of this prime minister, just as of the country he leads, is found in what seems ordinary or imperfect.

But we hope this book will be read by people of all parties and of none because at its core is an effort to find a real-life and humbler version of England which belongs to everyone or, at least, to no one in particular.

Runnymede
The English Invention of Liberty

The exact spot where England's liberty was supposedly invented is not in the centre of London with all its grandiose symbols of political power, but an hour or so away on the far side of the suburbs.

Set off from the Houses of Parliament with its statues of Richard 'the Lionheart' and Oliver Cromwell holding their swords, cross the river towards Lambeth Palace, then head towards the secret-but-not-secret MI6 building and a disused gay sauna called Chariots that once claimed to be the biggest in Europe. At Vauxhall station, catch an overground train going further west – past new blocks of flats, parks and the stadium where England plays rugby – before arriving at Staines, the home of the fictional Ali G and where that most sub-urban of household furnishings, linoleum, was once made. Wander up this town's pedestrianised high street, then take the path along the River Thames, the artery of the Home Counties, where you can see the backs of villas with big French windows opening out on to lawns decorated by endless varieties of garden furniture.

Not long after passing under the M25, there is a bend in the river where at last you are in the water meadows at Runnymede, the site for the first myth we will examine in this book, one about this country's relationship with freedom and which, in its most inflated form, claims the whole idea belongs to England.

On 15 June 1215 these fields were where King John was forced to seal Magna Carta. This is a document that through history has been mythologised by conservatives and revolutionaries, as well as liberal intellectuals and populist charlatans. It is still being exploited today as the supposed source of everything from jury trials and freedom from false imprisonment to parliamentary democracy.

The myth-makers say this shows England 'invented freedom' and has a special claim on it now. But anyone reading Magna Carta's sixty-three clauses will only discover that medieval barons had an outsized interest in the navigation of rivers, bridge construction and the location of fish traps. And, far from being uniquely English, the showdown at Runnymede was really between some French-speaking barons and their French-speaking king. One popular theory is that these muddy fields were chosen precisely because the ground was not firm enough to bear the weight of heavy armour and meant they were less likely to turn up ready to kill each other. It was also just a convenient place to meet. The barons had largely got control of London while John had a castle at Windsor, just as Charles III does even now.[1]

For all Magna Carta's often starring role in England's national story in the 800 years since, nobody thought to make a fuss over Runnymede itself until quite recently. From time to time, the water meadows would be used for disreputable activities like duelling. Horse racing was banned from the site at the end of the nineteenth century because it attracted too much crime.[2]

The symbolic significance of this particular patch of land only began to creep up again when Rudyard Kipling, a writer ever keen to burnish England's identity, composed a poem about it in 1911 for a children's history book.

At Runnymede, at Runnymede,
Oh, hear the reeds at Runnymede:–
'You mustn't sell, delay, deny,
A freeman's right or liberty.'
It makes the stubborn Englishry,
We saw 'em roused at Runnymede![3]

Even so, after the First World War a cash-strapped government was still trying to sell the site off to housing developers when a Tory MP and his oil-enriched American wife stepped in to buy the land before later donating it to the National Trust. But that didn't stop twentieth-century suburbia creeping up along the A308 or the site falling under the flightpath of planes heading to nearby Heathrow Airport.

After the Second World War, visitors from the United States, where Magna Carta has long been venerated as an inspiration for its Declaration of Independence, would sometimes arrive and be puzzled to find there was nothing to see. Eventually, in 1957, lawyers from the American Bar Association took matters into their own hands and decided to build their own tribute to the invention of liberty. The result was a scaled-down version of the grand marble memorials found in Washington DC, a floodlit neoclassical rotunda over a stone pedestal bedecked with a blue star and carved with the words 'freedom under law'.

Next came a 1965 tribute to the assassinated President John F. Kennedy, on a symbolic acre of Runnymede gifted by Parliament in perpetuity to the United States in gratitude for his Cold War efforts to defend liberty from Communism. This would later have to be rebuilt after anti-Vietnam War protesters blew it up in 1968. By the time Queen Elizabeth II came to plant an oak there in 1987 as part of National Tree Week, it was really only because the Americans were also doing so – with soil imported from the site of the first English settlement in Virginia – to mark their constitution's bicentenary.

This sense that Magna Carta was something that mattered a whole lot more to the United States than to England was reinforced as recently as 2012 when David Cameron became the first serving British prime minister to appear on a US talk show. The host, David Letterman, asked him to translate 'Magna Carta' from Latin into English. 'Ah, you're testing me there,' said Cameron who had studied Latin at Eton, within rowing distance of Runnymede. There was a pause and laughter from the audience. 'Boy, it would be good if you knew this!' said Letterman. 'Yes, it would, wouldn't it!' replied the prime minister, as it became clear he really couldn't.[4]

All this ignorance and understatement over Magna Carta was, however, about to change.

In 2015, for the 800th anniversary of it being sealed, millions of pounds were scattered by the British government on heritage festivals, historical pageants and library exhibitions to celebrate. A global tour was arranged for some of the surviving original copies of the document. Schools were issued with new teaching materials issued by the government, with pupils being encouraged to debate the idea that 'Magna Carta was the foundation stone for modern democracy' as part of their new commitment to expounding 'British values'.[5]

The government's celebration of Magna Carta included Morris dancers, and church bells being rung, while the National Association of Flower Arrangement Societies did a floral tribute depicting all the different shields of the barons. Events called 'LiberTeas' were organised in places as diverse as Basingstoke, Islamabad and the Falkland Islands where people could 'celebrate, debate or reflect' on the nature of freedom over a hot beverage and a slice of cake.[6] The gift shop at the British Library did a trade in Magna Carta T-shirts, tea towels, quills and, in a bizarre piece of marketing, 'King John pillows'.[7]

But there was nothing particularly 'British' about this 800th commemoration. It blew hot air into the mythology of an English document, sealed by an English king, in which other countries are mentioned primarily as places from where hostages had been taken. The commemoration committee found only one project worth funding in Scotland: a £3,000 information board at the site of Tongland Abbey founded by Alan, Lord of Galloway, whose role in Magna Carta appears to have been on the 'wrong side' as a trusted adviser to King John.[8]

The elements of a national story that get celebrated change over time and there is always a reason when one particular myth is suddenly inflated. That summer's festivities were sandwiched between the Scottish referendum on independence in 2014 and one on membership of the European Union in 2016. It came just a month after David Cameron had surprised himself by winning the first Conservative majority in Parliament for twenty-three years with an election campaign in which he had successfully stoked English fears about the influence Scotland would have wielded if he had lost.

The centrepiece of the Magna Carta commemoration was a summer's day ceremony on 15 June 2015 attended by a full list of the Establishment: ranging from the queen, Prince Philip, Prince William and Princess Anne to the Archbishop of Canterbury, the Master of the Rolls, David Cameron and a Spitfire.[9] When Cameron rose to speak, three years on from his debacle on American TV, he was as powerful as he had ever been or ever would be again. This David Cameron was in no doubt about the significance of what he now effortlessly translated as the 'Great Charter'. 'Eight hundred years ago, on this day,' he said, 'King John put his seal to a document that would change the world. We talk about the "law of the land" and this is the very land where that law – and the rights that flow from it – took root.'

His government had chosen to mark this moment very deliberately. And, unusually for an event involving the queen, Cameron decided to play politics with a speech that fumbled around in Eurosceptic erogenous zones. He took aim at the previous Labour government's Human Rights Act, which was loathed by many Conservatives for, as they saw it, empowering European courts and importing foreign concepts of law. 'Here in Britain, ironically, the place where those ideas were first set out,' he said, 'the good name of human rights has sometimes become distorted and devalued. It falls to us in this generation to restore the reputation of those rights – and their critical underpinning of our legal system.'[10]

Cameron was not the first English politician to press this old document into his service and it's a safe bet he won't be the last. But it didn't do him much good. Barely a year later, he was announcing his resignation as prime minister after losing the referendum he had called on membership of the European Union.

By invoking the myths of an especially English form of freedom, he had been playing with fire. Within twenty-four hours of his Runnymede commemoration, Magna Carta was being warmed up to make the case for Brexit. An editorial in the *Sun* anticipated the Leave campaign's famous slogan of 'Take Back Control', declaring: 'Britain created human rights. When King John set the seal on the Magna Carta 800 years ago today, he made it clear: Nobody is above the law. Not even the King himself … It came about because the people rose up and said they would not allow their rights to be crushed by a faceless body beyond their control … *We say we must take control again*.'[11]

The *Sun* was able to use an old document written in a foreign language for an attack on the European Union because, in common with all the myths of England in this book, Magna Carta is both familiar and obscure. Although most people have heard of it, the details flicker, half-remembered, in and out of national consciousness. A poll in that same commemorative year suggested just 15 per cent of the British public think the Charter is 'well understood'. Given a list of rights it is supposed to have guaranteed, 45 per cent of people identified trial by jury, 40 per cent said protection of private property and 29 per cent freedom of speech. Around a quarter suggested freedom from slavery, freedom of religion, free elections or the freedom to protest. One in nine said it was about 'non-discrimination'.

Not one of those rights was mentioned in Magna Carta, let alone guaranteed by it. Probably the most accurate answer in the whole poll was the 38 per cent of the public who were honest enough to admit they did not know what it meant at all. Given how powerfully this story has resonated through history, though, it is worth spending a little time finding out.

A 'BAD KING' AND 'BAD HISTORY'

In the build-up to the 2015 commemoration of Magna Carta, new – and this time distinctly English – memorials began to mushroom in the water meadows of Runnymede. The first of these was a four-metre-high bronze statue of Queen Elizabeth II, portraying her as she was in the 1960s. It was plonked down beside the Thames at a cost of £300,000 and paid for largely by anonymous private donors. Alongside, a stone pathway was laid called a 'democracy timeline', tracing 'the rulers of England and Great Britain' back to Aethelred the Unready in 978 and taking in a series of disconnected events including the abolition of slavery and publication of Karl Marx's *Communist Manifesto* before declaring Runnymede to be the 'birth-place of freedom'. A nearby cafe provides an antidote to such pom-posity with a choice of 'normal tea' or Earl Grey and warm sausage rolls, alongside a neon sign advertising fish and chips, as well as a brightly lit picture of the Leaning Tower of Pisa to let everyone know it sells ice cream.

The statue did not enjoy universal support locally and most comments at the planning stage objected to the memorial. One said it was 'bizarre and ridiculous' to use a statue of the queen to com-memorate a moment in history usually seen as the first time any one reined in the power of an English monarch. Others worried about the cost of insurance, warning 'there's a real good chance it's going to be graffitied'.[12] But the scheme had enthusiastic backing from Runnymede's Conservative councillors who swatted away the results of the public consultation as unrepresentative nit-picking that 'we did not feel … was particularly significant'.[13] Philip Hammond, then the local MP and foreign secretary, helped unveil the statue on a wet day when dignitaries stood holding umbrellas and council officials struggled to get the plastic sheet off Her Majesty's likeness. Hammond later told his local newspaper there was nothing incongruous in celebrating the events of 1215 with a tribute to royalty. 'The development of our monarchy from King John to Queen Elizabeth represents the principles of Magna Carta,' he said.[14]

The story of Magna Carta and the English invention of liberty usually starts with King John. Since the mid-twentieth century, his place in the national imagination has been guaranteed not only by the history books or the national curriculum, but also by the Disney cartoon *Robin Hood*. Voiced by Peter Ustinov, Disney's John is a mangy, cowardly lion, with a foolish aristocratic accent and a propensity for sucking his thumb, who is outwitted by everyone, including the outlaws of Sherwood Forest. Even his trusty servant and adviser, a snake called Sir Hiss, turns against him. When King Richard 'the Lionheart' triumphantly returns from the Crusades, both John and Hiss are locked up in jail.

In real life, King John was part of a spectacularly dysfunctional French Norman family whose problems put more recent royal scandals to shame. Nicknamed 'Lackland' because his father cut him out of any inheritance, and for years largely ignored by his mother, John spent his youth plotting against his brothers, including Richard, whom he eventually succeeded in 1199. By almost any measure, John's subsequent reign did not go well. He swiftly lost much of England's territory in France, spawning a new nickname: 'Softsword'. He raised taxes and fines to fight wars in an effort to reclaim it, probably murdered his nephew, then fell out with nobles whose families he sporadically kidnapped and killed. He had a particular penchant for starving hostages to death in dungeons. A row with the pope got so intense that weddings and funerals were banned across England, like a medieval version of a Covid lockdown, before John eventually made a humiliating peace by offering up the whole country as a papal fiefdom.[15]

As is the way of these things, some historians claim that John has been treated unfairly. But if Magna Carta is always being venerated as 'good', it seems logical the king who was forced to surrender to its demands must have been 'bad'.

Despite Magna Carta's mythological status, historians are pretty much unanimous in saying that the deal made at Runnymede achieved very little of immediate consequence. The document sealed there was intended to prevent fighting between the English monarch and his barons. In practice, this event signalled the start of internecine violence that lasted for centuries.

Indeed, the fighting began almost as soon as the wax was dry as John went back on his promises. He proceeded to lose the crown jewels in the Wash, another muddy patch of England far away in East Anglia, while leading his army against the rebels. Then he died from dysentery or possibly a 'surfeit of peaches'.

The Charter had to be reissued as early as 1216 by John's successor, his nine-year-old son, Henry III, as an indication of his willingness to govern fairly, only for war to break out again. Another version, with half the original clauses removed, was published in 1225 when Henry came of age. This was just the start of a process in which Magna Carta would be revived and reconfirmed as a means of resolving violent crises before invariably being overridden once more. The legal document most people regard as Magna Carta today dates from 1297 and even that has long since been mostly repealed.

Popular understanding of Magna Carta's contents was not helped by it being written in Latin. This was not even translated into English until three centuries later.[16] Some of its clauses are markedly at odds with modern conceptions of liberty or rights. 'If a man dies owing money to Jews, his wife may have her dower and pay nothing towards the debt from it,' states one. Another says: 'No one shall be arrested or imprisoned on the appeal of a woman for the death of any person except her husband.'

But there are two famous clauses, sometimes known as the Charter's 'golden passage':

No free man is to be arrested, or imprisoned, or disseised, or outlawed, or exiled, or in any other way ruined, nor will we go against him or send against him, except by the lawful judgment of

his peers or by the law of the land. To no one will we sell, to no one
will we deny or delay, right or justice.

Those words have echoed through the history of England and much
of the world over the last 800 years. Even so, they are not what they
seem. Those who think they are an assertion – or reassertion – of
legal principles like a right to trial by jury or release from unlawful
imprisonment through habeas corpus – 'you shall have the body' – are
wide of the mark. Legal scholars say those ideas had not even been
conceived at the time.[17]

Magna Carta was less a charter of fundamental rights than a list
of baronial grievances against what they saw as John's abuse of the
feudal system and a revolt against his tax increases. Barons valued
the privilege of being judged by their 'peers' – or equals – because
medieval England was so manifestly unequal. When they were in
dispute with the king, they didn't want just anybody settling the
argument – they would only allow fellow nobles to judge them. Far
from Magna Carta being evidence of ordinary people rising up to
demand their rights, it was a consequence of a deeply hierarchical
society in which a medieval aristocracy – akin perhaps to modern-
day Russian oligarchs – sought to rein in the use of unbridled power
against them.[18]

Nor was it unique in this regard: similar concepts were bubbling up
through continental Europe at the time. At best, some of the privileges
it granted the barons extended to 'free men', while some historians say
the sheer length of the document was unusual. But the vast majority of
people, the *villeins* or serfs who lived in semi-slavery – not to mention
women of all classes – got nothing.[19]

This has not, however, stopped the myth of Magna Carta having
lasting appeal to people seeking a justice that always seems just beyond
reach. Tom Bingham, a twentieth-century Lord Chief Justice who is
venerated as one of this country's greatest jurists, remained convinced
'Magna Carta was an event that changed the constitutional landscape
in this country and, over time, the world'.[20] And that was because,
not in spite, of what he called all the 'bad history' surrounding it. The
importance of Magna Carta, according to Bingham, is the mythical
power of what people imagine it said, rather than anything that was
actually written down on goatskin in 1215.

One example is the story of English common law. Much has been made over the years of Magna Carta's role in upholding or reasserting the 'law of the land' which is handed down case by case rather than based on abstract codified principles as is more usual in continental Europe.[21] This is one of the mainstays of the myth of English exceptionalism and the distinction did help shape attitudes to liberty over time, even if it came in a rather roundabout fashion.

When Magna Carta was sealed criminal trials were far from being the contest of evidence associated with modern juries. More often it took the form of 'ordeals' of combat, fire or water because God was the best judge of all. The trial of fire was to make the accused hold a hot coal with guilt determined by whether the wound became infected. The trial of water entailed being lowered into a flooded pit by a rope. If those accused floated, they were guilty. If they sank, they were innocent. Modern researchers have discovered the trick of winning such a trial was to avoid eating too much beforehand and not to hold your breath – provided you didn't then drown.[22] After the pope forbade priests from participating in trials by ordeal, they began to be used less frequently across Europe and other methods had to be invented to determine guilt. Roman canon law put more emphasis on the need for at least two witnesses or a confession. England's common law required a lower standard of proof. The consequence was that the English had less need to torture suspects to get a confession, even though they still often dealt with those convicted in the most gruesome fashion.

In the centuries that have passed since, a blurry association with common law has established the idea that Magna Carta somehow guaranteed human rights protecting citizens from unlawful imprisonment or torture. This mattered at moments like the Reformation when England did not – usually – resort to the methods of the Inquisition. It even still mattered when American intelligence officers made sure that waterboarding terror suspects took place on sites like Guantánamo Bay far away from any legal jurisdiction touched by the principles of what people think was in Magna Carta.[23]

Similarly, King John's promise to seek 'the common counsel of the realm' before imposing taxes has been seen over the centuries as laying the foundation stone for parliamentary democracy and the doctrine of 'no taxation without representation'. At the time, this nebulous clause meant no more than consulting a bunch of hereditary barons and wealthy bishops which, at best, might have been some embryonic version of the deeply undemocratic House of Lords. But, as with habeas corpus and jury trials, this aspect of Magna Carta has been built up into another towering and mythical edifice of the origins of England's democracy.

The myth's most ardent proponents have wrapped it up with a story of a distinct English identity and culture slowly reasserting itself after suffering under the 'Norman yoke'. Some have tried to connect Magna Carta with Wat Tyler's Peasants' Revolt or John Wycliffe translating the Bible into his native tongue in the fourteenth century.

But Magna Carta has dropped out of history as often as it dropped in. People whose worldview is based on the idea of this English invention of liberty are sometimes shocked to discover that Magna Carta is not mentioned in any of the historical dramas of the Elizabethan era, including William Shakespeare's *King John*. That began to change with the accession to the English throne of the Scottish Stuart dynasty at the start of the seventeenth century which, along with the Protestant reformation, had begun to complicate England's identity. When the Scottish-bred King Charles I started locking up powerful English people in the 1620s, the story of Magna Carta made a dramatic comeback.

Sir Edward Coke, formerly a crown prosecutor in the trials of both Sir Walter Raleigh on trumped-up charges of treason and the leaders of the Gunpowder Plot, was sacked from his judicial posts for being a little too free-thinking. He responded by reaching back into England's past and dusting down Magna Carta to justify an argument calling for limits on royal power. In his celebrated *Institutes of the Lawes of England*, he claimed that Magna Carta was the basis of English common law and the independence of courts from royal control. Coke invoked Magna Carta again in defiance of absolutist monarchy as he framed the 1628 Petition of Right and what would become the essence of Parliament's case against Charles as England, along with Scotland, Ireland and Wales, descended into a civil war that, given the size of the population, remains the bloodiest conflict ever fought in the British Isles.

The name of Magna Carta was emblazoned on Parliamentarian battle standards alongside anti-papist slogans and was, rhetorically, made flesh during the war. 'Magna Carta is such a fellow,' declared Coke, 'that he will have no "sovereign".'[24] Sir Thomas Fairfax, the commander-in-chief of the New Model Army, described the Charter as 'that which we have fought for' and in 1647 fetched a copy of it out of the Tower of London. When the king was put on trial and sentenced to death in 1649, it was on the grounds that he had subverted 'the ancient and fundamental laws and liberties of this nation'. And when the severed head of Charles I was held up to the crowd in Whitehall on the chilly morning of 30 January that year, it was proof that no man, not even a king, was above the law. Instead of '*Rex* is *Lex*' – the king is law – *Lex* would now be *Rex*: the law was king. The ghost of Magna Carta and its tradition of English liberty, 'the good old cause', had constrained absolute power. Or, at least, so it was said.

MISSION CREEP

Back in 2015, amid all the hype of David Cameron's expensive commemoration, a second new memorial was installed on the water meadows at Runnymede. *The Jurors* is formed of twelve bronze chairs designed to challenge people 'to consider the ongoing significance and influences of Magna Carta'.[25] It was unveiled by Prince William despite its Guyanese British creator, Hew Locke, saying his 'feelings about the Royal Family are ambivalent'.[26]

On the front and back of each chair are symbols depicting the struggle against oppression not just in England but around the world. One has a portrait of suffragette Lillie Lenton in Holloway prison and Oscar Wilde's poem while incarcerated in Reading gaol for homosexuality. There is a tribute to blind trade unionists and a commentary by the scientist Sir Tim Berners-Lee who has called for 'Magna Carta of the internet'. It has nods to the eighteenth-century African American poet Phillis Wheatley, and to Mary Prince, a Black woman who presented an anti-slavery petition to Parliament in 1828. There is an image of the portable spinning wheel for cotton designed by Mahatma Gandhi in resistance to the laws of the British Empire, as well as the loudhailer used by the first openly gay man to be elected to public office in California, Harvey Milk. Another chair shows the house in Yangon where Aung San Suu Kyi was held under house arrest in Myanmar and a *xiezhi*, a legendary figure in Chinese mythology symbolising justice. Still more show Nelson Mandela's prison cell on Robben Island, the *Exxon Valdez* tanker whose oil spill led to new environmental principles, the emancipation of Russian serfs, a boat carrying refugees and another filled with slaves, a place used by British police to imprison indigenous Australians, protesters fighting for the release of political dissidents, the ancient Egyptian goddess of truth and some Chinese script describing Confucian principles of humanity.

The barons who gathered at Runnymede would have been utterly confused by such ideas and any suggestion that this is what they stood for would have been dismissed in some sort of Old French as 'mission creep'. But the message visitors are supposed to take away from such a memorial is that Magna Carta and liberty in England are part of the global battle waged through the ages by the people against the powerful.

This has always been bitterly contested territory. Those for whom it is enough that the king is subject to the law do not need a new monument telling them about Nelson Mandela or Harvey Milk. Others, including some Marxist historians, see Magna Carta and the execution of a king as being about a clash between emerging economic interests because the civil war – like every war and everything – is 'class war'. Still more believe Magna Carta came to symbolise a fundamental belief that it was not enough for the king to be subject to the law but that the law itself should serve the people.

This is not just an academic argument because it goes to the heart of ideas of England and freedom. The historian Quentin Skinner, who has done more than anyone to remind modern generations of this tradition, quotes from the charge sheet laid against the king at his trial where he was accused of trying to 'destroy and inslave the People'.[27] In the aftermath of Charles' head being chopped off, this more radical view of English liberty was powerfully expressed by John Milton. These days he is best remembered for writing the epic poem *Paradise Lost* but he was also a vigorous political pamphleteer who argued any truly 'free nation' must have 'the power to remove or to abolish *any* governor supreme'.[28] Puritan agitators like the Levellers were beginning to worry that they had not secured enough of this kind of liberty. In the Putney Debates held in 1647, they demanded that every Englishman – or even, according to the most radical, every Englishwoman – should be treated equally because 'the poorest hee that is in England hath a life to live, as the greatest hee'.[29] Not all of these Levellers draped themselves in Magna Carta, tainted as it was by the aristocracy of the past. But one of the most celebrated participants, John Lilburne, 'Freeborn John' as he was known, claimed to draw as much inspiration from Magna Carta as he did from the Bible.

And there were others seeking to revive the myth of Magna Carta during those feverish years. Just a few miles from Runnymede is St George's Hill where Gerrard Winstanley and his Diggers, a socialistic breakaway from the Levellers, set up camp and planted crops to show they did not recognise private land ownership. Winstanley had said he wanted the common people to share the privileges secured by the rich in 'Magna Charta' which he described as 'best laws that England hath … got by our forefathers' importunate petitioning unto the kings'.[30] Local landowners swiftly hired some heavies and the Diggers were evicted. These days St George's Hill is a temple to private property with a gated community and golf course where homes have been sold to Russian oligarchs for up to £30 million.

Both the Levellers and the Diggers emerged in the turmoil and excitement after the civil war when the execution of a king briefly made anything seem possible. There were Fifth Monarchists preparing for Christ's Second Coming, groups with names like Ranters, Seekers and Muggletons, long since disappeared, along with others like the Quakers and the Baptists who are still around today. In this explosion of ideas, with competing visions of Utopia and expectations of violent apocalypse, the myth of Magna Carta became so overheated it has been fused ever since into the national story and what it means to be English. Christopher Hill, the twentieth-century Marxist historian who wrote of this time as the 'World Turned Upside Down', described how the civil war transformed Magna Carta 'from a baronial charter of privileges into a declaration of the rights of all free Englishmen'.[31]

As so often before, it did not last long. Shortly after the death of Cromwell, the monarchy was restored under Charles II and the idea of English liberty reverted to a more conventional form. Magna Carta, however, did not disappear. Another, if somewhat tempered, version of it was invoked during the 'Glorious Revolution' of 1688. King James II had enraged Parliament by not only being Catholic but also producing a son and opening up the prospect of a 'papist' succession. He was ousted in favour of his Anglican daughter, Mary, and her Dutch husband, William of Orange, who had sailed up the Thames with a large foreign army of Protestants just to make sure. Parliament then passed a 'Bill of Rights' to guarantee there would never again be a 'papist prince' on the throne, as well as what the philosopher John Locke was by then describing as a new 'social contract' with English citizens.

But this was not a revolution handing power down to the people. Instead, it merely transferred sovereignty from the crown to a government accountable to Parliament 'under the Crown'. Nor did this version of English liberty do much to protect those groups who were out of favour with their rulers. Few of the Irish Catholics who were systematically discriminated against during the subsequent Protestant Ascendancy would have regarded themselves as living in a free country where the law tracked their fundamental interests as much as it did those of the Establishment. Nor would the Scottish crofters forcibly evicted in the Highland Clearances, the Welsh whose language and identity were being systematically suppressed, or the poor English rural labourers being denied access to common land by the Enclosure Acts.

If Parliament taking power from the crown did not protect people living in these isles from tyranny, then – at least technically – nor did it guarantee citizens of this country any inalienable rights. Even the narrowest parliamentary majority could theoretically pass legislation abolishing jury trials, habeas corpus and free elections. For all the endless invocations of Magna Carta over history, this country is a system where Parliament reigns supreme with power borrowed from absolute monarchy.[32]

But the radical version of Magna Carta's myth was powerful enough to cross the Atlantic. When the English who settled in America revolted against their king, their battle cry of 'no taxation without representation' claimed to be sourced directly from the principles established at Runnymede. Magna Carta was also used as a primary source for the later Declaration of Independence by the United States of America and the first ten amendments to its constitution, even if the 'English liberty' it guaranteed was sometimes regarded as 'a birthright' that excluded foreigners in general and Black people in particular.[33]

Back in England, arguments about the principles supposedly under-pinned by Magna Carta would surface in the emerging debate about slavery and the celebrated case of James Somerset who was eventually allowed his freedom after escaping from a ship bound for Jamaica's plantations.[34] More often, however, the idea of Magna Carta in the eighteenth and nineteenth centuries was cited as proof that liberty was at heart something distinctly English or, at least, Anglo-Saxon. It became part of Merrie England's misty heritage that entranced society at a time when the public joined archaeological societies, enthusiastic-ally translated *Beowulf* and gave children Saxon names like Cuthbert, Edgar, Edmund, Edward, Alfred and Wilfred, or Audrey, Edith, Ethel, Hilda and Mildred.

Victorian society revelled in the myth that Anglo-Saxon 'Englalond' was a freedom-loving country where warriors had gathered around oak trees in a *folkmoot* democracy. Historians sought out evidence of an embryonic system of law that by the eleventh century had grown incrementally into some written legal codes. They seized upon the so-called *witans* – councils of wise men – that approved the succession of kings, settled disputes or tried cases. They pointed out how Runnymede itself was a place that had hosted open-air councils dating back to the time of Alfred the Great.

All of which was a bit of a reach. To the extent that England was a country at all before William's conquest in 1066, it was one living in constant fear of raids or invasion by Vikings who were being bought off with Danegeld provided by punitive levels of taxation. More than one in ten of the English population were slaves and punishment by savage mutilation or killing was commonplace. Aethelstan, who some regard as having been the first proper king of England in the tenth century, was no liberal. He decreed the death penalty for petty child criminals, said that women harbouring thieves should be thrown off a cliff or drowned, while ordering delinquent slaves to be stoned to death by other slaves, 'and if any one of them fails three times to hit him, he himself shall be scourged three times'.[35]

Even so, the notion of Magna Carta restoring Anglo-Saxon freedoms suppressed by the 'Norman yoke' resonated across England. It inspired the name of the 'Chartist' movement as it campaigned for working-class emancipation. For instance, the Methodist preacher Joseph Rayner Stephens told an 1838 rally in Leeds: 'We stand upon our old rights, we seek no change, we say give us the good old laws of England unchanged. And what are those laws? What is that constitution by which we seek to abide?' Back came the answer from the cheering crowd, 'Magna Charta! Magna Charta!' And on he went, saying: 'Aye, Magna Charta! The good old laws of English freedom – free meetings, freedom of speech, freedom of workshops, freedom of homesteads, free and happy firesides – and no workhouses!'[36]

Instead of resorting to violent insurrection, as many similar movements did across Europe, these English Chartists – or, at least, most of them – focused on changing the law through Parliament with a series of restorative, even patriotic, demands for change. As such, it has been the invocation of Magna Carta that has arguably helped stave off revolution. And, while it is possible to sentimentalise such democratic traditions, there is something remarkably self-confident about the way Britain's belief in freedom meant that, without any border controls, it welcomed as many as 7,000 refugees – radical, nationalist, republican and socialist – from the failed continental revolutions of 1848 including a German philosopher called Karl Marx who had just written *The Communist Manifesto* with Friedrich Engels.

As the nineteenth century aged, different ideas of Magna Carta continued to swirl around concepts of nationhood. A much more conservative account of Anglo-Saxon liberty was used to justify an Englishness which stuck freedom in stodgy, constipated concepts of property rights, obedience to custom and a settled social hierarchy. It was the England described by Alfred, Lord Tennyson as the land that 'sober-suited Freedom chose'.[37] Edward Freeman's vast *History of the Norman Conquest of England* in 1870 said Magna Carta had restored ancient liberties that had been lost by invasion. There was only a 'temporary overthrow of our national being' by the Normans, Freeman insisted, and that within a few generations Anglo-Saxon values, sustained by the continuity of the English language, had roared back so they 'led captive our conquerors'.

At the start of the twentieth century, Henrietta Marshall sought to stitch these competing myths of liberty into one coherent national identity with her celebrated children's book, *Our Island Story*. 'When the barons forced John to grant the Magna Carta, they fought, not for themselves, as barons and Normans, but for the whole English people,' she wrote. 'For the first time since the Conquest, the people of England acted as one people.'[38] And yet even she felt it necessary to include a warning: 'this is not a history lesson, but a story book', based on what were 'only fairy tales'.[39]

After all the confusion and conflation of Magna Carta by both radicals and conservatives, Marshall knew there has never been anything simple or singular about English liberty. For all the boasts about England's court system, access to justice was denied to many of the poorest victims of crime who, until late in the nineteenth century, had to pay for prosecutions, as well as criminal defendants who were often not given legal representation. And there were many other fundamental battles about freedom which had yet to be fought, let alone won, in that Edwardian era.

Industry was paralysed by strikes and lockouts; suffragettes were throwing themselves in front of royal racehorses and starving themselves in their fight for the right to vote; Britain teetered on the brink of a civil war over Irish home rule. Working-class men in Britain got the vote much later than those in Australia, New Zealand or the United States, while women did not get equal suffrage until 1928. And even as an Anglo-centric Britain congratulated itself for being free, it was the axis of an empire where many tens of millions of still colonised, subjugated and exploited people longed to be freed *from* England.

Confronted by this muddled reality, English historians of the time admitted the story of English liberty was a mess. As early as 1904, Edward Jenks' *The Myth of Magna Carta* described 'the hollow truce of Runnymede' as a conspiracy of self-serving and reckless barons. He said that any idea of the Charter creating real freedom for ordinary English people was largely the invention of a seventeenth-century Parliamentarian propaganda machine.[40] Such a view became established over the years that followed, with notions of a distinctive English liberty further eclipsed by the political realities of international alliances. When Britain and France lined up against Germany in the First World War, the royal family changed its name from Saxe-Coburg-Gotha to Windsor and Victorian notions of a distinctive, ethnic Anglo-Saxon freedom slunk away in shame.

By the time W. C. Sellar and R. J. Yeatman, two veterans of that war, came to write their parody of school history in *1066 and All That*, the prevailing idea of Magna Carta could be summarised in a few sentences of brilliant snarkiness:

That no one was to be put to death, save for some reason – (except the Common People). That everyone should be free – (except the Common People) … Magna Charter was therefore the chief cause of Democracy in England, and thus a Good Thing for everyone (except the Common People).

'DID SHE DIE IN VAIN?'

In the years since the 2015 commemoration, through all the ructions of Brexit, Covid and much more besides, yet another tribute to Magna Carta has been built at Runnymede.

Writ in Water is reached by walking up a muddy track and, from the outside, looks like it might be a concrete machine-gun bunker or possibly a public toilet. Visitors who enter must walk anti-clockwise around its dimly lit internal wall before they come to a pool of dark water reflecting light from a circular hole in the roof and words from the Magna Carta. Mark Wallinger, the artist who designed it, says this was to demonstrate how 'intangible' rights are when they have not been written in a constitution or carved in stone: 'We can see how threatened they can be by the appeals of populism or fundamentalism.'[41]

Whatever the intentions of various myth-makers in this uneven story over the past 800 years, the baronial privileges agreed in Runnymede in 1215 are clearly different from the Protestant rights that Parliament thought it was defending in the seventeenth century, or the liberties used to provide the justification for American colonialists to break away from England in the next. And this memorial is perhaps the best representation of how Magna Carta's myth has flared intermittently and in irregular fashion through the more recent past.

The Second World War's blood-soaked struggle for freedom saw Winston Churchill trying to give an original copy of the old charter to the United States as part of his effort to entice President Franklin Roosevelt into the conflict. He was thwarted by the stubbornness of Lincoln Cathedral's Dean and Chapter who 'unexpectedly' made it clear they were 'unwilling to surrender their Magna Carta'.[42] In 1948, when democracy was on its victory lap, the former First Lady, Eleanor Roosevelt, drew up the Universal Declaration of Human

Rights in the hope it might 'become a Magna Carta of all mankind'. The European Convention which was drafted two years later also incorporated the key clauses of Magna Carta guaranteeing that no one should be deprived of their liberty except 'in accordance with a procedure prescribed by law'.

Much of that was at the insistence of David Maxwell Fyfe, who had been a prosecutor at the Nuremberg trials where he cross-examined Hermann Goering and went on to become a Conservative home secretary in the 1950s. In that latter role, however, he launched a zealous campaign to 'rid England of this plague' of homosexuals who, he told the House of Commons, were 'exhibitionists and proselytisers and are a danger to others, especially the young'.[43] Maxwell Fyfe's career underlines how ideas of what constitutes liberty in England have been as stable as a royal marriage.

As England began to liberalise its attitudes to sex and much else besides in the 1960s, everyone was so confused that the comedian Tony Hancock asked: 'Does Magna Carta mean nothing to you? Did she die in vain?'

For a time in the late twentieth century, efforts to rekindle a specifically national sense of pride around Magna Carta were led by the left in politics. In the 1960s, the Runnymede Trust was established to track how ethnic minorities remain grossly over-represented in an English criminal justice system that supposedly protects everyone's rights, but significantly under-represented when it comes to securing access to the best opportunities in education or work. A few years later, perhaps in reaction to Margaret Thatcher's apparent monopoly on patriotism, there was talk of a 'golden thread' in the history of English liberty that was flecked with the deepest red. For them it ran from Magna Carta through the Peasants' Revolt, the Levellers and the Diggers, the Chartists and the Suffragettes all the way to the foundation of the NHS. Billy Bragg, a socialist songwriter best remembered for the lines 'I don't want to change the world/I'm not looking for a new England', has written about 'the struggle for rights that has gone on in England since Magna Carta'.

Even the long-time left-wing MP Tony Benn, who had previously dismissed what happened in Runnymede as merely a victory for 'feudal barons' against monarchical 'dictatorship',[44] felt moved to invoke the Charter against efforts by Gordon Brown's Labour government to extend the time terror suspects could be detained without trial from an already unprecedented 28 days to 42 in 2008.[45]

This was when the pendulum began to swing back the other way. The Conservative Party discovered they were now defenders of a specifically English brand of liberty against this 'authoritarian tendency' of Blair and Brown's New Labour. David Davis, the then shadow home secretary, felt so strongly about the government's detention of terrorism suspects without trial that he resigned his seat so that he could fight and win a by-election on the issue. In 2009, he gave a speech about Magna Carta in which he described how the 'greatest history of freedom in the history of the world' was in danger from an all-seeing state controlling internet data, DNA samples and CCTV footage.[46]

Dominic Raab, the future Conservative foreign secretary, who was then not even an MP, wrote a book that same year ramming home his belief that England was special when it came to freedom. 'Centuries before the Enlightenment gave birth to the French Revolution and American Declaration of Independence, and with a fraction of the bloodshed, English nobles persuaded their monarch to cede rights and freedoms that charted a course towards liberal democracy,' Raab wrote. He went on to warn that an alien concept of freedom had been introduced to England by 'importing the European approach to human rights'.[47] Here was the distinctly ethnically and culturally inflected Magna Carta, one that had seemed dead a century before, sitting back up in its coffin.

Eventually Brown's exhausted government petered out to be replaced by a Conservative-led administration under David Cameron who, as we saw at the start of this chapter, swiftly caved into demands for a referendum on Europe. Part of the reason for this was that he was under pressure from a resurgent Eurosceptic right whose idea of sovereignty laid claim to freedom as a specifically English birthright and creation. It reached an intellectual climax, of a sort, in 2013 when Daniel Hannan wrote an influential book, *How We Invented Freedom and Why It Matters*.

Hannan is an unusually focused Conservative writer and politician who, despite never being elected to any position other than that of a member of the European Parliament, has been described as one of the 'godfathers of Brexit'.[48] His book on England's invention of liberty made the case for a new alliance of English-speaking nations – what some have called the 'Anglosphere' – based on their shared reverence for such freedoms together with the common law and parliamentary government. This is how he described events at Runnymede 800 years before:

> In a field near Windsor, an event of truly planetary significance took place. For the first time, the idea that governments were subject to the law took written, contractual form. The king put his seal to a document that, from that day to this, has been seen as the foundational charter of Anglosphere liberty: Magna Carta.[49]

Such a desire to claim liberty as an English invention was not just a piece of patriotic boasting. Hannan was seeking, like so many of those who had gone before him, to defend an 'Anglo-Saxon' concept of limited government, in which individuals were free from excessive interference by the state, against continental ideas which led to so-called enabling rights like education and bigger governments. His exceptionalism even went so far as suggesting this English liberty was unrelated to 'human rights' but was a special feature of English-speaking nations, including the United States. He shrugged off the famous lines in the Declaration of Independence about 'self-evident' truths and 'inalienable rights' to claim that the American revolutionaries were merely fighting for 'the privileges bestowed on them by Magna Carta' as Englishmen. 'The rights we now take for granted – freedom of speech, religion, assembly and so on – are not the natural condition of an advanced society. They were developed overwhelmingly in the language in which you are reading these words. When we call them universal rights, we are being polite,' he wrote.[50]

Hannan was not the only Conservative politician busy making the case that Magna Carta somehow made the English special. Ahead of the Brexit referendum campaign of 2016, Priti Patel, who would soon become home secretary, declared her support for leaving the EU by saying it would restore 'values of democracy and self-determination which date back to the Magna Carta'.[51] And when Covid struck in 2020, the then prime minister Boris Johnson answered a question about why Germany was doing better at 'track and trace' by telling MPs: 'There is an important difference between our country and many other countries around the world: our country is a freedom-loving country ... virtually every advance, from free speech to democracy, has come from this country. It is very difficult to ask the British population uniformly to obey guidelines in the way that is necessary.'[52] In fact, polling showed many in the public were supportive of lockdowns to control infection and often wanted the government to go further. While there were riots in continental countries like the Netherlands against the daily infringements of their personal liberty, a similar movement in England never got much further than the conspiracy fringe of far-right libertarians and Piers Corbyn, the brother of the left-wing former Labour leader. The only time the bulk of people in this country got properly angry about the lockdowns was when they found out that staff in Downing Street, including the prime minister himself, had been repeatedly breaking the rules they had written for everyone else.

In the political crisis that followed, cabinet ministers rushed out policy proposals that might distract attention. Up popped Dominic Raab, who was then justice secretary and had finally been given the chance to shoot directly at a Human Rights Act he had been fulminating against for two decades or more. He boasted that his proposals for a new 'Bill of Rights' would, by being 'quintessentially British' rather than foreign, restore traditions that 'stretch back from Magna Carta in 1215'. Yet even he was entirely unable to find a compelling reason to sever all links to the European Convention that he once found so terrifying.[53]

One of the reasons why Conservatives were so keen on this argument was that it gave them a dividing line with Labour's leader, Keir Starmer, who had once been one of the 'lefty lawyers' they so despised and supported the UK Supreme Court's verdict that plans to send asylum seekers to Rwanda violated their human rights. Starmer himself remains dismissive of the Magna Carta myth, saying it is based on a 'fundamentally flawed analysis' of history. 'England did not "invent" freedom, as some of today's more far-out politicians like to say, nor are the rights we have in the UK part of an exclusive racial birthright.' He prefers to see human rights as part of inclusive, patriotic tradition which has helped England always be at the heart of a debate about what freedom means and says their incorporation into international conventions has made nations 'stronger ... not weaker.'[54] The European Convention on Human Rights is something Starmer has defended consistently at every stage of his career. It inspired him as young law student in Leeds in the 1980s and he wrote a book about it when he was a human rights lawyer in the 1990s. He used it to advise police on balancing the rights of different communities in Belfast during the 2000s and used it as the basis for his first speech to parliament in 2015. After becoming prime minister in 2024, his first significant foreign policy intervention was to host a summit for European leaders at Blenheim where he reaffirmed support for ECHR as being 'built on the blood bond of 1945 and our shared sacrifice for freedom' and adding it described 'the very essence of what it is to be human'.[55]

Such an approach didn't stop further calls from the Conservative party for the UK to leave the convention, nor the myth of Magna Carta to boil away in the people's imaginations on the fringes of politics as it had for much of the previous decade. Even as David Cameron was shaking hands with the royal family on that 2015 summer's day in Runnymede, police were blocking access to what locals called a 'hippy village' in the wooded hillside above which consisted of tents made from plastic sheeting, an Anglo-Saxon long house and some makeshift huts. Residents of the camp, some of them veterans of the anti-capitalist Occupy movement, had been planning to put on an alternative 'festival of democracy' complete with a reggae stage which they said would be 'a celebration of the Magna Carta in its truest sense, in the spirit of the rights of the individual against the government'. The landowner was taking them to court that day to evict what they said was 'a squat' and the police were encircling them. But the campers claimed they had a right to do what they wanted there according to the Charter of the Forests, a companion document to Magna Carta passed in 1217.[56]

During the Covid lockdowns, a man called Graham Moore who, under the moniker 'Daddy Dragon', posts a lot on the internet about Europe, the deep state and the danger of vaccinations, turned up at Runnymede with some flags. He went to the John F. Kennedy Memorial to claim protection under the US constitution because he was standing on 'American soil' before launching a petition for England to be declared a 'captive nation'.[57] At the same time, businesses ranging from a hair salon in Oakenshaw, a tattoo parlour in Bristol, a martial arts centre in Wigan and a Christian bookshop in Gedling called The Mustard Seed all refused to obey Covid lockdown rules. They placed identical notices in their window claiming that Clause 61 of Magna Carta allowed them to opt out of any law to which they did not consent. It did not, of course.

The clause in question gave twenty-five barons the right to 'distrain upon and assail' the monarch if they decided he had breached the agreement. But a hairdresser, a tattooist and a bookseller are not medieval barons. And anyhow, that clause was excised from the original document after 1215, never to appear again in scores of reissues.[58] Tens of thousands of pounds in lockdown fines later, it emerged the business owners had been inspired by an internet conspiracy group called Freemen on the Land with links to white supremacists that believe people can declare themselves independent of all government.

And then there was Giles Fraser, a self-styled 'radical rector' with an undeniable talent for publicity, doing something similarly meaningless with a different Magna Carta clause ahead of his Easter Service in 2020. On the door of St Mary's in Newington, south London, he pinned Article 1 of the Charter which promised the 'English church shall be free'. This was because he had been upset by reports that the police had barged into churches to break up religious gatherings deemed to breach Covid lockdown rules. He told parishioners to come along anyway and braced himself for the arrival of the forces of repression and, excitingly, his possible arrest. 'As it would happen, the police didn't show up,' he later wrote in a slightly wistful column for a right-of-centre website entitled 'How the Left gave up on Freedom'.[59] Fast forward four years and self-styled defenders of freedom were making even wilder accusations that the newly-elected Labour government of 'erasing Magna Carta' because some of their number who stirred up that summer's riots with racist or false information got arrested.[60]

But maybe it is too easy to mock such antics because a hairdresser in Oakenshaw or a radical rector in Newington have as much basis for using an 800-year-old document to claim their rights are being impinged as anyone else. The left-wingers who think the Charter inspired the NHS or justifies overthrowing the aristocracy are as equally wrong-headed as those who believe Brexit will restore the *folkmoot* democracy of some Saxon *witans*. Constitutional experts who say it does not really matter that Magna Carta failed to mention jury trials and habeas corpus just so long as ordinary people believe it did, are going to struggle to win an argument with a man who says he's going to keep his tattoo parlour open in Bristol because he has read something on the internet.

Even if no one really agrees on what it means and all this history has become a muddle, a question remains: can the myth of Magna Carta be brought down to earth and still mean something for England's future?

FREEDOM, GRANTED

These days the anarchists camping out in their eco-village at Runnymede have been moved off the land by bailiffs and police. In their place has risen a monument to property capitalism: Magna Carta Park, an exclusive £130 million community spread over 60 acres where the price for its mock-seventeenth-century homes starts at £1 million and rises up to five times that amount. Next door is a retirement complex for the over-fifty-fives that includes a swimming pool, spa and tennis courts.

The high iron gates outside serve as a reminder of how myths that help build a sense of national identity can also divide people or make others feel shut out of a country's story. Now, as over the centuries, many sub-categories of English people – 'poor', 'Black', 'gay', 'female' or maybe just 'different' – have not had an equal chance to enjoy all the 'freedom under the law' that supposedly goes with being a citizen of this country.

Even so, in highlighting what's wrong it's also possible to miss what's right. The overwhelming majority of citizens in this country have – and, usually, know they have – certain freedoms.

Escaped convicts are not free, even if they are at liberty. Someone with reason to worry about the secret police knocking on their door in the middle of the night is not living in a free land, even if the knock never comes. Perhaps, ultimately, no one is properly free until they can take it for granted.

As the next chapter will show, there are places in England today where people fight over memorials, but no one does that in Runnymede. Fears that the new statue of the queen would be vandalised have not materialised. And, when the sculptor of *The Jurors* said it was an 'invitation to sit, reflect and to discuss together the implication of the histories and issues depicted', he hadn't reckoned with the National Trust which issued a guide to it that told visitors firmly 'please do not sit on and touch the artwork'. The Trust has a nearby tearoom with standard-issue flapjacks, chocolate biscuits and cheese scones, along with a notice in the toilets, ordering people not to flush hand towels or wet wipes because it causes drains to block, adding: 'It costs us £125 + VAT to call a plumber, money we could have used to care for the garden.'

Other instructions to be found on the site commemorating the invention of freedom include signs saying: 'Keep your dog on a lead', 'Do not light fires', 'No barbeques', 'Caution: paths may be slippery when wet'. But it is doubtful many people want to see fires being lit there, let alone someone's grandmother fall over on a wet path. And, in any case, this is the kind of place where most visitors seem much too polite to break any rules. Passing each other on footpaths, they surprise anyone who has just come from London by looking up and saying, 'hello'.

The muddled ideas represented in these Runnymede monuments and the benignly petty interference with personal freedom of an organisation like the National Trust may yet prove a safer foundation on which to stand. They are, at least, preferable to others that have sometimes been painted in sharper relief both in this country and elsewhere.

The inflation, conflation and deflation of England's idea of liberty over eight centuries has made it a worn-in, over-stretched myth, like a hand-me-down jumper that is still the most comfortable thing to wear even if it is only at weekends. So much has been made of Magna Carta by so many people in so many different ways that it ends up meaning nothing very much and still mattering nonetheless. The strength and value of this story lies far more in its confusion than its clarity.

England did not invent liberty, because no one did. It's not an object like the lightbulb or the printing press but an idea that has existed, in some form or another, ever since human beings started dreaming of a life free from the slavery or torture imposed on them by others. And, in an age of angry certainties where people insist their version of the truth must trump every other, it is worth remembering that much of what defines England has never been the invention of a single mind or served a single purpose. Like the common law and the English language, it has evolved slowly, under pressure from all kinds of demands and struggles, into the familiarly lumpy shapes of today.

One way to understand this is to wander the semi-suburban countryside on the Berkshire–Surrey border where Magna Carta was sealed. There can be few places on the planet where people are more certain of their individual freedom. Dotted around are golf clubs like Worplesdon or Walton Heath or the more exclusive Wentworth, St George's and Queenwood that – not entirely unfairly – evoke the image of diamond-patterned sweater-wearing men and blow-dried women making liberal use of their right to free speech to speak their mind over a few drinks at 'the 19th hole'. A little further back towards London there is Surbiton which, for anyone of a certain age who watched the BBC sitcom *The Good Life*, always summons up memories of Margo Leadbetter, that caricature of the 1970s southern

English Tory, declaring: 'I am not a citizen, I am a *resident*.' Access to basic liberties has never been equal in England.

Among the rhododendron bushes of the Home Counties, however, it's still possible to see why England's mundane, everyday freedom matters. That is because a new wave of immigrants, from what had been one of the last parts of the British Empire, are now fleeing tyranny and choosing to settle in those same suburbs. And, if you make a mistake in how you describe them, they will quickly point out – in an unconscious echo of Margo Leadbetter – 'we are not Hong Kong Chinese, we are *British* Hong Kongers'.

When Hong Kong was handed back to China in 1997, millions chose to retain their status as British nationals even though they were not given the right to live in the UK. After China introduced new security laws clamping down on basic freedoms and sending the police in to break up pro-democracy demonstrations in 2020, Britain announced it would let them live and work in the UK, with a pathway to full citizenship after six years. The government expects around 300,000 Hong Kongers to move here over the next few years – a third of whom will arrive aged under eighteen – making them by some margin the fastest growing group of permanent immigrants in Britain.[61]

Several thousand British Hong Kongers have already settled in the Surrey town of Sutton and a similar sized community has established itself in Kingston upon Thames, just a few miles from Runnymede. No one has suggested their attraction to Surrey has anything to do with Magna Carta. Instead, as with all migrant communities, people naturally cluster around friends and family who have already arrived. Sometimes this is about schools and housing. Others come because they prefer to live outside big cities to avoid the all-seeing eye of the Chinese Communist Party, as well as the dead eyes of white racists with twisted notions of what it is to be English.[62]

Over a cup of tea in a café less than an hour's walk from Runnymede, Elise Kong explains why her family decided to move here. She is a doctor and says many of her colleagues went out on the streets of Hong Kong to treat injured protesters who were not only afraid of the police but were also 'afraid to go to hospital'. She does not want her children growing up in a society where the 'government can hurt people or arrest people for no reason', adding: 'We were a colony under the British, but we did have rights.'

They live in Chertsey and at weekends she likes to visit the English countryside with her husband, Ming Wong, and their children Sean and Stanley. Has she been to Runnymede yet? 'I don't know – what's that?' she asks. Oh, it's quite close to here. Magna Carta, King John – you know – the barons! 'Maybe we've heard of this place,' she says, looking needlessly embarrassed. 'We've much more we want to learn because this is our home now.'

She is planting a garden with roses and hyacinths, as well as trying to make friends with her 'very nice' neighbours who she would like to invite to dinner – 'they've told us how much they like the smell of our cooking'. Then her eyes well up, as she says: 'We will now be British Hong Kongers, but I hope we can go back sometimes to see my parents. They are too old to leave.'

Emily Lee, known to her friends as 'Duckie', shares a similar story. She left Hong Kong because she did not want to live in a place where 'you have to obey'. Asked what freedom means to her on an average day in the Surrey suburbs, she laughs and talks about her ageing poodle, called Coffee. 'I like taking my dog to the shops. Coffee is getting quite old and he goes everywhere with me because he has separation anxiety. Sometimes I put him in my bag so he can come to the restaurants that are pet-friendly. A lot of people here are not too strict about rules on that sort of thing because the English love dogs, don't they?' Does Magna Carta mean anything to her? 'No.'

Richard Choi, a phone designer who has lived in the UK for fourteen years, helps run a Hong Kongers group in Sutton which has more than 5,000 members, although he points out not all of them will end up in this Surrey town. Much of his work is coordinating with schools and local authorities because 'we have a responsibility to let them know' about new arrivals. Choi produces graphs about anticipated numbers of newly arrived children and spreadsheets of where school places might be available. His idea of freedom is heroically suburban. 'On Sundays, I go to church and then take the kids to the park. Maybe we will then go to the pub, it's about family, it's about having nothing to worry about.' And, no, he has not heard of Magna Carta either.

One person who does know all about the events at Runnymede 800 years ago is Simon Cheng. He had been working in the British

Consulate back in Hong Kong when a shrivelled copy of Magna Carta was exhibited there. This was when the document was doing a world tour as part of the commemoration which David Cameron had invested so heavily in during 2015. The next stop was scheduled to have been an appearance at Beijing's People's University but this was blocked at the last minute by paranoid Chinese authorities.[63]

Although he talks eloquently about how Magna Carta made an impression on his youthful political identity because it set 'limits on royal power', Cheng doubts that his taste for English medieval history had much to do with an arbitrary arrest three years later. After crossing into mainland China, he was interrogated and tortured for fourteen days before being released. He then fled to Britain where even now he sometimes thinks he is being followed.

Cheng leads 'Hong Kongers in Britain', an organisation that not only provides support for immigrants but also seeks to integrate them with events such as raising money for Poppy Day. Halfway through the conversation, he goes off to find his Union Jack beanie hat, as well as a jumper of similar design. 'We want to show we are part of this country,' he says. 'It has shortcomings – just look at some of the transport systems – but I would not trade the humanity I have found here for all the high-speed trains in China.'

In time, these Hong Kongers will once again change ideas of England. Unlike many previous waves of immigrants, those arriving usually have some savings and two-thirds possess a degree-level qualification.[64] Cheng, who leans to the left himself, suspects most Hong Kongers are believers in a 'laissez-faire economy' and quite 'right-wing'.

Such attitudes are one of the reasons the Conservative government enthusiastically supported immigration from Hong Kong in a way it noticeably did not for others. For instance, when it comes to discussing Hong Kongers, Daniel Hannan – the Tory politician who thinks England invented freedom – has hardly been able to contain his excitement, saying the economic 'miracle' of the former colony was due to its imperial inheritance. He has called for Hong Kongers to be given somewhere in England to build another 'self-governing city', maybe on the Isle of Wight. 'The most industrious population in the world, a population that brings its own global business networks, is looking for a new home. An opportunity like this will not come again. Who will seize it?'[65]

There is little sign of Hong Kongers flocking to the Isle of Wight just yet. Their former island off a different south coast 6,000 miles distant was only ever 'British' in the first place because China had been forced to cede this territory after being battered by British gunboats in the nineteenth century's Opium Wars. That conflict was not mentioned on any of the 399 pages in Hannan's book on English liberty. Nor, it is worth pointing out, was Hong Kong ever properly free or democratic in its entire 155 years as a British possession.

For all that, there is still hope in a story about Hong Kongers wanting to come to England now, one which is testament to the sense of security and everyday freedom – 'the peace and quiet' – that Britain is giving them once again.

The myth that freedom was invented here has sometimes been used to imply it is a uniquely English inheritance, a 'birthright' to which other people who are neither white nor Anglo-Saxon have no automatic entitlement. It is one of the reasons why so many people of colour in this country, including newly arrived Hong Kongers, still prefer to call themselves 'British' rather than embrace an 'English' identity. Yet there is still room for a humbler relationship between England and liberty that claims neither parentage nor inheritance, just a deep and lasting affinity. Such freedom expresses itself in countless everyday actions by people getting on with their lives without a moment's thought about the meaning of Magna Carta.

None of this would have come as a surprise to Bernard Williams, the mid-twentieth-century English political philosopher who was for a time married to that liberal political icon Shirley Williams. He spent much of his life trying to explain the fragility and limits of freedom, reminding us that 'somewhere someone is being tortured right now'. Stopping humans doing the most terrible things to each other so that we can each live an ordinary life is ultimately more important, he said, than dreaming of a perfect future or celebrating a glorious past.

As such, the dowdiness of England that can be found in Runnymede and so many other places is not only a safeguard against the excitable and the extreme, it also offers a kind of freedom itself: the right to be comfortably bored in some waterlogged fields on a damp Sunday afternoon.

Inside the new *Writ in Water* memorial are some stone benches. There, on one such day, two women could be found with their English bulldog. Have they come to see this monument in particular? 'No, we just came for a walk,' says the first. Are they interested at all in Magna Carta? 'We're from Feltham, so we had to drive.' A few drops of rain are beginning to fall through the hole in the roof into the reflecting pool and there is a pause as everyone ponders just how awkward this conversation has become. Eventually, the second woman speaks: 'It's nice and peaceful here, isn't it?'

2

Plymouth
England and the Sea

THE BOWLING GREEN

A few years ago, when waves smacked into the coast and twisted and tore up the railway tracks at Dawlish, there were panicked reports that Plymouth had been cut off from the rest of the country. The wildness of the wind and the sea can make this city seem a long way from anywhere. But the relationship Plymouth has had with those same elemental forces once made it England's gateway to everywhere.

It is pretty much impossible to escape reminders of a maritime past in this city. Go down Armada Way, past the Armada Sundial and the high battlements of the Royal Citadel, then on to Plymouth Hoe. This is where Sir Francis Drake was said to be playing bowls on a July evening in 1588. The Spanish Armada, a wooden wall of ships almost two miles wide, had been spotted by lookouts on the most southerly tip of England and beacons had been lit on hills all the way up the coast to warn that invasion was imminent. Breathless subordinates raced up to the famous admiral, shouting: 'The Spaniards! The Spaniards!' The game paused for a moment as all eyes turned towards the sea. 'Come,' Drake is supposed to have said, 'there is time to finish the game and to beat the Spaniards, too.'

The Battle of the Armada was a moment of maximum danger for England when it faced not only invasion but subjugation by Europe's greatest and richest power. Almost half a millennium later, this means that Plymouth is still guaranteed a place in the national story. And the city makes the most of it. The official name of its still-vast naval base next to the Devonport shipyards is HMS *Drake*. Then, out in Plymouth Sound sits Drake Island. A big shopping mall in the middle of the city is called 'Drake Circus'. Then there is Drake Primary School next to Royal Navy Avenue, the Drake Ward of the local council, a park and garden called 'Drake's Place', as well as Drake Reservoir and Drake Memorial Park which describes itself as 'one of the first fully-lawned cemeteries in the country'. Even the modern university has a cafeteria called Drake's Kitchen, offering Full English breakfasts, fish and chips and Drake's classics, which include 'Italian-inspired pasta dishes.'

At the Hoe itself there is a slightly dilapidated bowling green which announces itself with a wooden sign showing Drake – portrayed in Elizabethan garb of colourful tunic, pantaloons and pointy beard – lunging forward to finish the game. But for all that tourist tat, nothing really detracts from the beauty of this great green and windy space high on limestone cliffs above the sea. As the Hoe opens out to the water below, there is a white granite monument to the victory over the Armada and a large statue of Drake gazing out towards the sea. His left hand hovers above a sword, the right touches a globe in recognition of his circumnavigation of the world, the first by an Englishman, that saw Drake eventually – triumphantly and sensationally – sail back into Plymouth, his ship laden with a fortune in plundered Spanish gold.

Drake is not simply a heritage brand for the city of Plymouth. In recent years, his legend has been stirred back into life as a symbol of a seafaring England kicking free of all the tangles that held it back for so long at home. This is the second myth of this book.

Like that of Magna Carta, it is a story that was co-opted by those who led a campaign to leave the European Union in 2016. These 'Brexiteers' used that extra 'e' to make themselves sound more like swashbuckling 'buccaneers', who had once sailed so close to the wind. As a scrappy underdog who nonchalantly defied a sinister continental power, Drake is not just a statue for them, he is a role model. As an English adventurer who came home richer after a journey into the unknown, Drake's legend gives them faith that huge and reckless gambles do, sometimes, pay off. And above all else, invoking it just makes everything seem so much more patriotic. The Brexiteers use

Drake's name like sea salt to be scattered across the media, sprinkled into speeches, or flung in the face of anyone who dares doubt them.

This was a time when politicians channelled their inner Drakes to declare the nation's destiny has always been in the wide expanse of the oceans beyond rather than in Europe. David Davis, who was put in charge of negotiations to leave the EU, said, 'our history is a trading, buccaneering history – back to Drake and beyond – that's what we're good at'.[1] In 2018, when Davis resigned from the government in protest over what he thought was too soft a Brexit deal, he went off to watch the Formula 1 motor racing at Silverstone and compared himself to 'Drake going to play bowls before going to sink ships'.[2] The following year, Nigel Farage, the leader of the Brexit Party, stood on Plymouth Hoe to publicise his party's 'battle plan' for defeating any fainthearts who might seek a compromise with the Continent.[3] He later revealed that the old sea dog had always been 'one of my heroes' because his 'house' at private school had been known as 'Drake's'. Ahead of the 2019 General Election, the cabinet minister Jacob Rees-Mogg wrote an article in the *Daily Express* extolling the virtues of his new prime minister, Boris Johnson. 'Just as the inspiration of Sir Francis Drake transformed England's naval fortunes under Elizabeth I,' he wrote, 'so the UK now has a new leader under Elizabeth II who can finally take us to victory.'[4]

This mixture of different stories produced something called 'Global Britain' in which, like anything that has been overcooked, the different ingredients are hard to identify. Some bits appear to be about trade deals with faraway countries, while others hint at sending warships 'East of Suez'. It has the spice of an Elizabethan age when England was small and nimble, like Captain Jack Sparrow of *Pirates of the Caribbean* who prospered through banter and derring-do. But there is also the savoury gravy of nostalgia for an empire that was once so mighty and rich.

Some supporters present Global Britain as a kind of free-market Thatcherism based on low taxes and even lower regulations. Others suggest it is a cornerstone of their 'Anglo-sphere' alliance of English-speaking countries, including the United States and members of the 'Old Commonwealth', that is all about protectionism rather than free trade or enterprise. A few make out that it's both, because Global Britain is not a coherent policy so much as a feeling.

'The ship of state has been moored in harbour since 1973,' declared Rees-Mogg in reference to the date when Britain joined Europe, but now 'can once again take to the high seas and look at the whole world rather than the narrow European sphere.'⁵ If the international consensus on the referendum result was summed up by the cover of the *New Yorker* magazine showing bowler-hatted and buttoned-up Englishmen resembling Rees-Mogg himself silly-walking off the edge of a cliff, Brexiteers preferred a different image, one of an English nation preparing to fling off its continental straitjacket, defend its salty difference and prepare once more to find fresh fortune in far-flung lands. It is a mindset that goes a long way to explain the disproportionate attention paid by Brexiteers to the fate of Britain's tiny fishing fleet, the continued use of offshore tax havens in the Caribbean by the wealthiest, or the fury that seizes hold of so many of them at the sight of refugees trying to 'invade' by crossing the English Channel in rubber dinghies.

Post-Brexit Conservative governments cut foreign aid budgets to fund the warships that would 'restore Britain's position as the fore-most naval power in Europe', launched a new aircraft carrier HMS *Queen Elizabeth* adorned with an English Tudor rose, and suggested that if only the rest of the country could resemble their myth, England could be made great again.⁶ In a speech to the Royal Naval College in Greenwich, the then prime minister Boris Johnson began by pointing out to the audience how 'above and around us you can see the anchors, cables, rudders, sails, oars, ensigns, powder barrels, sextants, the compasses and the grappling irons' of an era 'when it all took off' for this country. He then added, laying metaphor upon metaphor, 'this can be another such moment on the launching pad … this is the moment for us to think of our past and go up a gear again, to recapture the spirit of those seafaring ancestors immortalised above us whose exploits brought not just riches but something even more important than that – and that was a global perspective'. Johnson ended his speech by misquoting Alfred, Lord Tennyson, the laureate of the Victorian Imperial age, as he declared: 'There lies the port, the vessel puffs her sail … the wind sits in the mast.'⁷

These twenty-first-century Brexiteers were not, however, the only people fixated about what the English did at sea long ago. In 2020, after the murder of George Floyd by police in the United States,

Black Lives Matter protests erupted around the world. A hundred miles to the north of Plymouth, a crowd in Bristol pulled to the ground a statue of Edward Colston, whose eighteenth-century philanthropy meant he had been celebrated with schools, a concert hall and even special buns named after him. The protesters tied a rope around the statue's feet, sprayed the word 'prick' down its side and rolled it through the streets and into the city's harbour. Colston had bequeathed to Bristol a fortune made in part through his role in the Royal African Company where he had helped enslave an estimated 84,000 people, of whom almost a quarter died in the 'middle passage' on their way across the Atlantic to the Caribbean and the Americas.

Briefly, the next target of the statue-toppling culture warriors seemed to be Drake. He had taken part in three slaving trips to West Africa led by his cousin, Sir John Hawkins, in the 1560s. Those voyages, the first by English ships to transport African slaves across the Atlantic, had resulted in between 1,200 and 1,400 people being captured and sold to Spanish colonies in the Caribbean.[8] Back then, Elizabeth I had been so pleased she rewarded Hawkins with a special coat of arms depicting a naked Black man bound in rope. In California, which Drake had claimed for England during his round-the-world voyage, a statue of him was taken down in the town of Larkspur and a school carrying his name covered up its signs.[9] Back in England, a petition signed by more than 2,000 people called for the removal of Drake's statue on the Hoe. 'If I, a white person, am offended by seeing these statues on the streets of our hometown,' wrote the lead petitioner, Fiona Roberts, 'just imagine what a young Black person, already marginalised in a town with less than 2 per cent people of colour feels passing that statue every day on their way to school.' And, a few days after the Bristol protests, someone put the statue of Drake on Plymouth Hoe in chains and shackles along with a sign that stated: 'Decolonise History'.

As with Magna Carta, Drake's story has ebbed and flowed through the centuries. At various times, he has been presented as a free-spirited buccaneer of a little island nation that survives on its wits, the explorer who steered his country towards a maritime empire, or the admiral defending England and its queen against the might of Europe. But at least for some, he was also a symbol for all the crimes committed in that country's name.

Any effort to get a grip on him or England's identity needs to examine the mythology of this country's relationship with the sea and the world it opens up beyond.

PROTESTANTS AND PATRIOTIC PIRATES

A nation with a coastline as long and a landmass as small as that of England is always going to be defined by the waters around it. There are historians who argue that was true as far back as Alfred the Great, who built a fleet of ships to see off the Vikings who had for centuries been terrorising his Saxon *Angelcynn* subjects. But then came the Norman invasion and, for a long time afterwards, the English Channel was a bridge that linked it to the Continent rather than a barrier.

The idea of the sea acting as England's safeguard against continental invasion really took off in the Tudor era. It started with Henry VIII's break with Rome and the investment of some of the money he made by looting monasteries in a 'navy royal' to protect himself from continental Catholic kings. One of the ships Henry built was the *Mary Rose*, a name remembered by all those who watched it being raised from the floor of the Solent live on the BBC in 1982, more than 400 years after it sank. Henry's eldest daughter, Mary I, sat on the throne only long enough to lose Calais – England's last remaining foothold on continental Europe – and terrify Protestants with her Catholic Counter-Reformation. And then came her sister, Elizabeth I, that most storied of all England's queens.

Elizabeth never travelled abroad, was declared a Protestant heretic by Rome, and famously refused to marry a string of foreign suitors to seal a military alliance with continental power. She defied invasion by the Spanish Armada, telling assembled troops at Tilbury that she would offer only 'foul scorn' if 'any Prince of Europe should dare to invade the borders of my realm'. This Elizabethan Age, bound up with a belief in Divine Providence, was a time when the narrow strip of the Channel – 'a sanctuary and a springboard' – kept England safe and then became a path to riches thousands of miles away.[10] It was when England began a programme of 'Protestant Plantations' and land seizures to make it safer from Catholic Ireland. And it was when the queen would sign the charter for the East India Company as Drake's fellow Devonian adventurer Sir Walter Raleigh began to dream of a global empire based on English naval power. 'Whosoever commands the sea commands the trade,' he wrote, 'whosoever commands the trade of the world commands the riches of the world, and consequently the world itself.'[11]

Shakespeare's plays written at this time often feel close to the sea. The water's depth is a metaphor for love, its expanse the route to exploration of 'unpathed waters, undreamed shores', and its wildness the cause of shocking change as in his three shipwreck plays, *The Comedy of Errors*, *The Tempest* and *Twelfth Night* – 'what country, friends, is this?' But the 'sceptred isle' speech of John O'Gaunt in *Richard II* pays homage to the 'precious jewel set in a silver sea' which acts as a 'moat defensive' for England. In the intense nationalism of *Henry V*, Shakespeare wrote about the 'threaden sails' and 'lofty surge' of the navy as his 'band of brothers' crosses the Channel to make war on the French who have dared to underestimate the English.

Like much of his country, Drake himself used the sea as a defence against the world and a way of being upwardly mobile within it. As his fame grew, he gave English Protestants their own kind of hero, not an intellectual explorer like Raleigh, but a plain-speaking man from non-aristocratic roots, with red hair, a stocky build and piercing blue eyes. Many English people in those days were still attached to the 'old religion' of Catholicism, but Drake's farming family were proudly Protestants and later had to flee Devon to escape 'papist' rebellions that were spreading up through the south-west. One of the few books he is said to have carried on all his voyages was *Foxe's Book of Martyrs*, a polemic which depicts England as a defiantly Protestant nation whose people were protected by Providence from the evils of the Catholic Inquisition.[12] Although some of Drake's adventures cast doubt on the depth of his piety, this was a time when the idea of English liberty first became directly linked to protecting Protestantism from a continental Counter-Reformation.

It also granted his piratical greed a measure of divine national purpose. As the naval historian N. A. M. Rodger wrote, it was when 'Protestantism, patriotism and plunder … became a distinctive and formative part of the English national myth'.[13] An English ship's chaplain said that they 'cold not do God better service than to spoyl the Spaniard both of lyfe and goodes'.[14]

Much of that plundering has been obscured in the myth of England and the sea. In the 1960s television series *Sir Francis Drake*, the eponymous hero was depicted like an Elizabethan James Bond heading off aboard the *Golden Hind* on a series of secret missions for his queen. In one episode, a villain pretends to be Drake for the purpose of falsely smearing him as a pirate. In another, far from being a slaver, he leads a rescue mission to free white English people who had been enslaved by murderous Black Africans. The inspiration for that was probably the Barbary corsairs, another group of pirates operating out of North African ports like Algiers who made regular raids on ships and even on Plymouth itself. But Drake was a state-sponsored pirate, a 'privateer' who had been issued with 'letters of marque' authorising him to pursue vessels belonging to the queen's many enemies. If he traded at all, he did so with cannons primed and cutlass drawn. The Spanish felt so strongly that they would execute captured privateers with their letters of marque hanging around their necks.[15] And most historians generally accept that many of Drake's activities were 'unquestionably piratical'.[16] Once the romantic myth-ology is scraped away, the reality of England was 'cruelty at sea, deceit and betrayal ashore' where 'victims were tortured and killed, partners double-crossed and crews cheated'.[17]

The slave-trading conducted by Hawkins and Drake was largely an extension of this piracy as they started stealing cargos of humans from Portuguese ships they raided. And, although their three slave-trading voyages only amount to a tiny fraction of the human trafficking across the Atlantic that came later, that does not diminish the horror of what they did. The cruelty can be shown by statistics: for instance, of the 400 people Hawkins and Drake took from Sierra Leone in 1566, the filth and squalor below deck where they were held was so bad that almost half of them died.[18] But a better insight can be found in the story of their arrival at the little port of Rio de la Hacha, in what is now Colombia. Hawkins and Drake had returned to the Caribbean carrying a bigger cargo of African slaves on a trip in which the queen herself was a prime investor. But this time the Spanish were under strict orders not to buy anything from what they judged to be illegal English trading in their waters. Hawkins was facing financial ruin until he was helped by a slave who had escaped from the Spanish to the English ships and told him where the town's treasure was hidden. The

English seized it and only agreed to give it back if the Spanish bought 200 humans from his cargo. Far from rewarding Hawkins' informant or at least taking him to safety, however, the English handed him over to the Spanish, who promptly killed him.[19]

Perhaps these Elizabethan English seafarers regarded Africans as mere commodities to be bought and sold like animals, or Shakespeare's character of Caliban in *The Tempest* who is portrayed as savage and sub-human. Towards the end of her reign, Elizabeth wrote to city mayors warning that there were too many 'divers Blackmoores brought into this realm' and 'those kinde of people should be sente forth of the land'.[20] But ideas of ineradicable racial differences based on the colour of skin were scarcely formed in those days and the historical record is more ambiguous than at first it might seem.

For instance, on a voyage to Spanish America in 1573, Drake formed an alliance with escaped Black slaves called *Cimarrons* to intercept mule trains in Panama carrying gold. According to accounts from the time, they guided and sometimes carried the English through the jungle, fought and died with them, as 'they showed themselves to be no less valiant than industrious and of good judgement'.[21] One of them, known as Diego, accompanied Drake on his later voyages and appears to have been a paid servant and friend until he died from wounds incurred in battle with island natives during the circumnavigation of the world. More troubling is how, on that same journey, Drake seized 'a proper negro wench called Maria' and, for a while, she became the only woman on board the *Golden Hind*. When Drake found out she was pregnant, he marooned her with two other Black men on the desolate 'Crab Island' in Indonesia. Some have since suggested Drake may have been trying to spare them the fate of enslavement, others say he wanted to economise on scarce supplies of food and water, still more say he did not want to explain what his sailors had been doing below deck with her when he got back to Plymouth.[22] But even accounts written within a few years of the voyage described a 'crime laid to his charge' when Drake 'most inhumanely exposed on an island that negro or blackamore-maid, who had been gotten with child in his ship'.[23]

Whatever the truth of Elizabethan views on race, Spain's refusal to buy the Africans that Hawkins and Drake had kidnapped temporarily put paid to systematic slaving by English sailors. Instead, it was the chance to indulge in the more conventional piratical activity that appears to have been Drake's primary motivation for circumnavigating the world when he set off in 1577. Over the next three years, Drake raided six coastal towns, plundered thirteen ships and ran aground a further dozen. The loot he accumulated along the way was so immense, it represented a 4,700 per cent profit on an original outlay of £5,000.[24] Queen Elizabeth's share alone was greater than the English state's entire annual revenue, enabling her to pay off all foreign debts with some change to spare.[25] Little wonder that she resisted Spain's furious demand for its return and instead rewarded Drake with a knighthood on the deck of the *Golden Hind*.

Drake went on to purchase Buckland Abbey in Devon, acquire his own coat of arms – much to the disapproval of more aristocratic members of the royal court – then become mayor and later MP for his home city, Plymouth. The sea had proved, as he is said to have put it, to be 'the path to Fame, the proof of zeal, and way to purchase gold'.[26]

Even now it is impossible not to be awed by the epic qualities of Drake's voyage. This was like going to Mars and back: longer than any journey ever undertaken before; the first known trip around the world in which the captain had survived; a voyage that necessarily involved outrageously brilliant acts of seamanship. By the time Drake returned home, two years late in 1580, most had long since written him off as dead and his initial convoy of six ships had been reduced to one. He had navigated the deep, cold currents of the Strait of Magellan in the record-breaking time of just two weeks, before almost becoming shipwrecked in the Pacific by towering storms. Along the way, he conducted a show trial of the aristocratic Thomas Doughty whom he executed for mutiny and witchcraft, clapped his chaplain in irons for lowering morale, took an arrow in the face from indigenous Americans and claimed what is now California for his queen. He then sailed home 12,000 miles across the Pacific via the Cape of Good Hope with so much booty he had to chuck some of it overboard to prevent the ship sinking.

Drake's most celebrated moment, however, was still to come. By July 1588, the Spanish Armada invasion fleet was on its way and Drake joined other privateering sea dogs alongside his queen's 'navy royal' on the front line of England's defence in Plymouth. The ensuing battles saw their nimbler, better armed and more predatory vessels pursue the bulkier Spanish eastwards across the Channel for several days without either side delivering a knockout blow. Then, with supplies running short and sickness spreading across both fleets, a change in the weather pushed the Armada northwards around the coast of the Britain and Ireland where much of it was wrecked in storms. It was a victory that had more to do with the 'Protestant wind' than naval brilliance, so much so that Queen Elizabeth minted a special coin declaring, in Latin, that 'God blew and they were scattered'.

And if that appears a little fanciful today, so too is the story of Drake shrugging off the sight of the Armada to finish his game of bowls. There was no published account of him playing on the Hoe at all until 1736 and even that described Drake being forced to stop playing immediately as panic spread about the arrival of the Spanish.[27] For all its long overuse as an illustration of English sangfroid and calm in the face of crisis, the story is almost certainly invented, not least because playing bowls or any other kind of game on Plymouth Hoe was expressly forbidden by law at the time.[28] Nor is there evidence to suggest that Elizabethan England had much of that cool-under-fire, keep-calm-and-carry-on national character that later became central to this country's military myths both at sea and on land. Emanuel van Meteren, a Flemish trader in London at the time, concluded the English were 'cruel in war, fiery in attack' and also 'very inconstant, rash, vainglorious, light and deceiving'.[29]

The centrality of Drake's role in defeating the Armada has also been questioned, even by some of those writing at the time. There were accusations that his pirate's instincts led him to defy orders and endanger the English defences when he sailed off to capture the prize of a damaged Spanish ship that happened to be carrying tens of thousands of ducats in gold and silver.[30] His reputation as a naval commander took a further knock with the expensive failure of his 1589 mission to destroy what was left of the Spanish fleet and capture the Azores. And, although the conflict with Spain carried on until 1604, it was more often than not fought by proxy through privateers whose numbers quadrupled over those years to far exceed the size of Elizabeth's navy.[31]

Many historians believe England developed global reach precisely because it was a 'nation of pirates' and, while Drake was fêted for his achievements back at home, there was always a certain amount of diplomatic embarrassment and secrecy about his thieving. After he died from dysentery off the coast of Portobello in 1596 during another piratical voyage, Drake's legend was projected by contemporary writers like Richard Hakluyt as a chivalrous explorer who had scoped the potential for new settlements. His conduct towards the Spanish was presented as 'gentlemanly', as he relieved them of their gold by 'rifling' through their ships and their settlements.[32]

But England and its Protestant faith protected by the sea were scarcely more secure after Drake's death than during his childhood. The failure of an insurgent Catholic 'gunpowder plot' to blow up Elizabeth's successor, James I, and Parliament in 1605 was presented as another intervention of Divine Providence on behalf of the 'chosen people'. An Ipswich Puritan preacher called Samuel Ward designed an engraving called the *Double Deliverance.* On one side heavenly angels are shown blowing the Armada away, while the detection of Guy Fawkes is portrayed on the other. The pope and the King of Spain are depicted plotting with the Devil.[33] It is a tradition that continues with the macabre English tradition of children celebrating 5 November with explosive fireworks and the burning of an effigy called 'Guy'.

England's attitude to what has been called 'piratical imperialism' evolved further in the century after Drake's death. The country was emerging as a significant sea power and its navy could no longer tolerate rogue ships roaming the oceans when there were overseas settlements, trade routes, investments and valuable cargoes of slaves that needed to be protected.[34] By the start of the eighteenth century, men with names that shiver with legend like Captain William Kidd, Edmund Teach – better known as 'Blackbeard' – and 'Calico Jack' Rackham, most of whom had at one point or another been licensed privateers, were being killed or captured by the navy. These pirates were gibbeted, a practice that involved their rotting bodies being displayed in cages for several years at the entrance to docks as a warning for anyone considering piracy as a lifestyle choice.

No one – even the most fervent of Brexiteers – would suggest that a Global Britain of the twenty-first century should be involved in piracy, raiding Spanish settlements, let alone state-sponsored slave-trading. And even this brief examination of Drake's life surely shows how ridiculous it is to invoke his name as a guide to the kind of country some political leaders claim they can build now. By the same measure, however, it is also wrong to brand him with the word 'racist'. Drake's merit for anyone seeking to understand England lies precisely in his complicated reality rather than all the absurd simplifications and overstatements that surround his myth.

Both sides in today's culture wars want a symbol around which to drape their flags or hang their placards. In doing so, they ignore the necessary muddle of contradictions that define England today every bit as much as they did before.

SELLING SLAVES

In that summer of 2020, when protests erupted about England's slave-trading past, Plymouth City Council dug in behind Francis Drake, insisting not only would the statue of him stay on the Hoe but also that it would be floodlit at night.

This local authority did, however, promise to do more by way of explaining the context of Plymouth's historical role in slavery and announced plans to rename Sir John Hawkins Square in the city after Jack Leslie, a Black footballer. He had played for Plymouth Argyle in the 1920s and was chosen for an England squad until, it is said, selectors withdrew the invitation when they discovered the colour of his skin.

The desire to pin the blame on Hawkins was understandable given how invested Plymouth was in Drake. But the decision was still picked up by a campaign called 'Save Our Statues' which was already warning about the 'mob rule' and extremists trying to 'delete your history'.[35] There was a court challenge by Danny Bamping, a local businessman and lawyer, whose chief claim to fame had been an appearance fifteen years earlier on the BBC TV show *Dragons' Den*. Since then, he had dedicated much of his life to a lonely but multi-fronted war against the council, which he claims bankrupted him and to whom he sends around 1,000 emails a year.[36]

In a café near the station, where Bamping had arranged to meet us, he orders a mocha latte – 'no one buys them but you, Danny!' says the lady behind the counter – before embarking on a conversation that veers at breakneck speed from theories about the corruption of Parliament and the influence of local paedophiles to the illegality of

Covid lockdown laws and the danger of vaccines. Getting to the issue at hand, Bamping says changing the name of the square is an example of 'left wing cancel culture' by the council. He goes on: 'They don't like our history; they don't like how we have got roads and statues and all kinds of things celebrating the people who literally made this country great.' If anything, he thinks Hawkins deserves more recognition, not less, saying: 'He was a real English grafter. Drake was just a playboy pissing around on the bowling green when Hawkins was already out there fighting. People like Drake always take the credit but if it wasn't for John Hawkins, we would probably be speaking Spanish now.'

The square formerly named after Sir John Hawkins does not really seem worth fighting over. It is more of a thoroughfare than any-thing else; part of a 1980s redevelopment of the backside of the city's Magistrates Court. There are some trees and a series of benches which provide an outdoor seating overspill for Kitty O' Hanlon's Irish pub. It smells of stale beer and urine. On such an unprepossessing battleground, Bamping has stood for election and mounted multiple legal fights against it being re-named Justice Square. 'He's an idiot' is the short verdict of Tudor Evans, the city's Labour council leader. 'Bamping tried to do all that culture war stuff that the right like to do but it didn't work,' he says. 'We're not like that in Plymouth.'

Nonetheless, this city could have done without having even luke-warm controversy in 2020. The council was planning to launch a '100 journeys that changed the world' theme at a smart new £38 million museum called The Box. But there was one story, above all others, in which the city had invested millions of pounds. That summer marked the 400th anniversary since the Pilgrim Fathers had set sail from Plymouth and named their new settlement 3,000 miles away in America after it. The main exhibition at the new museum was going to be all about the *Mayflower* and its 102 passengers who, it said, procreated up to thirty million descendants living today (a figure that suggests those Puritans were busy doing more than reading the Bible and thinking godly thoughts when they arrived in America).

Although Plymouth's hopes of a bumper year for American tourists were wrecked by the Covid pandemic, the council still spent £750,000 on a twelve-foot-high cast-iron artwork called *Look II* which swiftly became known locally by the nickname of 'Rusty Reg'. It gazes thoughtfully out to sea from a jetty on the western edge of the Hoe, apparently to symbolise the Pilgrims' yearning for a new world. Inevitably, the council was criticised for the cost, as well as for failing to stop 'tombstoning', a practice by which young people climb up the sculpture to dive off it into the sea. Since then, twenty-four-hour CCTV surveillance has been installed to monitor the site, together with a sign that warns teenagers they face imminent death if they carry on like that. Meanwhile, Rusty Reg's creator, the leftish sculptor Antony Gormley, was himself turning away from England, applying for German citizenship because of 'the tragedy of Brexit'.[37]

The story of the *Mayflower* matters immensely to America, but it is also part of England's mythology of the sea. It revolves around the idealism of early colonialists, battling against repressive orthodoxy here at home, setting out onto the oceans and carving out a 'New England' founded on religious freedom and the ancient liberties of Magna Carta, while blessed by the Providence of a Protestant God.

Life for the early settlers was precarious and they would have been unable to survive without what has been described as 'an act of sharing that is almost unimaginable in its generosity'. The indigenous Americans not only gave 'the needy newcomers' their food, but also taught them hunting and agricultural techniques, knowledge of trade routes and local geography. There were treaties in which settlers promised in return to share the land with the people who had been there long before them.[38] In Plymouth, the new colony the Mayflower Pilgrims founded in what is now Massachusetts, the fifty settlers who had survived until the harvest of 1621 celebrated their first 'Thanksgiving' alongside ninety Wampanoag guests. Together, they feasted for three days on fowl, cod and lobster, as well as roasted venison from the five deer which had been presented to them by King Massasoit and his men.[39]

But these initially friendly relations deteriorated as settlements became colonies into a story of misunderstanding, betrayal, theft, massacre and war that would be repeated by the English across North America and then Australia, New Zealand and Africa in the centuries that followed. 'Natives' who remained 'faithful to their ethic of sharing', wrote James Tully, merely provided 'proof of their backwardness and the justification for policies of forced removal and assimilation'.

The wide-open spaces found by those who followed the Pilgrim Fathers, including abandoned fields and villages with providentially buried sacks of corn, were only empty because large numbers of the indigenous inhabitants were being wiped out in what they called the 'Great Dying'. They had no immunity to imported diseases like smallpox, measles or influenza and, by 1700, the original population in areas where they came into contact with settlers had been reduced by as much as 90 per cent.[40]

Few of the settlers who followed the *Mayflower* were motivated by either the piety or the pioneering spirit associated with the original Pilgrims. The vast bulk of them were escaping poverty. England's commoners, as well as people living in the subjugated Ireland and Scotand, lost rights to graze enclosed land. More than half of those who migrated to North America between 1650 and 1780 were convicted prisoners or indentured servants, effectively contracted slaves, needed to meet chronic shortages of labour.[41] Most initially headed for the Caribbean where the English had been picking off islands like Barbados or sometimes seizing them by force, as the navy did in the case of Jamaica in 1650. For instance, around 800 convicts were transported to the West Indies from the West Country by the so-called Bloody Assizes for the crime of supporting a rebellion against the restored monarchy.[42] Although some myth-makers would later regard the eventual prosperity of these settlers as evidence of unique qualities inherent in their 'island race', they generally ignored how many of the early colonialists had been rejected by England itself or were trying to escape the misery of life back home.

By the beginning of the eighteenth century, the English had also begun to settle in numbers along the eastern seaboard of the American mainland. A connected system had developed that has been described as 'the English Atlantic' in which these colonies acted as hubs for trade or supplied the hugely valuable sugar island plantations with produce.[43] This was the dark heart of England's first empire.

The Expansion of England by the Victorian historian J. R. Seeley is best known for suggesting that 'we seem, as it were, to have conquered and peopled half the world in a fit of absence of mind'.[44] He propagated a wholly false story about the 'unopposed occupation of empty countries by the nation that happened to have the greatest surplus population and the greatest maritime power'.[45] For Seeley, this was merely the 'extension of the English race into other lands, which for the most were so thinly populated that our settlers took possession of them without conquest'. Obscuring the reality of violent ethnic cleansing, such an 'empire of settlement' was not, he said, the same as an 'empire of conquest' which involved taking over lands with a large existing population.[46]

Such a baleful distinction between two different empires – one good, one not so good – suggested the 'colonies of settlement' were not only the inevitable consequence of an expanding and superior Englishness but also that a wholesome natural bond of ethnicity, culture and destiny exists across the oceans. By contrast, the 'colonies of conquest' found managing all those 'natives' burdensome; they were places that seemed dangerous, alien and of which Britain remains wary. This mythology of empire has infected attitudes to immigration in recent decades. Those from the empire of conquest – the 'New Commonwealth' – have often been regarded with suspicion and met with hostility. Those arriving from the empire of settlement – called variously the 'Old Commonwealth' or the 'White Commonwealth' – have generally received a warmer welcome.

Although slower than Spain and Portugal to start using slaves from Africa in large numbers, any sense of English high-mindedness was undone by their growing addiction to sugar. In 1700, the average consumption of sugar in England rose to 4lb a person, by 1789 it was 12lb, then 18lb in 1809 and over 90lb in 1901.[47] It was used to sweeten tea and make biscuits, jam, jellies, flavoured creams, chocolate, treacle, cake and puddings. As supplies increased, these were no longer just for the rich but increasingly available to everyone in a consumer revolution that not only defined English eating habits for the next two centuries but helped finance the industrial one that followed.

To feed this demand, a huge workforce was needed in the English sugar plantations that spread across the Caribbean from St Kitts, Nevis and Antigua to Jamaica. The supply of indentured labour was never going to be enough and, by most accounts, the sickly poor from Europe were unsuited to working in the Caribbean climate where they would often die from tropical diseases like malaria, yellow fever and dengue fever or the more prosaic typhus and dysentery.[48] The plantation owners turned to Africa to get slaves who they thought were better suited to tropical conditions and could, quite literally, be worked to death.

Slavery was not based on conceptions about the superiority of the white 'race'. Instead, racism was largely invented to justify slavery.[49] A legal code, hastily drawn up in Barbados and soon copied by other English colonies including in the American South, made clear that Black slaves had no rights. They were regarded as a form of private property, the owners of which were protected by common law and entitled not only to the fruits of their labour but also, in the case of women, the use of their bodies for sexual exploitation.[50] Africans were 'of a barbarous, wild and savage nature ... and wholly unqualified to be governed by the laws, customs and practices of the nation', stated the code. Any slave that retaliated against their treatment would be punished. 'For his second offence of that nature, he shall be severely whipped, his nose slit, and be burned in some part of his face with a hot iron.' No trial was necessary, and if they happened to die during the punishment, 'no person whatsoever shall be liable to any fine therefore'.[51]

Thomas Thistlewood, a manager on a plantation in Jamaica, detailed in his diary how he gave one runaway 'a moderate whipping, pickled him well, made Hector shit in his mouth, immediately put a gag in whilst his mouth was full & made him wear it 4 or 5 hours'.[52] Women not only worked the fields, cooked, cleaned and cared for children but were also subject to violence and rape. In 1765, Thistlewood is recorded as having administered twenty-one floggings to thirteen women in just one year.[53] His diary gave a meticulous account of his sexual abuse of enslaved women: over thirty-seven years, he had intercourse 3,852 times; in a typical year with fourteen different women. 'White men were expected to have sex with Black women, whether Black women wanted sex or not.'[54]

The Royal Africa Company had a Crown-sponsored monopoly on slaving until 1712 when MPs succeeded in opening it up to all comers by using an argument, without any apparent sense of irony, that Englishmen could not be deprived of their freedom to prosper from a lucrative trade in denying the freedom of others.[55] Estimates suggest that no fewer than 4.2 million people were kidnapped and taken thousands of miles away on English or British ships to be sold as slaves over the course of 150 years.[56] Sugar production in Caribbean colonies was joined by other cash crops that could be harvested by slaves and shipped back to England – coffee, tobacco, rice and cotton. The third leg of this trading triangle saw cheap manufactured goods and guns taken to West Africa where they would be exchanged for more kidnapped people.

Even in those days, some people sensed slavery was a grisly business. But, perhaps like today's middle-class cocaine addicts who would rather not know about the murderous activities of drug cartels, they could not work out how to stop a trade that was, wrote Daniel Defoe, as essential to the production of sugar 'as wind is to the ships that bring it home'.[57] Robinson Crusoe, the hero of Defoe's eponymous 1719 novel, is himself a shipwrecked slave trader, who eventually escapes from the desert island to reclaim his fortune from a sugar plantation.

Apologists still like to claim slavery was a long tradition in Africa, whose kings and chiefs had no problem in selling criminals or captives to European traders. But industrial-scale slave-trading of the kind carried out by the English in this period was wholly different from what had happened before. Cheap imports of European goods undermined Africa's own textile and ironwork industries, making them ever more dependent on trading slaves to buy weapons for the wars the slavers had often encouraged. An average of 161,531 guns were sold in West Africa every year between 1796 and 1805.[58]

All of which still matters enormously to the people from places where the wounds inflicted by England's sweet tooth have never healed. But it matters also to the identity of this country today as it clings to the myth of a seafaring trading nation.

Within England's diverse population, which includes the descendants of both slave owners and slaves, there are far too many people blindly refusing to recognise the grim reality behind the myth. For instance, this is how a 2022 pamphlet published by the conservative think tank, the Centre for Brexit Policy, made the case for new trade deals:

Britain became powerful through trade – albeit through its imports, not its exports. The British adventurers, privateers and trading companies searched the world for exotic foods, drugs and raw materials to sell in the UK – importing tea, coffee, sugar, tobacco, cocoa, quinine, potatoes, rubber, wine, raw cotton, wool, furs, timber and high-grade ores. Exports primarily served as ballast in ships and to get around the lack of an acceptable international currency. Later,

Britain used its colonies to produce these goods commercially as raw material for British industries.[59]

No mention there of the enslaved people producing sugar and cotton 'commercially', or that the 'ballast in ships' on at least one leg of this triangular trade comprised kidnapped men, women and children who this country's 'adventurers' had shackled in chains.

RULING WAVES

Hand in hand with the expansion of the empire was that of the Royal Navy and the Royal Dockyard next to Plymouth at the mouth of the River Tamar. It was there that the warships were built and refitted, where the first 'stepped stone' dry docks in Europe were constructed and a whole new town called Devonport grew up that for a while would become larger than Plymouth itself.[60] The impact on the land and oceans around it was profound. An entire hillside had to be cut away to make the dockyard bigger still while four million tons of rock were used in the construction of a gigantic breakwater to protect Plymouth Sound and make the bay a safe anchorage for the Channel Fleet.

All of this was so that the navy could wage transoceanic warfare anywhere across the planet. Those ships safeguarded the routes across the sea that made trade profitable, providing protection for sugar-slave plantations on one side of the world and new outposts in India on the other. They forced open markets and cowed the indigenous people in far-flung places that would form an empire eventually covering a quarter of the planet's entire land mass. And they made joining together with England a more attractive prospect for Scotland than ever before, or, some say, since.

Following the Act of Union in 1707, the Royal Navy provided the muscle for the hybrid new country of Great Britain. But the empire of the sea it built was not only founded by the English, it also enabled the Church of England, the English language, English common law, the English parliamentary system and the English monarchy to be spread to the four corners of the world more effectively than it had been to the four nations of the United Kingdom. When Alfred, Lord

Tennyson gushed over 'the mightiest Ocean-power on earth, Our own fair isle, the lord of every sea', it was still very clearly, 'the fleet of England' about which he wrote. The navy was 'her all-in-all ... And in her fleet her fate.'[61]

In England itself, the navy was usually popular as it was seen as not only the best way to protect this Protestant nation but one that also avoided the kind of land army that could enable a tyrant to seize control. Abroad, the navy increased market share for Britain's slave traders by cowing the Spanish into signing the 1713 Treaty of Utrecht – the kind of deal for which Hawkins and Drake would have happily killed – a contract known as the *Asiento* to sell 144,000 slaves a year to South America.

But the country still faced the threat of imminent invasion from the Continent for much of the eighteenth century. When James Thomson wrote a poem for a masque to be performed in front of the Prince of Wales in 1740 – including the words, 'Rule, Britannia! Rule the Waves' – it was more of an exhortation than a celebration. The subtle change to make it, 'Rule, Britannia, Britannia *rules* the waves!' so beloved of flag wavers even today, was a Victorian adaption to reflect what had by then become merely a statement of fact.[62]

A string of stunning naval victories saw Mediterranean bases like Gibraltar captured from Spain, while the storm-tossed Battle of Quiberon Bay in 1759 not only thwarted France's plan to invade England but also enabled the seizure of its colonies across America, the Caribbean and West Africa.[63] There were some notable setbacks and, as late as 1781, a continental coalition ganged up with rebel colonists against the Royal Navy to defeat it in the Battle of Chesapeake Bay – and Britain in the American War of Independence. Even as much of the empire was being lost in the west, however, a bigger and more lucrative one was being built in the east.

The Royal Navy's control of supply routes in the Indian Ocean enabled Robert Clive to win land battles against the Mughals on behalf of the largely unregulated East India Company. Once installed as Governor of Bengal, Clive began a vast extraction of wealth that put the thieving of Elizabethan pirates like Drake in the shade. This plunder, described by one historian as 'the supreme act of corporate violence in world history', was a primary cause of the Bengal Famine between 1769 and 1773 in which at least one million and possibly as many as ten million people died.[64] One of the biggest statues standing today at the heart of national government in Whitehall still celebrates the achievements of 'Clive of India' who did so much to make his country, as well as his employers and himself, very rich.

Even so, Clive's memorial is dwarfed by the statue atop a column in nearby Trafalgar Square, named after the battle won by Admiral Horatio Nelson in 1805. It left Britain so supreme on the seas that the Royal Navy destroyed or captured 139 enemy ships in the two decades that followed – and lost just one in return.[65] Such dominance was earned through raw courage, better warship design, diet and organisation, as well as discipline enforced by the lash.[66] At least half the navy's 120,000 sailors at the time of the Battle of Trafalgar were 'pressed' into service by being seized from merchant vessels and sometimes the streets. There is some bitter irony in singing 'Rule, Britannia!' and declaring 'Britons never, never, never shall be slaves' when the navy itself was reliant on 'enslaving' tens of thousands of those same Britons into life-threatening service for periods of several years at a time.[67]

Memorials for Nelson were dotted around imperial outposts from Bridgetown and Montreal as well as cities of the 'inner empire' like Glasgow and Edinburgh. Although 'Nelson's Pillar' in Dublin was eventually blown up by the IRA, more than a century after this slavery-supporting admiral's death, his appeal was so enduring that a young South African boy called Rolihlahla Mandela was given the first name of Nelson by his teacher at a westernised school in the Eastern Cape.

The navy was an engine of change in England, too. Huge investment in building or maintaining the fleet at dockyards such as Plymouth Devonport hastened the development of a state with its attendant bureaucrats and taxes.[68] The navy's needs accelerated an industrial revolution with foundries to make cannons, copper mines to strengthen hulls and eventually steam engines to power the ships, while transforming the landscape with no fewer than 4,000 oak trees – once plentiful in England – used in the construction of each ship of the line.[69]

And yet remorseless military logic pointed towards a fate like that of Nelson himself, who had various body parts blown off over the years, then famously declared that 'England Expects Every Man Will

Do His Duty', before finally bleeding out on HMS *Victory*. Even as the British Empire extended its reach to New Zealand and Asia, an expansion driven in part by the shipbuilders' insatiable demand for timber, the launch of the ironclad *Gloire* in 1859 appeared to have rendered much of the Royal Navy's wooden fleet obsolete. Within a year, Britain had built the all-iron HMS *Warrior* as it embarked on a fantastically expensive naval arms race.

This empire was a nervous giant. Bigger countries, including the United States and Germany, were already looking to challenge the Royal Navy's right to rule the waves and, eventually the 'balance of power' on the war-exhausted European continent in the nineteenth century would tilt in dangerous new ways. Concrete forts known as Palmerston's Follies were hastily placed in the water around coastal bases such as Plymouth.

The problem was that its military might was concentrated in bases resembling 'a vast archipelago strewn around the world' on islands such as Gibraltar and Malta in the Mediterranean; St Helena and Ascension in the Atlantic; Jamaica, Trinidad and Bermuda in the Caribbean. There were the naval outposts of Singapore and Hong Kong in the South China Sea, as well as Perth, Adelaide, Melbourne, Sydney and Wellington in the Pacific.[70] A foreign observer at the time concluded that Britain was an 'artificial' power whose colonies were held together only 'through the threads of the fleet ... threads that could all be broken or cut'.[71]

Even at Global Britain's zenith in the nineteenth century, trade with its imperial possessions was still less than that with its closest neighbours in Europe.[72] And all those maps coloured pinkish-red only served to conceal how loose was the empire's grip on the interior of the lands it nominally possessed.[73]

As for Plymouth itself, the days when the likes of Drake would sail into the Sound in a ship laden with looted Spanish gold did not last much beyond the sixteenth century. Anyone looking for evidence of the fortunes created by slavery should begin at the exquisite Georgian architecture of Bristol's Queen Square, London's Portman Square and the decorative frieze depicting African faces on Liverpool's town hall. Or, even better, they can visit the huge country piles such as Harewood House, the family seat of the Lascelles plantation owners, with its Robert Adam interiors, Chippendale furniture and collection of paintings by Turner, Reynolds, Titian and El Greco.

Such wealth did not trickle down as far as Plymouth because it was too far from the centres of population and industry to prosper.[74] The city had been built as a naval base for its access to the Atlantic, not to markets in England, and in vain did it make occasional pleas for a larger share of the imperial pie. For instance, in 1812, after the transport of slaves across the Atlantic was abolished, Plymouth lobbied Parliament for the East India Company's monopoly on oriental trade to be lifted and claimed its 'harbours, docks, stores, and warehouses' made it 'equal to any port of the British Isles for carrying on an extensive commerce'.[75]

But some were more 'equal' than others. Unlike the great commercial ports of London, Liverpool, Glasgow, Bristol and Hull, Plymouth was to be dominated by the public sector naval war machine. This stifled other private businesses and left it so reliant on government subsidy that the end of the Napoleonic Wars in 1815 saw rents plummet and workhouses overflow in the city.[76]

The local population, known as 'Janners', often lived in the most abject and overcrowded slums where the water was so dirty that children drank beer. Girls as young as eight had their bodies sold for sex in Castle Street, then known as 'Damnation Alley'.[77] In 1871 the home secretary claimed that in Devonport alone there were thousands of women and child prostitutes. New laws were applied to limit the spread of sexually transmitted disease not because of any concerns about their welfare but because of 'naval imperatives to efficiency'.[78]

It was around this time that all the different faces of Francis Drake – pirate, patriotic Protestant, upwardly-mobile trader, explorer and hero-admiral – began to merge into a bigger myth about England and Englishness. Inland from Plymouth, through Drake's hometown of Tavistock and across the wildness of Dartmoor to the north-facing coast of Devon, is a village that occasionally features as a quiz question as the only place in England with an exclamation mark in its name. Westward Ho! is so-called because developers wanted to cash in on the immense popularity of Charles Kingsley's 1855 novel of the same name which is set nearby. This was a swashbuckling romance all about privateers seizing Spanish treasure and then fighting with their lives to defend England. Kingsley presents Drake – 'at once manful and godly' – as eschewing the effete education of continental types, having him declare: 'Book-learning is not business; book-learning did not get me round the world; book-learning did not make Captain Hawkins, nor his father, neither, the best ship builders from Hull to Cadiz; and book-learning, I very much fear, won't plant Newfoundland.'[79]

Plymouth finally put up a monument to Drake on the Hoe three centuries after the Armada. This was during the Victorians' 'statue-mania' when it was thought the public needed some heroes to rally around and Rudyard Kipling, the myth-making poet of High Imperialism, was fretting about the fate of the empire.

'What should they know of England who only England know?' he asked in his lament at the ignorance of achievements overseas among the 'poor little street-bred people'.[80] Kipling would call upon the United States to 'Take up the White Man's burden' of 'new-caught, sullen peoples/Half devil and half child',[81] as an overstretched empire began to show cracks from India and South Africa to Ireland that hinted at the flaws in its construction. In the years that followed, Joseph Chamberlain would split the Conservative Party by campaigning for a new Imperial Federation that asked the white settler colonies to come to the aid of the Mother Country, 'a weary Titan' that had 'borne the burden for many years'.[82]

The twentieth century was when another set of monuments sprouted up around Plymouth. At first, the city's war memorials are easy to over-look because they are found in every English town and village. What sets those in Plymouth apart is their scale, range and sheer number. Close to Drake's statue on the Hoe is a tall obelisk beneath which are inscribed the names of tens of thousands of sailors who died in the twentieth century's wars and have 'no other grave than the sea'. Most were not from Plymouth and many were from former colonies who had died for an empire that has disintegrated in the years since. All along the Hoe are further memorials for those who died in South Africa, Norway, Dunkirk, Normandy, Crete, Korea, Algeria, Burma, Borneo and the Falklands, that final adventure for the old imperial navy.

Although the naval base and its now privatised dockyard remain Plymouth's biggest employer, successive cuts to defence spending mean there are far fewer jobs there than before. When the aircraft car-rier HMS *Ark Royal* was decommissioned and broken up for scrap in 1980, the city was presented with its giant ten-tonne anchor as a keep-sake. It now sits poignantly on the city side of the Hoe surrounded by flowering shrubs, like a well-tended grave.

If all these memorials are about sacrifice and loss, Drake still represents a lighter story which is less about remorseless warfare, where victory became determined by the size of guns or the tonnage of ships, than a twinkle-eyed defiance of the odds and maybe death, too.

Contemporary accounts sometimes suggested Drake had supernatural or, according to the Spanish, demonic powers. The Victorians elevated him to Arthurian status. 'Drake's Drum', an 1897 poem by Sir Henry Newbolt which was later set to music, popularised the idea that he would answer calls to return whenever England is in danger:

> Drake he's in his hammock till the great Armadas come,
>   (Capten, art tha sleepin' there below?),
> Slung atween the round shot, listenin' for the drum,
>   An' dreamin' arl the time o' Plymouth Hoe.
> Call him on the deep sea, call him up the Sound,
>   Call him when ye sail to meet the foe;
> Where the old trade's plyin' an the old flag flyin,
>   They shall find him, ware an' wakin', as they found him
> long ago.

English sailors claimed to have heard the drum beating at various epic moments in history including most recently during the evacuation from Dunkirk in 1940. And there really is a drum that, according to what tourist websites refer to as 'folk lore', Drake insisted must be kept in Buckland Abbey or 'Plymouth will fall'.[83] It was briefly removed for safekeeping during the Second World War and then hurriedly restored to its proper place by superstitious civil servants when the city started being heavily bombed.

It's a nice story but the drum now on display at his old home near Plymouth is a replica. The original was placed in cold storage at a warehouse somewhere in the Midlands a few years ago. And, if what has happened to Plymouth since hasn't been too bad, neither has it been particularly good.

Many of the worst slums were cleared by bombing during the Second World War and then by a vast reconstruction programme afterwards that erased what was left of the Victorian centre. In its place was built a new model city designed by Patrick Abercrombie, the master planner of his generation, to deliver what he called 'spaciousness and beauty for all'. But its grand boulevards always seemed too big for a place that had little private sector prosperity and the thirteen new housing estates separated by ring roads spreading inland loosened connections with the sea, even as Plymouth still seemed a long way from anywhere else.[84]

Today's modern city of 265,000 people has around 10,000 children growing up in poverty, pockets of deep deprivation and no strategic rail or road connections to the rest of the country.[85] Although the pubs are no longer filled with the navy's sailors – hard-drinking 'Jolly Jack Tars' with their 'hearts of oak' – the streets outside still pulse to the beat of past generations who were never too far from violence. A report commissioned by the local council in 2021 after a spate of murders found that 80 per cent of women and girls feel unsafe at night while two-thirds have experienced intimidating behaviour from men.[86]

Efforts to reflate the myths of buccaneering past have not done Plymouth many favours. When this city voted for Brexit in 2016, the political rhetoric about Drake and independence from the Continent was wrapped up with claims Global Britain would now prosper in a free trade area 'probably 10 times the size' of the European Union. That would have been bigger than the size of the entire global economy. The deal eventually signed with the EU settled for a free trade area that, without Northern Ireland, was smaller than the size of the United Kingdom.[87]

As we write this, there is no sign of the much-vaunted trade deal with the US and those that have been agreed represent a drop in the ocean compared to what has been lost by leaving the EU. Ideas of an 'Anglosphere' ignore how it makes little sense for Commonwealth countries to be doing exclusive deals with each other when there are other markets much easier to reach closer to home.

Similar promises that a fleet-of-foot country would once again head out across the oceans to find its fortune by undercutting Europe have gradually given way to the logic that aligning as closely as possible to EU standards will ameliorate the worst damage done to exports. The military focus also shifted away from distant shores and back towards defending Europe continental borders following Russia's invasion of Ukraine. The retreat from Global Britain rhetoric has seen many of the politicians who once advocated it shrink back into the idea of reinforcing the natural barrier of the sea to stop refugees' small-boat crossings.

Plymouth undoubtedly played its part in both protecting England from invasion in the sixteenth century and providing a springboard to

expand out to the world in those that followed. This involved depre-
dation and slavery, as well as swash and buckle.

But the elemental forces that once made this city so important to
the national story have not disappeared. Even when the wind is taken
out of this myth's sails, it is still a force of nature, one which might yet
propel this country forward to meet new challenges facing it today.

A WIND OF CHANGE

Plymouth is one of the most heavily memorialised cities in the
world and many of its monuments are for those who set out across
the oceans with varying degrees of success. They include not only
Drake and the *Mayflower*'s Pilgrim Fathers, but also Captain James
Cook to explore the coast of Australia and get stabbed to death in
Hawaii. Then there was Charles Darwin to find evidence for his
theory of evolution and keep quiet about it for twenty years for fear
of outraging conservative Christian opinion, Captain Robert Scott
to freeze to death in the Antarctic on a pointless race to the South
Pole and Francis Chichester to sail single-handed 'the wrong way'
around the world.

But none of these voyages by dead Englishmen have as much
relevance right now as one undertaken from the same city by a
Swedish girl.

Greta Thunberg left Plymouth in August 2019 hoping she might
persuade world leaders to stop the 'mass extinction' of species
including their own. Barely five foot tall and still only sixteen, she had
become a global figurehead for young people protesting against climate change. Invited to address the United Nations in New York on
the subject, Thunberg refused to fly because that would have meant
using fossil fuels for the journey and instead relied on the natural
power of the Atlantic's 'trade winds' to take her across the ocean on
a racing yacht.[88]

At a press conference held at the Mayflower Marina before her
departure, she endured journalistic enquiries about her clothes
and bathroom habits. No, she couldn't yet say what would be the
toughest aspect of the trip. 'Maybe seasickness,' she offered helpfully.
The yacht's skipper, who had already read out a prepared statement

about his previous adventures at sea, could be heard asking in a tone of puzzlement mixed with hurt, 'so, most of the questions are for *her*?'[89]

Polling consistently shows that women are more worried about the environment than men and Thunberg was the latest powerful female voice to make the case for urgent action on climate change. This annoyed some people, particularly self-consciously masculine politicians. When Thunberg sailed across the Atlantic from Plymouth, she attracted the scorn of everyone from the then US President Donald Trump to Arron Banks, who had bankrolled UKIP and the Brexit Party with millions of pounds. Above a picture of the teenager setting sail, Banks tweeted: 'Freak yachting accidents do happen in August …' He later claimed the outrage caused by his 'joke' about a child drowning only proved that his critics 'have no sense of humour'.[90]

What is less disputed, however, is that her campaigning helped move the dial on this issue. In the years since her voyage, even within a political class terrified of antagonising key groups of voters, a consensus of sorts was established about the need to make sustained investment in renewable energy. In 2023, the UK was second only to China in the amount of offshore power it had installed and new national targets were being set to build shoals of wind turbines in the sea which will generate enough electricity to heat and light every home in the country.[91]

Not all of this has had the greenest of motives. It is partly about the security of energy supplies, an issue that became more pertinent after Russia invaded Ukraine in 2022. It is also about commercial interests competing for a slice of a renewable market estimated to be worth upwards of £2 trillion by 2030.

But for Plymouth, it may be a matter of simple self-interest. The city is directly threatened by the problem with rising sea levels from unchecked climate change, forecast to cover large portions of it with water by 2050.[92] And Plymouth is also well placed to be part of the solution because, in addition to its natural coastline, the recently rebranded 'Ocean City' has an engineering skills base in Devonport, as well as a cluster of research centres including Plymouth Marine Laboratory, the Marine Biological Association and the University of Plymouth.

It may be significant that many of those blowing a wind of change through Plymouth's relationship with the sea are women. The university's female professors include Deborah Greaves, an ocean engineer who leads a national coalition of universities co-ordinating research on renewable energy. She is director of the COAST Laboratory which looks like a massive swimming pool but turns out to be where renewable energy technology is tested by subjecting it to a battering from simulated waves, currents and wind.

Greaves explains how Plymouth has helped develop new offshore designs, 'moored to the seabed and floating rather than fixed so they can be installed in deeper water', which will allow the UK to use far more of its coast. Ministers say they want a tenth of renewable energy to be generated from this form of floating offshore power by 2030, a proportion they expect to multiply many times over the decades after that.

Although this technology doesn't solve everything, it can be part of the answer for the country as a whole – and Plymouth in particular. Greaves says: 'I was born here and went to school here. I came home to be with my family and because I always missed the sea. It would be wonderful if these kinds of projects could help the economy in Plymouth and the whole country. The UK developed a lot of the original wind farm technology but we're mostly buying turbines from other countries ... We need to do better than that this time.'

Among the marine scientists and engineers who have recently studied at Plymouth was Emily Stevenson, who set up a project in Cornwall to remove ocean litter from a beach. Stevenson ended up pictured on the front of national newspapers with an intact Walkers Crisps packet that had been floating in the sea since 1997, the same year she was born. A subsequent campaign, which included Stevenson graduating from Plymouth in a dress made entirely from these seemingly indestructible little plastic bags eventually persuaded Walkers to begin a recycling programme.[93]

There are already signs of a different kind of English cultural identity emerging in some of the newer monumental architecture around the city which does not revolve around dead pirates, admirals and sailors. Outside Plymouth's Theatre Royal is a 23-foot-high image of a woman called *The Mighty Messenger* who is shown crouching and ready to spring forward. A century after Nancy Astor became the first woman to sit in the House of Commons in 1919, the city that elected her finally marked her achievement with a statue of her on Plymouth Hoe. And on the university campus at Portland Square, there is a modern artwork called 'Hope' showing an amorphous figure lifting up a child to represent the desire to 'protect the next generation'.[94]

Proponents of a greener economy can sometimes also be guilty of their own Global Britain vanity. More realistic is a humbler set of opportunities through collaborating with overseas scientists, supply chains and energy markets. But, if this country is to develop a new relationship with the wind and the sea, reheating myths about England's separateness or its naval power will only get in the way.

For instance, Trevor Hardcastle moved to Plymouth so that he could work with its scientists developing underwater robotics. He developed a floating renewable energy platform called the Marlin System to be used by small coastal communities in developing countries like Bangladesh and India so that they no longer have to burn wood or import propane gas. But the prototype his firm built was never tested off the coast of Plymouth because government funding was cut in 2020 along with the international aid budget – part of the Global Britain strategy of recalibrating spending towards the hard power of more warships. 'The project came close to being scrapped at that point,' says Hardcastle, 'we just didn't have the money to do it.' Hardcastle says he has now secured other investment for his invention, adding, 'the jobs we create will probably go elsewhere'.[95]

A couple of years later, Plymouth City Council was being led by a Conservative who appeared to disregard the threat of rising global temperatures altogether. Richard Bingley had described how 'some countries – Pakistan, the United Arab Emirates and Saudi Arabia – have adjusted for many years to living in barren, sandy landscapes', adding: 'I'm not really feeling that we should worry too much about climate change in itself.' Those remarks were made in a video for an organisation called the New Culture Forum, part of a network of up to a dozen right-wing groups notoriously based at 55 Tufton Street, London. One of them was the Save Our Statues campaign of which Bingley himself just happened to be general secretary. This generated endless publicity over protecting monuments like that of Sir Francis Drake on Plymouth Hoe from what it said was a left-wing mob trying to 'erase our history'.[96]

After Bingley became Plymouth's leader, one of his councillors resigned from the Conservative Party over what she called a 'misogynist and bullying culture'. She may also have upset him by routinely shortening his first name to 'Dick'. He was eventually forced to resign himself after running foul of local opinion and the courts over his order to cut down more than 200 trees lining Armada Way in the dead of night.[97]

The myth of Drake finishing his game of bowls on the Hoe before taking on the Spanish Armada will always be more vivid than the sight of some wind farms floating off the coast. But just as nations change over time, so do the stories that people tell about them, and it is ludicrous to suggest that Drake is being 'written out of history' just because historians are busy writing about how he was involved in slavery.

A deflated myth is more useful than one that has been blown up out of all proportion. It is probably not entirely coincidental that the conservative culture warriors who are fiercest about preserving mythology in stone are also those who deny the science of climate change or get into trouble for toppling, not statues, but trees.

To its credit, Plymouth's council has recently installed a memorial to remember the victims of the slave trade. This features a bronze engraving of how captured Africans were stowed in impossibly tight spaces on the British ship *Brookes*, and a plaque explaining how this 'shocking image' was first drawn in 1788 by the Plymouth MP William Elford. Elsewhere, the Drake display at the local museum has been modified with a sign that describes him in suitably muddled terms as a 'hero, pirate and slave trader', adding that the voyages he took helped lay the foundations for England later to dominate 'the European trade in forcibly transported Africans'. Another glass case filled with some historical detritus to do with Sir John Hawkins has been supplemented by a couple of old manacles and a reference to the Black man in his coat of arms.

Most people walk by these displays without pausing as they head for the bigger, flashier exhibits. Linger too long, however, and a volunteer guide appears to explain she had worked at Buckland Abbey for many years and has great affection for 'Sir Francis'. Pointing an accusing finger at the new sign about Drake, she whispers: 'I don't really like them talking about him like that and doing him down.'

Does she mean the bit about him being a slave trader? 'Well, I don't really know about all that,' she replies.

And then, in words that reduce all the hysteria and hyperbole over culture wars to a distant rumble, she adds: 'I just don't think it's right to call him a pirate.'

3

Hull

England's Moral Mission

Out on a limb and towards the end of a line, trains go slow through a flat eastern English landscape of fields 'too thin and thistled to be called meadows'. Eventually they give way and open out to the great brown breadth of the Humber into which much of the country has always drained its silt. This is where the poet Philip Larkin described 'the piled gold clouds, the shining gull-marked mud, gathers to the surprise of a large town'.[1]

Almost as startling for passengers arriving in Hull is that one of the first sights to greet them at the railway station is a statue of Larkin with his glasses twisted askew by what the local newspaper described as 'a drunken moron' trying to swing on them late one night.[2] Although Larkin's poetry is loved for the way it throbs with his particular kind of Englishness, his reputation as a person has never recovered since the posthumous publication of his letters. These showed him posturing as a woman-hating saloon-bar racist who stopped going to watch Test match cricket because, he said, there were 'too many fucking n—about'.[3] He had indulged his self-loathing scorn on Hull, too, when he first arrived in the city in the 1950s to be the university's librarian. 'I'm settling down in Hull all right,' he wrote. 'Every day I sink a little further.'[4]

There is certainly something about Hull that can seem as cussed and contrary as Larkin. The city is a stronghold of rugby league, that defiantly professional, working-class and northern breakaway from the once amateur, private school and southern code of English rugby union. Trains stop at a building named the 'Paragon Interchange' when 'Hull Railway Station' would surely have done. The city's telephone boxes are the only ones in England painted not red but an off-white shade of cream because the local council always refused to be part of the Post Office. In the centre of the city there is a memorial plaque to the first real military action of the English Civil War, when Hull locked its gates against King Charles I in 1642. Locals say that the royal family have been reluctant to visit ever since and perhaps it explains why the first bit of the city's proper title, *Kingston* upon Hull, is invariably omitted or forgotten.

Nor is Larkin the only poet memorialised in Hull. At Trinity Square there is a statue of Andrew Marvell who, as MP for Hull in the late seventeenth century, combined his contempt for the royal court with his frustrated passion for a 'coy mistress'. He imagined her gathering rubies on the banks of the Ganges in far-off India while 'I by the tide/Of Humber would complain'. And the great melancholic estuary itself has long marked the start of a boundary running down the River Trent that separates the southern half of England from the old kingdom of Northumbria and the rest of Britain that everyone – from the Romans, the Saxons and the Normans to Oliver Cromwell, the Established Church and even Margaret Thatcher – always found harder to control.

Hull is, therefore, not the most obvious spot for this book's third myth, one rooted in the nineteenth century when England claimed first moral redemption and then a moral superiority over other countries. It is a story not of the city's dank-humoured poets but of the Evangelical Protestant politician William Wilberforce who helped abolished the slave trade and became the embodiment of a civilising missionary purpose. This myth has not only resonated around the world and in people's idea of England but has also impacted everyday life on everything from the price of bread to our taste for tea. And, to the extent that these moralising values sought to impose a one-size-fits-all straitjacket on people, it still affects how the English judge each other now.

Much as Plymouth has done with Francis Drake, Hull has tried its best to build an identity around its most famous son. Wilberforce was voted what the *Hull Daily Mail* called the 'greatest ever Hullensian' after a poll of readers in which poets did not even make the short-list.[5] The city has a Wilberforce Drive running through its centre, the Wilberforce Sixth Form College and the Wilberforce Health Centre. There is 'Wilberforce Blend' fair trade coffee available at the Peloton Café in the new health club on Pickering Road. On the High Street, a bit further up from the unfortunately named Ye Olde Black Boy pub, is Hull University's Wilberforce Institute for the Study of Slavery and Emancipation where there is an annual Wilberforce Lecture given by a champion of human rights. Next door is Wilberforce House, a handsome red-brick building where the man himself was born in 1759 and which operates as a museum dedicated to his memory. In the garden outside is the first of two statues of Wilberforce, this one a life-sized white marble number, while the second – ten minutes' walk away – is mounted atop a 102-foot-high Doric column.

For all that, however, Wilberforce never really belonged to Hull. He was its MP for just four out of the forty-five years he spent in the House of Commons. And it was there that he earned his fame, doggedly tabling, then re-tabling, Bills to abolish the slave trade even when the cause seemed hopeless. Despite a shrimp-like stature and weak constitution, he was a powerful speaker and master of debate in an age when that really mattered. 'You may choose to look the other way,' Wilberforce famously told MPs in a four-hour speech describing the slave trade's sins, 'but never again can you say that you never knew.'[6] When the Commons finally approved the ban on 23 February 1807, tears rolled down his face and MPs on all sides rose to give him a rare standing ovation. It is why Wilberforce is not buried at Hull Minster but lies instead alongside dead kings, queens, prime ministers, admirals and poets in Westminster Abbey. And there, beneath a marble statue showing Wilberforce seated, with his body contorted as if in the throes of moral passion, are the words:

His name will ever be specially identified with those exertions which, by the blessing of God, removed from England the guilt of the African slave trade, and prepared the way for the abolition of slavery in every colony of the Empire.

It is for this, being the person who 'removed England's guilt', that Wilberforce has been so venerated. Endless biographies with titles such as *He Freed Britain's Slaves*, *A Hero for Humanity*, or *Statesman and Saint* kept the Wilberforce story handy for whenever it was needed to sponge clean a nation's conscience.[7] As the latter-day historian Linda Colley has written: 'Abolitionism became one of the vital underpinnings of British supremacy, offering – as it seemed to do – irrefutable proof that British power was founded on religion, on freedom and on moral calibre, not just on a superior stock of armaments and capital.'[8]

Like other myths, this one has waxed and waned with political fashions. It seemed to slip out of England's story during the carnage of the twentieth century when the end of colonial rule in distant lands coincided with the steep decline of organised religion in England. Although Hull marked the centenary of Wilberforce's death in 1933 with a ceremony attended by thousands of people, the giant statue and column commemorating him in the town centre had to be moved to a nearby park just a year later because it had been deemed 'a traffic hazard'. And, as the empire began to break up, the historian and future prime minister of Trinidad and Tobago Eric Williams felt bold enough to dismiss Wilberforce and white English abolitionists as mere functionaries of an emerging capitalism in which the sugar plantations had become unprofitable. Williams claimed that the high-minded principles associated with them were mere 'propaganda' and even took aim at Wilberforce's character, saying, 'there is a certain smugness about the man, his life, his religion'.[9] In the years that followed, the high column built in Wilberforce's memory suffered a further indignity when the incongruous and brutalist tower block that is Hull College rose up behind it.[10]

But Wilberforce and this myth of England possessing a civilising moral mission for the world has resurfaced in recent years. As the bicentenary of the abolition of the slave trade approached in 2007, there was a clamour to reinstate Wilberforce in the national pantheon. William Hague, the former Conservative Party leader, published a well-received biography of Wilberforce that reflected his admiration for a fellow Yorkshireman called William with conservative views. On the liberal left, the broadcaster Melvyn Bragg recorded a special edition of his popular BBC Radio 4 programme, *In Our Time*. He described how Wilberforce had come from provincial northern origins, perhaps similar to his own, before having more influence 'on the course of human history' than all the other Englishmen and Englishwomen buried in Westminster Abbey. 'He was truly a great man in his time and, I think, for all time,' concluded Bragg. The then prime minister Tony Blair also had a reason to revive the story of Wilberforce. He was entering his final months in Downing Street and his Labour government was fighting increasingly unpopular wars. As a politician with Christian convictions unusually deep for his country at the beginning of the twenty-first century, Blair was perhaps instinctively drawn to this story of redemption.

The museum at Wilberforce's old house in Hull was duly refurbished for the occasion and his Doric column illuminated, while tourists were given the chance to wander along the 'Wilberforce Trail' through a maze of old town streets next to the docks. But this story of England was regarded as too important to be left to Hull alone and the government wheeled out the full panoply of the state with £20 million spent on commemoration projects across the country. There was a Downing Street reception, along with special £2 coins and a new set of stamps honouring those who fought against the slave trade. John Prescott, the deputy prime minister and himself a Hull MP, toured slave heritage sites in West Africa and the Caribbean. A new International Slavery Museum was opened in Liverpool, while a group of young Christians walked 250 miles from Hull to Westminster in chains before being joined by the Archbishops of Canterbury and York for the final leg across Lambeth Bridge.[11]

The highlight was a National Service of Commemoration at Westminster Abbey in March attended by the queen where the congregation sang 'Amazing Grace', that Evangelical hymn of redemption.

> Amazing grace! (how sweet the sound)
> That sav'd a wretch like me!
> I once was lost, but now am found,
>   Was blind, but now I see.

As with the celebrations of Magna Carta or England's seafaring past, this commemoration also said much about the political climate of the time. Barely a month after the Wilberforce bicentenary in 2007,

for instance, there was no official effort whatsoever to commemorate the 300th anniversary of the Act of Union between Scotland
and England. The reason, perhaps, was that the pro-independence
Scottish National Party had just taken power at the Holyrood parliament in Edinburgh.

But the debate about Wilberforce's legacy was not confined to saying
simply that he made right what had been wrong. Some objected to
what they called the 'Wilberfest' because, for them, the British Empire
symbolised everything that had been and still was wrong with the country.
As the Archbishop of Canterbury began speaking at the Westminster
Abbey commemoration for Wilberforce, he was interrupted by Toyin
Agbetu, a community activist, who slipped past security guards to stand
three yards in front of England's monarch. 'You, the Queen, should be
ashamed!' he shouted. 'This is an insult to us.' The BBC dutifully averted
its cameras and Agbetu was dragged from the Abbey.[12]

Although Tony Blair had become fairly inured to such things by this
stage of his career, he might have guessed that trouble was brewing.
The prime minister had already resisted calls to make a full apology
for slavery because, he said, doing so might open up the prospect of
the government paying billions of pounds in reparations. Instead,
Blair issued a statement expressing 'deep sorrow' for the horror of
slavery, before adding, on a cheerier note, 'thankfully, Britain was the
first country to abolish the trade'.[13]

And, amid all the angry clamour from the anti-imperialist left, a very
different noise could be heard coming from the neo-conservative –
maybe even 'neo-imperialist' – right. For them, the abolition of the slave
trade was less a reason for hand-wringing regret over the wrong that had
been done, than evidence that the empire had, in fact, always been right.

Under the headline 'Recolonise Africa!' the historian Andrew
Roberts used a newspaper article to say: 'There is no country or race
that is expected to feel guilty about the moment their empire occupied the limelight of history – except, of course, the English-speaking
peoples.' The 'Left-liberal intelligentsia,' he said, was undermining
pride in an imperial past when Africa had 'never known better times
than during British rule'. He called for the 'old system of "informal"
empire to be re-instituted across the Dark Continent', adding that
'the "boyish tyranny" of the English-speaking peoples' would be

welcomed back in Africa, because people there had an 'overall memory of justice, sound money and fair dealing'.[14]

Roberts was writing in the middle of the American-led War on Terror that he and many like him regarded as a chance for the West – especially its English-speaking Anglosphere – to resume the moral leadership of a benighted world, not just to right wrongs but to reassert old power and restore old interests. Boris Johnson was another attracted at this time to the contrariness of arguing that the empire had been all about peace and prosperity. In an article he wrote about colonising Africa, he asked: 'Are we guilty of slavery?' Johnson answered his own question with the word, '*Pshaw*', adding, 'the problem is not that we were once in charge, but that we are not in charge anymore'.[15]

The revival of pride in the superiority of the British Empire was mostly an English phenomenon. It never really extended to Scotland, Wales and Ireland where nationalists usually shrug off their ancestors' imperial contribution by insisting they were victims of English colonialism, too. And, even though the most influential popular historian about empire in recent years has been a Scot, he is an expat who lives in America.

Niall Ferguson's bestselling 2003 book, *Empire*, acknowledged the empire had been guilty of many sins, but argued that the West still had much to learn from the nineteenth century's 'Anglobalization' in which an English system of values and institutions had been spread across the world. He regarded the abolition of the slave trade as the 'moral transformation of the British Empire' which saw the country going from being the world's leading enslaver to the world's greatest emancipator. 'It was almost as if a switch was flicked,' he wrote.[16] When an opinion poll showed 59 per cent of British people were proud of the empire, compared to just 19 per cent who said they were ashamed, it was greeted with a characteristically provocative two-word tweet from Ferguson: 'I won.'[17]

Roberts and Ferguson were tapping into a myth of a better empire whose adherents range from those who comfort themselves with the thought that at least Britain behaved better than the Belgians did in the Congo, to others who believe Anglo-Saxon values should be reimposed on the world now.

THE 'BETTER' EMPIRE

Arguments about how this country's imperial adventures should shape England's sense of itself are not new. From the very start there were those who took pride in the empire and claimed it was built on higher moral ground than others. England's first foreign settlements in the sixteenth and seventeenth centuries were defended as 'a civilising mission', even though 'in practice "civility" was equated with acceptance of English rule'.[18] It was then, too, that pamphlets circulated detailing atrocities committed by Spain in its conquest of Central and South America or the sadism of the Catholic Inquisition. This so-called 'black legend' was used to justify the milder empire of England.[19]

As it grew, however, so did the kind of doubts and self-criticism that represent another significant strand of England's tradition. There was an 'undertow of dissent' towards the empire that found expression in books like *Gulliver's Travels* by Jonathan Swift that, far from being the children's story it is often known as today, was a deeply unsettling story of indigenous innocence destroyed by slavery and conquest.[20] Then, in the 1770s, Edward Gibbon's gloomy verdict about the decline of the Roman Empire chimed with a successful revolt by American colonies to sow doubts about the righteousness and stability of this country's global ambition. In the 1780s, the philosopher-politician Edmund Burke began a long campaign against the imperial expansionism led by the East India Company and especially the governor-general Warren Hastings' abuse of power. Even then much of this dissent had a conservative impulse with Burke intent on defending traditional 'English liberty' against the dangerous 'Jacobin' freedom being fomented by the French Revolution.[21]

It was into this mix that the unimposing figure of William Wilberforce, little more than five foot tall in his stockings, stepped into history. He was born in 1759 when Hull was a prosperous place with docks infused with the smell of oilseed and the stench of processed whale blubber. Although the Wilberforce family fortune had been enhanced by refining some plantation sugar from the West Indies, this port's east coast location made it the wrong place to profit directly from the Atlantic slave trade. Instead, most of its business was conducted across the North Sea, importing timber and animal skins from Scandinavia, as well as wheat, peas, pork and butter from Holland and Germany, 'all to be washed down,' wrote William Hague admiringly in his biography of Wilberforce, 'with thousands of gallons of Rheinish Hoch'.[22]

Hull had a strong Protestant tradition which had resisted the Royalists in the civil war and later installed a gilded statue of William III – 'King Billy' – whose 'Glorious Revolution' of 1688 had seen Hull rise up against the local Catholic commander. When Robert and Elizabeth Wilberforce gathered around the medieval marble font at the Holy Trinity Church for the baptism of their new son, though, membership of the Church of England was more of a stodgy formality for someone of their social rank rather than anything too morally demanding. Wilberforce would later write that his mother 'had no true conception of the spiritual nature and aim of Christianity' and that 'her piety was rather of that standard to which the Church of England had then so generally declined'.[23]

Many believed England's state religion was sinking into a mire of corruption, with wealthy parishes allotted on the basis of nepotism or political favours while largely absentee clergy lived off a compulsory tithe imposed on people whether they attended church or not. The brothers John and Charles Wesley, along with George Whitefield, had begun a 'Methodist' revival of a purer and more disciplined approach to religion. A new urban working class, many of whom saw the Established Church as being too close to the rural gentry, thronged to their outdoor meetings and chapels.

For others, however, Methodism was not only a foolishly earnest sect but also one linked to dangerous radicals challenging the social order. Wilberforce himself had shown such tendencies as a boy which led to his mother feeling she needed to rescue him from a godly aunt and uncle who had taken him to revivalist meetings. He was withdrawn from the local grammar school because the teacher there was suspected of Methodism at a time when John Wesley, who had initially been greeted with a hail of stones and clods of earth when he first came to the town, returned to preach in Hull no fewer than fourteen times.

The family's intervention appears to have been initially successful because he grew up to be a conventionally rich young man who fully enjoyed the louche pleasures of theatre and balls.[24] He headed off to Cambridge University where he played harder than he worked, then London where he gambled, drank and frequented a variety of gentleman's clubs. In 1780, at the age of twenty-one, he bought himself a parliamentary seat by spending around £9,000 – equivalent to £1 million today – bribing the freemen of Hull to vote for him. Ironically, his election removed David Hartley, who was the first MP to have spoken out against slavery and one of a small minority who had been brave enough to support America in its war of independence.[25]

It was not until five years later, by which time Wilberforce had abandoned Hull for the more politically influential – if equally expensive – seat of Yorkshire, that he experienced a religious conversion or what he called his 'Great Change'. Seeking to explore his new feelings, Wilberforce then went to see John Newton, a former seafarer who had become a leading London Evangelical and the composer of the hymn 'Amazing Grace'. In the 2007 film version of Wilberforce's life, this meeting is treated as one of profound significance. Albert Finney hams up Newton as a barefoot, penitential, sackcloth-clad prophet when Wilberforce comes to his church asking advice about leading a campaign for abolition. 'Do it, Wilber! Take them on! Pull their dirty filthy ships out of the water! The planters! The sugar barons!' says Newton, his eyes wide and imploring. 'Do it for God's sake!'

In reality, Newton found God long before he found anything wrong with slavery. After his Evangelical conversion in 1748, Newton had been a slave ship captain himself on four transatlantic voyages and only got round to condemning the trade many years after his meeting with Wilberforce.[26]

But such details are irrelevant once scriptwriters get their hands on a myth. The film portrays Wilberforce as a dashing, if fragile, hero. Described in the trailer as 'the man who changed history', he is shown shaking his flowing locks in parliamentary debates and frolicking around the gardens of country houses.

Pointing out how ridiculous much of this now seems does not diminish the story of the real Wilberforce. Almost every account of his life recognises he was remarkably accomplished. He was a loving husband and father, a witty and charming companion with a beautiful singing voice and a generous heart. He could not bring himself to sack elderly servants, a dozen of whom eventually tottered uselessly around his family table, treated tenants kindly and gave a quarter of his income to charity. He was even a founder of the Society for the

Prevention of Cruelty to Animals long before it became fashionable enough to earn a 'Royal' prefix.

Wilberforce was at the heart of the so-called Clapham Sect, a group of wealthy Evangelical men that included fellow MPs Henry Thornton, Thomas Foxwell Buxton and James Stephens, as well as the crusading Granville Sharp, and a former plantation manager in Zachary Macaulay. No doubt their respectability, money and political connections contributed to the eventual success of their cause, not least because they were up against the entrenched and powerful interests of a slave-owning 'Plantocracy' that was said to be responsible for 80 per cent of England's foreign earnings.[27]

By giving Wilberforce such star billing, however, those propagating the myth of England's moral mission have ignored how the initial impetus against slavery came not from rich Evangelical converts but from dissenters like the Quakers and the Methodists. The early abolitionists included organised labour and enlightened capitalists, too. Henry Redhead Yorke told a rally of workers in Sheffield to avenge the 'wrongs done to our Negro brethren', as he declared: 'Let the African, the Asiatic, the European, burst asunder their chains, and raise a pious war against tyranny.'[28] Josiah Wedgwood, the industrial king of the Potteries, mass-produced medallions depicting the seal for the Society for Effecting the Abolition of the Slave Trade that showed a kneeling and manacled slave along with the words 'Am I not a man and a brother?'[29] Vast petitions were signed by almost a sixth of the entire population between 1787 and 1792, a painstaking triumph for campaigners who had to deal with parchment, poor communications and illiteracy in a way that would put today's online 'clicktivists' to shame. Much of the work was done by Thomas Clarkson who covered 35,000 miles in seven years on horseback as he travelled the country interviewing sailors from slave ships to find evidence of wrongdoing, as well as holding public meetings where he would brandish shackles and other instruments of torture.

And, if the cause of abolition was never about one man, nor was it just about men. More than a century before English women won the right to vote, hundreds of thousands of them used their power as consumers by refusing to buy West Indian sugar in an unprecedented boycott. The Quaker pamphleteer Elizabeth Heyrick inspired the formation of seventy women's anti-slavery societies, much to the disapproval of Wilberforce who thought political activism was 'unsuited to the female character as delineated in Scripture'.[30]

Also crucial was the testimony of former slaves and Black abolitionists like Mary Prince, Ottobah Cugoano and Olaudah Equiano, the last of whom wrote a bestselling account of being kidnapped in West Africa at the age of eleven before eventually securing his freedom in the Caribbean and settling in London. Equiano's description of the 'middle passage' across the Atlantic in the hold of a suffocating ship – with 'the galling of the chains ... and the filth of the necessary tubs, into which the children often fell' – remains as powerful as anything ever written about the trade.[31]

Two centuries later, the character of Equiano did at least briefly feature in the film *Amazing Grace* where he was shown at a dinner with Clarkson helping to persuade Wilberforce to take up the cause of abolition and later taking him to see a slave ship in London's docks. But there is no historical evidence that the two of them ever met or even that Wilberforce read Equiano's book.[32]

The hip hop star Akala has described how the failure to recognise the Black people who struggled and often sacrificed their lives for freedom still impacts ideas of England today. 'What does it say about our society,' he wrote, 'that after two centuries of being one of the most successful human traffickers in history, the only historical figure to emerge from this entire episode as a household name is a parliamentary abolitionist?' For all the statues of white men like Wilberforce over the years, there are none for those who suffered at the hands of this country's slavers or to the Black people who resisted them. In a country as heavily memorialised as this one, it is an extraordinary omission.[33]

If the mythology around Wilberforce himself is flawed, that of an empire proving its exceptional moral worth by leading the world against slavery is an even more dubious tale.

For a start, Britain was not the first European country to ban this 'trade in flesh and blood'. Denmark did so in 1792, fully fifteen years before Wilberforce's great triumph. Revolutionary France went further by abolishing slavery altogether in 1794, partly because it was already struggling to hold on to the sugar colony of St-Domingue – now Haiti – where as many as 100,000 slaves were in open rebellion led by Toussaint Louverture, the 'Black Spartacus'.[34]

The response of William Pitt the Younger, prime minister at the time and one of Wilberforce's closest friends, was to resist the uprising. He sent two invasion fleets to the Caribbean with the aim of reinstating slavery and making the colony British. When those missions ended disastrously, France – which had brought back slavery under Napoleon Bonaparte – went on to fight a vicious and genocidal war with the Black rebels.[35] Eventually, stopping France replenishing its stocks of human capital in the Caribbean was the patriotic, rather than humanitarian, reason why many MPs were finally persuaded to ban the slave trade in 1807.

Either side of that pivotal date for this mythical redemption story, there were repeated slave rebellions in Britain's own colonies across the Caribbean. It was not until 1833 that owning slaves, as opposed to merely trading in them, was outlawed by Parliament. Even then Wilberforce and his allies were uncomfortable about the idea of former slaves being given too much responsibility. The future prime minister George Canning, though an advocate of banning the slave trade, compared Black people to the monster in Mary Shelley's *Frankenstein*, a creature 'possessing the form and strength of a man, but the intellect only of a child'.[36] Wilberforce himself did not publicly endorse emancipation until 1823 and even then believed only in the gradual 'amelioration' of the worst abuses.

Once again it was often women who found clarity and purpose faster than the men. Elizabeth Heyrick published a popular pamphlet in 1824 called *Immediate, not Gradual Abolition* that attacked such 'slow, cautious, accommodating measures'. She mocked the 'politeness and accommodation' shown towards the West Indian planters in Parliament, saying: 'Truth and justice, make their best way in the world, when they appear in bold and simple majesty.'[37]

By the time Wilberforce succumbed to such demands, he had retired from Parliament and would die just days before the Emancipation Act was finally approved. MPs agreed to pay slave owners the astronomical sum of £20 million – representing 40 per cent of all government spending – in compensation for losing their 'property'.[38] Much was reinvested in the steam engines and railways, factories and spinning jennies, mines or land grabs that powered the empire forward to create scioned fortunes that continue to flourish into the twenty-first century.[39]

Freed slaves on Caribbean plantations received absolutely nothing, beyond the freedom that they should never have been denied. And they did not even get that in full. Instead, they were required by law to continue working as 'apprentices' for a further six years in conditions that were not much different from those that had existed before. When this provision was eventually revoked after sporadic revolts on the plantations, many were replaced by indentured workers insultingly known as 'coolies', of whom more than 1.5 million were shipped over from the Indian subcontinent and hundreds of thousands more from China.[40]

Supporters of England's moral redemption myth often point to the genuine heroism of the Royal Navy's West Africa Squadron whose sailors risked death – most often from tropical disease – as they patrolled that continent's Atlantic coast, boarded slave ships and broke the chains of those held captive. Although millions of Africans continued to be transported, often in ships flying the new flag of the United States of America, perhaps as many as 160,000 slaves were freed by the Royal Navy in the decades after 1807.[41] Those rescued were often resettled in Sierra Leone, which had been founded for this purpose by the Clapham Sect and was effectively still managed by them after it became a crown colony, Britain's first in Africa. The capital, Freetown, is now twinned with Hull and one of its main suburbs is named after Wilberforce. There is still an arch outside a hospital in Freetown with a sign saying it is there 'for Africans rescued from slavery by British Valour and Philanthropy'.[42]

Here, however, the mythology begins to get more ragged still. Many of those who passed through that arch went into a different form of slavery which also had the misleading title of 'apprenticeships'. They were bought and sold, did forced labour under threat of being whipped or beaten and, if they escaped to neighbouring African villages, they were brought back sometimes in chains. Although such apprenticeships usually ended after a maximum of fourteen years, that only made it 'temporary rather than permanent slavery'.[43]

The first crown governor of Sierra Leone was Thomas Perronet Thompson, an idealistic twenty-five-year-old army officer appointed in 1808 because Wilberforce knew his father, a prominent Hull businessman and Methodist lay preacher. Thompson was dismayed by the apprenticeship system in Sierra Leone but, when he tried to change it, was recalled to London and told by Wilberforce to keep his mouth shut. Thompson, who would later go on to become an MP for Hull himself, wrote to his future wife: 'Mr W. has thought that a little slavery might be connived at, a little breaking of a few Acts of Parliament, so long as the slaves were made good Christians in return for it, and that has been the Delilah which has seduced him ... Mr W. shall never again stand with me in the rank of honest men.'[44]

This is just one aspect of a flawed myth that the author Afua Hirsch calls the 'Cult of Wilberforce – an obsession that has become as famous as the truth of slavery has become obscure'.[45] As such, this story is neither about England's moral redemption nor being at the heart of a noble empire. It is about double standards. England continued to profit from the ownership of people long after it was abolished in the empire's dominions. Its shipyards built the vessels that carried slaves across the Atlantic, its banks financed them, its brokers insured them and its factories manufactured about 80 per cent of the goods traded for these kidnapped people. Above all, English consumers continued to enjoy cheap sugar, coffee and tobacco harvested by enslaved hands in Spanish Cuba or Portuguese Brazil.[46] As to those who say it was simply the ingenuity or work ethic of England's industrial revolution that enabled its economy to outstrip rival nations in the Victorian era, there is a simple, one-word answer – 'cotton'.

Lancashire's mills would not have been able to dominate global textile markets as they did by the middle of the nineteenth century were it not for nearly two million slaves engaged in picking and processing this raw material across the American South. Almost three-quarters of Lancashire's cotton imports came from the US between 1840 and 1858.[47] When the American Civil War began, imports plummeted and the 'Lancashire Cotton Famine' caused 330,000 workers to lose their jobs in the mills.[48] By the time that war had ended, however, England's mill owners had competed a rapid diversification to get their cotton from Egypt, Brazil and especially India which increased its exports of the stuff to Britain fivefold over this period.

This resulted in even more human suffering as workers lost their jobs in India's own once flourishing textile industry and peasants were forced off land previously used for food production. This was one of the causes, along with drought, behind the successive famines that cast such a long shadow over British rule in India and led to many millions of deaths. For instance, a decade after Berar province had been taken under British control, more than a fifth of its land was devoted to growing cotton. When famine hit it a few years later, one in twelve of the population died. As with other Indian famines under British rule, there was plenty of food – huge quantities of wheat and rice were still being exported – but prices determined by free-trading free markets had risen beyond the reach of cotton-picking peasants.[49]

Those who mourn lost national greatness, or proclaim how proud they are of the empire's achievements, rarely acknowledge how millions of people who had never asked to be 'civilised' paid for English pride with their freedom or their lives.

MANNERS AND MISSIONARIES

Visitors to Hull walking the 'Wilberforce Trail' today will eventually arrive outside his childhood home where the statue of him is inscribed: 'England owes to him the reformation of manners. The world owes to him the abolition of slavery.'

The first part of this tribute may seem a little puzzling, because slavery is surely something worse than merely being 'impolite'. But the importance of improving English manners, which in the widest sense of the word meant morality, was a core part of the religious revival of the late eighteenth and early nineteenth centuries. It went hand in hand with a civilising mission abroad and remains part of an overbearing moral superiority many English people impose on each other even now.

Wilberforce was appalled by the dissipation and debauchery of Georgian society. When he entered Parliament, it has been claimed that more than a tenth of London's one-million population were criminals, a seething mass of immorality that included tens of thousands of people forced by poverty into prostitution, many of them children.[50]

If Wilberforce regarded the slave trade as the 'foulest blot on our national character', that was because it was part of a deeper degeneracy. He declared the 'reformation of manners' as being of equal importance to his battle against shipping manacled Africans across the Atlantic. Wilberforce persuaded George III to issue a new royal proclamation in 1787 condemning 'excessive drinking, Blasphemy, profane

Swearing and Cursing, lewdness, Profanation of the Lord's Day, or other dissolute, immoral or disorderly Practices'. The Clapham Sect then formed the Society for the Suppression of Vice with a particular focus on enforcing Sabbath laws, clocking up 623 prosecutions between 1801 and 1802 before extending the range of their targets to include gingerbread fairs and nude sea bathers.[51]

According to his latter-day admirers, Wilberforce helped usher in an age of moral accountability when society thrived through 'Victorian values' of duty and rigid morality. He said England's role as the sanctuary of morals was 'the pledge of our superiority'. There have been suggestions that the civilised 'manners' of the Englishman 'whose word was his bond' were one of the reasons why nineteenth-century Britain prospered as a trustworthy trading partner for the rest of the world. Others claim, slightly more convincingly, that the moral improvement of England contributed to a healthier, better-educated, more law-abiding nation as the nineteenth century progressed.[52]

As with the empire overseas, though, not everything was as it seemed. The Evangelicals of the Clapham Sect notably failed to constrain the antics of the rich and powerful in London upon whose support and patronage they depended. The essayist William Hazlitt wrote:

> Mr Wilberforce's humanity will go all lengths that it can with safety and discretion; but it is not to be supposed that it should lose him his seat for Yorkshire, the smile of Majesty, or the countenance of the loyal and pious. He is anxious to do all the good he can without hurting himself or his fair fame.[53]

And for all Wilberforce's concerns about the decadence of London society or the growing importance of temperance to England's religious revival, his own behaviour was – at best – only ever moderated. In November 1786, when he was in the full throes of his religious conversion, he went over to Downing Street for a customarily long dinner with his friend Pitt, who was known to drink up to three bottles of wine a night. After withdrawing to his room, Wilberforce wrote a note confessing that he fallen again to 'temptations of the table' and listed his 'so-oft repeated resolutions'. These still allowed him a fair amount of leeway: 'Never more than six glasses of wine; my common allowance two or three.' A fortnight later, he was chastising himself once more for slipping off his wobbly wagon after stopping at a series of friends' houses on the road from London to Bath. 'On Monday the very day after that in which I had tasted the pleasantness of the ways of religion, I gave in to intemperance and this was the beginning of a week that has been spent in one vicious course or another, leaving my mind at this moment in a state of life-lessness and complete ineptitude to spiritual things.'[54]

In short, his own practice of Evangelical Christianity was never that well mannered. He was more 'happy' than 'clappy' and appreciated the privileges of being part of an Establishment whose priority continued to be keeping the English working classes in check. Even as Wilberforce campaigned against slavery, there were riots back in his birthplace of Hull as starving people attacked grain stores or desperately fought off the Royal Navy's press gangs.[55] Wilberforce backed imprisoning political activists without trial and voted enthusiastically for the Combination Acts during the Napoleonic Wars that punished striking workers with two months' imprisonment. The radical pamphleteer William Cobbett branded Wilberforce a 'cold-blooded hypocrite' who had 'never done one single act in favour of the labourers of this country'.[56]

This does not mean Wilberforce or those like him lacked compassion. He campaigned to improve conditions for child chimney sweeps, visited Newgate jail with the Quaker prison reformer Elizabeth Fry and persuaded his fellow Evangelical Hannah More to open schools to teach children the Bible in the hope that it would make England a more 'civilised and Christian country'.[57]

But the myth-makers hoping to find some burning passion for social justice in Wilberforce are likely to be disappointed by their very conservative hero. He wrote that the 'lower orders' needed to be 'diligent, humble, patient [because] their more lowly path has been allotted to them by the hand of God'.[58] He denounced the 'delusive and wicked' doctrines of the French Revolution, had little sympathy for the plight of Irish immigrants who he said suffered from 'irreligion and immorality', and was never persuaded by arguments for the 'rights of man' – let alone what Mary Wollstonecraft was already calling 'The Rights of Woman'. All this is why the Christian conservatives in the United States have recently sought to drape themselves in Wilberforce's mantle and co-opt him into their campaign against the legal right to abortion, or why Mike Pence, the vice-president to Donald Trump, has described Wilberforce as one of his 'personal heroes'.[59]

Indeed, the aspect which most upset Evangelical Christians about the Caribbean plantations was the failure to teach this captive workforce about Christianity. For a long time, the Church of England's Society for the Propagation of the Gospel focused missionary efforts on raising the piety only of white colonialists while owning hundreds of slaves on its own Barbados sugar plantations right up until emancipation in 1833.[60] By contrast, Evangelicals and the growing army of Nonconformists who were beginning to pull away from the Established Church saw every heathen as a candidate for salvation.

After winning the battle to outlaw the slave trade, the Evangelists' next great campaign was against the East India Company, not for bleeding the country dry or inducing famine, but because it refused to allow Protestant missionaries to preach the gospel there. They organised another mass petition to free India from what Wilberforce described as 'obscene and bloody rites'.[61] Although the East India Company protested that interfering in such matters would be bad for business, in 1813 Parliament voted once more to put Christianity ahead of the interests of commerce.

Thousands of missionaries would set sail from England's shores, armed with little more than a Bible and a broad-brimmed hat, to risk their lives and their health in propagating such beliefs to 'the Heathen'. In India, they targeted the practice of suttee among some Hindus in Bengal in which widows of wealthy men would be burned alive with their dead husbands. Graphic reports appeared in pamphlets across Britain and the Baptist William Carey joined forces with Wilberforce in Parliament to save such 'degraded Hindoo women'.

In the Caribbean, these missionaries often received a frosty welcome from slave owners who feared teaching Black people to read Scripture might 'enflame their minds' with ideas about the Israelites freeing themselves from bondage. In the years between the abolition of the slave trade and full emancipation, rumours swirled across the plantations that the King of England had already freed them or that Wilberforce was next in line for the throne.[62]

Jamaica's Baptist Rebellion over Christmas in 1831 was led by Sam Sharpe, one of several enslaved men who had been encouraged by the missionary Thomas Burchell to preach at his church. The revolt resulted in the deaths of around a dozen white settlers and many hundreds of Black people. The following year Burchell had to flee the island to escape reprisals, while churches and chapels in Jamaica were set on fire by white militias who beat up missionaries or sometimes tarred and feathered them.[63]

One woman caught up in all this fervour was Eliza Ann Clarkson, an intense-looking but broad-shouldered young Methodist from Hull. Her letters and diaries were full of the most expansive versions of England's moral myth with passages quoting psalms and a variety of exhortations to be a better Christian. 'So panteth my soul after God,' she wrote, 'O for more faith!'[64]

Most missionary societies liked their men to be married so that they could 'withstand the alluring temptations of "licentious savages" in hot climates'. Clarkson was engaged to one of them and she prepared for 'the many dangers' ahead by organising a ladies' sewing society to raise money for 'Negro school-houses in the West Indies' or attending chapel where she heard the testimony of freed slaves from Sierra Leone and a 'Hottentot Chief' from South Africa.[65] After her wedding, she sailed through storms to Jamaica in January 1841 to live in a mission station high in the hostile tropical forest at Guy's Hill. While her husband preached, she taught children to read the Bible, even though she could 'scarcely understand all they say; they are so fond of altering words ... it is sometimes very difficult to know their meaning'.

Her letters contain hints of the 'privations' she suffered ranging from clouds of gigantic mosquitos to infestations of rats, impassable roads and mortal illness.[66] By the end of the year she wrote: 'Three of our Missionaries, and two of their wives, have been taken away by death, since our arrival on the island, and many others have been dangerously ill. Poor Mr Lofthouse, who went out from Hull, is now called to appear before God.'[67] And then Eliza Ann died, too, at the age of just thirty and barely a year after her arrival in Jamaica, along with her baby son. The tablet erected for her at the Ebenezer Chapel back in Jamaica is inscribed, naturally, with lines from the extraordinarily dutiful output of 9,000 dour poems and hymns that Charles Wesley poured out in his lifetime:

> To patient faith the prize is sure
> And all that to the end endure
> The cross, shall wear the crown.[68]

Stories like hers were far more common than might be imagined. Many of them were published by missionary societies in the expectation they would inspire others to 'endure the cross'. Through meetings in churches and chapels across provincial towns and cities, people heard these tales of exotic lands filled with 'savages' as they raised money for the ardent men and women who saw it as their Christian duty to venture onward and outward to 'propagate the gospel'.

Those using the pathways cut by missionaries deep into the interior of continents were not, of course, confined to those seized by the need for moral improvement. They were followed by legions of profiteering traders, freebooters or those hunting for gold, ivory and fame like those travelling up the Congo in Joseph Conrad's *Heart of Darkness*. And all that energy and righteousness surging around the empire when so many Englishmen and Englishwomen wanted to change the world would, in turn, change ideas of England, too.

This was the richest country on earth and at the centre of an empire so large that politicians were already boasting 'the sun never set' on it. But England was going through the industrial revolution, a transformation that no country and no one had ever experienced before. The advance of technology saw labourers forced off the land into increasingly overcrowded urban slums. And, for all the efforts of Wilberforce's Society for the Suppression of Vice, much of England was filled with the moral degradation that is so often the direct result of poverty. The Corn Laws, imposed as the Napoleonic Wars reached their climax, made life harder for the poorest by protecting the price of grain for landowners. Cheaper bread was one of the demands made by the tens of thousands of demonstrators who gathered at St Peter's Field, Manchester, in 1819 before a dozen of them were killed by the cutlass-wielding cavalry of the 15th Hussars in what became known as the 'Peterloo Massacre'.

There were widespread fears of political revolution the following year when police uncovered the Cato Street Conspiracy, a plot involving a Black man from Jamaica, to kill the prime minister and all the members of the cabinet. By the time slavery was finally abolished in 1833, farms were being set on fire by unemployed agricultural workers inspired by the mythical 'Captain Swing', while discriminatory laws against Catholics were scrapped amid fears of a full-scale Irish insurrection. MPs felt the pressure and passed the first big

Parliamentary Reform Act, abolishing so-called 'rotten boroughs' that had so few voters they had been essentially the gift of the local landowner.

In the midst of this tumult, the man at the centre of the myth of England's moral mission, William Wilberforce, remained bound tightly to the mast of the Establishment. He backed the Corn Laws, after taking the precaution of posting five armed guards outside his home to protect it from mobs of angry protesters.[69] Wilberforce not only opposed a public inquiry into the Peterloo Massacre but helped draft the Sedition Act that followed by which any protest of more than fifty people was punishable with seven years of transportation to a penal colony. Although no longer in Parliament when the 1832 Reform Bill was passed, Wilberforce was worried that extending voting rights even to a very limited number of property owners was going too far. And, in any case, the last constituency he had represented had itself been a 'rotten borough'. According to what is probably an apocryphal anecdote from a Victorian guidebook, he only ever visited the village of Bramber in Sussex by chance and, on hearing its name, exclaimed: 'Why, that's the place I'm member for!' More likely, he never went there at all.[70]

And Wilberforce remained equally remote from the reforming energy running through urban northern England in those years. By the time he was buried with great honour in faraway Westminster Abbey in 1833, the Methodism that had once so appalled his family had become dominant across many of the industrial towns and cities north of the River Trent. In Hull itself, Nonconformists outnumbered Anglicans by at least two to one.[71]

The following year, Parliament approved changes to the Poor Law that had been administered by the Church on a parish-by-parish basis since Elizabethan times. The new regime was intended to remove the 'outdoor assistance' that supposedly had encouraged idleness and stipulated how the poorest would only get 'indoor' assistance at workhouses designed to be so harsh that they would deter anyone in their right mind from relying on them. It became illegal to celebrate Hull Fair each October with 'plum pudding for the paupers and pennies for the children'. Women seeking medical aid from the workhouse a second time were humiliated by being made to stand locked in the wooden frame of a pillory for 'at least one hour'. One account from the time described a pregnant woman being told to go away after repeatedly hammering on the door of Hull's workhouse at Whitefriargate asking for help. She ended up giving birth on the steps outside where her baby initially 'appeared to be dead, but on the application of warmth, it came about'.[72]

Such conditions were most famously dissected by Charles Dickens in *Oliver Twist* with sarcasm that still cuts cleanly almost two centuries later. He described how the 'very sage, deep, philosophical men' on the Board of Governors who ran the workhouse had 'found out at once, what ordinary folks would never have discovered – the poor people liked it!' One tells Oliver to 'pray for the people who feed you and take care of you – like a Christian', even though the child trembling before them did not know how Christians were supposed to behave 'because nobody had taught him'. Another, 'the gentleman in a white waistcoat', says Oliver's request for more gruel had revealed a latent criminality which meant 'that boy will come to be hung'.[73] Those novels broke new ground as Dickens elevated England's poorest children into central characters using the language of the everyday. He made the conditions of English poverty so vivid that anything similar since has been routinely labelled 'Dickensian'.

But the novelist himself always loathed what he called the 'sour-faced women', disapproving do-gooders and temperance zealots from the Dissenting churches. He preferred those red-faced jolly gentlefolk who allowed moderate consumption of alcohol because it led to 'kindness of feeling and openness of heart'.[74] Later left-wing historians like E. P. Thompson, himself the son of Methodist missionaries, could also be dismissive of the impact of all that Nonconformist moralising. Thompson described how young people were held back by 'psychological atrocities' and religion, and contorted by sexual repression. He attacked the frugality and diligence that helped create an orderly, obedient workforce, as well as the conservatism of many Methodist leaders, for merely doing the bidding of capitalist factory owners. There was always a 'dark side to the Protestant work ethic' by which those who were idle failed to do God's will and are morally suspect.[75]

Both Dickens and Thompson, however, were probably too dismissive of how the moralising mission provided much of the impetus for lasting social reform in England over the nineteenth century. This was the age driven by a desire for respectability and a thirst for

improvement at least as much as it was characterised by the helpless-
ness of Dickens' paupers. It was when the spirit of thrift and persever-
ance was captured by Samuel Smiles with *Self Help*, a book he wrote
in Leeds that went on to sell hundreds of thousands of copies across
Victorian England. Smiles extolled self-made Englishmen from Francis
Drake to George Stephenson – the 'father of the railways' – because
'heaven helps those who help themselves'. He described how 'strong
individuality' and 'indomitable spirit of industry' were a 'marked feature in the English character and furnishes the true measure of our
power as a nation'. The 'greatest slave', said Smiles, was 'he who is in
thrall to his own moral ignorance, selfishness and vice'.[76] Often 'self-
help' found its expression in the local co-operatives for savings, loans
and insurance that Smiles had backed in Leeds as an alternative to
'external assistance'.

   As early as the Napoleonic Wars, Hull's workers were setting
up their own co-operative flour mills 'to preserve ourselves from
… covetous and merciless men in the future'.[77] And a series of such
movements or friendly societies found their locus in the Methodism
of towns like these across the north of England. Hull's churches and
chapels were behind local initiatives to tackle not only the destitution
and crime that came with being a port town but also the causes of
it. For instance, when presented with statistics showing the bulk of
those people being taken into custody were more or less illiterate, no
fewer than five schools were founded in the town by the Wesleyan
Methodists and two more by the Congregationalists.[78]

   An account of the pride people felt about Hull's moral and material
progress can be found in the memoir of the Rev. James Sibree, who
arrived there as a Congregationalist minister in 1831 and initially
thought it was the 'fag-end of the world'. But, like others since, he
learned to love a place 'where men know and understand the priceless
value of English liberty and English character'. Sibree described at
length how the arrival of the railways in the 1840s allowed for better
docks to be built, as well as the visit of some awe-struck African
converts to see the Wilberforce monument.

   He wrote about a much-improved workhouse on Anlaby Road
where, he said, 'I spent some of the happiest hours of my ministerial
life' because of 'the well trained voices of the children, the smiles of
welcome from the aged, and the hope of doing some good'.[79] And he

recalled the terrible impact of a cholera epidemic in the town in the summer of 1849 that killed one in fifty of Hull's population. Sewerage had long been a problem in this low-lying port where open drains went straight into the river and stinking excrement was dumped into what were known as 'muck-garths', one of which covered about three acres, where it was left to decompose in the open air in an area surrounded by houses.

Sibree refused to believe the epidemic was a divine judgement on Hull's sinfulness, but he saw the disease in more positive – if mundane – terms as 'a call to better sanitary arrangements'. Like the nursing pioneer Florence Nightingale who said she felt 'called by God' to help others and campaigned to improve sewerage systems in London, religious conviction in Hull did much to improve life for its poor. Sibree's own son would work as a civil engineer for the town's Board of Health improving poor drainage and sewers, before, true to type, heading off to Madagascar as a missionary.[80]

Although Sibree was angry about the activities of James Acland, an 'agitator' whose scandalous *Hull Portfolio* newspaper stirred up mobs protesting about everything from the corruption of local officials to the impurities being added to bread, he wrote more approvingly of Chartists campaigning for an extension of voting rights and the Anti-Corn Law League, at whose meetings he listened 'with pleasure' to speeches from its leaders, Richard Cobden and John Bright, who he said were among 'England's greatest benefactors'.[81]

Their campaign for cheaper bread had resonated with people's lives in the same way that the women's boycott of West Indian sugar had done during the fight against slavery. Both were staples of everyday life and made politics matter in a way that abstract moral theories never could back then – and often haven't since. No one, therefore, should be too surprised that this was also when another consumer product had a similarly profound impact on nineteenth-century England. It was tea, a commodity that even today marks out the passage of so many people's days from the first moment they wake, through breaks at work, to the evening meal at home.[82]

Tea became embedded in ideas of what it means to be English during the nineteenth century partly because the Temperance Movement transformed it from merely a hot beverage into a source of moral purification. Church leaders wanted better observance of the Sabbath on Sundays – which had become the publican's most lucrative day of the week – and bigger congregations. They were supported by the middle class who wanted an industrious, orderly and healthier work-force, as well as Chartists who saw temperance as proof the working class could be trusted with the vote.

In 1869, there were growing concerns about the drunkenness and debauchery spilling out from Hull's 287 'beer-houses', 309 gin shops and 306 brothels. People were encouraged not only to 'temper' their intake of alcohol but to be 'tee-total' from all forms of it. Tea parties, sometimes involving hundreds or even thousands of people, saw men gather with their wives and children to sing hymns, sip sober brews and take the pledge of 'total abstinence'. By the end of the century, the People's Public House Company which did not serve any alcohol had nineteen outlets in Hull, where one of them was predictably named 'The Wilberforce'. The Salvation Army, founded in London by Methodists behind the banner of *Onward Christian Soldiers!* began to operate in Hull from 1881, with William Booth himself conducting packed meetings at a disused ice-house in the town's Cambridge Street. Guy Hayler, a radical Congregationalist preacher who ran a teetotal hotel on Albion Street, was so devout he was said to have delivered no fewer than 127 different sermons and addresses across Hull on one Sunday alone.[83]

But temperance campaigners also sought other ways to keep men out of the pub. They were part of the driving force behind new museums, toilets, better housing, cleaner drinking water and organised sports like cricket, football and rugby. Many of the chapels also provided libraries with one on Waltham Street containing 1,800 books. There were numerous philanthropic organisations like the Temporary Home for Fallen Women, a Young People's Institute to promote 'intellectual, moral and religious improvement', not to forget the extraordinarily named 'Society for the Relief of Really Deserving Foreigners'. Sometimes there was opposition with mobs, or what were described as 'friends of the beerhouse interests', protesting against plans to spend ratepayers' money on Hull's public library during the late 1850s. Undaunted, Hull's Methodist mayor Zachariah Pearson donated the land for the town's first public park in 1860.[84]

Once again, however, social reforms in England cannot be disconnected from the impact of the English abroad. Pearson, that philanthropic park-building mayor, went bankrupt two years later after an ill-fated effort to run guns to America's slave-owning Confederates. And the English not only added milk to their tea, they also took it with a dash of full-fat hypocrisy because these bitter leaves were harvested by people who were little better off than those on the Caribbean slave plantations a century earlier. The 500,000 Tamils brought from southern India to work on tea plantations in what is now Sri Lanka, for instance, were indentured labourers forced to live in crowded shacks without sanitation, medical facilities or schools for their children.

Nor was that the end of the double standards. One reason why the British Empire made such efforts to grow the tea so beloved of temperance campaigners on plantations in India, Ceylon and Kenya was the vast trade deficit that England's tea imports had opened up with its traditional supplier of China. And the way the empire sought to close that gap by getting millions of Chinese people addicted to opium could not have been further from either the idea of moral improvement at home, or a civilising mission abroad.

THE POWER AND THE GLORY

Back in the days when William Wilberforce was fighting an unconvincing battle against the temptations rising out of his friends' wine cellars, he had also been developing a pretty serious drug habit. The great abolitionist was taking 'four grains of opium three times a day' and would continue to do so for the rest of his life. Missing a single dose would mean Wilberforce spent twenty-four hours in bed with the 'signs of spasm' familiar to anyone who watched *Trainspotting*, Danny Boyle's 1996 film about a group of young heroin addicts.[85]

The use of opium was perfectly legal and respectable in England at the time, with notable abusers of the drug including the likes of the poet and philosopher Samuel Taylor Coleridge, as well as Robert Clive – 'Clive of India' – who is thought to have died either from an overdose of it or by cutting his throat with a blunt paperknife under its influence. But, as this chapter has shown, England's missionary purpose abroad and the campaigns to improve morals back at home were mired in hypocrisy and entangled with acts of deep inhumanity.

As Christian campaigners proselytised the virtues of tea to the poor of Hull and missionaries pressed the Bible into the hands of heathens, Britain's empire was pushing drugs. Indeed, the East India Company's effort to balance a trading deficit that had soared because of tea was the explicit reason why its exports of Bengal-grown opium increased tenfold in the first few decades of the nineteenth century.

The Chinese authorities tried to ban the drug, confiscated it and showed a justifiable lack of respect towards the British diplomats who complained they were interfering with the cherished principle of free trade. London's response was to send in Royal Navy frigates. By the time the first Opium War ended in 1842, China had been forced to cede the island of Hong Kong to the British Empire, open up its ports to the empire's drug dealers and, of course, allow the entry of Protestant missionaries.

Lord Palmerston, who had consistently supported the abolition of slavery, saw nothing wrong with using the language of a moralising mission to justify Britain's destructive assault. 'These half-civilised governments', he said, 'require a dressing every eight or ten years to keep them in order. Their minds are too shallow to receive an impression that will last longer than some such period, and warning is of little use. They care little for words and they must not only see the stick but actually feel it on their shoulders before they yield to that argument that brings conviction.'[86]

The second Opium War, which began in 1856 when Palmerston was prime minister, saw that stick wielded to great effect. It resulted in access for foreign merchants to China's previously closed interior, the plundering of art and treasure for British museums – often *the* British Museum – and a victory for a free trade in a highly addictive narcotic. When Richard Cobden warned that England was becoming 'little better than brigands, murderers and poisoners', Palmerston brushed him aside. Such remarks, he said, were characterised by 'an anti-English feeling, an abnegation of all those ties which bind men to their country and to their fellow-countrymen', as if 'everything that was English was wrong, and everything that was hostile to England was right'.[87]

Within a month of Palmerston expressing his breezy confidence, however, England's righteousness and mightiness were both challenged by the trauma of the Indian Rebellion of 1857. One of the sparks for the revolt was new rifle cartridges supposedly greased with pork or beef fat. Such substances were polluting for Muslim or Hindu soldiers and their rumoured use in the Indian army was seen as part of a wider conspiracy including missionaries to turn them into Christians. As stories emerged into an ever-excitable London press of English women being raped and hacked to death by rebellious 'Sepoys', or live children being thrown to their deaths down wells in Cawnpore – now Kanpur – much of the British public lost its appetite for a civilising mission.

Although Charles Dickens had enthusiastically backed the abolition of slavery and the Corn Laws, his scorn for the moralising Evangelicals and Nonconformists became more intense. In *Bleak House*, Dickens describes how Mrs Jellyby neglects her family as she devotes her energies to setting up a mission in 'Borrioboola-Gha' while 'orphaned Jo' sits on the doorstep of the Society for the Propagation of the Gospel in Foreign Parts eating a 'dirty bit of bread'.[88] In *The Pickwick Papers*, Dickens has the hypocritical alcoholic Rev. Stiggins constantly demanding money to pay for another 'tea drinkin'' event, the proceeds of which he promises will be used to furnish 'infant negroes in the West Indies with flannel waistcoats and moral pocket-handkerchiefs'.[89]

During the Indian Rebellion, Dickens was at the vanguard of those demanding revenge against the Indian rebels. He said if he was commanding the military, his response would be: '[I] have the honor to inform you Hindoo gentry that it is my intention, with all possible avoidance of unnecessary cruelty and with all merciful swiftness of execution, to exterminate the Race from the face of the earth.'[90] And, when the rebellion was eventually crushed, the British commanders were scarcely more merciful. Some of the captured Indians were forced to lick the blood of white victims from the ground at Cawnpore before being executed. Others were tied to cannons and blown apart.

It was all a long way from a civilising empire bringing forth moral and economic progress, an idea that had underpinned the writing of Thomas Babington Macaulay. His popular epic *The History of England* stitched together a story of how English liberty, parliamentary sovereignty and the 'moral effect of the Protestant Reformation' had created a form of government that would make a better world.

The son of Zachary Macaulay – one of the leading figures in the Evangelical Clapham Sect and a governor of Sierra Leone – he had served as a colonial administrator for the East India Company. The younger Macaulay had described how 'a great and stupendous process was underway – the reconstruction of decomposed society'. He set about reforming education to teach a new governing class that will be 'Indian in blood and colour, but English in tastes, in opinions, in morals and in intellect'.[91]

Liberal imperialists like him were on the defensive again as disillusionment with the 'experiment' of a civilising mission was crystallised by events back in the Caribbean. In 1861, Edward Eyre, the son of a clergyman and a child of the abolition movement, became the colonial governor of Jamaica. Faced with a Black population discontented over political disenfranchisement and poverty, Eyre told them – as Wilberforce had told the English working classes before – to reform their 'social habits', smarten up their 'ordinary daily dress' and generally undertake an 'improvement in civilisation'. When protest marches in 1865 to the Morant Bay courthouse turned violent, Eyre imposed martial law and ordered the kind of indiscriminate slaughter that had characterised the suppression of revolts on the island during the time of slavery. For instance, a man called George Marshall who, in response to 'receiving 47 lashes, ground his teeth and gave a ferocious look of defiance' was immediately ordered 'to be taken from the gun and hanged'.[92]

Eyre was recalled to London but efforts to hold him to account for such cruelty were frustrated by a Defence Committee that had been set up by Thomas Carlyle, the philosopher-prophet of Victorian Anglo-Saxon manliness, who attacked the soft-headed pity for 'ignorant, uncivilised and grossly superstitious people'.[93] The Black and brown people of the empire, who had once been objects of pity for abolitionists or targeted as souls to be saved by missionaries, were re-cast as savage threats to civilisation.

Hopeful ideas about the potential of all men to be raised up to liberty were being replaced with a pessimistic view of the ineradicable nature of racial difference or the innate superiority of even the humblest Anglo-Saxon settler. And there was growing support for those who suggested, just as many do today with international aid, that the beneficiaries of philanthropy should be found at home rather than abroad. Benjamin Disraeli's novel *Sybil* asked why missionaries were not as concerned for the children killed in England as they were for those who died 'on the banks of the Ganges'.[94]

As prime minister after the 1874 General Election, Disraeli would lead an era of Tory populist imperialism which elevated Queen Victoria to 'Empress' and celebrated British power while upholding the patriotic working Englishman's right to enjoy the pleasures of the beer house or the racecourse. Although William Gladstone's Liberals sought to distance themselves from the empire's excesses, when he returned to power that did not stop him setting Alexandria on fire to protect British interests in Suez.

In recent years there has been a lengthy academic argument about the extent to which the empire mattered much to ordinary English people at the time, as well as whether it has much relevance to England's sense of identity now. Bernard Porter, an historian who spent much of his career teaching in Hull, said that for most of the nineteenth century only a very small minority were actively involved in the imperial project. Everybody else, he suggested, was too busy 'starving, striking, getting rich, struggling with new working conditions, agitating for reform, anticipating utopia, fearing the mob, bemused or exhilarated by all the profound social and moral changes going on'.[95]

Other historians have countered that such an analysis just lets the country off the hook for a period in which the empire's subjugation of other people reached new heights and was justified by a commonplace racism that found its way into just about every kind of popular culture. A Pears Soap advertisement, for instance, showed a missionary holding out a bar of soap to a squatting Black man wearing only a loin cloth, along with the legend that it was busy 'brightening the dark corners of the earth as civilisation advances'. Another such advert has a child 'washing the blackamoor white'.[96]

Beliefs in the inferiority of other civilisations or the incapacity of 'savages' to govern themselves became entangled with the advance of science. Humanity was divided up into different races according to inherited physical features that denoted intelligence, the control of sexual impulse and the ability to exercise moral choice.[97] Phrenologists placed England's Anglo-Saxons at the top of the evolutionary pyramid because of something to do with the shape of people's skulls, while even more insidious eugenicists sometimes warned the empire would degenerate if it allowed inter-racial marriages or the feeble-minded to breed.[98] A new literary genre of 'science fiction' novels in this period included Robert Louis Stevenson's story of the civilised Dr Jekyll turning into Mr Hyde with his ape-like body and dark, hairy hands, as well as H. G. Wells' time traveller who visits a future where the English working classes have evolved into terrifying subterranean Morlocks.[99]

Although Charles Darwin generally tried to steer clear of applying his evolutionary theories to human society, he predicted the 'civilised races of man will almost certainly exterminate, and replace, the savage races throughout the world'. This was a time when the competing theories of race, nation and class that would wreak such havoc in the twentieth century were born. They ranged from the 'social-Darwinism' of the Victorian libertarian Herbert Spencer who coined the phrase 'survival of the fittest', to the 'scientific' economic philosophy of Karl Marx and Friedrich Engels who regarded religion as a 'bourgeois construct'.[100]

The challenge this presented to the Established Church can be shown by the careers of two of William Wilberforce's sons. Samuel, the Bishop of Oxford – known as 'Soapy Sam' for his oleaginous and unctuous speaking style which involved repeatedly wringing his hands – took part in a momentous debate about the theory of evolution at the university's Museum of Natural History in 1860. Wilberforce is said to have asked Thomas Huxley, one of Darwin's colleagues, whether he preferred to describe his descent from monkeys as having come from 'the father's or the mother's side'. Huxley reportedly replied he 'would sooner claim kindred with an Ape' than with a man like the Bishop who used his debating tricks to obscure 'a matter of truth'.[101] Robert Wilberforce, who had briefly been Archdeacon for the East Riding in Yorkshire, including Hull, found cover in the unseeable mysteries of religion by becoming part of the 'Tractarian' Oxford Movement with figures like John Newman and Henry Manning who, like him, eventually abandoned the Church of England altogether for Roman Catholicism.[102]

Throughout this time, however, there was always a more pragmatic side to religion in England, one chronicled by writers like Anthony Trollope. His description of a parochial life has since continued to provide comfort for moderately conservative figures such as John Major.

For instance, Trollope's portrait of what he nostalgically insisted should be called a church 'parson' with a supply of 'old crusted port' and a tendency to be in 'mild opposition to the bishop' is recognisable in people seen as 'pillars of their communities' across England even today. 'He dislikes zeal; and of all men whom he hates, the over-pious young curate, who will never allow ginger to be hot in the mouth, is the man whom he hates the most.'[103]

Such a softer version of Englishness was contained – even repressed – within the increasingly brittle shell of High Imperialism and its hard-hatted military heroics. It is a version of the British Empire myth that has been kept alive by films like *Zulu*, which the current generation of politicians would have watched growing up, portraying the Battle of Rorke's Drift in 1879 when barely 100 British soldiers held out against 4,000 African warriors. The movie was filmed on location in apartheid South Africa with real Zulus acting alongside a contingent from the country's military playing the part of white soldiers.[104] It opens with a Bible-clutching missionary watching a Zulu wedding when news arrives about a massacre of a British infantry column. 'While I stood here talking peace, a war has started,' he says, before hurrying back to his mission station where he is exposed as a secret drunk and a coward. The heroes include Lieutenant Gonville Bromhead played by Michael Caine who, despite being a foppish aristocrat, turns out to be very brave and 'a good shot', as well as the humbler Lieutenant John Chard of the Royal Engineers. At the end of the film, Chard is shown shaking his head regretfully at the piled-high bodies of dead African warriors and repeating: 'I came up here to build a bridge.'

There were a lot of bridges, dams and courthouses constructed during the course of colonial rule which seem to matter deeply to the myth of a civilising mission. Examples of its spread of concrete and iron are endlessly celebrated in TV programmes invariably hosted by shirt-sleeved white presenters like the former Tory politician Michael Portillo. Even his beloved railways, however, were not so much about the generous beneficence of the empire as an exercise in power, and built against a backdrop of shocking indifference to the wellbeing of the Indian people.[105]

In those years at the end of the nineteenth and beginning of the twentieth century, 'the Great Game' came to be seen as more important than any civilising mission. The crazed, death-obsessed General Charles Gordon was hailed as a martyr to English manliness after he was killed by 'dark hordes of Islam' in Khartoum in 1885.[106]

Cricket was exported around the empire as an improving example of 'fair play' along with young Englishmen who were encouraged to risk their lives in battle with as much insouciance as they might muster in the face of hostile bowling. It was advice followed in the Boer War by the British commander in the defence of Mafeking, Robert Baden-Powell, who would go on to create the Boy Scout movement. When asked to surrender after a siege lasting more than 200 days, he replied: 'Just now we are having our innings and have so far scored 200 not out.' When the siege was finally lifted in 1900 there was riotous public rejoicing back in England – 'mafficking' – that propelled Salisbury's Conservatives to re-election at the so-called khaki election later that year, even as Kitchener implemented a new policy of concentration camps in South Africa in which more than 20,000 children would die and never get the chance to learn the finer points of cricket.

This was the England when King Edward VII himself would suggest to Edward Elgar he needed some patriotic words fitted on to his latest tune:

> Land of Hope and Glory, Mother of the Free,
> How shall we extol thee, who are born of thee?
> Wider still and wider shall thy bounds be set;
> God, who made thee mighty, make thee mightier yet!

The jingoism reached Hull, too. The names of streets built in the city at the beginning of the twentieth century are like an honour roll of the battles fought in the Boer War: Rustenburg, Pretoria and Kimberley. There is even a Middelburg Street, named after one of the places where Kitchener's deadly concentration camps were located. In 1903, two years after her death, a massive bronze statue of Queen Victoria was unveiled in the centre of the city. She is shown wearing the imperial crown, flanked by allegorical symbols of power, 'Mistress of the Seas' and the 'Dominion of the Land'.

The belief in common humanity that had characterised the anti-slavery campaign had largely evaporated by then. Instead, Hull's trade unionists declared solidarity with the white miners and railway workers in Africa, saying they should not accept a reduction in conditions 'to the level of that of coloured or Chinese labour'.[107] Nor did the principle of 'free labour' that was so precious to the abolitionists mean much to the workers of Hull. Strikes were routinely broken by so-called 'free labourers' – 'scabs' as trade unions prefer to call them – brought in from outside. One such dispute in 1893 by dockers and seafarers resulted in 7,000 free labourers being recruited from as far away as Sweden and the Netherlands, two navy gunboats being stationed in the Humber estuary and soldiers patrolling the streets.[108]

The distant rumble of military conflict in faraway lands grew closer in those early years of the twentieth century. A memorial on Hessle Road commemorates the incident at Dogger Bank in the North Sea, a name now usually only known to people who have listened to the ever-magical rhythms of the *Shipping Forecast* being broadcast late at night or very early in the morning on BBC Radio. In 1904, some fifty Hull trawlers had been eight miles out from Hull at Dogger Bank when they saw the Imperial Russian Baltic Fleet approaching. Captain Whelpton, one of the skippers, described the excitement on deck of what they thought was going to be 'a brilliant spectacle'. Then the Russian ships began firing on them in the belief that Hull's trawlers were Japanese submarines. Two men were killed and Whelpton later 'died from shock'.[109]

The First World War brought a much deeper and disorientating sense of grief, spelled out on the walls of the railway station where there are twenty-two varnished wooden boards listing the names of all those who died fighting for their country between 1914 and 1918. The accompanying sign says they all 'left Hull Station and never returned' without mentioning where they went or the grand purposes for which their lives were sacrificed.

In the next war, more than a thousand of Hull's citizens were killed by bombing raids that damaged 90 per cent of the city's houses and were far worse than anything that happened to London in the Blitz. But Hull's suffering never got much attention with wartime radio and newspaper reports usually referring to it only as an anonymised 'north-east coastal town', perhaps because it was always at the end of the line and disconnected from the national story.

A more insular identity was also detectable among Hull's business leaders at this time. Many of them came from staunchly Nonconformist stock, like the strictly Methodist Thomas Ferens, a Liberal MP for Hull who supported women's suffrage and temperance, and was so critical of overseas military spending that he was attacked for being a 'little Englander'. He helped establish Reckitt & Sons as one of Britain's biggest makers of household products like laundry blue and starch and used his money to found the city's art gallery and Hull University. Another devout and even wealthier Methodist in the city was Joseph Rank, who made a fortune crushing grain into flour at the giant Clarence Mill that he opened on the banks of the River Hull. Although he donated generously to the Missionary Society, his official biography describes him as a firm believer in self-help and 'survival of the fittest' when it came to social policies at home. In contrast to the idealism of the campaigns against the Corn Law, Rank backed Joseph Chamberlain's campaign for 'imperial preference' that protected British business against foreign competition so that 'this country would be able to look after itself'.[110]

The flour-making business eventually merged into Rank Hovis McDougall, a multinational that mass-produced archetypal English comfort food such as Bisto gravy granules, Paxo stuffing, Mother's Pride sliced bread and Mr Kipling cakes. It produced a classic 1970s TV ad that has been voted the nation's favourite, featuring a boy pushing his bike up a cobbled hill to deliver loaves of Hovis bread along with music from a Yorkshire colliery brass band playing what sounds like an old Methodist hymn.

It might be regarded as a symbol of how England's crusading mission for the world had turned into misty-eyed, inward-looking nostalgia for cobbled lanes and brass bands, buttery toast and warm cups of tea. But the real history of a country is never so tidy. The advert was filmed not in a northern mill town but in Dorset and its music was, far from being an English working-class anthem, Antonín Dvořák's Symphony No. 9, 'From the New World', inspired by what the composer called the 'negro melodies' of slavery's African American descendants.

The myth of England's moral superiority is, like the previous two myths discussed in this book, also a patchwork of contradictions. The empire wrecked indigenous cultures, incubated racism and caused endless suffering to millions of people. Yet there was also genuine idealism and sacrifice from missionaries, as well as division and dissent inside England itself.

Once again, there are clues in the monumental architecture of a city like Hull to its relationship with the bigger story of nation and empire. Many of the people memorialised in stone or bronze are, like Wilberforce himself, those who achieved fame only after leaving the city. For instance, there are two memorials to Amy Johnson, the pioneering female aviator who flew off far away to Australia, South Africa and India, before dying when her plane crashed in the Thames Estuary.

Even more tenuous are efforts to link Wilberforce with great deeds done elsewhere. A Humanitarian Wall has been built at Hull University's Institute on Slavery round the back of the Museum which is made up of stones engraved with the name of Wilberforce and other people who have fought for freedom around the world. They include the likes of Nelson Mandela, Sylvia Pankhurst, Abraham Lincoln and Dr Martin Luther King. One of the stones on this 'Humanitarian Wall' has been covered up with what looks like a piece of laminated cardboard so that no one can see it says 'Aung San Suu Kyi', whose status as Myanmar's democracy icon was tarnished by the succour she gave to genocidal attacks on the Rohingya minority. 'She is a little lesson to us in how people's trajectories can change,' says Trevor Burnard, the director of the institute.

As Burnard describes the institute's work in exposing the scale of modern slavery, he admits that Wilberforce – whose 'motive was really about cleansing England of its sins' – is not much of an inspiration. Although he says Hull still has a 'proprietorial interest' in the Great Abolitionist, Burnard explains this is probably based on 'little more than a coincidence' of history that 'he happened to be born here and then was its MP for a while'.

And if Wilberforce himself was not quite the man that latter-day admirers would like him to have been, the city of his birth has a similar dissonance – an absence of harmony – with the national story.

Indeed, the real flavour of Hull is much less syrupy than the moral sanctimony that oozes from this myth.

HERE AND NOW

The reason why the likes of Wilberforce moved on from Hull is perhaps the same as why Philip Larkin chose to stay there, drinking
cheap whisky, eating his favourite lettuce sandwiches and two-timing
his girlfriends while writing extraordinary poetry about the ordinary
in his top-floor flat at 32 Pearson Park.[111] Although his statue at Hull's
railway station shows him striding forward as if in a hurry to catch a
train – maybe the 'one-twenty on a sunlit Saturday' immortalised in
The Whitsun Weddings – Larkin never did leave for long. The poet
once remarked he wouldn't mind seeing China provided he could
come home the same day.

Larkin, who kept two cardboard boxes filled with bondage-themed
pornography under his desk, would not have fitted in well with the
Clapham Sect or the Society for the Suppression of Vice and his story
was never going to be one of redemption. He feared death every bit
as much as Wilberforce was said to have been almost 'luminous' in
his final days with the 'enjoyment of heaven within'.[112] But Larkin
always had a far better sense of the beauty found in the mundane
than any moralist. He came to understand how his homeplace had a
'different resonance' that 'neither impresses nor insists'.[113] In 'Here',
he described mid-twentieth-century Hull in rapt fashion as somewhere in which 'residents from raw estates' crowd into department
stores:

> Push through plate-glass swing doors to their desires –
> Cheap suits, red kitchen-ware, sharp shoes, iced lollies,
> Electric mixers, toasters, washers, driers –
> A cut-price crowd, urban yet simple, dwelling
> Where only salesman and relations come
> Within a terminate and fishy-smelling
> Pastoral of ships up streets, the slave museum,
> Tattoo-shops, consulates, grim head-scarfed wives …[114]

Apart from that single, snarling reference to the 'slave museum',
Wilberforce does not feature in either Larkin's poetry or his published
letters. The 'raw estates' were prefabricated concrete places like
Orchard Park or Bransholme built at the edge of the city where a

combination of poverty and post-war planning was steadily unpicking ties of community. The 'grim head-scarfed wives' probably included Lillian Bilocca – 'Big Lil' – the leader of women from the Hessle Road community who successfully led a campaign for better safety regulations in a fishing industry where thousands of Hull's husbands, fathers and son had been killed.

Within a few years, the fishing industry had been sacrificed in what were known as the Cod Wars of the 1970s, severing the connection Hull once had to the shared purpose of the nation even as a decline in its economic fortunes accelerated. The old fish docks are now deemed part of the city's 'maritime heritage', while all those department stores – Thornton-Varley, British Home Stores, Littlewoods, Woolworths, C&A, Debenhams, Marks & Spencer – have shut, one by one, and now none are left. Like Plymouth, this city has sought to revive its economic fortunes by harnessing the power of the wind and sea off its coast. Hundreds of millions of pounds have been invested by Siemens in turbine production at Alexandra Dock and there are ambitions to turn the Humber into Britain's renewable 'Energy Estuary'. Nonetheless, much of what has been trumpeted as solutions often turns out to be vainglorious. There was talk for a while of Hull becoming the 'Gateway to Europe', but that evaporated after the Brexit for which the bulk of the city's electorate had voted.

Larkin wrote bitterly about a country that 'brought its soldiers home for lack of money' and an England 'where all that remains/For us will be concrete and tyres'.[115] Despite his poetry tingling with this sense of resentment or loss, however, his England is still a better place to find answers than in ideas of moral superiority or instant redemption. Not only has the Wilberforce myth obscured the deep harm caused by the British Empire, it also gets in the way of this country coming to terms with the challenges of today.

Nowhere is that more obvious than in the church that bears England's name. A consequence of the nineteenth century's civilising mission that Wilberforce inspired is that Anglicanism is the world's third largest Christian denomination. But barely one in fifty of those taking its Communion across the planet these days are in England and the average, if not archetypal, Anglican today is a twenty-five-year-old Nigerian woman. The 'English' quotient of this church has not just been diluted, but also diminished. As recently as the 1980s,

40 per cent of the English population described themselves 'C of E', a proportion that had fallen to just 12 per cent by 2021 and more people now go to a mosque each week than attend an Anglican church.[116] As Larkin himself asked in 'Church Going', how long would it be before there were only a handful of cathedrals left on show, 'A shape less recognizable each week/A purpose more obscure'?

Hull itself, once so filled with Evangelicals that it was known as the 'Garden of Our Lord', is now said to have the smallest congregations in the country.

And it has witnessed two very different efforts to revitalise this religion in recent years.[117]

The Holy Trinity Church in Hull is where Wilberforce was baptised over a vast medieval font carved from a single block of marble. More than 250 years later, an Anglican vicar conducted the same ceremony by running up the nave and trying to kick a football into it.

'I wanted to show that this baby Harry was the newest member of our team as Christians and we needed to teach him some skills,' explains Matt Woodcock, whose voice always seems to be in danger of toppling over into self-induced hilarity. 'I probably went a bit far by trying to chip the ball into the font at the end,' he adds, 'and – anyhow – I missed!' Similar moments saw Woodcock busking Oasis songs outside the church and climbing down from a high pulpit to liven up a harvest festival service as the organist played the theme tune of *Mission: Impossible*.

When he first arrived in the city, he was told this church was one of several facing the prospect of being mothballed or even closed. The congregation had fallen to barely a dozen people while the building itself needed a refurbishment costing several million. 'This was the biggest parish church in the country – I called it God's aircraft hangar – but it was only open for a couple of hours on weekdays and for Sunday services,' says Woodcock. 'Hardly anyone was coming because it could not have been further removed from the everyday life of people in Hull.'

England's moralising religious mission has, much like the marble font in which Wilberforce was baptised, appeared to be carved into an unyielding block of stone that told people what they should be doing, who they were and where they were placed in the world. Woodcock, by contrast, went out to reconnect with people by meeting them, wherever and whoever they were, or whatever they were doing. He describes wearing his dog collar while propping up a series of local bars, holding services in a pub called – ironically – the Mission, as well as weekly meetings in a Wetherspoons named the William Wilberforce. 'We've retreated from the council estates and poorer areas,' he says, 'it's time to jump back into people's joy and despair; to be part of the mess – just join in.' One of his breakthrough moments was when he opened the doors of Holy Trinity Church to a real ale festival. Another came when he hired camels for a nativity procession through the city that ended up outside yet another pub.

Not everyone was happy with what they saw as this 'trendy vicar'. Some stopped giving money to the church while others moaned about the noise being made by a new youth group. There were further complaints that the beer festival was irresponsible and, more pedantically, that camels had never been part of the Bible's nativity story.[118] Such opposition crystallised around Woodcock's antithesis, another Anglican priest in the city named the Rev. Melvin Tinker. He had built a big congregation at St John's Newlands Church for everyone who wanted a more traditional form of Evangelicalism.

Like Wilberforce before him, Tinker said religion should primarily be concerned with 'raising the moral tone of the nation by clamping down on offences such as the publication of indecent or blasphemous literature and the desecration of the Lord's Day'. And, though he recognised the importance of charity, he said opening a food bank for the poor should never be 'exalted to the same status' as the necessity of spreading the Gospel.[119]

Tinker was opposed to the Church devoting too much time to social action because it undermined what he saw as his primary purpose of spreading 'Biblical truth'. He described how it was the 'Will of God' revealed in scripture, not societal pressure, that had inspired his fellow Evangelical to oppose slavery in the eighteenth century. And those same gospels, he insisted, would have shown Wilberforce that women priests or homosexuality were also inconsistent with Christian faith.[120]

Before his death in 2021, Tinker split from the Church of England to join a breakaway network of conservative Anglicans. He complained that too many clergy could no longer 'distinguish vice from virtue' and 'there are certain things you can't love if you're going to love God'. When a service conducted at Holy Trinity Church to mark Gay

Pride Week was addressed by a trans activist, Tinker took to the air-waves to compare homosexuality to paedophilia.[121]

Woodcock, who has since moved on from Hull and presents 'The God Spot' on Zoe Ball's BBC Radio 2 *Breakfast Show*, admits: 'I had to find somewhere to hide when I saw Melvin coming.' But he still looks forward to the day he can officiate over a marriage between two people of the same sex because 'loving people is a non-negotiable part of being a vicar'. Most people in this country agree with him. Polling shows the public support gay and lesbian marriage by a margin of three to one, while even the ageing community of Anglicans back it by two to one.[122] Justin Welby, the Archbishop of Canterbury, has recently travelled to the Caribbean to deliver hand-wringing apologies - 'we are deeply, deeply, deeply sorry' - for the church's historic role ownership of slaves. He is such a moderniser that he presides over an organisation that doesn't even like to refer to new places of worship as 'churches' with a recent report describing them only as 'things'.[123]

But Welby has felt compelled to reaffirm how 'homosexual practices' are 'incompatible with scripture' and, while same-sex couples can now receive a blessing in church, they are still not allowed to get married in one. Welby has effectively acknowledged he cannot move much fur-ther without causing a schism with millions of Anglican worshippers in Africa and elsewhere, whose homophobic religious dogma was exported from England by his church's missionaries 200 years ago.[124]

Arguments about who can get married in church might seem to be low on a list of Hull's problems that include some of the worst school results, lowest wages, poorest rates of political participation and least healthy people anywhere in the country.[125] But this chapter has shown how England's religion lay behind a sense of national moral super-iority that has often showed little compassion for those in most need. If the myth of a moral empire spreading English civilisation around the world still ripples through debates about military intervention or development aid abroad, the influence of it can still also be felt across cities like Hull, both in small ways and large.

For instance, Woodcock remembers the reaction when he invited a homeless man in for a cup of tea at Holy Trinity. He says one of the so-called 'welcomers' at the church sidled up to him to say he shouldn't offer kindness to such people because 'you'll only encourage them'. And such views bared their teeth on a national scale during the 2010s when there was a concerted political campaign against so-called 'benefit fraud' which David Cameron, the then prime minister, described as a 'moral mission' for the country. It was used to justify slicing fully a fifth out of the income of England's poorest families and underpinned by more than a thousand newspaper articles a year about 'cheats', 'scams', 'fiddles', 'scroungers', 'spongers' or 'skivers'.[126] One such story was about a woman called Amanda White from Hull. The *Daily Mail* described her as 'shameless' even though she was 'tearful when she was led away' to jail for fraudulently claiming tax credits while earning the less-than-astronomical sum of £850 a month as a cleaner. The newspaper's fury seemed to have been triggered by how she had managed to pay for a holiday when more deserving members of the working class did not.[127]

This belief that poverty is a sign of moral weakness, so that people should be discouraged from falling into its vices and punished if they do, is as much rooted in the piety of nineteenth-century Evangelicalism and the myth it generated as Wilberforce's campaign to abolish the slave trade. The conformity required to feel morally superior to other people does not allow much room for England to breathe.

But a football being dribbled up the nave of a church or a same-sex couple walking up the aisle to get married serves to loosen those constraints a little. And they are part of a different Christian tradition in England that, rather than imposing an unbending idea of morality on unwilling supplicants, helps people live their lives or overcome challenges.[128]

Elements of such religion could be found among the Victorian Nonconformists who set about creating local schools, parks and libraries or tried to improve sanitation after cholera epidemics. During the twentieth century, when the supposedly scientific ideologies of Communism and Fascism dressed entire nations in uniform, this gentler Christianity often provided a sanctuary. It was William Temple, the Archbishop of Canterbury during the Second World War, who coined the phrase 'welfare state' as a contrast to the 'power state' of Nazi Germany. His bestselling *Christianity and Social Order* set out to take the sharpest edges off the post-war 'national settlement', as well as being hugely influential on English social policy from R. H. Tawney and Richard Titmuss to A. H. Halsey. It is why, even now, the Church of England still runs local schools and provides social services that maintain a sense of community, individual dignity and the vestiges of a voluntary society.[129]

The Rt Rev. Andrew Rumsey, a present-day Anglican bishop, has described how the Church remains embedded in the English imagination through 'national ceremonies, the names of our streets, schools, places and much of the built heritage we wish to preserve'.[130] He says: 'Over the centuries we've too often been on the side of power and privilege. Our public role has now receded and that's good for us, good for our soul. Maybe we needed to learn to be on the losing side a bit more.' He talks about ways a society can be 'resilient without being defensive – "little" without being narrow' – and an England best conceived as 'a scaled-up parish', with a responsibility for everyone, whatever their beliefs. Rumsey believes this can yet help define a humbler version of both England and its Church, which is 'a blend of justifiable pride, aching regret and, in maturity, understanding and acceptance of the whole'. What does all that mean in practice? 'It means,' replies the bishop, 'we run half the food banks in the country.'

Heather Black, at a church initiative in Hull called Mustard Seed, say she is too busy setting up parent-and-toddler groups in poorer parts of the city to be interviewed about the legacy of Wilberforce. 'Lots of families have broken down, lots of kids are struggling,' she says. At St John's Church in the Bransholme estate, the Rev. Andrew Silley holds a morning prayer service where only a couple of worshippers turn up and then a food bank an hour later which attracts forty people. 'More come in at the moment because they are so hard up,' he says. 'Some just pick up a bag and say "hi" – it doesn't matter if they're not religious – others stay for a chat.'

There are, of course, many other denominations or religions working in urban environments like Hull to help people in need and, perhaps, restore 'faith in the city'. Although fewer people these days think religion can solve every problem, a greater degree of humility about the Church's role might mean it is better placed to help solve some of them. And, in any case, Christianity no longer has a monopoly on bringing meaning to people's lives.

At the city council's offices on George Street is a branch of a national organisation called Pause which seeks to break the destructive cycle of women repeatedly having children taken into care. Sitting in a meeting room (inevitably named after Wilberforce) and listening to some of their stories, it is impossible not to be moved. Many of these women have grown up in abject poverty, have been sexually or physically assaulted, have faced issues of drug and alcohol abuse, or suffer the isolation that comes from a breakdown of family and community ties.

Practitioners like Hope Brown work one to one with these Hull women so they are no longer defined merely as people whose children have been taken away. 'It might be taking them to the hairdressers and some fun on the beach, or getting them a hobby for the first time,' she says. 'They've constantly been told that they're not good enough – that they are failures – with that subtle undertone which suggests they're bad.'

Sophie Humphreys, who founded the organisation, says: 'At the heart of our work is a professional relationship with each woman as an individual in her own right. But it has to be a genuine relationship if it is to bring change; it's about giving people love.' Her use of that word 'love', as well as her focus on what makes people different, is striking. Too much of this country's social policy, as with religion, has always been about making everyone fit into the same moral strait-jacket. Often, Pause practitioners have to battle the local benefits office trying to apply 'sanctions' to a vulnerable woman because she 'failed to attend' a job interview. But far more public money can be saved if another child does not have to be taken into care.

In similar fashion, a casual glance at Hull City Council's 'Corporate Plan' shows much of it is indistinguishable from those of countless other places dotted around England. In the breath-freshened, homogenised language of such documents, it describes a series of 'employability aspirations', a 'continuum of opportunities and needs', as well as a 'reconceptualised library offer'.[131]

At one stage, the council wanted to demolish an ugly and asbestos-ridden old BHS building as part of an elaborate Albion Square redevelopment. That would have meant losing a unique 1960s mosaic, said to be the biggest in England, representing three trawlers, which meant a lot to many people in this city. The demolition was stopped by local campaigners including the photographer Esther Johnson, who remembered sitting in a nearby café eating fried-egg sandwiches while her trawlerman father pointed at the artwork and told her tales of his voyages to the edge of the Arctic Circle. The mosaic might just be seen as 'a symbol of what's been lost' in the city, she said, 'but I see it as a symbol of achievement and hope'.[132]

The real lesson to draw from Hull, then, lies not in the myth of a moral superiority that has been applied both across the world and to the less fortunate citizens of England itself, but an appreciation of the end-of-the-line contrariness of a real city rather than the myth of its most famous son. Ultimately, people do not love each other because they are the same; they do so because everyone is a bit different.

Hull was where a pop band would adopt its name from the slogan used by Turners store on Beverley Road offering to sell 'Everything But The Girl' – and the Housemartins made their debut album, *London o Hull 4*. It was also where the industrial music pioneer Genesis P-Orridge met the performance artist Cosey Fanni Tutti. Their resulting collaborations, Coum and Throbbing Gristle, were so obscene – live performances involved enemas with blood or milk – that they were accused by a Tory MP of being 'a threat to Western Civilisation'.[133]

Maybe such cussedness is what helped this city remain resilient in the face of German bombs, Icelandic fishing trawlers and media scorn. When Hull was chosen to be the UK's 2017 City of Culture, the decision was greeted with predictable snobbish derision even by some of those who usually claim to speak for the people. The *Sun* branded Hull the 'Scrapital of Culture' with a double-page spread about the binge-drinking of 'boozy revellers', 'lashed-up louts' and girls 'flashing their knickers'.[134] Amid all the sneering, however, the proportion of Hull's inhabitants who felt pride in coming from this city from rose from 45 to 75 per cent while visiting football fans were taunted with the chant: 'Here for the culture, you're only here for the culture!' Parts of the old town like the mysteriously named street Land of Green Ginger were done up nicely with recobbled road surfaces, while cafés on the Fruit Market and Humber Street now showcase a distinctive local idea of art.[135]

One has some rusty corrugated iron sheets rescued from the demolished sheds at Alexandra Dock on which the rough image of a bird on its back along with the words 'A DEAD BOD' had been daubed in white paint. It was painted in the 1960s by Len 'Pongo' Rood after a voyage where his captain had spent weeks nursing an injured bird back to health. When the time came to set it free, everyone retreated so they could watch it fly off. At which point, so the story goes, the ship's bosun turned up, screamed 'what the fuck is that!' and kicked it into the sea. 'A dead bod,' replied one of his shipmates.

That image of a bird's corpse subsequently appeared on everything from T-shirts to vodka bottles, representing the value of a 'Hullness' that owes nothing to piety and moral superiority. And it finds expression everywhere you go in this city.[136]

On an autumn day outside Hull's further education college, beneath the 100-foot Doric column dedicated to England's Great Abolitionist, leans a teenaged student. Did he know who is commemorated on top of it? 'Yes,' he says, showing justified disdain towards the question and questioner. What's your name? 'Dan.' What about your surname? 'I don't want to tell you. That would be weird.' Another silence. He checks his phone. So, are you proud to be from the same city as Wilberforce? 'I'm not proud of him or Hull,' replies Dan, finally making eye contact and sort of smiling in bleak triumph as he says, 'I'm just part of it – I'm here.'

4

Wolverhampton
The English, Alone

Wolverhampton is not overburdened with claims to fame. It was where Queen Victoria ended years of mourning in 1866 to unveil a statue of her dead husband, Prince Albert, which locals call 'man on the horse' or just 'MOTH' for short. It's where takeaways sell 'orange chips' which are fried in a batter that looks like it might glow in the dark. It's where Wolverhampton Wanderers, always known as Wolves, pioneered floodlit matches in the 1950s against teams from the Continent – or, as their fans will tell you, 'invented European football'.

Outside the club's Molineux stadium there are three statues. One is of Stan Cullis, the club's post-war manager, dapper in trench coat with trademark trilby held out in his hand. Another is of the captain of Wolves and England in that era, Billy Wright. A third is Sir Jack Hayward, known as 'Union Jack', who once said he wanted to bring back 'the cat o' nine tails and the empire' but mostly just sunk his family fortune into restoring the fortunes of this football club.[1]

But there is no monument of any sort to Enoch Powell who, for a time back in the late 1960s and early 1970s, made it seem as if Wolverhampton was the axis on which the future of England would turn. In recent years, there have been calls to give him a blue plaque in this city where he was MP for a quarter of a century. A poll in the local newspaper, the *Express & Star*, generated a huge response with 70 per cent of the 20,000 who voted saying they supported the idea.[2] Despite – or maybe because of – this evidence of Powell's enduring appeal, the proposal was quashed amid fears that wherever any memorial was put would become a magnet for protest.

The reason Powell cannot be commemorated is also why he became so notorious: his so-called 'Rivers of Blood' speech, delivered in April 1968. He warned that 'whole areas, towns and parts of towns across England will be occupied' by immigrants, leaving white people 'strangers in their own country'. He insisted it was a 'ludicrous misconception' to think the idea of integration even 'enters the heads of a great and growing majority of immigrants'. He claimed that the only way to stop inter-racial conflict was to prevent more coming in and encourage those already here to return to 'their countries of origin' or, as some of his supporters preferred to put it, 'send them home'.[3]

Wolverhampton is the setting for the fourth myth of this book because these ideas tapped into a deep tradition of thinking about England, one which sees the country as standing alone, looking after only its own and owing others nothing. Powell believed in an England that was truly 'sovereign', not only in the technical or constitutional sense, but a place and a way of life for which, he said 'men, if necessary, fight and, if necessary, die'.[4] Sometimes known as 'little England', even by its advocates, this myth has regularly burned across the political spectrum, culture and everyday life. In Powell's time, it carried the scorch marks of the twentieth century's world wars and the decline of empire. And it has flared again in our own.

Powell's antipathy to supranational politics, to prioritising economic growth over cultural difference and, above all, to immigration, were key themes in the campaign to take the UK out of the European Union. His warnings that 'local people' are losing in a fight for public services and jobs to new arrivals from overseas has had its own recent champions, too. And the resentment he stirred up against liberal journalists, bishops and race-relations lawyers represented the attack on 'wokery' of its time. One seasoned conservative thinker called Powell 'the Baptist of the Brexit movement'. *The Economist* went further, describing the 2016 referendum as his 'posthumous success' after a campaign that was 'soaked in the blood of Powellism'.[5] In 2018 the BBC controversially broadcasted the 'Rivers of Blood' speech again, to mark the fifty years that had passed since he delivered it, in recognition that what had essentially been a reaction against events of the last century had become relevant again to this one.[6]

Powell certainly knew what he was doing. In 1968, he told the editor of his local newspaper he was planning to make a speech that would 'go up – "fizz" – like a rocket' adding that while such things usually fall back to earth, 'this one is going to stay up'.[7] His defenders have always insisted there was nothing explicitly racist in this speech. But he quoted the most racialised comments of anonymous Wolverhampton constituents. Powell recounted a conversation with one – 'a middle-aged quite ordinary working man' – who predicted how in the next twenty years 'the Black man will have the whip hand over the white man'. He then read out a letter from a woman that said her mother, whose sons and husband had been killed in the war, was the last remaining white person on her Wolverhampton street and she was being victimised for refusing to let rooms to immigrants:

> She is becoming afraid to go out. Windows are broken. She finds excreta pushed through her letter box. When she goes to the shops, she is followed by children, charming, wide-grinning piccaninnies. They cannot speak English, but one word they know. 'Racialist,' they chant.

And, if it is true Powell never uttered the phrase 'Rivers of Blood' by which the speech is usually known, that is because like other politicians since he cloaked bitterly divisive sentiments in a Classical quotation – a prophecy from Virgil's *Aeneid* – as he said: 'I am filled with foreboding. Like the Roman, I seem to see "the River Tiber foaming with much blood".'

It was all too much for the Conservative leader of the time, Edward Heath, who sacked Powell from the Tory front bench while students and anti-racism groups marched against him. Ever since, his name has become a trigger word on the liberal left, instantly conjuring up images of his staring eyes and a moustache that he grew to 'convey an impression of Nietzsche'.[8]

The speech's most sulphurous claims never bore much relation to reality. A local school, described by Powell as having a class where there was only one white child, could not be identified because almost certainly it did not exist.[9] He consistently refused to disclose the name of the war widow whose daughter he said had written to him. But decades later a BBC documentary based on a deep dive into city archives decided she was probably someone called Drucilla Cotterill, a widow, short of stature and someone who had suffered mental health issues. Some West Indian children in her street probably did tease her. The excrement, however, was pushed through a different letterbox and was part of a family row, not a racial one. Cotterill got on so well with her Black neighbours that she babysat for them, and they, in turn, had sent flowers to her funeral. Cotterill did not have any sons, let alone two killed in the war, but she did have a drink problem. As for the claim that the only English word the children knew was 'racialist', what other language – as immigrants from the British Caribbean – would they have been expected to speak?[10]

But if his story was largely false, it had immense power. The speech did not 'go up – "fizz" – like a rocket', as Powell had predicted, so much as 'off – bang – like a bomb'. It wasn't just Drucilla Cotterill who was 'becoming afraid to go out' and face a changing world, but much of England itself. An opinion poll showed three-quarters of the country agreed with him, while wildcat strikes broke out among London's dockers and meat porters, as well as at some Black Country factories, in support.[11] Protesters marched from Wolverhampton to Dudley singing: 'Send them back to Pakistan, hallelujah.'[12]

Powell's version of this insular myth has continued to froth away ever since. There were always those who saw him as a prophet who had drawn on the secret strengths of the nation. As an old man he went to a lunch at the *Spectator* which descended into an Enoch Powell impersonation contest with journalists for whom imitation really was their sincerest form of flattery. He finished in third place. His death in 1998 was marked by a *Daily Telegraph* leader gushing that his legacy 'will survive more surely than any other British politician of the 20th century except Winston Churchill'. Even if political and parliamentary culture was destroyed, it added, 'those brave few who wish to restore it will find in the thoughts of Enoch Powell something approaching the Bible'.[13] Indeed, in the years following his death, he seemed to matter more than ever. Boris Johnson, perhaps unconsciously, echoed Powell's language in 2002 by referring to Africans as 'piccaninnies' with 'watermelon smiles'. As the issue of immigration surged back into politics, UKIP's leader Nigel Farage took relish in declaring that Powell was his 'political hero'.[14] David Starkey, a professional historian and then popular public intellectual, appeared on national television to denounce inner-city riots in 2011 and declared Powell had been right to warn of England turning into 'literally a foreign country'. He said: 'A substantial section of the chavs have become black. The whites have become black. A particular sort of violent, destructive, nihilistic gangster culture has become the fashion.'[15]

The myth examined in this chapter had more innocent origins. It began with a yearning for a pastoral England as an imagined place of liberty and peace, where the sovereignty of its 'mother of parliaments' guaranteed stability and security for a nation that was always steadfast in the face of terrifying external threats. Powell's peculiarly noxious contribution to the myth was to add a concept of the English nation rendered in very narrow terms. He may have elided race and ethnicity so that he could always claim the most prejudiced remarks of his followers were not really what he meant, but he openly sought to define Englishness as a set of cultural differences so great that no outsider could share them. He portrayed the arrival of immigrants as the root cause of disorder and a threat to England's civilisation, as he offered the English what one recent historian has described as the myth 'that their society was in a state of perpetual existential crisis'.[16]

This version of it had begun to take form as early as 1961 when he delivered a speech to celebrate England's patron saint at the annual dinner of the City of London's branch of the Royal Society of St George. Then he urged the English 'standing at the heart of a vanished empire, amid the fragments of demolished glory', to rediscover 'England herself' now that 'looser connections which had linked her with distant continents and strange races' had fallen away.[17]

Speaking at a time when Britain was losing its grip of its remaining imperial possessions, Powell was clear there was only one direction in which the English people should be looking.

'Backwards travels our gaze,' he said, telling his audience to seek guidance from their ancestors who lived before 'Elizabethan adventurers' had begun exploring the world. 'We find them', he said, 'in many a village church, beneath the tall tracery of a perpendicular east window and the coffered ceiling of the chantry chapel. From brass and stone, from line and effigy, their eyes look out at us, and we gaze into them.'

> What would they say? They would speak to us in our own English tongue, the tongue made for telling truth in … They would tell us of that marvellous land, so sweetly mixed of opposites in climate that all the seasons of the year appear there in their greatest perfection; of the fields amid which they built their halls, their cottages, their churches, and where the same blackthorn showered its petals upon them as upon us; they would tell us, surely, of the rivers, the hills and of the island coasts of England. One thing above all they assuredly would not forget; Lancastrian or Yorkist, squire or lord, priest or layman; they would point to the kingship of England, and its emblems everywhere visible. They would tell us too of a palace near the great city which the Romans built at a ford of the River Thames, to which men resorted out of all England to speak on behalf of their fellows, a thing called 'Parliament'.[18]

In his 'unique' continuity of people, buildings, language and landscape, Powell believed that 'the slow alchemy of centuries' had created a set of political and legal institutions that 'appear in England almost as works of nature, spontaneous and unquestioned'.[19]

For Powell, as so often for those who obsess over sovereignty, there were a great many people living on this island excluded from such a mystical vision of England. For a start, he was denying access to Englishness for anyone from those 'strange races' in 'distant continents' because they had not shared in his slow alchemy of ethnic ancestry. 'The West Indian or Asian does not by being born in England become an Englishman,' explained Powell later, 'in fact he is a West Indian or an Asian still.'[20] Moreover, his ideas of a national identity were emphatically about England. His was not a Britain that might have included Scottish, Welsh or even Irish identities. 'English it is, for all the leeks and thistles grafted upon it here and elsewhere,' he said. 'The stock that received all these grafts is English, the sap that rises through it to the extremities rises from roots in English earth, the earth of England's history.'[21] Nor was there ever much of a role for women in Powell's England, other than for old Mrs Cotterill. When he was a student at Cambridge, Powell could not understand why the university bothered educating female students and, years later, could never fully reconcile himself to Margaret Thatcher's premiership in part because he thought women were unsuited to politics.[22]

And, if all of this was not exclusionary enough, Powell was largely uninterested in how he could reconcile his romantic, pastoral England – the imagined England of cottages, perfect seasons, oak trees, fields, village churches and showers of blackthorn petals – with the realities of post-war, urban life. Indeed, one of the ironies of Powell's grotesquely distorted idea of England is that it resembled neither the existence of the 'quite ordinary working man' nor the Midlands city he had thrust into the spotlight.

And the best way to shrink this myth is to reveal more of that reality.

'THE LAND OF LOST CONTENT'

Long before Powell arrived in Wolverhampton, it had already become an industrial place, part of the 'Black Country' which got its name from the grime of a coal-fired industrial revolution that covered its grass and made its canals foam, not with blood, but with pollution.

Queen Victoria is said to have kept the blinds drawn on the royal train when travelling through it because she found the sight of 'smoking and burning … intermingled with wretched huts and carts and little ragged children' too disturbing.[23] The steelworks and blast furnaces of the Black Country may even have been the inspiration for J. R. R. Tolkien, who grew up nearby, when he invented Mordor – the Dark Lands – for *The Lord of the Rings*.[24] This was a place that specialised in the production of metal goods. The image of a chain is now part of the Black Country's official flag, an unfortunate reminder that it also once made fetters, collars, manacles and shackles for the slave trade.

A sense of how tough life was can be found in the way the town of Willenhall became known as 'Humpshire', because workers bent over the intricate locks and keys for which it was famed ended up with crooked backs. Some pubs still have hollows in the wall behind the wooden bench seats to allow their customers to sit comfortably with their hump.[25] The whole soot-blackened place is said to have been the model for 'Wodgate' that Benjamin Disraeli conjured up for his 1845 novel *Sybil, or The Two Nations*, which he described in these terms:

> So, a population gathered, and rapidly increased, in the ugliest spot in England, to which neither Nature nor art had contributed a single charm; where a tree could not be seen, a flower was unknown, where there was neither belfry nor steeple, nor a single sight or sound that could soften the heart or humanise the mind.[26]

When Disraeli wrote those words, England's artists were already grappling with how the industrial future was upheaving – often defiling – their country. These efforts spawned great masterpieces, including John Constable's paintings of the Stour Valley and J. M. W. Turner's spectacular visions of a rapidly transforming England, as well as, later on, the Pre-Raphaelites' adoration of nature or the Arts and Crafts movement of William Morris. In literature, it inspired poets like William Wordsworth romanticising daffodils in the Lake District; the novels of Jane Austen chronicling the village life of 'four or five families' in Hampshire; the furious fiction of the Brontë sisters sweeping across wild Yorkshire moors; and then, in the twentieth century, the stories of Thomas Hardy and D. H. Lawrence in which England's countryfolk fight for survival.

Although these artists had very different political and spiritual views, they all stood defiant against the deadening corruption of the modern world. This was when the country had become the most urbanised place on the planet, with more than three-quarters of the population living in towns or cities.

At the beginning of the twentieth century, what was left of the countryside was riven by injustice. Just 4,000 families owned more than half the land in England, while 95 per cent of people owned nothing at all. The neat hedgerows and empty moorland that for so many defines the beauty of English countryside are also symbols of the cruelty by which rich landowners enclosed common land and ordered clearances of people's homes to make way for sheep. For all today's *Downton Abbey* nostalgia, the largest estates operated in almost feudal fashion with vast staffs of domestic servants bound by the most rigid and petty class distinctions. Almost a third of all

English women in employment were servants, a whole way of life that now exists only in almost parody form within a few households like that of the royal family.[27]

But the myth of a 'Merrie' and little England prevailed nonetheless. And, in the furnaces of the First World War, it was forged into a weapon. The soldiers arriving at the Western Front, recruited disproportionately from the blighted urban landscape of the working class, were given popular anthologies of verse designed to boost morale that told them they were fighting for the kind of rural idyll most of them had never experienced.

The Old Country: A Book of Love and Praise for England published for the military in 1917 claimed it would help 'the average man in our forces', even when sitting in trenches or sheltering in a shell hole, to use his imagination so that he can still 'see his village home'.[28] The England presented was that of Rupert Brooke's Grantchester and his 1914 poem, 'The Soldier'.

If I should die, think only this of me:
    That there's some corner of a foreign field
That is for ever England. There shall be
    In that rich earth a richer dust concealed;
A dust whom England bore, shaped, made aware,
    Gave, once, her flowers to love, her ways to roam;
A body of England's, breathing English air,
    Washed by the rivers, blest by suns of home.

This 'golden-haired' poet's death a year later, ingloriously caused by an infected mosquito bite, triggered a burst of patriotic enlistment for what was then still a volunteer British army. In Wolverhampton, torchlight processions were held to mark his death and encourage enlistment, while every man aged between eighteen and forty got a visit at home from the local recruitment committee to explain the necessity of joining up – and the shame they would face if they refused to do so.[29]

The real horror of a war in which one in eight British soldiers would die was being chronicled by the likes of Wilfred Owen, Robert Graves and Siegfried Sassoon – some of the extraordinary number of 2,225 poets published in that time. Their later prominence helped build the 'lions led by donkeys' account of blundering generals and an incompetent elite popularised in the film *Oh, What a Lovely War!* or the TV comedy *Blackadder Goes Forth* where soldiers were expected to lay down their lives to move Field Marshal Douglas Haig's 'drinks cabinet six inches closer to Berlin'.

Nowadays, that debate about whether the war was a patriotic duty or senseless slaughter is represented almost as competing versions of national identity. But it is also possible to see them as different sides of a single story of sacrifice, the enduring power of which has ensured the names of the Western Front battles closest to home – Ypres, the Somme and Passchendaele – are still seared on the national memory in a way that other parts of this global war are not. The squalor and carnage of Gallipoli is better remembered by Australia and New Zealand, while the East Africa campaign in which at least 100,000 Black 'native carriers' or porters were killed is hardly remembered at all. Unlike white soldiers, who are buried in cemeteries of some foreign fields still lovingly tended by the Commonwealth War Graves Commission, the African porters' graves are now often overgrown by scrubland.

The way war is commemorated matters greatly to any nation. After the First World War, the statues of generals sitting on horses slowly gave way to memorials which emphasise ordinary soldiers and the places from where they came. The national cenotaph and the 'tomb of the unknown warrior', buried among the dead kings and queens in Westminster Abbey, came to be seen as a mark of respect to 'the many Multitudes who ... gave the most that Man can give'. The annual act of remembrance, universally known as 'poppy day', still culminates in small ceremonies on village greens or the centre of towns and cities where a usually out-of-tune trumpet player sounds 'The Last Post'.

Indeed, one of the more revealing statistics about the UK is that there are an estimated 100,000 war memorials scattered across it, almost all of which were erected in the early twentieth century.[30] Cities like Wolverhampton have dozens upon dozens of them, as do all the places visited in this book. This country is far from unique in this regard but, whereas other nations have undergone subsequent traumas of revolution, dictatorship and defeat, the 'War to End All Wars' remains England's greatest human catastrophe and a still-vivid reminder of the difference between an imaginary gentle home and a violent destructiveness abroad.

All of which brings us back to Powell, who was just six years old when that war ended and, like so much of his generation, grew up in its shadow. An only child of two teachers, then a solitary scholarship boy at King Edward's School in Birmingham, he spent much of his childhood going for long walks alone along the lanes of rural Worcestershire. By the time he was eighteen, Powell was proficient in five languages as well as being an admirer of Nietzsche's philosophy. But his greatest enthusiasm was reserved for the poetry of A. E. Housman, whose *A Shropshire Lad* describes an English country landscape – the 'land of lost content' – strewn with the corpses of tragic 'lightfoot boys' and broken-hearted 'rose-lipt girls'.[31]

Riven with their author's agonisingly repressed homosexuality – 'Because I liked you better/Than suits a man to say' – these poems that gave shape to this myth of England evoked what Housman acknowledged was 'not exactly a real place'. Some were written from his home in north London before he had set foot in Shropshire and, even after he finished all sixty-three of them, the poet said he had 'never spent much time' in the countryside where they were supposedly set. The 'blue remembered hills' that Housman described had less to do with his memory than his imagination.[32]

When Powell left school, he went to Cambridge University to study Classics where Housman himself could still be found as a revered, if remorselessly severe, professor of Latin. According to Powell's official biographer, he 'modelled himself on Housman', became a fixture at his lectures and sent letters to him about Virgil's *Aeneid*, the same poem from which he would later derive his 'foaming with blood' line. He wrote his own pastoral poetry modelled on Housman's not least because it was filled with Powell's intense longing for a male student called Tommy Thomas.[33]

> While yesteryear I tarried
> In a garden in the south,
> I met a youth who carried
> A rose-bud in his mouth.
>
> I gave him chase and caught him,
> And would not set him free,

But held him and besought him
To give the flower to me.

He smiled, and broke a petal
And laid it in my hand
It seared like molten metal,
And here is yet the brand.[34]

Many years later, when he was close to death after a long and apparently happy marriage, one of Powell's last public acts was to unveil a window dedicated to Housman at Poets' Corner in Westminster Abbey.[35] Even as other passions dimmed, that poetry could still move him to tears, and he continued to talk about visiting pastoral treasures like Lilleshall Hill as 'homecoming to me, to my own people, to my own country'.[36]

Such admiration for Housman's poetry and the mythical England it described was shared by many at the time. Among them was the young Eric Blair, then a pupil at Eton, who would later become famous under his writing name of George Orwell. 'I probably knew the whole of the *Shropshire Lad* by heart,' he said, 'we used to recite [it] over and over, in a kind of ecstasy' as part of what he called an 'enormous gush of "country" sentiment'.[37]

After the Armistice was signed in 1918, the prime minister, David Lloyd George, went to Wolverhampton to launch his re-election campaign in front of an adulatory crowd where he promised to build 'a fit country for heroes to live in'.[38] But such optimism did not last long as this cultural turn inwards and backwards spilled over into politics.

A victorious nation stumbled into the next few years as a sadder, poorer and more insular place bereft of the confidence it had once felt. A global pandemic killed upwards of 250,000 people in the UK, especially the young. Britain's economy was saddled with debts ten times higher than before a war in which more money was spent by the government than in the previous forty years. Border controls introduced properly for the first time during a war when every alien was regarded as a 'potential subversive' remained in place afterwards to protect England from a continental Europe stricken with revolution and civil war.

Trade unions grew in size and militancy, with a wave of industrial action culminating in Britain's first General Strike in 1926. Upper-class suffragettes who had once asked, 'My butler can vote, why can't I?' had been enfranchised after the war but were then confronted with a new problem of finding their servants increasingly had ideas of their own. It was said that these 'lower classes' had become too 'uppity'.[39]

While all this was going on at home, the empire abroad was notionally bigger than ever, swollen by the addition of 500 million more people and tracts of land across Africa and the Middle East that had once been run by the Germans or Ottomans. And, for a time, it seemed there was still life in the old imperial myth even as it rubbed up against this more insular one. The 1924 British Empire Exhibition, held in Wembley, was the biggest national celebration since the Great Exhibition seventy-five years earlier, with seventeen million people attending. Exhibits, including the newly discovered tomb of Tutankhamun, were connected by miles of railways whose stops had names given to them by Rudyard Kipling.[40] But the feeling was not quite the same as before. Noël Coward's play about ordinary English families between the wars, *This Happy Breed*, has a character complaining about going to the Wembley exhibition with his children. 'I brought them here to see the glories of Empire,' he says, 'and all they think about is going on the dodgems.' And the empire itself was changing, too. In 1926, the white settler communities in the colonies of Australia, New Zealand and Canada were granted Dominion status and, five years later, the Statute of Westminster renounced the Imperial Parliament's right to legislate for them.[41]

Instead, a new sense of security was offered by turning inward to the myth of 'the old country'. This was best expressed by the future Conservative prime minister Stanley Baldwin in a speech to the Royal Society of St George. He began by stating 'profound thankfulness that I may use the word "England" without some fellow at the back of the room shouting out "Britain"'. Baldwin went on to declare that 'England is the country, and the country is England' before launching into a description of the 'one eternal sight' of this country:

The tinkle of hammer on anvil in the country smithy, the corncrake on a dewy morning, the sound of the scythe against the whetstone, and the sight of a plough team coming over the brow of a hill, the sight that has been in England since England was a land, and may be seen in England long after the Empire has perished and every works in England has ceased to function.[42]

No matter that, far from being 'eternal', much of that England had long since disappeared, Baldwin was tapping a potent combination of nostalgia for the past and anxiety about the future. Hundreds of popular books, novels, pamphlets and poems bore 'witness to the dying arts of the countryside'.[43] This was the moment when Vaughan Williams and Cecil Sharp began collecting the embers of folk culture to reheat fifteenth century traditions of Morris dancing so that even now the sight of beer-bellied bearded men with bells attached to their ankles can be seen in village fêtes across southern England. The same sentiment inspired landscape artists like Graham Sutherland, Paul Nash and John Piper, the last of which collaborated successfully with John Betjeman who wrote softly of a certain kind of Englishness in his *Shell Guides* for newly mobile motorists. His writing was, he said, intended to represent a 'redemptive insularity' of humane values at a time when people sought refuge from the barbarism of the world. His England was an imaginary one, heavily romanticised, characterised by craft, care and community.[44]

The real country was often riven by snobbery and deeply undemocratic. Evelyn Waugh's *Brideshead Revisited* captures the resentment England's upper classes felt between the wars. It chronicled how, having sacrificed the flower of their youth on the fields of Flanders, they were having to sell their land and lose their servants or their stately homes 'so that things might be safe for the travelling salesman, with his polygonal pince-nez, his fat, wet handshake, his grinning dentures'.[45] In a mid-market but equally snobbish category was the popular prose of H. V. Morton who set off in his Bullnose Morris to write a semi-fictional account of warm beer, country lanes and village greens surrounded by thatched cottages that became the bestselling *In Search of England*. And, if Morton quite deliberately skirted around the 'Black Belt' of the industrialised North or Midlands to reinforce an idea of the 'beautiful Old England that I love',[46] he also concealed his frequent trips to brothels and his private sympathies for Adolf Hitler.[47]

This fear of slaughter dominated so much public culture in these years between the wars, whether in the disorientation described by T. S. Eliot's *The Waste Land* or the anger of F. R. Leavis towards the forced 'standardisation' of life. Similar sentiments were found in the idea of 'deep France' – *La France profonde* – or the *Heimatschutz* movement of German traditionalists. Much of this had far-right connotations such as the overtly racist 'blood and soil' back-to-the-land fantasies of Eliot's farming friend, Viscount Lymington, or the desire for order voiced by Thomas Sharp who said: 'The crying need of the moment is the re-establishment of the ancient antithesis. The town is the town; the country is the country; black and white; male and female.'[48]

But the fetish for England's countryside was shared by left-wing radicals, too, who packed rucksacks to stay in youth hostels amid remote and windswept hills, sent their children off to join the Woodcraft Folk, or campaigned for ramblers' rights of way as in the famous 'mass trespass' of Kinder Scout in the Peak District.[49] George Orwell may have been irritated by such people but he was nonetheless attracted to the idea behind it. His novel *Coming Up for Air* saw a middle-aged everyman, George Bowling, travelling back to the village of Lower Binfield to seek the 'calmness' of the life he remembered growing up.

Another socialist, J. B. Priestley, indulged a twentieth-century version of the myth with his book *English Journey*. He described an emerging homely suburbia filled by 'bungalows with tiny garages, cocktail bars, Woolworths, motor-coaches, wireless, hiking, factory girls looking like actresses'.[50]

But Priestley knew there could be no return to a rural past and nor did he think industrial England, scarred by depression, was anything about which to wax lyrical. As someone who grew up in Bradford, he felt qualified to pronounce on the human consequences of poverty. 'If I declare that Coketown is a horrible hole, I do not merely mean it cannot be fitted in to some private fairy-tale Merrie England of my own: I mean it is a damned horrible hole,' he wrote in *English Journey*, by way of introduction to a section on the Black Country.

You looked into an immense hollow of smoke and blurred buildings and factory chimneys. There seemed to be no end to it ... the earth has been left gaping and bleeding; and what were once bright fields have been rummaged and raped into these dreadful patches of waste ground ... The places I saw had names, but these names were merely so much alliteration: Wolverhampton, Wednesbury, Wednesfield,

Willenhall and Walsall. You could call them all wilderness and have done with it.[51]

Priestley's England was far more democratic and generous than the patronising versions offered by either conservatives or the liberal intelligentsia in Bloomsbury. But his version was never very inclusive or outward looking. He questioned whether the emerging new lifestyle of the suburbs owed too much to America and not enough 'to this particular island'. And what would now be called multiculturalism disgusted him. Priestley recalled reaching Liverpool and recoiling at 'the wooly curls of the negro, the smooth brown skin of the Malay, the diagonal eye of the Chinese' before launching into a demand that would have made Enoch Powell blush for the repatriation of Irish immigrants. 'What a grand clearance there will be in all the western ports,' he wrote, 'what a fine exit of ignorance and dirt and drunkenness and disease.'[52]

'A FLAVOUR ALL OF ITS OWN'

In spite of all this inward-looking Englishness, barely two decades after the Armistice the country embarked on another world war in 1939. Holding that paradox tight, the nation's favourite song was Vera Lynn's 'There'll Always Be an England', the lyrics of which combined the pastoral themes of 'a country lane', 'a cottage small' and 'a field of grain' with the idea that 'England shall be free/If England means as much to you/As England means to me'.

A sense of 'what England meant' at that terrifying time can be found in a collection of paintings preserved in London's Victoria & Albert Museum. The government began commissioning them from artists deemed unfit for military service and who suddenly found themselves unemployed – some were apparently 'close to starvation' – so the essence of the country could be captured before it was destroyed by German bombers, modernity, or both.[53] The resulting 1,549 watercolours are known collectively as *Recording Britain* but they are overwhelmingly about England, with just seventy-six of Wales and none at all of Scotland.[54] They reflect the preoccupations of this myth of English insularity. In four boxes of paintings recording scenes in

Staffordshire, for instance, there are pictures portraying farms, fields, churches, locks, hotels, hills, mills, distant potteries and grand country houses, but not a single one of anything deemed worth preserving for posterity from anywhere in Wolverhampton or the Black Country.

But this was a very different war in which the entire civilian population had good reason to fear they might be killed. Even though Wolverhampton was largely ignored by the *Luftwaffe*, just as it had been by those unemployed watercolour artists, the city was an obvious target because its factories had been turned over to the production of tanks, shells and aircraft. Local people watched neighbouring Coventry and Birmingham burn, then nervously waited night after night for bombers that they had warned would 'always get through'.

The shock of it was summed up by a woman who recalled for a BBC archive project growing up in Bilston, one of the towns that make up Wolverhampton, during the 1940s. When she was five, sirens woke her up and she raced into an air raid shelter as a stray German aircraft flew directly overhead before dropping its bombs nearby. 'The flares lit up the scene. My mother screamed and we looked up to see the face of the pilot clearly,' she said. 'And he waved to us!'[55]

George Orwell and J. B. Priestley were among those who recognised early on that the myth they had helped shape before the war could now be put to use. They drew on the daily experiences of citizens in towns and cities, describing patriotism not in terms of glory or imperial salvation, but in the value of English ordinariness. Orwell's essay *The Lion and the Unicorn* is the most celebrated of these efforts not least because of its famous opening sentence. 'As I write, highly civilized human beings are flying overhead, trying to kill me.' This was written during the Blitz of 1940 and captured that same astonishment felt by that five-year-old girl in Bilston watching a German bomber pilot wave at her. Orwell recognised that behind behaviour seemingly so alien in the modern world was an 'overwhelming strength of patriotism' that Hitler had understood better than his opponents. But Orwell also described a gentler, 'unofficial', form of pride; and Englishness 'somehow bound up with solid breakfasts and gloomy Sundays' that had 'a flavour of its own' and, he wrote, 'above all it is your civilisation. It is *you*.'[56]

Priestley's celebrated *Postscripts* radio broadcasts mined this same seam. 'When the enemy bombers come roaring at us at all hours, and it's our nerve versus his,' he said, 'we're not really civilians any longer but a mixed lot of soldiers – machine-minding soldiers, milkmen and postmen soldiers, housewife and mother soldiers – and what a gallant corps that is – even broadcasting soldiers.'[57] He enlisted his listeners into 'the strangest army the world has ever seen ... doing quite ordinary things, an army of all shapes and sizes, but nevertheless a real army'.[58] His most telling *Postscripts* broadcast was the first one he made, in the darkest hour of June 1940 after the fall of France and the chaotic evacuation of troops from the beaches of Dunkirk inverted the myth of Francis Drake. He told the story of how an English 'armada' of little ships and seaside pleasure craft, plucked from familiar everyday life, had come to their country's aid to turn an ignominious retreat into something that felt like a victory.

Much like the story of playing bowls on Plymouth's Hoe, the one about Dunkirk was never wholly true. Although more than 310,000 British, French and Belgian soldiers were taken across the Channel, two-thirds of them boarded big passenger ferries and warships at the docks. And, since those years, academics have devoted much of their careers to trying to debunk the wartime mythology.

The 'Blitz Spirit' has taken a particular battering in recent years. Recorded crime of all kinds, including murder, rose by 57 per cent during a time when everyone was supposed to be cheerfully singing along with each other in Tube stations. There was hoarding, looting of bomb sites and profiteering through a black market. Even an iconic photograph of a stoical milkman picking his way through the London rubble to maintain his deliveries was never quite what it seemed. On the October morning in 1940 when it was taken, the photographer, Fred Morley, knew the censors would not approve a morale-sapping picture of firefighters trying to douse the flames of blasted London buildings. But he had earlier seen a milkman in the area and asked him if he could borrow his coat and a crate full of milk bottles. It was Morley's assistant who then posed in the coat, with his eyebrows raised and his left arm swinging wide, while he pretended to go about his rounds.

The mythology of this time was manufactured in a process as much part of the war effort as the factories making tanks back in Wolverhampton. Britain was focused on the strategic need to bring the United States into a war which Britain was never going to win alone; these stories were aimed at the US, as much as 'us'. For instance, the story of the Blitz was constructed around ordinary people partly to convince Americans that England was not a class-ridden waning imperial power but a freedom-loving country fighting for its life. *London Can Take It*, a brilliantly successful Ministry of Information film, was aimed squarely at US opinion with the title originally an American phrase and the words narrated by Quentin Reynolds, an American journalist.

Those who take too much relish in unpicking the myths of 1940, however, risk missing the point. Few countries had ever put the everyday struggles of ordinary people at the heart of their identity as England did in those days. For many British people who survived the Second World War this was a time when they felt a common purpose and pride they never really felt again. A total of 1.5 million people volunteered for civilian emergency services, another million for the Home Guard, while millions more donated into community Spitfire Funds which raised enough money to build 2,600 such aircraft.[59] An opinion poll conducted by Gallup when the Blitz was at its most intense found 77 per cent rejected the idea of making peace with Germany and 82 per cent thought Britain would still win the war.[60] It was a mood summed up by David Low's iconic cartoon showing a soldier standing on a cliff with raised fist against the storm-tossed sea as the dark shapes of German bombers fly overhead. The caption beneath declared: 'Very well, alone.'[61]

Most importantly of all, Britain was still, more or less, a democracy. Together with its empire, it stood up to Fascism in 1940 when America was still in thrall to isolationism and the Soviet Union was busy picking over the carcass of Poland it had divided up with Germany. There was a relatively free press and parliament that succeeded in ending some of the worst excesses of war such as the denial of basic civil liberties to thousands of innocent foreign nationals who had been interned. A certain sort of pride can also be taken in the treatment of some Nazi spies that had been caught in the midst of a panic over 'Fifth Columnists' in 1940. All of them had displayed various levels of incompetence after landing on the south coast with one giving himself away when he knocked on the door of a seaside pub at 9 a.m. to demand, in a foreign accent, a 'Champagne cocktail'. At their Old Bailey trial, the judge said they should all be convicted and three of them were duly sentenced to death. But Sjoerd Pons was acquitted in a remarkable display of the independence of an English jury.[62]

Rationing, the sight of Churchill in his siren suits or that of the king and queen visiting bombed-out East Enders also helped build an idea of a nation sharing a burden. Although all kinds of snobbery and privilege continued unabated, some of the gentler stories were real enough. For instance, on 15 September 1940, around 100 Communist protesters stormed the Savoy Hotel's luxury shelter where guests were bedding down in linen sheets. A stand-off with police was defused when an air raid began and sympathetic waiters eventually served the demonstrators tea and toast on silver trays for a specially negotiated price of 2d, the same amount they would have been charged at a Lyons Corner House café.[63]

Nor were Orwell and Priestley mere cogs in a war propaganda machine as they instinctively reached for change.[64] Laid on top of the idea of England as a place – the 'sovereign isle' – was that of an increasingly sovereign people, too. 'Zweee – BOOM! What's that?' asked Orwell. 'Oh, only a bomb on the Stock Exchange. Zweee – BOOM! Another acre of somebody's valuable slum-property gone west.' There was an assumption that the war would create a better country, one that could reconcile the peace and domesticity at the heart of this myth by delivering a fundamental shift in the balance of power and the distribution of wealth. The Beveridge report of November 1942, *Social Insurance and Allied Services* – which, despite its title, sold more than 600,000 copies – set out a programme to eradicate 'the five giants' of 'Want, Disease, Ignorance, Squalor and Idleness'.[65] By the end of *The Lion and the Unicorn*, Orwell had fully reconciled his wartime patriotism to the cause of progress. In lines that could have almost been a Leave campaign slogan in the Brexit referendum seventy-five years later, Orwell declared: 'England has got to assume its real shape ... to take charge of its own destiny.'[66]

When Labour unexpectedly won a landslide majority in 1945 and Clement Attlee's government began a programme of national reconstruction, the mythology of 1940 and 'standing alone' was as important as ever. A line was traced from the emergency wartime measures taken on rationing and 'digging for victory' to the new housing, nationalisation of key industries and the creation of the post-war welfare state. The National Health Service, which Aneurin Bevan said would mean other countries would learn 'from us in the 20th century as they learned from us in the 17th', remains a unifying and enduring symbol of this country.

The problem was that there was still a very narrow definition of who was included in the 'imagined community' of the nation. The story of 1940 was always overwhelmingly about England and largely the southern half of it, symbolised by the White Cliffs of Dover. The contribution of 500 million people in the British Empire and the vast imperial supply chain scarcely got a look-in. The Bengal Famine of 1943, in which up to three million Indian civilians died as Japan took control of the Burmese rice fields and desperate pleas for help were largely ignored by Churchill, was not part of the popular history of the war. Nor were the experiences of Black people in the Blitz, at least one of whom wrote to Churchill to complain they had been thrown out of air raid shelters 'as if they were Jews from Germany'.[67] Orwell himself, although a lifelong campaigner against empire, sometimes appeared to revel in xenophobia. 'The English working class are out-standing in their abhorrence of foreign habits,' he wrote. They refuse to 'accustom themselves to foreign food' and think 'it effeminate to pronounce a foreign word correctly'. Such insularity, said Orwell, 'is the same quality in the English character that repels the tourist and keeps out the invader'.[68]

As such, this wartime story of England 'standing alone' both cleared the way for thinking anew about a better country and stood as an obstacle to reform. At vast and unaffordable expense, Britain developed its own atom bomb in a desperate effort to maintain world power status. 'Whatever it costs,' said Labour's foreign secretary, Ernie Bevin, 'we've got to have the bloody Union Jack on it.'[69] As that Labour government fought Malayan insurgency by ordering the internment of half a million people and covering up massacres, it began to run out of steam back at home. Enthusiasm for building a 'New Jerusalem' had been overtaken by frustration with bureaucratic inertia, rationing and shortages. In 1950, MPs moved back into a new House of Commons that had been designed to look almost identical to the old one destroyed by German bombing in the war. Virtually the last act of the Labour government was the 1951 Festival of Britain. A sharp departure from the great exhibitions London had seen before, it contained scant reference to the empire or the rest of the world but instead celebrated the optimism of a smaller country. Its highlights were Magna Carta and rural folklore, as well as the futuristic Skylon sculpture and the Dome of Discovery. The imperialist Churchill, of course, hated it and ordered the whole site to be dismantled as soon as he was returned to Downing Street later that year.[70]

Churchill launched an effort to restore Britain's global status that, even though it was often frustrated, went on to overshadow English culture and British politics for the rest of the twentieth century. In tune with the country's reduced circumstances, it invoked the backs-to-the-wall days of insular wartime adversity and is why Dunkirk and the Blitz, when the country 'stood alone' in adversity, are more important to national mythology than moments of Allied triumph like D-Day.

Such an idea has been reinforced by countless commemorations and endlessly repeated TV series like *Dad's Army* with its title sequence of spidery Nazi arrows surrounding the south coast to its theme tune song – itself a piece of retro pastiche written in 1969 – of 'Who do you think you are kidding, Mr Hitler, if you think old England's done'. Almost every night, one of the main TV channels will show a documentary, a drama or one of the 200 feature films made about the conflict which betray none of the post-First World War doubts about Britain's moral purpose. All of which has left a lasting impression on the national psyche with a 2015 poll showing no less than 50 per cent of British people believing their country contributed most to the defeat of Germany in the war. By contrast, Germans overwhelmingly said it was the US and Soviet Union who beat the Nazis, with just 7 per cent saying it was Britain.

Even today, middle-class kitchens are decorated with 'Keep Calm and Carry On' posters (even though they were never actually used in the war). Amateur cooks busy themselves by 'blitzing' the onions and garlic together for dinner. Around the table, arguments about almost anything invariably end up with someone mentioning the Nazis. Some foreign visitors find it all a bit strange that a country can be so utterly and remorselessly obsessed about events that happened eighty years ago. But retelling the many exaggerations and half-truths is usually done at a volume that defies the existence of uncomfortable facts with as much determination as London was once said to have faced the Blitz. Sometimes, this expresses itself in a kind of national

masochism like that of Ant Middleton, the former Special Forces soldier and star of Channel 4's *SAS: Who Dares Wins*, who declared he
wanted the toughest Brexit possible: 'It would force us into hardship
and suffering which would unite & bring us together, bringing back
British values of loyalty and a sense of community! Extreme change
is needed!'[71]

This is a country that has been unable wholly to move on from,
or measure up to, its wartime story of close-knit, resolute, sovereign
England. Indeed, if that was England's 'finest hour', wasn't it inevitable that everything that happened afterwards would be worse?

'GET BACK TO WHERE YOU ONCE BELONGED ...'

At the end of the Second World War, five-year-old Ken Clibery watched
a convoy of Americans soldiers pass through Wolverhampton. 'They
came by in trucks waving to us and throwing cigarettes and chocolates,
and an orange rolled towards me,' he said. 'I picked it up and went to
throw it back, and then my mum said, "Don't throw that." It was the
first time in my life I had seen an orange. I hadn't a clue what it was.
It was like a ball.'[72]

The awe felt by a child watching American GIs tossing oranges and
sweets around underlined the straitened circumstances and reduced
status of this nation. Even in the moment of victory, a deep sense of
loss was wrapping itself around many people. And few were gripped
more tightly by it than Enoch Powell.

Having reputedly been the youngest professor in the empire at the
start of the war, Powell embarked on a similarly meteoric rise through
the ranks of the military from private to brigadier even though, as
a military intelligence officer, he never experienced combat. Years
later – in true Housman style – he was still insisting, 'I should like to
have been killed in the war'.[73] Undeterred by his continued existence,
Powell then set himself the alternative and spectacularly immodest
ambition of becoming Viceroy of India where he had been stationed
for much of the conflict.[74]

On his return to England, he swiftly got a job with the Conservative
Party for whom he wrote a 25,000-word memo on how Britain
could reconquer India with ten divisions in the event of it claiming

independence. 'The forces of disorder are endemic,' he argued. Indians 'look to British order as a welcome salvation from chaos and strife' and would continue to do so 'for at least 50 years more'.[75] On his insistence, it was shown to Churchill who found it slightly unsettling, with one account saying he 'seemed distressed and asked if Powell was "all right"'.[76]

When, the following year, the Labour government announced India's independence, Powell said he suffered a 'shock so severe that I spent the whole of one night walking the streets of London trying to come to terms with it', occasionally sitting 'down in a doorway, my head in my hands'.[77] This was a personal disaster that convinced him the empire was over. It saw Powell steadily turn away from being an arch-imperialist into a politician who would believe an English-centric Britain should never depend again on anyone, or anything, except itself.

After the Anglo-French military effort to seize back control of the Suez Canal in 1956 collapsed into diplomatic ignominy and retreat, Powell wrote: 'The Tory party must be cured of the British Empire, of the pitiful yearning to cling to relics of a bygone system.'[78] During Britain's suppression of Kenya's Mau Mau rebellion in the late 1950s, Powell condemned the murder of prisoners at the Hola camp in a speech often taken as proof that he was no racist. But, as one of his many biographers has pointed out, Powell's outrage was sourced not in a humanitarian mission to the world so much as his concern that such 'un-British' behaviour by white and Black people in Africa should be kept very separate from this country's 'civilised way of life'.[79] At the same time, he became increasingly sceptical about Britain prioritising nuclear weapons over conventional forces not least because under Harold Macmillan's deal with the Americans to buy Polaris, these missiles were effectively controlled by NATO.[80]

Powell's sense of England's existential crisis was, at least initially, at odds with the experience of millions of people who were enjoying rapidly rising living standards. Motorways were cutting a swathe through the countryside and vast construction projects like the bridge over the Humber were linking the north and south of England like never before. There were more hospitals, schools and universities, while 250,000 new homes were built in England every year for two decades from 1953. Those homes were filled with fridges, washing machines, telephones and televisions. Car ownership soared, rationing ended in 1954, the same year that the first Wimpy Bar opened selling hamburgers and sardine sandwiches. Chinese takeaways opened and lager arrived in pubs. There was frozen chicken, peas and fish fingers in supermarkets, as well as free milk for children in schools.[81]

In the Black Country it was a time when the worst slums were cleared, Wolves won three football league championships in five years and the economy boomed. It made the steel and bricks needed to rebuild Britain, the cookers and car components that post-war consumers demanded and the BSR turntables with which teenaged children danced to rock and roll music. By 1961, household incomes in the area were 13 per cent higher than the national average. Vast factories owned by multinational firms like Goodyear and GKN competed for workers by offering ever-higher wages, sports grounds and smart new canteens with subsidised lunches.[82] Although Wolverhampton itself, sandwiched between the Birmingham suburbs where Powell had grown up and Housman's imaginary 'land of lost content' in Shropshire, may not have looked much like anyone's pastoral ideal of England, it was a shared prosperity sustained by a welfare state, strong trade unions and interventionist governments.

But there was also unease and it once again found expression in that inward-looking myth of England standing alone against a hostile world. Harold Macmillan is often remembered for being the prime minister who said that 'most of our people have never had it so good'. The words that followed from that 1957 speech are less often quoted. He asked: 'Is it too good to be true? ... Is it too good to last?'[83] That was the year when six continental countries signed the Treaty of Rome to create the European Economic Community. It was when the Union Jack was being lowered for the last time in colonies across the world and manufacturers were facing new competition from resurgent foreign rivals who had been defeated or rescued in the war. West Germany's growth rate overtook Britain by the mid-1950s and even France, which had been lagging behind since the days of Napoleon, did so a few years later. Although Britain's economy was still growing, the speed with which Europe had caught up created a deep sense of pessimism about the future.

And there was another, very visible, sign of change. When the SS *Empire Windrush* had docked in London with 500 Jamaicans on board, the post-war Labour government had swiftly passed legislation confirming they were British citizens with the right to come to the 'mother country'. At first, numbers of new arrivals were low but by the early 1960s – at more or less the same time as the economy began to slow and unemployment was creeping up – tens of thousands of immigrants began to arrive each year.

By 1962, when gangs of Brylcreemed Teddy Boys were smashing the windows of Black and Asian people's homes in Dudley, Macmillan's government began restricting entry for people who did not have a job offer or what were deemed useful skills. Rab Butler, the home secretary, told colleagues the measure was 'intended to, and would in fact, operate on coloured people almost exclusively'.[84] When Labour got back into power a couple of years later, it introduced the Race Relations Act but began to wobble over immigration controls when the Conservatives' Peter Griffiths won a by-election in Smethwick where his leaflets said: 'If you want a n—for a neighbour, vote Labour.'[85]

Both Dudley and Smethwick are Black Country towns just a few miles from Wolverhampton where Powell was an MP who, for most of this period, remained noticeably quiet on the whole subject. He was a self-consciously intellectual politician who listened to Wagner, wrote poetry, studied ancient Greek texts, conversed with Indian constituents in Urdu and spent most of the time living in Belgravia. Socially liberal on issues such as ending capital punishment and legalising homosexuality, he regularly risked serious injury falling off his horse as he rode out with hunts such as the Albrighton in Shropshire and the Old Berkeley East on the edge of the Chilterns, travelling to the latter on the London Underground 'dressed in his full kit'.

Powell was no instinctive anti-immigration populist. When minister for health in the early 1960s, he had actively recruited NHS staff from Asia, as well as the Caribbean and Africa. As a local MP, he lobbied officials to help immigrant constituents bring members of their families to Wolverhampton.[86] They included Tarsem Singh Sandhu, one of the first British Asians to become a member of the MP's local Conservative Association. 'Enoch Powell was my friend,' Sandhu later explained on BBC radio. 'He helped get two of my cousins into England.'[87]

There is a healthy debate among historians about what caused such a politician to become one who, more than any other in the past half-century, symbolised an England defined by an insular cultural ethnicity. Perhaps it was gaining just a handful of votes in a Tory leadership contest in 1965 that made Powell want to raise his profile. Maybe it was the influx in that decade of Kenyan and Ugandan Asian refugees, including the parents of future Conservative home secretaries Priti Patel and Suella Braverman, that tipped his views on immigration over the edge.[88] Possibly it was the sense of global chaos that made him believe racial integration could never succeed. The year before he gave his 'Rivers of Blood' speech, Powell had visited the US as the civil rights movement gathered speed. Nineteen sixty-eight itself had begun with Harold Wilson's government announcing military withdrawal from bases 'east of Aden'. There was civil war in Nigeria, Viet Cong victories and massacres in Vietnam, as well as the start of the Troubles in Northern Ireland. In America there were riots in Detroit, the rise of the Black Panthers movement and the assassination – just a fortnight before the speech – of Martin Luther King.

And, in the months before, Sandhu – the Sikh man who described Powell as his friend – had been turned away from his job as a bus driver in Wolverhampton because the transport company would not let him wear a turban. It became a celebrated national and international cause that saw 5,000 Sikhs march through the city centre, 50,000 gather outside the British Embassy in Delhi and one activist threaten to set himself on fire.

Powell condemned the campaign, linking it to the 'communalism' that had caused so much bloodshed during the partition of India. He referred to it again in the 'Rivers of Blood' speech describing 'the cloud no bigger than a man's hand, that can so rapidly overcast the sky [which] has been visible recently in Wolverhampton' as he raised the spectre of race war coming to England.

Sandhu, even as an old man looking back fifty years later, still insisted that Powell 'was not a racist' – merely an opportunist – saying: 'I think he just gave that speech for political reasons.'[89]

What seems confusing now is that the late 1960s is generally remembered as a time when England was at the forefront of a global cultural revolution. Young people the world over listened to the Beatles and the Rolling Stones, men grew their hair longer, women went out to work and some took contraceptive pills. The Wilson government legalised sex between men and abortions for women, divorce for both was made easier and capital punishment for murderers was abolished.

But the 1960s were not 'swinging' for most people. Best estimates suggest that less than 5 per cent of the country experimented with drugs and, even as students rioted in Paris and Mexico, only a few thousand people followed the bandana-wearing Vanessa Redgrave when she led the Anti-Vietnam War demonstration into Grosvenor Square in London.[90]

The old English elite was satirised by a new one that was no less exclusive as the products of private schools who had met at the universities of Cambridge and Oxford spawned TV shows like *That Was The Week That Was* and *Monty Python's Flying Circus*, or magazines like *Private Eye*. And, if bands like the Beatles were inspired by Black American and later Indian music, their lyrics often returned to the provincial England about which Lawrence, Orwell and Priestley had written. Songs like 'Penny Lane' and 'Strawberry Fields' or the '4,000 holes in Blackburn, Lancashire' from 'A Day in the Life' combined modernity with a deep sense of place and everyday life. Their own story – friends grow up in English suburbia, fall out, feel regret – was instantly recognisable, or as Paul McCartney later put it in an interview with the softly pornographic *Playboy* magazine: 'The fact is, being ordinary is very important to me. I see it in millions of other people. There's an appreciation of common sense. It's really quite rational, my ordinariness. It's not contrived at all. It is actually my answer to the question, what is the best way to be? I think ordinary.'[91]

Barely a year after the 'Rivers of Blood' speech, early versions of the Beatles' song 'Get Back' were dreamed up as a riposte. 'Dirty Enoch Powell said to the immigrants, immigrants you better get back to your Commonwealth homes', along with the ironic 'don't dig no Pakistanis'. But they scrapped those lines in part because they might be taken literally, as some online conspiracy theorists subsequently did. The version eventually famously played live on the roof of their new studio in London's Savile Row only had a hint of this anti-racist protest. It said: 'So get back. Get back. Get back to where you once belonged.'[92]

Perhaps the reason for McCartney's caution was that there was still a big chunk of England that did not believe the old and the new could be combined in the way that the Beatles did. They were shocked and appalled by the permissive society in the 1960s and they wanted to 'get back' themselves.

It may not be entirely coincidental that Powell lived for a number of years next door but one to the similarly polarising figure of Mary Whitehouse in Wolverhampton's Merridale Road. She would go on to lead a national campaign to 'clean up' television of sex, violence and general immorality but, in those days, she was teaching at a secondary school in the city and fulminating to herself about the 'filth' on the radio or TV.

Whitehouse later recounted how she liked to observe her local MP through her back window. 'Mr Powell had only a tiny garden, but we watched with fascinated interest and respectful awe the care with which he planted out his lettuce seedlings.' She was less impressed with the way he shook fruit off a tree which hung over her wall, although she eventually concluded 'the falling apples simply demonstrated the direct Powellian approach to an immediate problem'.[93] It all ached with the kind of insularity chronicled so well by Alan Bennett, who has the fictionalised exiled spy Guy Burgess saying: 'So little, England. Little England, little art. Timid, tasteful, nice. But one loves it, one loves it.'[94]

After Whitehouse had moved out to nearby Claverley and achieved national fame, one of her sons perhaps inevitably joined a commune and got arrested for possessing drugs.[95] Although sneering about her role has declined in recent years when progressive opinion has become more concerned itself about pornography, it is difficult to disentangle Whitehouse's unease about the breakdown of traditional values with the fear many people like her felt about immigrants. Social conservatives worried about the young listening to Black people's music, 'primitive dances' and, in their view, the resulting promiscuity of women.[96] In 1968, even as Powell was igniting the immigration issue, Whitehouse had written to broadcasters complaining about the airtime given to Tariq Ali, the Pakistani-British socialist, Ruth First, the anti-apartheid activist and Stokely Carmichael, the Black Power leader.[97]

But to the extent there was inter-racial violence in England, much of it can be laid squarely at Powell's door. For instance, one week after his speech, fourteen men attacked a British West Indian christening party in Wolverhampton. They punched the father of the child and slashed the face of the grandfather, Wade Crooks, with a razor. 'The crowd were shouting "Powell, Powell" and "why don't you go back to your own country?"' Crooks said that 'nothing like this has happened before' in his thirteen years in England, adding: 'I am shattered.'[98]

In 1968, there was still not a single Black or Asian person in the House of Commons, the West Midlands police force or among the 1,000 members of staff at Beatties, Wolverhampton's biggest department store.[99] Just twenty-four hours after Powell delivered the 'Rivers of Blood' speech, the North Wolverhampton Working Men's Club reiterated a 'colour bar' policy by a unanimous vote of its 800 members. It was only being discussed because a Black woman, Ruth Saxon, complained she had been turned away when she tried to enter with a friend who had been invited to perform for the club as a 'strong man'. George Hall, the club secretary, explained to the *Observer*: 'We've the right to keep them out … Our members live by them and they know what it's like. All this dirt and sex.'[100]

This was never a sentiment universally shared in Wolverhampton, of course. Students from what was then the city's polytechnic joined together with young Asians to break the 'colour bar' in pubs around the town. Nor was resistance confined to students. When the press camped outside West Park Primary School in the city, having decided this was where Powell thought there was only one white child in a class, reporters got little change from the formidable headmistress, Eileen Llewellin-Davies. She told them the school not only loved all its children but also that 'we have a lot to learn from them'.[101]

Nonetheless, Powell had touched a nerve in Wolverhampton and in England as a whole. He received more than 100,000 letters in the month following his speech, the overwhelming majority of which were supportive. Although a sympathetic piece of research conducted soon afterwards found little evidence of prejudice, more recent academic analysis from the historian Amy Whipple has shown the support he had tapped into was wrapped up with the imperialism he had rejected, anger over Britain's diminished status and what would today only be described as racism. 'What's happened to *Great* Britain?' asked one. 'We have our back to the wall and are being bent over it. Isn't it high time we lashed out instead of being so damned soft and weak-minded about it?' Another said: 'As I see it, with the run-down of the once great British Empire which owes nothing to the coloured people after all we have done for them in the past, we are now being kicked in the teeth by one and all.'[102]

Immigrants were not the only people blamed for the widespread sense of decline that washed over the country in those post-war years. Across all parts of the political spectrum, it became a conventional wisdom that Britain had been let down by a bumbling elite who had contrived to 'lose the peace' as much as the people had 'won the war'. Scientists like Sir Barnes Wallis, famed for the 'bouncing bomb' featured in the film *The Dambusters*, toured the country giving popular lectures fulminating against short-sighted bureaucrats who had not followed through on his idea of giant cargo submarines and folding wing aircraft. Although the real causes of relative economic decline had more prosaic origins in a long-term failure to invest and reform management, Harold Wilson's Labour Party also caught the virus. It promised to transform a creaking Britain through the 'white heat of technology'. The subsequent experiments with hovercraft, air-cooled nuclear power stations and the Anglo-French supersonic airliner Concorde all cost taxpayers a fortune while receiving precisely zero export orders, even as national prestige received another blow with the devaluation of the pound in 1967 and trade union strikes challenged the wage policies that had been used to control inflation.

Wallis ended up with Sir Frank Whittle, the inventor of the jet engine, as embittered guest speakers at meetings of the racist Conservative Party faction known as the Monday Club where they could moan on against immigrants, unions and socialist governments.[103]

But it was Powell who wove together all these feelings into a new, radically right-wing economic programme. Long before it became Conservative Party orthodoxy, he was an advocate of the cleansing power of free markets and the purity of monetarism to free the English from 'bondage'. A sovereign nation, he said, should be independent of international obligation and debt. 'Give us a money system which will tell us the truth about the consequences of our choices and decisions,' he told businessmen in 1967. 'Give us this and we can do the rest ourselves,' he said. 'We would hear no more about a weak economy, about being "the sick man of Europe" … What we are would speak for itself.'[104]

None of this is separate from the myth of 'England alone'. Powell believed there were hereditary or, at the very least, deep-set Anglo-Saxon dispositions for orderly free markets and limited government. His obsession with the differential birth rates of ethnic groups and the make-up of the working-age population had more than a flavour of eugenics. He saw policies allowing immigration as diluting the national character with 'communal' values because of what he regarded as some deluded prioritisation of prosperity over national identity.

Above all, he was utterly at odds with all those who saw a multicultural society as a logical consequence of being at the heart of an empire for the previous 300 years, or, as the anti-racist campaigner and novelist Ambalavaner Sivanandan put it, 'we are here because you were there'. Instead, Powell regarded 'Asiatic and Negro immigration' as an alien, invading force and ridiculed the suggestion that the English should have to 'sink on their knees to apologise for being civilised'. He wrote a book with Angus Maude, *Biography of a Nation*, that mentioned slavery just once and then only in reference to how Britain's eighteenth-century naval superiority helped it get a bigger share of the trade.[105] He locked himself into such a painfully narrow idea that even his treasured English institutions were exposed to Powell's fury if he deemed them complicit in undermining the nation.

He attacked the queen for a Christmas message featuring images of her trip to a Commonwealth meeting in India, saying it showed she had the 'affairs and interests in other continents as much, or more, at heart than those of her own people'. The *Sun* helpfully translated his words into a front-page headline that said she 'should speak up more for whites'.[106]

When he received a letter from the Wolverhampton Council of Christian Churches, asking him to sign up for a Declaration on World Poverty, in the best traditions of that Victorian civilising mission discussed in the previous chapter, Powell replied that all their propositions were 'meaningless and absurd'. It was, he said, an example of 'woolly thinking and self-righteous nonsense' that was destroying the Church of England's authority and the Anglican mission to spread the gospel in 'heathen lands afar' was now needed at home.[107] Indeed, this was when Peter and Janet Hill, two Evangelical missionaries to India, returned to found the Christian Festival of Light campaigning against pornography and moral pollution alongside Mary Whitehouse and the pop star Cliff Richard.

The Tories regained power in 1970 in an election where they were probably helped by Powell's appeal to the anti-immigration sentiments of voters. Edward Heath's government duly passed legislation under which only those 'patrials' who were British by place of birth or parentage could come to live in the UK. Everyone else had to apply for a work permit. It meant the old imperial concept of the British subject-citizen was dead. In other words, if Powell could no longer become Viceroy of India, an Indian had no right to work in a Wolverhampton factory.

Powell, however, was infuriated by the Heath government's failure to follow through on plans for deep spending cuts. Having by then recanted his earlier support for the European Economic Community, Powell became incensed when the government negotiated the UK's entry because, more than anything, he could not bear the thought of England's sovereignty being shared. Powell longed for sharp lines, hard borders and a single source of power, derived from the medieval absolute authority of the crown that he said resided in 'the Parliament of the United Kingdom, or, to name it less exactly but more truthfully, the English Parliament'.[108] In 1974, he quit both the Conservative Party and Wolverhampton in a prolonged act of self-immolation that has burned itself onto the imagination of many Conservatives since. He went on to become an unbendingly English MP for South Down in Northern Ireland where he ended up defying his new party, the Ulster Unionists, by arguing against devolution or any power-sharing deal that might impinge on that 'English Parliament' in Westminster.

Powell's political genius was to combine such a stark political ideology with a mystical rendering of nation and ethnicity that resonated so far beyond the political orthodoxy of the time. This new version of the 'England alone' myth chimed with people's anxiety over the closed branch railway lines, the abolition of old counties like Middlesex and Rutland, or the replacement of the wonky-shaped coins and dyslexia-inducing imperial measurements with metric systems.

But his idea of England was always a delusion and as much a product of imagination as A. E. Housman's Shropshire had been in the nineteenth century or, for that matter, those 'blackthorn petals' which Powell's backward-travelling gaze had once seen being scattered over the smokestacks of his constituency. It nonetheless left a mark on this country. The comedian Lenny Henry grew up just six miles away from Wolverhampton and, as a young Black man in the mid-seventies, used to open his act with a gag that is frequently cited as a proof of progress. 'Enoch Powell says he wants to give me a thousand pounds to go back where I came from. Which is great, because it's only twenty pence for me to get on the bus from here to Dudley.' The next line is less often quoted: 'You'd better laugh, or I'll come and move in next door to you. That'll bring your rent down.'[109]

Henry's first regular work on TV came with the BBC's *The Black and White Minstrel Show* that, until it was axed in 1978, pulled in vast audiences to watch white men in blackface make-up and women doing high kicks in fishnet stockings. He remembers now being embarrassed at being 'the only real black person among all these fake ones', as well as slowly realising he was used by producers so they 'could point at me and say, "How can we be racist? Look – we've got Lenny Henry in the show."'[110] In his memoir, Henry writes about how he may have started doing impressions because of a desire to fit in, reassure white England, show them he could even 'talk like them'. When he married his fellow comedian Dawn French, a white woman, someone smeared the letters 'NF' – for National Front – on their door in excrement. And maybe, he wonders now, he should have done more to 'stand up and tell people to back off'.[111]

Through the 1970s, into the 1980s and sometimes beyond, the hatred he felt was real. Believers in the myth of 'England alone' took it as vindication of Powell's belief that 'we must be mad, literally mad' to have allowed in so many ethnically different immigrants.[112]

Finding people still willing to parrot those lines is still not too difficult. On Merridale Road, where Powell once lived, Geoff Bingham is drinking a mug of tea outside a friend's motorbike workshop and says: 'We've become a wet race, we're not looking after our own. Enoch was right.'

It is noticeable, however, that Powell is so often spoken about in this fashion, using the past tense rather the present. His grimmest prophecies about England have emphatically not come true. 'Rivers of blood' have not flowed and foamed in this city, or anywhere else.

In recent years, his former constituency in Wolverhampton has been represented in Parliament by an Asian Tory man and a Black Labour woman. The old Conservative Party offices in Clifford Street where, some say, Powell wrote the 'Rivers of Blood' speech are now an African-Caribbean Heritage Centre. It has a bar stocked with a dozen different types of rum along with a sign explaining the Jamaican Patwa 'Wha yu ah doh yah?' means 'What are you doing here?' There are pictures of Malcolm X, Barack Obama and Nelson Mandela.

There is also a blue plaque on the wall. And, no, it's not for Powell. Instead, it bears the name of Paulette Wilson whose life perhaps best sums up the patchy progress England has made in the years since Powell was the city's MP. She was born in Jamaica before being sent to live in England as a citizen of the British Empire at the age of ten. She went through school, raised a family, worked as a cook in the House of Commons dining rooms where she might have made Powell his dinner, and paid taxes for thirty-four years. But in 2012, Wilson was declared an illegal immigrant and became homeless after having her rights to housing and to work suspended under the Conservative government's 'hostile environment' policy for immigrants.

Five years later, she was arrested and held in a detention centre while she awaited deportation to Jamaica, a country she had not visited for fifty years. Her case led to an outcry, both locally and nationally, that helped expose what became known as the Windrush scandal in which hundreds of people were threatened and thrown out of the country on the most spurious grounds. Wilson became a campaigner who helped expose other cases, eventually forcing the home secretary to resign. When she died in 2020, there were tributes to her from all of Wolverhampton's MPs and the local newspaper started an appeal to raise money for her funeral.

Wolverhampton and the Black Country is also home to England's biggest and most successful Sikh community which has started paying for its own war memorials to celebrate their contribution to the armies of the British Empire. One of them, in Smethwick, commemorates those killed in the First World War. Another, in Wednesfield, is a monument to the last stand of twenty-one Sikh Indian soldiers in the face of some 10,000 Afghans on behalf of the Raj Saragarhi in 1897.

Memorials to a Windrush campaigner or Sikh soldiers might be seen as the best riposte to the insularity of anti-immigration campaigners. And yet, spend any time in Wolverhampton and it's hard to miss other new monuments that have sprouted up there in recent years that also commemorate a very different England from the one imagined by Powell. They are for the factories, foundries and collieries that once made this city prosperous.

The badges of Sunbeam Motors and bronze murals depicting various world land speed records decorate St John's Retail Park where cars were once made. A 'lone rider' artwork marks the site of the former AJS motorbike plant at Blakenhall. In Bilston's main shopping street, there is a sculpture of a nineteenth-century woman worker bent over so that her head is an anvil, as well as a Job Centre decorated with images of the cog wheels, steel girders, chains, drills and chimney stacks that no longer provide much work in this part of the city. On the bridge at Church Street there are cast-iron panels with words from an oral history of the steel industry. Morrisons supermarket has panels above its car park showing metal working, mining and workers pouring molten iron. Most of those jobs have long gone in the towns of the Black Country today.

Some of the metal-making and niche engineering firms were taken over by Caparo, a multinational steel business founded by the Indian immigrant and Labour peer Lord Swraj Paul who has been the chancellor of – and biggest single donor to – Wolverhampton University since 1999. But even these businesses eventually became insolvent, too, and Caparo went into administration in 2015.

The closure of Wolverhampton's factories cannot be separated from Powell's monetarist ideology that did so much to wipe out manufacturing industry from the late 1970s onwards. The following chapters will examine in greater detail what that did to England, but there is a circularity between the reasons why Powell's former constituents lost their jobs and the revival of his myth that contributed to the city voting by a 63 to 37 per cent for Brexit in 2016.[113]

Average earnings in Wolverhampton, which used to keep pace with those in London, are now 20 per cent below the UK average. Beatties, the big department store that was once at the heart of the city's shopping district, now stands shuttered and empty opposite a pawnbroker. The site of the giant GKN Sankey's plant at Bilston has been re-wilded as a meadow and the air is less polluted, so that on a clear day it's possible to see 'those blue remembered hills' that A. E. Housman had imagined in *A Shropshire Lad*.

But there is a strong sense that many people are now yearning less for an imagined pastoral past than an industrial one. No matter how hard and dirty the work was, there is now nostalgia for times when their communities felt strong, there was money for a good night out and hope that better days lay ahead.

'I'M JUST FROM WOLVERHAMPTON'

On a late summer Sunday afternoon in Wolverhampton a dreadlocked, brown-skinned man can be seen locked in a brief but ecstatic embrace with a slightly overweight white one. Although they have never met before, they have enough in common to share a few seconds of joy with each other. And 25,000 other people around them are all doing much the same.

If you haven't already guessed, they are all at a football match and one of the multi-racial multinational millionaires playing for Wolves has just given the team a 1–0 lead against Newcastle United. As he walks home after the game, Tyler Dayil explains that 'hugging this total stranger is not something I would do anywhere else' but is because 'the feeling I get when a goal goes in is like nothing else'. As he puts it, 'football brings this whole city together'.

A shopfitter by trade – 'we do Morrisons, Sainsbury's, all of them' – he says football means more to him 'than any religion; it's what I live for'. Dayil describes his roots as 'half-Indian, quarter-Jamaican, quarter-English' before saying how 'my nan came here from the Punjab' and 'my grandad's mum was on a boat from the West Indies'. Where does he say he is from? 'Me?' he says, breaking into a broad smile at the discomfort of a white liberal writer asking this question. 'I'm just from Wolverhampton!'

The final section of this chapter returns to where it began, at Molineux. It is a huge cathedral to more than sport in this diverse city where the football club has perhaps unexpectedly emerged as a symbol of unity rather than division.

When we ask Dayil what he thinks of Enoch Powell, he says: 'I've heard the name, but to be honest I don't really know the ins and outs of it.' Has he ever suffered racist abuse at games? 'Sometimes there'll be people who take the piss out my hair,' he says, pointing to his dreadlocks. 'But nothing worse.'

It was not always so. This football club once had supporters who wore white pillowcases on their heads with cut-out eye holes in the style of the Ku Klux Klan. The writer Sathnam Sanghera remembers growing up in the city and not being allowed out on match days or being hidden in the local Sikh temple to protect them from roaming gangs of skinhead hooligans. And for a long time, football's obsession with specific traditions and peculiarities seemed to make it a perfect host for a most insular kind of identity.[114]

Minute differences or perceived historic slights between people have always been amplified through football. There are still ferocious 'local derbies' that sometimes spill over into violence. If Wolves fans hate West Bromwich Albion because it is nine miles away in a different corner of the Black Country, think how intense the loathing can be when a team represents a different country or its players have a different skin colour and religion.

Certainly, no one who has spent any time watching English football will think it is some sort of panacea. In almost every crowd there are people – too drunk to stand up, or eyes popping from cocaine – who want to hurt others. For all the globalised modernity of the Premier League, fans often behave like a very old-fashioned mob. And racists have found a new platform on social media where some players are still subjected to the vilest abuse.

But overt inter-racial hatred at football matches is nothing like as bad it was during the 1970s and 1980s when there were routine monkey chants if a Black player touched the ball. When Jamaican-born John Barnes scored one of England's greatest individual goals in a 2–0 win against Brazil, the National Front skinheads following the team chanted about a 1–0 scoreline. For them, only 'white goals' counted.[115]

Wolves themselves perhaps began to open England's national sport up when they pioneered floodlit European games in the 1950s. And real progress began at Wolves' rivals West Bromwich Albion where three Black players – Cyrille Regis, Lawrie Cunningham and Brendan Batson – broke through with spectacular effect into the first team during the 1970s. Even then, however, when the least offensive of their nicknames was 'the Three Degrees', Batson has recalled how fearful Powell's speech had made members of his community. 'He must have known the impact it was going to have,' he said, describing how Black players would be spat at as they got off the team coach or showered by bananas.

All of which makes it so remarkable to see crowds streaming into Molineux these days who do not give a second glance to a billboard advert for Sky Sports outside the ground showing two turban-wearing Sikhs celebrating a Wolves goal. In the 'fan zone' by the entrance, Mr Sizzle's sausage van stands next to others offering curry wraps, samosas and 'Balti Pies'. Inside the stadium, there is a 500-strong Punjabi Wolves Supporters Group who bring their *dohl* drums with them to away games.[116] A stand named after a local hero, Steve Bull – the 'Tipton Terrier' – displays a dozen flags representing all the different nationalities in the team: Portuguese, Spaniards, Malians, Mexicans, Montenegrins, Colombians, Brazilians, South Koreans, Austrians, as well as some Irish, Welsh and English, too. The message is clear from endless signs dotted around the ground: the Wolves are 'one pack'.

Attached to the club is a charity called the Wolves Foundation which has independent funding of £2.5 million a year and more than fifty full-time members of staff. Will Clowes, who has been running it for the past twenty years, estimates the foundation is responsible for more than a third of the food bank stock across the city. The club's former head coach, Nuno Espírito Santo, gave it £500,000 out of his pocket to keep the most vulnerable in the city fed during the Covid pandemic. Projects range from improving physical health to getting dementia patients to meet the former players they once idolised. Clowes says: 'Football means something to everybody and in this small city we are a big brand that can have a positive effect.' He describes how the foundation sends staff into the city's bus station to prevent fights between schoolchildren or gather evidence on a recent stabbing, because young people will talk to someone from Wolves even if they don't trust the police. And the club knows full well where some of the divisions lie. Clowes says: 'We're abundantly clear of the Enoch Powell legacy in Wolverhampton and the challenge it represents.'

The foundation works with African-Caribbean groups and Sikh temples to raise participation in grassroots sport among people who can't afford a gym membership or have not had opportunities to play football before. It has formed an alliance with local GPs to send out information in six different languages about its Active Through Football programme, specifically aimed at those, including Muslim women, who might feel uncomfortable taking exercise in front of an audience. It has launched an annual 'One Pack Week' which celebrates all the different supporters who wear the Wolves shirt with pride. There are also many more women going to watch games. Emma Milton sits behind the goal in the Stan Cullis Stand and has been a season ticket holder for twenty years, ever since she started going with her husband. She reckons 'I'm more into it than him now'. She sometimes goes to women's games but prefers to watch the men. 'If someone uses bad language and then apologises to me, I ask them why they're not saying sorry to everyone else?'

Clowes says: 'I've been here a long time and the diversity of our fan base – in every way – is more visually apparent every year.' And that is more than matched by the players on the pitch. The team's recent captains have included Danny Batth, a centre-back who grew up in the city and whose father is Punjabi. The current squad has a number of Muslims for whom the club provides prayer rooms inside the training ground, help for those fasting during Ramadan and Halal food. But Clowes admits that the Muslim community 'has proved harder to reach' for football as a whole. The reasons cited range from cultural questions about clothing and the presence of alcohol, to more practical ones about the importance of Friday night prayers when there is a big game on Saturday.

Enoch Powell never had any time for football, preferring to dress up in pink for countryside pursuits like fox hunting. One of the reasons why football clubs like Wolves have been so effective at telling a different story of England from that presented by the city's former MP is that they are rooted in the urban life of the town and cities where most people live. For similar reasons, football with its long-running 'Kick It Out!' campaign against racism has been a significantly more effective platform for meaningful multiculturalism than any number of awareness training courses, diversity questionnaires or much of the publicly funded inclusive street art that gets routinely – and sometimes deservedly – parodied in the press.

All kinds of prejudice and inequality still scar England. Prisons contain a greater disproportion in the number of Black inmates than even those of the United States. People of colour are three times more likely than those who are white to be denied entrance to restaurants, pubs and clubs. Nor should anyone forget that football clubs are ultimately commercial businesses. There are plenty of Premier League clubs that were once at the heart of their communities who have sold the naming rights of gleaming new stadiums for the petrodollars of authoritarian Middle Eastern regimes, with Manchester City playing at 'the Etihad' and Arsenal at 'the Emirates', as well as Newcastle United, now owned by the sovereign wealth fund of Saudi Arabia.

But the national team, as one of the few clear expressions of England itself, can still feel like it has a higher purpose. At a time when big national events often fail to draw large audiences, more people in the UK watched England lose to Italy in the European Championship final in July 2021 than any other moment in television history except the funeral of Princess Diana. And the capacity of live football to bring the country together was demonstrated again in 2022. That was when Chloe Kelly's winning goal for England women's team in their European Championship final looked destined to be the most watched event of 2022 until it was trumped by another royal funeral, that of the queen, three months later. Gareth Southgate, the manager of the men's team, even wrote an essay that sought to bridge the patriotism of his grandfather with the growing 'discussions on race' that meant 'young kids of today ... grow up baffled by old attitudes'. He said that in modern England 'everyone has a different idea of what it actually means to be English', adding: 'I understand that on this island, we have a desire to protect our values and traditions – as we should – but that shouldn't come at the expense of introspection and progress.'[117]

It is just one example of a society where people not only celebrate their differences but are also able to bridge them and evoke the best of the parochialism of England that so appealed to Orwell and Priestley a century ago. And it is in normal settings – offices, factory floors, shops, cafés, schools, community centres, as well as football stadiums – that this society takes hold, as people meet, mix, get to know, even trust or like each other. Football's story is not one of multiculturalism of grandiose statements or empty idealisations. Rather, it's about ordinary life which gets energy and brilliance precisely because people are not required to pretend they are cut from the same cloth.

Pat McFadden, a senior Labour politician, has been one of Wolverhampton's MPs for two decades despite making no claim to being English. His parents spoke Gaeilge growing up in Donegal before immigrating to Glasgow. He sounds Scottish but his allegiances in sport shift depending on which is being played. 'Who you are can be your family, your city, your football team, your religion, your nationality and many other things. You can be Scottish and British, English and British, European and British or whatever,' he says.

In the summer of 2024, when far-right riots made a rumpus in town centres across the country, Wolverhampton was noticeably quiet. But the racism that Enoch Powell articulated so powerfully has not disappeared entirely. David Hall, a retired engineer from Wolverhampton, was prosecuted after sending a series of menacing messages to MPs including Eleanor Smith, a Black woman representing Powell's old seat who he told to catch 'the first banana boat to the jungle clearing you came from'. Hall also warned David Lammy, Labour's most senior Black politician that he would 'suffer the same fate' to another MP who was murdered by a white supremacist during the Brexit referendum, saying: 'As you attack the White population of Britain in your aims to gain Black Supremacy in this country, remember what happened to Jo Cox.'[118]

When Hall was eventually put on trial, Lammy decided to watch. 'I felt sorry for him. He cut a pathetic figure,' wrote the MP after hearing how the man who had made such lurid threats had lived on his own for 48 years and whose limited contact with the outside world had shrunk further since retirement. 'His vicious messages were an expression of the impotence he felt about a world changing at a rate he could not comprehend,' said Lammy.[119]

As someone born in London with Guyanese immigrant parents, Lammy locates his identity not in ethnicity but in what he calls a 'civic nationalism' that combines formal aspects of British citizenship and shared institutions like the Monarchy, the NHS and Remembrance Sunday, with English values and culture. For him, that includes everything from fish and chips, pints of beer in country pubs, Walker's crisps, Ribena and, of course, football. He is a season ticket holder at Tottenham Hotspur in his constituency and also sometimes goes to watch the lower league Peterborough United because he has affinity for that place too having been a chorister boy at the city's cathedral school.

When we interview him, however, Lammy says that he still feels held to a more exacting standard of Englishness than white colleagues. Recounting a moment in 2021 when he and Keir Starmer were filmed being jostled by 'anti-vax' conspiracy theorists outside the House of Commons, he says: 'Everyone praised us afterwards, saying, "Oh, God, weren't they dignified and respectful and restrained". It was all very English, wasn't it? But if I had thrown a punch – and, boy oh boy, I felt like it – that would have gone all wrong for me as the only Black man there, wouldn't it? John Prescott got away with hitting someone in the 2001 election but me – it would have been different.' He suggests creating an 'England where people engage with other people who look, sound, think and live differently from themselves' is still a work in progress, not least because many people of colour in England still prefer to identity as British. But he insists: 'My humour is English, my sensibility is English, my education has been over-whelmingly English, my friends and my wife are all English, my kids are English. So, even though I hold my links to the Caribbean dear, I'm not really West Indian, I'm an Englishman.'

McFadden is immensely proud of the city's Sikh community, he has regular meetings with the Sedgley Street Gurdwara in the Blakenhall district of the city, the top item on the agenda is a long-running complaint about the temple's car-parking problems. For years, it has been trying to buy a patch of land opposite to create more capacity, but the council says it will not concrete over what is a small patch of grass and children's play area for car parking. The committee's members remain frustrated that the council, controlled by the Labour Party which they have loyally supported over the years, will not give them the bit of land they want. McFadden tells them carefully, 'I'm not going to make the mistake of being disrespectful to you by promising something I can't deliver'.

This is a deeply parochial planning battle of the kind that exists in every community in the country. But it is also a mark of how far Wolverhampton has come if car-parking problems are the biggest issue for this Sikh Gurdwara. It is a dispute in which neither side has 'the whip hand', as Powell would have put it, because ultimately that would serve no one. What might seem to be bureaucratic inertia around a set of arcane laws is, in fact, an example of how different interests remain balanced in a healthy democratic city. One member of the temple's committee later talks of how India's politicians make the country 'too corrupt' to do business in these days. Another describes how the relative stability of Wolverhampton's political institutions has allowed him to build a good life. 'I came here with £4 in my pocket and I now have four cars, four houses, four shops,' he says. Would that have been possible if rules were bent for this or that interest? He smiles and shakes his head. Asked if he thinks of himself as English, he replies carefully: 'I am a British Sikh, but England is my home.'

Visit the Sedgley Street Gurdwara on a Sunday and you will see families crowd around the entrance, teenagers pour out of the back of cars and run excitedly inside. Trays of home-cooked sweets are being taken in for what will later be a wedding party. A notice in the window of the evening school where children are taught Punjabi reads: 'Congratulations, you have taken your first step to maintain our Sikhi Culture and Identity.'

Gurdwaras matter greatly to a city like Wolverhampton but so do parks, even little ones like this one, a reminder perhaps of that yearning for a fresh air and pastoral England that had such influence through the previous century. And balancing these needs is what a multicultural society is about.

A couple of streets away is a big Victorian church, St Luke's, that has long since been abandoned by its congregation and is now only used as an antiques centre. But this was the same building that was once so much at the heart of its community. It was where the football team that is now Wolverhampton Wanderers was founded in 1877 as St Luke's FC by some boys at the church's school.[120]

On the Sunday we visited, when tens of thousands of people were packed into the club's Molineux Stadium a mile or two away and nearby the Sikh temple was throbbing with life, the only person at the disused church was a man trying to fix a car that had been vandalised by what he claimed were 'our local drug gangs'.

Writers such as Krishnan Kumar have shown that searching for a 'moment of Englishness' is pointless in a country that has never been homogeneous in either its culture or ethnicity.[121] But walking through Wolverhampton on a sunny weekend can make you feel part of a modern English moment that is the very opposite of what Powell prophesied. This is a cacophony of history, people and culture not least in the city's 'Desi pubs' that combine English beer and football with Punjabi food. There are different tastes, smells, sights, sounds at every corner in a city of Balti pies and fish 'n' chips, Steve Bull, the St Luke's Boys' Team and the Sedgley Street Gurdwara.

This is England, in all its real, everyday brilliance. It is not a problem that has to be managed but a country that can transcend the most evil of myths. There is real hope here and, when the ball hits the back of the net, just a bit of glory, too.

5

Greenwich

Old England, New Britain

'A NEW DAWN HAS BROKEN, HAS IT NOT?'

The final big bend in the Thames before London turns into Essex, where the river begins to widen out and speed towards the open sea, is a spot you might expect to be teeming with England's past. On one bank were the busiest docks in the world, where thousands of workers unloaded cargoes of exotic spices and tea from India or sacks of slave-cut Caribbean sugar which so badly chafed the porters' backs that the streets next to warehouses were known as 'blood alley'. On the other side is the once marshy Greenwich peninsula where the corpses of gibbeted pirates captured by the Royal Navy were hung out as a warning to others, where oil extracted from the blubber of slaughtered whales was landed and black gunpowder was stored. Later it was where factories manufactured the giant underwater telegraph cables that spanned the Atlantic to connect the New World to the old, then where coal was transformed into foul-smelling gas to heat London's homes or light its streets.

Yet all that history was flattened a few years ago with just about everything, as far as the eye can see, covered in a mixture of concrete, glass and steel. Ahead are the silver arches of the automated Thames Flood Barrier while, where the Victorian Royal Docks once stood, there are smart modern apartment blocks followed by the ExCeL exhibition centre stretching its bulk out long and low. Behind, Canary

Wharf has been rebuilt as a huddle of high towers topped by the logos of global finance – HSBC, Citi, Barclays – with a flashing red light to warn passing aircraft not to get too close. The derelict flour mills where Derek Jarman filmed his melancholic lament to a lost urban landscape, *The Last of England*, have been redeveloped and, beneath them, workers are digging the Silvertown Tunnel so that cars can travel faster from one end of England's capital to the other.

But the most futuristic sight of all, resembling an upturned space telescope, is found on the northern tip of the peninsula. Now called the O2 Arena after a corporate sponsor, this building once attracted more fury than just about any in England before or since. It had another name in those days: the Millennium Dome.

Back in the late 1990s, much was made of how it was being built on a site reclaimed from the contaminated toxic sludge of the old gas works. The great white Dome cut across the Prime Meridian which, when Britain was powerful enough to do such things, had given the world the concept of 'Greenwich Mean Time' – the reference point for time zones across the planet. One of its architects, Mike Davies, who always dressed head to toe in red, explained how the building revolved around the concept: 'Twelve months of the year, so 12 masts, 365 metres in diameter, and with 24 scallops, like 24 hours in a day,' he said.[1]

The whole structure – skin, cables, masts – weighed less than the air inside and moved with the wind to symbolise how the heavy baggage of the past would no longer be a drag on progress. The Dome scarcely seemed to touch the ground and was, concluded an admiring writer at the time, 'a container for that most literally insubstantial of things – a moment when the days change'.[2]

Today, there is no obvious sign or monument to what it once was. And maybe that's how it should be in a place that was never meant to be about looking back or glorifying the past. It is why we chose North Greenwich as the site for our fifth myth.

In contrast to those considered in the previous chapters, this one is about England shedding history and bypassing time so that it could stride unburdened into a global future. It is the myth of a new country, one most obviously associated with Tony Blair and his New Labour government but which owed much to the decades before.

If the twentieth century had seen more lives mown down and minced up in the cause of various strains of nationalism than ever before in the violent history of the human species, there were good reasons to believe the next one would be better. The fading light of the old millennium had shown the Berlin Wall being pulled down and apartheid in South Africa collapsing into its own contradictions. To many, the glow of globalisation coming over the horizon promised a new era of peace through prosperity and connectivity across the world. In the United States, this myth expressed itself through the writing of thinkers like Francis Fukuyama who pronounced 'the end of history' with liberalism, both economic and political, the winner.³ But there were few places on earth where hope flared brighter than England. It was difficult to be youngish and leftish in this country at the turn of the new millennium without feeling at least a little bit of joy. Eighteen years of uninterrupted Conservative government had not merely ended in 1997, it had been swept aside as the new prime minister Tony Blair emerged blinking into the light of landslide Labour victory and the sun breaking over London with the words: 'A new dawn has broken, has it not?'

Great cities, the likes of Manchester, Birmingham, Newcastle and Bristol, as well as London, were throbbing with energy as the new millennium approached. It was when Noel Gallagher from Oasis turned up to a party to celebrate the success of Britpop in Downing Street and then snorted cocaine off a toilet seat normally reserved for the queen.⁴ It was when Kate Moss paraded around in a Union Jack designer jumper to launch London Fashion Week, then brushed her hair away from her eyes and laughed at the photographers whose stepladders trembled with excitement. It did not seem to matter that the old flag itself was being lowered in the empire's last meaningful possession of Hong Kong. New universities were opening, old ones expanding, as the internet flooded homes with the knowledge of the greatest library ever assembled. Office workers, freed from their desks by the invention of mobile phones, were spilling out onto the streets into gastro pubs, pavement cafés or trendy estate agents that opened late and served complimentary espressos in little porcelain cups.

After decades in which England had been known for its stodgy food, sugary tea, failures at sport, rotten teeth, repressed emotions, stilted conversation and incompetent sex, this was a country that seemed to be getting better by leaving the past behind and being less, not more, 'English'. Suddenly it was confident enough to learn from Indian chefs, Italian baristas, French football coaches, American dentists, Austrian psychotherapists, South American drugs and internet porn. Nigella Lawson was spooning marsala-flavoured morsels into the mouth of a nation for whom pasta had replaced fish fingers as its favourite meal.[5] Arsène Wenger arrived at Arsenal FC armed with continental nutritional science just in time to save some of his players from descending further into alcoholism. Wenger remembers the time with a professorial smile and kindly understatement, saying: 'From 1997 onwards, England became more open to the rest of the world.'[6]

Here was an old, brittle nation beginning to bend and sway again in tune with the times, as it wriggled free of its dry old skin. There were new rights for people who were gay, people who were disabled, people of colour – human rights for *all* people – being enshrined in statute. Female executives like Nicola Horlick – dubbed 'superwoman' by the press because, by some previously unimagined power, she had managed to be a mother and have a career, too – were shattering glass ceilings. Even the red leather benches of the House of Lords felt a little gust of change with most of its hereditary peers losing their centuries-old privileges. The stiff upper lip was replaced with wobbling bottom lips of a nation's 'un-English' grief over the death of Diana, the 'People's Princess'. Queen Elizabeth II herself was being forced to take crisis media-management advice from the staunchly republican Alastair Campbell. Scotland and Wales were given new powers to govern themselves. Northern Ireland, whose Troubles had seen the IRA trying to blow up Canary Wharf as recently as 1996, was at peace for the first time in decades. This was not only because two communities had overcome generations of sectarian hatred, but also because the UK and Ireland had – on the assumption of a shared European identity and single market – transcended their own borders in the Good Friday Agreement.

People not only cared more about climate change and famine, but for a while at least it seemed as if nations could come together to help fix global problems. Blair persuaded Bill Clinton to join an international military effort to halt a genocidal Serbian invasion of Kosovo. His chancellor, Gordon Brown, cancelled the debts of countries too poor to pay them. Britain sent troops to fight in Africa for the first time since the end of empire, not as some vengeful imperial power but to protect democracy in Sierra Leone, the former colony that had been created with the help of William Wilberforce for freed slaves.

The New Labour-friendly think tank, Demos (whose director of research at the time had changed his name from David Ashworth to 'Perri 6' for reasons too obscure to understand even then) was coming up with ideas to 'rebrand Britain'. It said the country should become a creative, global hub with embassies, airports and the design of postage stamps modernised to 'further the transition from a backward-looking imperial style'.[7] Another think-tank report suggested the term 'British' was 'hopelessly outmoded' and should be replaced by '*Pretanic*', a Greek name for the British Isles and which better reflected the 'mongrel pattern of [its] people'.[8] Historians were getting in on the act, too. Norman Davies published *The Isles* which argued that the old 'Anglocentric straitjacket is bursting at the seams', while Linda Colley opened a lecture in Downing Street by saying that many were already asking: 'What can a new millennium do for British national identity except confirm and complete its disintegration?'[9]

On the platform in Bournemouth where the Labour Party conference was held in the last months of 1999, Tony Blair set out his project to forge a more liberal, multicultural, European and modern country; to drain the nation of its old marshy myths and concrete over history. He talked of making this a 'young country' again as he promised to build a 'model 21st Century nation' set free from the 'old class divisions, old structures, old prejudices, old ways of working and of doing things'. He had a name for it, too: New Britain. There would be no more obsessing over Magna Carta, fantasising about swashbuckling privateers or looking inwards to a singular national sovereignty here. Blair said it was time to adapt to the 'global forces of change driving the future' that 'don't stop at national boundaries, don't respect tradition, they wait for no-one and no nation ... because what threatens the nation-state today is not change, but the refusal to change in a world opening up, becoming ever more interdependent'.

Blair's speech, though, showed signs of impatience at the slow pace of progress and the obstacles that still stood in its way. Cutting loose the myths of England's past was already proving difficult. The prime minister identified the enemies of modernisation as 'the forces of conservatism'. He even named a time and place for the coming conflict between these two forces, declaring 'the battlefield is the new Millennium'.

'EUROPE OR BUST!'

There is nothing new about the new. The history of England has been as much about upheaval as it has been one of continuity. The Norman Conquest, the Reformation and the English Civil War all ripped up England's past while, in much less brutal fashion, governments of left and right through the twentieth century had sought in various ways to change the country and renew. Although Blair claimed to be embarking on this great battle with the forces of conservatism, the myth of a New Britain had been forged a quarter of a century before in 1973 when Britain joined the European Economic Community.

Some of the fiercest resistance had come from the Labour Party where entry was opposed by most of its MPs, trade unions and voters. Many of them were instinctively hostile to the transnational capitalism they believed was behind what was pejoratively called 'the Common Market'. In the February 1974 General Election that followed little more than a year after the UK joined, Enoch Powell had urged people to vote Labour as the last best chance of stopping Britain becoming a 'province in a new European superstate'.[10] And, when the re-elected Harold Wilson called a referendum on his revised terms for membership in 1975, this single indivisible version of nationhood was invoked heavily by a 'No' campaign dominated by figures from the Labour left ranging from Michael Foot to Tony Benn. In Yorkshire, the union chief Arthur Scargill led miners, wearing helmets begrimed with coal dust, door to door in pit villages telling people to vote against the European 'capitalist ramp'.

The issue of sovereignty was emblazoned across the front of anti-Market leaflets under the headline 'The Right to Govern Ourselves'. Other leaflets referenced both Francis Drake and the Blitz, saying: 'The British people have fought to remain free and independent for centuries. They will never accept alien rule.'[11] It was a view summed up by Barbara Castle, a Labour cabinet minister who campaigned against membership, writing in her diaries that year about how relieved she felt that the government had at least decided not to proceed with the Channel Tunnel: 'It is a kind of earthy feeling that an island is an island and should not be violated. Certainly, I am convinced that the building of a tunnel would do something profound to the national attitude – and not certainly for the better.'[12]

Indeed, for many of these years, children were brought up in a state of high anxiety about terrifying dogs that had caught rabies on the Continent. A Central Office of Information TV advert intoned: 'Only the English Channel stands between Britain and rabies.'[13] Another had pictures of cat shows being cancelled and a terrified woman hiding in a red telephone box from a foaming-mouthed Labrador. 'Just one animal smuggled in could lead to all this,' it warned.[14] Ferry ports were covered in posters showing a human skull with the words, 'Rabies kills people'. The message was that enduring English values of diligence, watchfulness and wariness of foreigners would keep these shores safe.

Yet, for all the froth generated about sovereignty in the 1975 referendum, the public did not bite. Polls consistently reported sovereignty was 'low-salience' for voters, with fewer than one in seven of even those most opposed to European membership mentioning the subject.[15]

The 'Yes' campaign at this time was backed by every national newspaper except the *Morning Star*, and had cash rolling in from business. The historian Robert Saunders has detailed the way entering Europe was linked to the modernity of sexual freedom. The *Daily Mirror* hired a twenty-two-year-old model called Beverley Pilkington who posed for pictures in her underwear and a tight white T-shirt emblazoned with the slogan: 'Europe or Bust!' Others appeared reclining on racing cars along with placards saying, 'I will always say YES! to Europe'.[16]

And if the referendum ultimately revolved around everyday issues like food prices and jobs, there were many who felt entering the EEC was a chance to escape the gloom of a country that had made Jim Callaghan tell the cabinet in 1974 how, 'every morning when he shaved he thought he should emigrate but by the time he had breakfast, he realised there was nowhere else to go'.[17] When the results were in, the 'Yes' campaign won by a margin of 67 to 33 per cent. Remarkably, the proportion in favour of being part of the EEC did not drop below 60 per cent anywhere in England.[18]

The leaders of the major parties had all fallen into line behind the European membership, but it was the position of one of them that remains intriguing in this story.

Although she would later become the standard-bearer for a revival of Euroscepticism, Margaret Thatcher was evangelising for precisely the opposite back then. She had wrested the Conservative leadership from Edward Heath less than four months before the 1975 referendum and her identity, other than being the first female leader of a major political party, was not yet fully formed. Any doubts about the depth of her pro-membership convictions, however, were dispelled when she appeared at a rally in Hendon and tackled directly the question of sovereignty. She attacked those who said by leaving the EEC Britain would get back 'independence by return of post', saying they were ignoring 'the fact that almost every major nation has been obliged by the pressures of the postwar world, to pool significant areas of sovereignty so as to create more effective political units'.[19]

This was exactly the kind of sharing that had so incensed Enoch Powell. But what was so interesting about her speech is that she framed it as part of a much bigger argument about restoring national greatness, playing into many of the myths of England's past that infuriated other modernisers.

She relished telling other countries what it meant to be free and longed for the days when the Royal Navy's power meant that 'our business spanned the world'. She felt keenly the loss of an empire and the way Britain's economy had been eclipsed by countries like Germany or Japan, who had lost the war. In a BBC documentary before her General Election victory in 1979, she said: 'I can't *bear* Britain in decline. I just *can't*. We, who either defeated or rescued half Europe, who kept half Europe free when otherwise it would be in chains. And look at us now.'[20]

Thatcher tapped into a patriotic impulse that was finding expression in the most unlikely places. In 1980, British Leyland – a nationalised carmaker that had become a by-word for national failure – launched the Austin Metro with a TV advert. To the tune of 'Rule, Britannia!' it showed a saluting war veteran with medals on his chest and all-white crowds waving British flags as the plucky little hatchback repelled a landing-craft invasion of foreign cars – 'Italians, Germans, Japanese and French' – from the White Cliffs of Dover. It ended with the words: 'A British Car To Beat The World'.[21]

Two years later, Thatcher channelled her inner-Metro and sent a Royal Navy task force off to recapture the Falkland Islands. After victory was won, Thatcher lost no time in rebuking the 'waverers and the faint-hearts' who dared say 'Britain was no longer the nation that had built an Empire and ruled a quarter of the world'.[22]

But she also recognised that restoring prestige and prosperity in the modern world required trading some sovereignty for a slice of the influence Britain had once enjoyed as a global imperial power. Just as the empire had made the country part of something bigger than itself, she argued, so did membership of an increasingly prosperous capitalist European community which would act as a bulwark against trade union militants, Labour left-wingers seeking to establish 'socialism in one country' and the Communist bloc.

Thatcher's Cold War alliance with the US president Ronald Reagan was as much about global capitalism as it was about democracy, and Britain remained very much the junior partner in the 'special relationship'. She understood the limits of British influence in an era when the English Channel, so symbolic of 'standing alone' in the Second World War, had long since been rendered irrelevant by the prospect of a global nuclear war. Symbolically, it was under her leadership that a deal was done with France to dig a tunnel beneath it that finally breached Shakespeare's 'moat defensive'. And, within two years of the Falklands War, Thatcher signed a deal to hand the colony of Hong Kong to a Chinese government that was far more autocratic than any Argentinian junta. She later justified her decision by making a 'prophecy for the future', that China's lurch towards capitalism would soon extend to political liberalism, too, because 'many, many more nations … are coming up to full democracy and the rule of law'.[23]

Still more significantly, this was the prime minister who, even in the midst of rows over the EEC budget, had pushed hardest for the creation of the European Single Market – with its 'four freedoms' of goods, capital, services and people – to wipe away subsidies and unfair competition. She sacrificed the national veto at European Council meetings in order to speed through the reforms, taking the UK deeper into the process of European integration for the sake of free-market capitalism.

Margaret Thatcher became the standard-bearer for a modern global version of capitalism that replaced an old system of English virtues with a new one. Power, money and success were the values she promoted as she embarked on a mission to root out outdated working practices and invigorate moribund management. She would euthanise 'lame duck' subsidised industries and tidy away 'yesterday's jobs' into a bin.[24] England would never be the same after her decade in power. She crushed the trade unions that had improved workers' living standards ever since the General Strike. She blasted holes in the proud municipalism of local government to which her beloved father (as an independent councillor) had once belonged. She attacked revered national institutions – from the BBC and the higher ranks of the Civil Service to the Church of England – for being complacent and stuck in the past. The Archbishop of Canterbury briefed against her and Oxford University refused her an honorary degree, but their powerlessness was confirmed by Thatcher's second, then a third, consecutive General Election victory.[25]

Perhaps most crucially for the future, she deregulated the City of London for the advantage of international finance with the Big Bang of 1983. Paunchy Englishmen wearing bowler hats were replaced with the shoulder-padded and – self-styled – 'masters of the universe'. On the surface, at least, this was an enormous success. It generated vast wealth as stocks exchanged hands at rapid speed. The economist Duncan Weldon recalls that 'trading volumes soared from around 50 per cent of all listed stocks in 1985 to 90 per cent by 1990, with the value of companies listed on the exchange rising by around 25 per cent over the same period'.[26] Thatcher also privatised industries that had first been brought into public control in the 1930s, transforming both their value and their ethos as she did so. In the case of British Telecom, the change was clear for all to see as it promptly abandoned the 'British' brand to go global and become 'BT'. This greed-is-good culture was summed up by the comedian Harry Enfield's Cockney 'Loadsamoney' and the Chelsea football fans who waved £20 notes when they went to away games in the North.

Thatcher's real genius, however, had been to cover all of this modernising in the most reassuringly English of wrappers. It was akin to a lavender-scented grandmother offering you a slice of sponge cake laced with amphetamine.

VICTORIANS ON SPEED

Under the headline 'The Good Old Days', Thatcher described the lessons of a childhood growing up in the Lincolnshire town of

Grantham with a list including 'cleanliness is next to godliness' and 'tremendous pride' in the country. 'We were taught to work jolly hard. We were taught to prove yourself; we were taught self-reliance; we were taught to live within our income,' she said. 'All of these things are Victorian values. They are also perennial values.'[27]

The economic creed of Thatcherism was portrayed as a restoration of the laissez-faire she claimed had made Britain such a powerhouse before the twentieth century's experiment with big government. One of the most interesting historians to write about this time was Raphael Samuel. Although a member of the Communist Party, he never agreed with those Marxists who insist that everything is always determined by economics. Instead, he was fascinated by cultural ideas of England. Assessing who really stood for 'Victorian values' during Thatcher's time in office, he concluded: 'In terms of family solidarity, the dignity of work, the security of home, or simply the right of the free-born Englishman to stay put, it would not be the Prime Minister but the miners defeated in the strike of 1984–85 – her "enemy within" – who would have the stronger claim.'[28]

That strike, measured by working days lost as well as the fury it attracted, was the biggest industrial action in British history.[29] There was fierce fighting between pickets and police, breakaway unions among miners and deep wounds cut into many working-class communities especially across the North and Midlands from which some have never recovered.

Through most of this period, however, Thatcher was supported by sections of the working class. This was not just because of popular policies like the sale of council homes but also because she seemed to stand for these ethics of the small town, her grocer father and the Methodist town chapel she attended as a child – rather than the aristocratic hunting lodges, banking houses or high churches of other Tories. In a speech to the City of London, for instance, Thatcher made no apology for preaching 'the homilies of housekeeping or the parables of the parlour', saying they 'would save many a financier from failure and many a country from crisis'.[30]

Matthew Parris, a newspaper columnist for *The Times*, was once a Conservative MP and before that worked in Downing Street as Thatcher's correspondence secretary. He has described how his job for her was to summarise the thousands of letters she received, saying the prime minister was sustained by the 'fine lacework of British opinion, prejudice and sentiment, as flimsy and as persistent as gossamer' found in those letters.[31]

Talking to us for this book, Parris says: 'She was really looking for evidence that people agreed with her. She would read everything I gave her with a pen in her hand so that she could underline things she liked, as if to say, "there we are, he thinks so too."' But he also explains the nuance in this caricature of Thatcher. 'She was a very modern woman of the 1950s,' he says. 'This was someone who went to Oxford University to study science, a subject not many women did then. She married a divorced man – probably for money rather than love – had children, as well as a career. I don't think she really believed in God and, as an MP in 1967, she voted for the legalisation of homosexuality which, though she still regarded it as a misfortune, thought was not a matter for the police.' He recalls how, on the bus into work from Clapham one day, he had built up the courage to tell her, 'I am homosexual, a lot of our colleagues and a lot of natural Conservative voters are too, but our party shows us all a very unsympathetic face.' He describes the way she then placed her hand on his wrist and replied, 'Matthew, that must have been very difficult for you to say.' And he remembers, too, how the Conservative Chief Whip, who had been watching the exchange, later asked him for details of all those homosexual colleagues he had mentioned.

Thatcher could evoke some of the more insular anxiety towards the intrusion of modernity felt by people like Mary Whitehouse. This sometimes expressed itself as outright discrimination such as with the infamous Section 28 of the 1988 Local Government Act that prohibited local authorities from 'intentionally promoting homosexuality' or, in other words, making it illegal for a teacher to tell children it was okay to be gay. According to Parris, however, this was 'about politics, not culture – she saw it as a useful way to attack what we called "looney left" councils'. And he says Thatcher always kept Whitehouse 'at arm's length because she didn't want to be seen as someone like that'.

Even more significantly, as someone who came from a provincial grammar school-educated background, the then prime minister was never a good fit for the Establishment. She was sensitive to the condescension or satire of those who were trendier, more liberal or simply posher. Caroline Stephens, Thatcher's diary secretary, used to warn new colleagues their boss worried incessantly about matters like how she should curtsey when she met royalty. 'The first thing you have got to bear in mind is that Mrs Thatcher is a very ordinary woman,' she would tell them.[32] Such subtle distinctions of class were probably why, at least initially, Thatcher is said to have had a difficult relationship with the queen. For instance, when the countryside-loving monarch was asked if her prime minister would be joining the royal family on some waxed-jacket-and-wellies yomp up a Balmoral hill, she replied tartly: 'I think you will find that Mrs Thatcher only walks on the road.'[33]

Thatcher planted one impractically clad foot firmly in a mythical past and the other in an equally mythical future. This may explain her bizarrely close relationship with Jimmy Savile, the television entertainer who was later revealed to have been one of Britain's worst sexual abusers of children. Given that the former prime minister did not really have many friends or much sense of humour, it was odd that Savile could pop into Downing Street for tea and was a regular guest at festivities in the prime minister's country retreat. Even more remarkable was the way she fought, on no less than four occasions, to secure him a knighthood against the objections of civil servants who feared he would 'not be able to refrain from exploiting it'.[34] When he eventually received the honour in 1990, 'Sir Jimmy Savile' did an interview with the journalist Lynn Barber who, to her credit, asked him directly if it was true 'you like little girls'. His response said much about a modern celebrity's identity. 'I've got to be the most boring geezer in the world because *I ain't got no past,*' he told Barber. 'And so, if nothing else, it was a ginormous relief when I got the knighthood, because it got me off the hook.'[35]

It would be wrong, of course, to suggest Thatcher knew about – let alone deliberately enabled – Savile's predatory paedophilia, but there were some similarities between the two. Like Thatcher, Savile dressed up what he was really doing in the reassuring iconography of England's myths of the past. He copied the way Winston Churchill smoked his cigars, flaunted his Rolls-Royce and decorated his jewel-encrusted track-suited form in the Union Jack.[36] This hybrid identity, summed up unintentionally in his catchphrase of 'now-then-now-then-now-then', ruthlessly exploited a permissive sexual culture and was a pioneer for ostentatious displays of wealth, cynical manipulation of the media and status of 'being famous for being famous' that has since taken so many far further than their talent deserved. And, again like Thatcher in the 1980s, Savile instinctively understood how to manipulate petty snobberies. For instance, a subsequent report into his activities at Leeds General Infirmary shows how hospital consultants basked in his presence and only complained once, when he parked his Rolls-Royce in the car park reserved for them. Hospital porters were often bought off with free TVs or holidays at caravan parks. Nurses who had sometimes caught him sexually abusing patients were scared to speak out because, in that era when so many people lost their jobs or were bullied by management, they feared he had the power to get them sacked.[37]

The friction generated by this myth of a modern nation grinding against old national stories generated an immense and sometimes transformative energy throughout Thatcher's eleven years in power. Sparks flew around England's national sport of football where 'the imagined community of millions' had already seemed 'more real as a team of 11 named individuals'.[38] For a time it seemed that football hooligans might define England itself in the eyes of the world. Certainly, the idea that this country symbolised a sense of 'fair play' had long since gone in the foreign cities its football fans smashed up in the 1980s. English clubs were eventually banned from Europe after rioting Liverpool supporters caused a wall to collapse and the death of thirty-nine Italians at the European Cup Final in 1985.

Thatcher never really got the point of sport in general but her attitude to football in particular is said to have been one that regarded it as a 'law and order issue' with its fans part of an old-fashioned and violent working class. She pursued a policy largely conceived by David Evans, a self-made millionaire Tory MP, and chairman of Luton Town FC, who had introduced a membership card scheme and a ban on away fans at his club. The government wanted to roll it out across football and be overseen by a new body with the power to control fans' travel as the police had done with striking miners' flying pickets.[39] The nadir in this destructive relationship was at the Hillsborough stadium in 1989 when senior police officers – with the connivance of a right-wing Conservative MP, the *Sun* newspaper and Thatcher's press secretary – tried to cover up their mistakes by falsely blaming the deaths of Liverpool fans on other Liverpool fans.[40]

But, as so often in the Thatcher era, disaster and destruction coincided with change. A subsequent report into what happened at Hillsborough by Lord Justice Taylor recommended crumbling stands be rebuilt as all-seater stadiums and reforms of the police, as well as opening up the possibility that football fans might be treated as people or even paying customers.[41] Within a couple of years, England's refreshingly modern performance and Paul Gascoigne's tears in a World Cup semi-final defeat against Germany had earned the sport some form of redemption in the eyes of the media. Thatcher's favourite media mogul, Rupert Murdoch, began to pour hundreds of millions of pounds into the sport in return for the exclusive rights to broadcast live games from the new Premier League. Although traditionalists hated such commercialisation of English working-class culture, not least because Thatcher had been the catalyst for change, the sport changed over the next decade into one that was not only safer and more economically sustainable but also suddenly attractive to the middle classes and new markets across the world.[42]

The capacity for transformation was apparent, too, in the city from where those fans who had been killed at Hillsborough had come. Throughout the 1980s, Liverpool was portrayed as in Alan Bleasdale's lament to post-industrial decline, *The Boys from the Blackstuff*. What remained of its industry was at war with the trade unions and its council was controlled by a far-left Militant Tendency that blamed capitalism for all Merseyside's problems. Some members of Thatcher's cabinet advocated 'managed decline' and partial evacuation of a city that had turned so far inwards it was eating itself.[43] But the Toxteth riots in Liverpool terrified a nation unused to civil disorder and eventually Thatcher allowed one of her ministers, Michael Heseltine, to spend time there seeking a more future-oriented solution.

Heseltine was the tall, blond, privatising darling of the party's annual conference and a hammer of the miners. But he was also a moderniser to his core. In Liverpool, he produced a list of thirty ideas, including the regeneration of Albert Dock where the water-front collection of museums, conference centres, upmarket shops and restaurants has since become one of the most visited tourist locations anywhere in the UK.[44]

Back in the east of London, the most visible and lasting symbol of this decade of upheaval was slowly taking shape on another disused port. Once again, the London Docklands Development Corporation was largely the brainchild of Heseltine and was inspired by the myth of the future. Special planning powers were used to bull-doze the homes of the East End families who once worked there while a brochure for potential investors had a full-page photo-graph of a vast empty landscape of mud below a headline that said simply: 'Progress'.[45]

This gigantic development was often in trouble as property markets rose or fell, but Downing Street always came to its rescue. When Thatcher herself turned up to inaugurate the building of Canary Wharf on post-industrial wasteland, she promised 'this is going to be the biggest commercial development in the world' which would enable Britain 'to lead Europe at the beginning of the next century'.[46]

For all Thatcher's globalist instincts, however, she would also be the prime minister who lit the long fuse of Tory Euroscepticism. An address – now known as the 'Bruges Speech' – that she delivered to the College of Europe in 1988, included the famous line, 'we have not successfully rolled back the frontiers of the state in Britain, only to see them re-imposed at a European level with a European super-state exercising a new dominance from Brussels'.[47] But even in that speech she continued to insist: 'Britain does not dream of some cosy, isolated existence on the fringes of the European Community. Our destiny is in Europe, as part of the Community.'[48]

Europe was regarded as the future and her party was still so pro-European that it was her resistance to further integration, as much as her insistence on imposing the poll tax, that saw her ousted from power in 1990. And her replacement was partly a reaction against that roller-coaster convention-shattering decade of the 1980s.

The new prime minister, John Major, used his own St George's Day speech in 1993 to reassure people that the future would not be so different from the past. 'Fifty years from now,' he said, 'Britain will still be the country of long shadows on county grounds, warm beer, invincible green suburbs, dog lovers and pools fillers and – as George Orwell said – "old maids bicycling to Holy Communion through the morning mist".'[49] But he delivered this speech in the face of a rising tide of Conservative Euroscepticism that, in spite of his best efforts, would drift his party away from a European future and back into England's past.

At the same time, the Labour Party was heading in the opposite direction. Under the leadership of Neil Kinnock, it had been warming to Europe for precisely the same reason that many Conservatives were becoming hostile: the prospect of uniting with a social democratic Continent to temper the impact of free-market economics. This was when the centre-left began to outline the shape of a country with blurred national identities, more personal autonomy from the top-down structures of the state, as well as a greener and more feminist politics.[50] Much emphasis was placed on constitutional reform with the Charter 88 movement – less a distant echo of Magna Carta than a globalised version based on the demands of east European dissidents – demanding electoral reform, a Bill of Rights, an elected House of Lords and devolution of power across the United Kingdom.[51]

A self-consciously modern, progressive version of a country was beginning to crack through what seemed like the eggshell-thin crust of conservatism. The bland suburban pop of Duran Duran was being overtaken by sounds that were simultaneously more metropolitan and cosmopolitan. House music – influenced by African Americans in Chicago, Techno pioneers in Berlin and gay clubs in London – was joined by Indie bands from Manchester like the Happy Mondays, the Stone Roses and later Oasis, as a series of illegal raves and Class A drug-taking swept the country.

Some have tried to trace the decline of football hooliganism and racism in the early 1990s to the number of MDMA pills that 'loved-up' young people were swallowing on Friday nights before turning up for matches on Saturday with surreal plastic inflatables like bananas and haddocks.[52] Whether or not much of that is true, it was certainly the case that football was fashionable again. At the 1996 European Championships, fans replaced the Union Jacks that usually accompanied them with the Cross of St George (largely because England were in the same qualifying group as Scotland). Those red-and-white flags did not seem excessively nationalistic or nostalgic in that year. They flew from the windows of houses both posh and poor, black cabs driven by English white men and minicabs driven by English Asians, working-class pubs and student halls of residence. They were wrapped up in the gentle humour of two comedians, David Baddiel and Frank Skinner, who had an unlikely hit single 'Three Lions (Football's Coming Home)' with another Manchester Indie band, the Lightning

Seeds. It was a song rooted less in a sense of superiority for inventing the game – the 'football's coming home' bit – than in the humility that comes from being let down ever since the World Cup win of 1966. The lyrics were not about England being better than other nations, but about fresh hope springing eternal in defiance of history.

> Everyone seems to know the score
> They've seen it all before
> They just know
> They're so sure
> That England's gonna throw it away
> Gonna blow it away.

The English football team eventually lost to Germany (again) on penalties (again) at the semi-final stage (again) as the noise of 'Three Lions' being belted out across Wembley that summer night finally faded. But English football had been redeemed to such an extent that Germany's fans began singing the song, too.

It was around this time that Michael Heseltine, who had emerged as deputy prime minister from the ashes of Margaret Thatcher's immolation, was handed a billion pounds of lottery cash to plan a celebration for the year 2000. His mind was still focused on transforming the old Docklands amid the humming glass towers of Canary Wharf. And he chose another bit of decaying post-industrial London, a site he described as '300 acres of dereliction' on the opposite bank of the Thames, for a national exhibition. And it was Heseltine again who went to see Tony Blair before the 1997 General Election, begging him not to pull the plug on his Millennium project.

A BEACON TO THE WORLD, WITH PLASTIC PUBIC LICE

Once inside Downing Street, Tony Blair hesitated several times before giving the Dome his final approval and even then just about everybody in his cabinet thought he was making a mistake. 'If we hadn't inherited it, we would probably never have embarked upon it,' he said, before eventually reasoning, 'I thought the pain of cancelling too great.'[53]

But one of those who was in the room when the decision was made to go ahead recalls how larger issues were at stake. 'It was about not being so English any more,' he said. 'It felt that, if we were to become more European, we should do these modernist *grands projets* like the Louvre Pyramid in Paris.'[54] And there did seem something symbolic in Labour's choice not to pay for a replacement of the Royal Yacht *Britannia*, in which the queen had sailed to old imperial outposts, while instead funding a gleaming white modernist bubble, one which Blair promised would be 'truly a beacon to the world'.[55]

The ambition was to turn the country's gaze away from the insular myths of the past so that it faced outwards to the world and ahead to the future. But costs spiralled upwards to £850 million of public money amid endless disputes between artistic and commercial priorities. For instance, designers for the Mind Zone wanted to use the artist Helen Chadwick's *Piss Flowers* – bronze moulds taken from the cavities created when she peed in the snow – while corporate sponsors like the military manufacturing giant GEC Marconi did not understand how such sculpture would help them sell their weapons around the world.[56] Peter Mandelson, who was briefly the minister in charge, painted an enticing picture of futuristic attractions for visitors including the chance to play something he described as 'vast, huge in scale … an interactive attraction which comes under the working title of "Play at Surfball: The New 21st Century Sport" '.[57] Loyal or ambitious New Labour MPs got very excited, with one of them speculating it might involve 'virtual headgear' and 'gloves that are connected up or a bodysuit so when you move you feel as if you're part of the balls running in the headset'.[58] Only later did it emerge that Surfball had never got beyond a presentation by a consultancy team pitching for work. A faint echo of such unfulfilled fantasies could be found in the Dome's most popular attraction, the 'Body Zone', that had to be entered through vast androgenous legs and painted hair that, for reasons never properly explained, had been infested with foot-long plastic pubic lice.

A thousand years before, Christians had feared that the new millennium might mean the end of the world. But as the clock ticked down towards what was supposed to be the opening night for not only the Dome and the twenty-first century but also for New Britain, the biggest worry in this increasingly technology-driven country was that a programming error, known as the millennium bug, or 'Y2K', might cause computers to crash. On the big day itself – 31 December 1999 – the IT was fine but officials panicked, first over a credible bomb threat which to their relief did not result in an explosion, then over expensive fireworks that, to their dismay, also failed to go off with a bang. Thousands of VIP guests, including irate and self-important newspaper editors, were kept waiting for hours after an underground train broke down. Blair then spent much of his evening convinced that a trapeze artist was going to fall from the roof of the Dome and 'flatten the Queen' before he joined hands with the monarch to sing 'Auld Lang Syne' in a display that merely underlined the stomach-cramping awkwardness of the entire occasion.[59]

The next day's coverage from the newspapers set the tone for the rest of the year by being unforgivingly hostile. Although the Dome was never as bad as the press made out and eventually attracted more than six million visitors, there was still a sense that it symbolised how modernity was a great big white space and not much else. As Blair himself later admitted, in words that perhaps carried more meaning for his political project than he intended, 'the futuristic theme we wanted was fine at the broad-brush level, but elusive in detail'.[60]

Unlike Thatcher and Major, he was a prime minister who appeared not to have a nostalgic bone in his body as he began the process of 'sweeping away all the detritus of the past'.[61] Much of Blair's appeal was based on the understanding that he had accepted the modern free-market precepts of Thatcher but would combine that 'economic competence with social justice'. The latter would be underpinned by the European Union, so that the fruits of success were more fairly distributed across the country with 'schools n' hospitals' getting the sustained investment they had needed for long. Supposedly gone, too, were the old ideological divisions and class politics because his project was not just a challenge to the 'forces of conservatism' on the right but those in the Labour Party, too. Blair had no time for the nostalgia, defensiveness and insularity that had caused much of the party to campaign against Europe in 1975, entrench structures that ignored women and new voices in politics, or dole out favours to sectional interests like the trade unions.

The Millennium Dome itself, where the government adopted an even-handed approach to both public and private sectors, was an early test of this new national story. Blair later claimed that 'if I had my time again I would have listened to those who said governments shouldn't try to run tourist attractions'. But, in a sign of how politics had become as amorphous as the giant sculpture in the Dome, Michael Heseltine thinks the problem was precisely the opposite. This privatising Conservative told us it would have been better if 'the state had been allowed to organise its own event' because most of the problems came from having to work with a 'private sector who wanted to celebrate their own achievements rather than those of the country'.[62]

Blair's embrace of progressive global modernity was symbolised by his enthusiasm for what he called 'this explosion of activity and freedom' on the internet and a communications revolution that many hoped would replace a corrupt old right-wing press with a more democratic and accountable new media. Alastair Campbell remembers winning a bet that, if he wrote the words 'information super-highway' into one of Blair's Labour conference speeches, it would earn applause – even though he wasn't even sure what they meant. As in the United States, this new technology was allowed to develop unchecked by any form of government regulation because of a belief in the cleansing power of free markets. What they got in the years since was a social media that is even less attached to facts and more exploitable by political extremes of both right and left.[63]

Indeed, it is one of the reasons why Blair had surely been right when he had warned back in 1999 that his effort to create a New Britain was far from secure and predicted an epic battle with the 'forces of conservatism' in the new century. He knew 'Old England' was preparing for a comeback.

The Eurosceptics who prioritised a singular version of sovereignty above every other consideration ranged from the likes of Bill Cash, an MP who could sometimes bore his opponents into submission but whose defence of Parliament and the Common Law was at least intellectually coherent, to polemicists such as Boris Johnson. The future prime minister was then making his name inventing stories for the *Daily Telegraph* about the threat posed by Europe to English traditions like prawn cocktail crisps and pink sausages. He even claimed Brussels wanted to force Englishmen – perhaps not including himself given his record of extra-marital paternity – to wear undersized Italian condoms.[64] The fightback by Old England was all the more assertive for having been placed on the back foot. Andrew Roberts, the conservative historian, published a novel, *The Aachen Memorandum*, in which an 'English Resistance Movement' fights a European superstate that was trying to proscribe fish and chips, stop women shaving their armpits and had arrested a character he called 'Michael Gove'.[65]

For many, the Dome took on an obsessive significance even greater than its own circumference. Roger Scruton, the right-wing philosopher, said it represented the essence of everything that had gone wrong with the country, a 'Babylonian temple to Nothingness' which 'many Englishmen view with revulsion'. He wrote: 'The exhibits match the architecture: the past of the country, its institutions, monarchy, and religion, its imperial triumphs, its achievements in war, and its leading role in the spread of law and democracy – these are either reduced to insignificance or ignored.'[66]

The following year, in 2000, Scruton published *England: An Elegy*, which he described as a 'funeral oration' for a dead or dying 'enchanted realm' filled with green fields, societies of amateurs, lovers of nonsense and collectors of everything from stamps to vintage cars.[67] Scruton's enchantment included England's class system, the monarchy, the hereditary principle, high church Anglicanism, the small family farm and the mysteries of common law, all of which, he argued, were being *forbidden* by a combination of political correctness, faceless multi-national corporations and, of course, Europe.

Those swaggering around the late-night clubs of London's Soho in those days, a group including the self-consciously brightest young things from both Labour and the Conservative Party, generally regarded the views of such 'Domophobes' as some weird form of English ancestor-worship. And, for a long time, there were lots of reasons to suppose that their new myth of the modern would prevail. Sociologists said that demographics were pointing to a progressive political future; there was a shift in the population away from towns and villages to multicultural cities; more young people were going to university; immigration was making the country increasingly diverse. When Conservatives protested, it did not do them much good. Conservative leader William Hague chose to make his first speech in the 2001 General Election outside the Millennium Dome which he condemned as a monument to Labour's attempt to 're-invent 1,000 years of British history in their own image'. He made a net gain of just one seat and Blair swept to a second landslide.[68]

Nor was Labour's majority damaged by events earlier that year when a large chunk of the traditional English countryside, that pastoral story examined in the previous chapter of this book, went up in smoke. The government's response to an outbreak of foot-and-mouth disease saw farmers forced to slaughter more than six million cattle, pigs and sheep. The animal carcasses were then burned on vast pyres, the smell of which hung for days in the air across traumatised rural England.

But it began to mobilise conservatives against the new myth of an England stripped clean of its past. They became an active force rather than a wistful form of 'pick and mix' nostalgia. Hundreds of thousands marched under the banner of the Countryside Alliance in what was then the largest rally Britain had ever seen. It was not only a protest at a Labour government, it was also a defiant rallying call to defend an older idea of England they felt was disappearing.[69]

All of this meant that New Britain and the project to create a 'young country' was far more fragile than it seemed. In that 2001 General Election, turnout fell from 72 to 59 per cent with more people failing to vote than doing so for Labour. It was not just rural England that felt disconnected from the modernity of New Britain. Many industrial areas of Britain had never recovered from the Thatcher era and manufacturing industry was still disappearing at a faster rate than ever. As the next chapter will show, many in these parts of the country felt their cries of pain were being ignored in New Britain, too.

Of course the Thatcher and Blair eras were not wholly or even mostly the same, whatever their latter-day critics say. The economy grew just as fast and more consistently, but the Labour government invested enormous sums of money in hospitals and schools, raised the status of public services, as well as introducing a minimum wage and the tax credits that helped families living in poverty. And yet this myth of the future meant that they never fully understood the need to replace the sense of belonging, meaning and identity that had been ebbing away since the Thatcher decade. People from industrial communities who had once been proud of holding skilled jobs in manufacturing industries as part of that national story increasingly felt dependent on – and distant from – all the success of a weightless 'knowledge economy' that seemed more international than anything to do with them.

In London, huge wealth was being created but many of the richest people were from overseas, including the best footballers in the new Premier League. Even some of the clubs themselves were floated on the stock exchange and bought by overseas investors. Before Arsenal were taken over by the US billionaire Stan Kroenke, the old chairman Peter Hill-Wood, who had been educated at Eton and served in the Coldstream Guards, issued this last cry of defiance: 'Call me old-fashioned, but we don't need Kroenke's money and we don't want his sort. Our objective is to keep Arsenal English.'[70] There were lots of new jobs being created in the 1990s and 2000s, but they were often in factories assembling foreign-made components into foreign cars, in warehouses distributing foreign-made mobile phones and TVs, in airports to take people to foreign countries, or in shops selling foreign-made clothes and foreign food. And some were beginning to complain that foreigners were taking lots of the new jobs, too.

These concerns drew, both consciously and subconsciously, on the contradictory myths of the past already examined in this book. But it was too easy to dismiss them as representing merely a xenophobic backward-looking version of England. Modernisers needed to recognise that they were themselves bound to their own myth, one about the future. And they also failed to see that some of the measures they took to build a New Britain only served to make it more likely that Old England would prevail.

Devolution for Scotland and Wales stirred a sense that the English were missing out. Patrick Tripp, of royal flag-maker Turtle & Pearce, told the *Observer* in 1998: 'Since Mr Blair has decided to let Scotland go its own way, we in England have said "sod you, we'll go our own way too, we'll look after ourselves". I think England is discovering a sense of itself.' He left it to others in that same article to point out that most flags – whether English or British – were by then being made in Taiwan.[71]

Even more important was the decision Blair's government took in 2004 on immigration. In an effort to strengthen Britain's position among the former Communist countries then joining Europe and sustain the voracious demand of a deregulated labour market for low-paid workers, the UK was one of only three in the EU to waive its right to apply temporary restrictions on immigration from the new member states. The result was hundreds of thousands of new arrivals crossing Britain's borders – far more than had been expected – as the UK population was boosted by more than 2.2 million immigrants between 1997 and 2010.[72] Such numbers represent twice the population of Birmingham and almost ten times that of a city like Wolverhampton where Enoch Powell had once festered people's fear.

At the same time as this pull of the past was getting stronger in parts of Old England, the combination of two events in America did much to fray support for New Labour. The first was the narrow defeat of Al Gore in the US presidential election in November 2000. The second was the terrorist attacks on New York and the Pentagon on 11 September 2001. There is little doubt that almost any US president would have attacked al-Qaeda bases in Afghanistan. It is doubtful that a President Gore would have sought to widen the 'war on terror' to Iraq as Bush did – and unlikely that Tony Blair would have been knocking on his door demanding he do so. When he was asked about it a few years later, Blair for once stumbled over his words. 'I don't, I can't … I can't be sure,' he said, before eventually concluding, 'so I don't know how it would turn out with a different American president'.

The decision to back the US-led invasion of Iraq that followed in 2003, despite more than a million people marching through the centre of London in protest, meant that many among the self-styled progressive segment of the country began to turn their backs on Blair. The prime minister's view was that liberalism had to fight for its place in an interdependent world. Some of this undoubtedly sprang from his genuinely Christian beliefs and reanimated the myth discussed in Chapter 3, that civilising mission harnessed to raw military power that characterised Britain's approach to the world during the second half of the nineteenth century. But it was also based on Blair's hardening conviction that global challenges, from Sub-Saharan poverty and climate change to Islamist terrorism, transcended national borders. 'We are all internationalists now, whether we like it or not,' he said. 'We cannot turn our backs on conflicts and the violation of human rights within other countries if we want still to be secure.'[73]

Blair himself now accepts that it was 'finely balanced' whether the criteria he set out then for a 'just war' had been met ahead of the Iraq invasion.[74] The geo-strategic expert who drafted his speech, Professor Lawrence Freedman, would later be one of those who sat in judgement on Blair during the Chilcot Inquiry into the Iraq War. His own view was that Blair probably saw preserving an alliance with the US as the interest that trumped 'all other considerations'.[75]

This revealed a deeper level of unease which went to the heart of ideas of nationhood, namely that Britain was not in charge of its own destiny. Blair had promised Bush and the neo-conservatives that surrounded him that 'we will be with you whatever'.[76]

The discomfort many felt at the sight of Blair standing shoulder-to-shoulder with Bush was strong enough to pierce even the once impregnably feel-good metropolitan bubble of Richard Curtis's romantic comedies. His earlier films like *Four Weddings and a Funeral* and *Notting Hill*, as well as his charitable efforts for Comic Relief, had helped define a well-meaning modernity that generally dovetailed with the image of New Britain and Blair in particular. But in the 2003 movie *Love Actually*, the actor Hugh Grant was cast as a foppish prime minister who casts off his shackles at a Downing Street press conference and stands up to a smug US president who has just praised the 'special relationship' with the UK, saying:

> We may be a small country, but we're a great one, too. The country of Shakespeare, Churchill, the Beatles, Sean Connery, Harry Potter. David Beckham's right foot – David Beckham's left foot, come to that. And a friend who bullies us is no longer a friend.

Blair later told his party conference, 'I know there's a bit of us that would like me to do a Hugh Grant in *Love Actually* and tell America where to get off,' he said, 'but the difference between a good film and real life is that in real life there's the next day, the next year, the next lifetime to contemplate the ruinous consequences of easy applause.'[77]

This, then, was the hard-boiled reality of his modern foreign policy. Britain neither ruled the waves nor could claim a redeeming moral purpose as it had when banning the slave trade. Instead, this country was a post-imperial European nation seeking to preserve as much influence as it could through its alliance with the genuine superpower of the United States. Blair hoped that Britain could be a 'pivotal power' between America and Europe 'at the crux of the alliances and international politics that shape our world'.[78] But Iraq forced him to make a choice and, perhaps too eagerly, he chose America over much of the EU – including France and Germany – which was opposed to the invasion. Instead of being pivotal in a new era of internationalism, Britain was in a narrower and shakier alliance of the Anglosphere, following the US into its 'coalition of the willing'. And many people did not feel, as a sovereign nation should, that they were in control.

What this meant in practice is best told by one of those who had to implement it. Hugh Powell was a Foreign Office diplomat whose father, Charles, served as Margaret Thatcher's foreign policy adviser and whose uncle, Jonathan, was Blair's chief of staff. Later he would become a senior national security adviser to David Cameron. But in 2005 he was posted to the front line in Helmand province in southern Afghanistan as the senior British representative, a position of power over some two million people and a territory three times the size of Wales that some critics said made him 'viceroy of Helmandshire'. Powell is quick to reject any suggestion that his time in Afghanistan was any kind of imperial throwback, let alone a 'civilising mission' like those of the late nineteenth century. For a start, Britain was the junior partner even in areas like Helmand which were supposedly under its control. 'Once you sign up to be deputy sheriff,' he says, 'you have to go along with what America wants to do.'

He describes how talk of winning hearts and minds or how Britain was better at the 'soft beret stuff' was soon dismissed by military and civilians who spent any time in Helmand. Elections were humoured by the locals so long as a Pashtun ended up as president. 'When we insisted women should have the vote, they sort of rolled their eyes and said it simply meant more ballot boxes had to be stuffed.'

'The thing that haunts me most is the fate of young boys, aged about 10 or 11, who turned up at our gates having run away from sexual slavery,' say Powell. 'These boys were basically catamites and their "uncle" would arrive 24 hours later looking for them. I was always clear that, however awful this sounds, we had to hand them back. In this medieval society we could not interfere with that sort of tribal law stuff without losing local support in the fight against the Taleban. So, don't accuse me of having a "civilising mission".'

None of that made it easy for politicians trying to persuade British voters of the case for a continued participation in America's War on

Terror. Powell says: 'Communications experts would arrive from London and tell us the best way to sell the mission to the public back home was to emphasise how we were building new schools and hospitals. I would say, "fine, but don't kid yourself that's why we're here".

'It's probably inevitable that politics and the media try to boil it all down to something that makes sense to them with ideas that we're special or have something to teach the world. But we talked about it in a different way: the world is fucking chaotic and we are one of very few countries ready to roll up our sleeves and actually do something to make it less dangerous.'

Such a chilly version of reality, where British officials hand young boys back into medieval sex slavery, was a long way off from the warm glow of fulfilled idealism that once seemed to be the future.

BRITISH WORKERS AND ENGLISH LAWS

The slow realisation that it was impossible to build a new nation in a far-off land like Afghanistan was being matched by one that doing so at home might also be more difficult than many had expected.

Tony Blair still went on to win a third election in 2005 but within a couple of years he was handing over to Gordon Brown, who found himself being drawn back towards many of the myths of the past that his predecessor thought he had put to rest.

A New Labour agenda that had been decades in the making had lost much of its potency by this stage and, when he took over in 2007, the new prime minister decided his first priority was to distance himself from Blair as he presented himself as more sceptical of Europe and invoked older patriotic ideas of a global military power to shore up support for overseas operations in Afghanistan.

In his first speech as leader to the Labour Party conference, Gordon Brown mentioned 'Britain' or 'Britishness' no fewer than seventy-one times. In response to growing public hostility towards immigration, he promised 'British jobs for British workers'.[79] He tried to rename Remembrance Sunday as 'Britain Day', then he poured Magna Carta into a bucket labelled 'British values' along with tolerance, local pride, civic duty, George Orwell, the defeat of Fascism, citizenship ceremonies and the NHS. 'For years we didn't think we needed to debate or even think in depth about what it was to be a British citizen,' he said, 'but I think more and more people are recognising not just how important their national identity is to them but how important it is to our country.'[80] Brown's effort to shore up notions of an historic British identity was itself a tacit admission of the United Kingdom's fragility. Here was a Scottish prime minister, who relied on Scottish Labour MPs for his parliamentary majority, trying to dampen the appeal of Scottish independence with often factually threadbare bits of an overwhelmingly English history. It was also a sure sign that the project to run a country while bypassing its past was running on fumes.

This was when Jez Butterworth's 2009 play *Jerusalem* captured the essence of a bewildered England. It portrays a Wiltshire village with Morris dancers, bacon butties and real ale on St George's Day, as a drug-addled benefit-claimant Johnny 'Rooster' Byron hides out amid the oak trees of the greenwood forest. 'Rooster' promises to bestow 'free booze, bangers, draw, whizz and whatnot, for all the minions of my kingdom' and then puts milk in his mug before pouring his tea. At the end of the play, as a Spitfire flies overhead, he places a curse on the bureaucratic busybodies from the council evicting him from his caravan because of complaints from the nearby new-build estate. He summons the spirits of an enchanted land:

At my back is every Byron boy that e'er was born an Englishman. And behind them bay the drunken devil's army and we are numberless. Rise up! Rise up, Cormoran. Woden. Jack-of-Green. Jack-in-Irons. Thunderdell. Buri, Blunderbore, Gog and Magog, Galligantus, Vili and Ye, Yggdrasil, Brutus of Albion. Come, you drunken spirits. Come, you battalions. You fields of ghosts who walk these green plains still. Come, you giants![81]

In reality, however, it was the excesses of the behemoths of modern finance that did for New Britain rather than the heroism of imaginary giants from the past. The culprits that caused the financial crash in 2008 – Lehman Brothers, Merrill Lynch and insurers AIG – all had offices at that monument to Thatcherism at Canary Wharf in east London's old docklands. Barclays' investment bankers were jailed for helping to rig the 'Libor' short-term interest rates through insider dealing.[82] The big accountancy firm on the Wharf, KPMG, was fined $456 million for tax fraud.[83] HSBC, which has its global headquarters there, was caught laundering hundreds of millions of pounds for drug cartels.[84] So it was ironic that Brown tried to fix the crisis in 2009 at an emergency meeting of the G20 at the ExCeL exhibition centre on the site of the old Royal Docks and opposite the Millennium Dome. There, he persuaded world leaders to act together by injecting more than a trillion dollars to stabilise an international financial system that was rocking on its heels. Though the summit was a diplomatic triumph and helped save modern capitalism, it also reinforced the suspicion that ordinary families would eventually foot the bill for bailing out the banks.

Exhausted by war, crisis and scandal, Labour eventually slumped out of office in 2010 after a General Election when Brown was recorded off-camera describing Gillian Duffy, an elderly white woman from Rochdale who had upbraided him about immigration, as 'just a sort of bigoted woman who said she used to be Labour'.

The new Conservative-Liberal Democrat coalition was led by David Cameron, who regarded himself as a moderniser in the mould of Tony Blair. And there were still glimpses of the kind of country New Britain might have been. To his credit, Cameron overcame resistance to legalise gay marriage and increase overseas aid. In 2012, the year *Time Out* magazine named London 'the greatest city on earth', the Olympics were held on a patch of once blighted but now reclaimed land in east London.

For a few weeks, these Games cheered the nation up in a way that the Millennium Dome had not. The opening ceremony, scripted by Frank Cottrell-Boyce and directed by Danny Boyle, managed briefly to forge together the new myth of the future with the old myths of the past. It included elements of the stories we have explored in this book: the pastoral ideal of Arthurian Glastonbury Tor; games of cricket; the industrial revolution; suffragists demanding the vote; soldiers dying in world wars; Caribbean immigrants disembarking from the *Empire Windrush*; the BBC weather forecast; children bouncing on NHS hospital beds; and Tim Berners-Lee inventing the World Wide Web. It featured national cultural icons – everyone from Paul McCartney, the Sex Pistols and David Beckham to Mary Poppins hitting Lord Voldemort with her umbrella. Most spectacularly of all, it had James Bond parachuting with a body-double of the queen into the Olympic stadium. A Tory MP who tweeted that it was all 'leftie multicultural crap' was soon shot down by everyone else who, briefly, felt unusually good about their country. Boris Johnson, the then London mayor, said he found it all so moving that he was left 'crying like a baby'.[85]

But these were also the years when the government was implementing a programme of deep spending cuts to tackle a deficit that Cameron presented as an existential threat to the nation. The extra money that had been pumped into public services, local government and tax credits for the low-paid over the previous thirteen years was clawed back while right-wing newspapers whipped up hatred towards 'scroungers' and 'benefit cheats'.

Cameron was shrinking away from New Britain in other ways, too. Even before he entered Downing Street, Cameron had introduced a new logo for the Conservatives of a very English oak tree, severed his links with mainstream centre-right parties in Europe and promised to limit net immigration to 100,000 people a year when he had no idea how to do it.[86] As prime minister, he told interviewers that his favourite childhood book had been *Our Island Story* as he approved cuts in funding for diplomats and the BBC World Service or picked fights at European summits to please his backbenchers and the anti-EU press.[87] And, most significantly of all, Cameron was allowing the Eurosceptics in his party and UKIP – what might be called Old England's political wing – to drag him ever further from a modernising global liberal ideology. In 2013, it was pressure from this right-wing faction, not the public as a whole, that forced Cameron to promise an in/out referendum on membership of the European Union.[88]

Before the Brexit vote could happen, Cameron also agreed to let Scotland have a referendum on whether to stay in its three-centuries-old Union with England. After a bitter fight in which opponents of Scottish independence eventually ground out a victory, the prime minister might have been expected to deliver a message designed to heal divisions. Instead, Cameron stepped out into Downing Street on the morning of 19 September 2014 to announce he was stripping Scotland's MPs of their right to vote on legislation that only affected England. This never meant much in practice and has since been quietly repealed. At the time, however, Cameron's 'English votes for English laws' was widely regarded as a masterly way to counter the rise of UKIP, whose leader Nigel Farage had complained because 'they're getting our money' and 'they're being horrible about us'. And when he said 'us', everyone knew he meant England, while Scotland had become 'them'.[89]

Later in that same year, at the Rochester & Strood by-election, the Islington Labour MP Emily Thornberry came across a house bedecked in English flags with a white van parked outside while campaigning; she decided it was a sight unusual enough to post a picture of it on Twitter. Farage said this was proof that the 'sneering' Labour Party 'hates the concept of Englishness'.[90] Thornberry was forced to resign from the shadow cabinet by Ed Miliband, whose spokesperson issued a series of slightly implausible quotes about how much pride and respect the then Labour leader felt for English flags and white vans.

Cameron, by contrast, did everything he could to show he was standing up for England. In the 2015 General Election, his party ruthlessly and relentlessly highlighted the prospect of a minority Labour government propped up by the Scottish National Party. It was an issue mentioned in no less than 60 per cent of Conservative press releases before polling day when the party won its first majority for twenty-three years.[91]

But this was a prime minister who never believed in much. Here was a politician who presented himself as a moderniser but always found pressing political reasons to take his country back to the past. He put £50 million of public money into a commemoration of the 100th anniversary of the First World War in 2014, followed by still more in 2015 to celebrate the 70 years that had passed since the end of the Second World War, the 200 years since the Battle of Waterloo and the 800 years of English liberty since Magna Carta was sealed. These events saw Cameron, who had once told his party to 'stop banging on about Europe', contorting himself into ever-stranger shapes as he bent over backwards to present an English and conservative version of history.[92] For instance, a private memorandum circulating in Whitehall at the time emphasised that commemoration events should not give 'credence to the myth that European integration is the outcome of the two world wars'.[93] Little wonder that when he held his referendum on Europe in 2016 and tried – belatedly – to make the case that the EU had preserved peace, very few believed him.[94]

The expensively botched party to celebrate the dawn of a century at the Millennium Dome was followed by sixteen years in which the project to create a New Britain was largely confounded. Pretensions that this country could be an enforcer of liberal values around the world were exposed by unpopular wars in Iraq and Afghanistan. Confidence in unending growth and prosperity was shattered by a world financial crisis. Belief that interdependence was indelibly dyed into the nation's future dissolved in that referendum that voted to leave the European Union.

Back on the northern tip of the Greenwich peninsula, the modernity left behind by those modernising leaders – Thatcher and Heseltine, Blair and Cameron – feels a bit hollow, even desolate.

The area has been developed by the Hong Kong property firm Knight Dragon in an £8.4 billion project to complete a regeneration begun thirty years before. Publicity brochures herald what it calls 'new London: a new destination for modern urban living' together with promises of '34,000 new settlers, creating a diverse community' and photographs of people eating sushi while wearing sunglasses or practising their swings on the 'state-of-the-art' golf driving range.

Testament to lasting change can be found at the aluminium tile-clad Ravensbourne University offering art and design courses, part of an enormously optimistic expansion of higher education during the first decade of this century. And there is a buzz around the place when big global acts like Rihanna perform or tennis tournaments are held at the O2. But take away that and this south-eastern corner of England's capital could be a district of any modern city, anywhere in the world. Just about the only clues that you are in London are the street signs, cars driving on the left and the fact that the metro station is called the Underground.

The music venue itself is dominated by a circular shopping mall with netting draped from the ceilings to stop those clean lines that once earned architectural awards distracting consumers from buying more stuff. The cable car connecting the peninsula to the other side of the river, built when New Britain flickered again during the London Olympics, now has scarcely any passengers.[95] A raised walkway called 'The Tide', an imitation of New York's High Line with works by artists like Damien Hirst, seems similarly forlorn with its Harlequin-painted air vents and spindly trees. There are restaurants serving every kind of food imaginable from all around the world – Argentinian steak, Thai noodles, Japanese sushi, Indian street food, Italian pizza, Mexican burritos, Brazilian churrascaria – but only a tiny Tesco and slightly larger Co-op for those tens of thousands of 'new settlers'.

Greenwich council seems more interested in promoting its status as a royal borough than answering any of our questions about 'New London'. A mile or two away are heritage sites like the Royal Observatory designed by Christopher Wren, the Old Royal Naval College, as well as the Royal Chapel where kings and queens once worshipped.

Across the strange futuristic expanse of the North Greenwich peninsula, however, there are no churches, mosques, synagogues or temples. Not one. There is only a 'Multifaith Prayer Space' on the second floor of a building that houses multiple gyms. There is a community room which is often booked for yoga, but the prayer space is used most for Muslim prayers on Fridays and usually closed on Sundays.

Plans for three sweeping towers designed by the Spanish architect Santiago Calatrava that were supposed to be the crowning glory of the scheme have been scrapped because they were 'too difficult to build'.[96] At the same time, Knight Dragon has negotiated down commitments on the proportion of affordable homes, even though it says the overall number will be higher because it is building more apartment blocks on the peninsula.[97]

There are some cheaper apartments at the Lighterman Building on Pilot Walk, but their residents complain about having to enter through a so-called 'poor door'. The owners of more expensive flats, by contrast, go in through a marble lobby with a concierge, soft furnishings and access to a rooftop garden. Knight Dragon points out, with impeccable free-market logic, that if people want lower-cost homes they shouldn't expect to have everything available to those who pay more.[98]

On top of another building is a brand new basketball court decorated in bright primary colours. A public relations woman called Eleanor is organising a photo shoot when we visit. She seems perfectly nice but is suspicious of anyone holding a notebook. 'Are you a journalist?' she asks. Well, no. Not really, not any more. 'I think it's best you contact Victoria in the press and marketing department,' she says.

At this point some teenagers in hoodies turn up and ask politely if they can play football there. Maybe they live in some of the new blocks of flats nearby with great views of the river. 'You're not allowed to be here,' the PR woman tells them firmly, before her voice softens a little and says: 'We're looking into doing something further down the road.' They nod, unsure of what that means, and walk away. Later, we are told some children had been spotted trying to set the basketball court on fire but that a keylock booking system is being set up and improvements made. The new millennium may not have delivered yet. But it still might, 'down the road', at some point in the future.

'PARKLIFE'

Stare closely at the Teflon-coated fibreglass covering of the O2 Arena and you realise it is not so much a dazzling white than a very pale shade of grey. That's because, after a quarter of a century of exposure to the wind and the rain, it has become weathered; there even appears to be some lichen growing there.

Only older people now still call it the Millennium Dome but there is something to admire in how a building that was meant to be a temporary structure has survived everything flung at it over the years. The O2 is not only a commercial success and an established part of London's cultural scene, but also instantly recognisable, especially for anyone who watches the BBC soap opera *EastEnders* where it is the focal point of the opening credits.

And, like this building's ageing space-age exterior, little green shoots of community have begun to appear amid the glass and concrete in ways that are surprisingly – and even a bit sentimentally – still recognisably part of England.

A good place to start is at one of the very few bits of the peninsula that survived the new millennium's bulldozers. The Pilot Inn dates back to 1801 and, when we visited it, was serving Sunday roasts to groups of friends and families. This pub flaunts the old maritime connections of the area with a ship's wheel on display amid drawings of sailing vessels on the walls and, for reasons that are not immediately obvious, framed covers of Billy Bunter books from the 1960s. Right next to the Pilot is a small row of similarly old terraced houses that, according to the fading paint of the street sign on the corner, was once called Ceylon Close.

These buildings provided the backdrop for the 1994 music video *Parklife*, the hit by Britpop band Blur that seemed to define the classlessness of those modern times with its mockney chorus line of 'Aaa-all the peo-ple/So maaan-y peee-paal!' The video also featured an ice-cream van, a red pillar box and a double-decker bus. It showed Damon Albarn and Phil Daniels sharing sandwiches out of Tupperware and drinking tea from a Thermos as they cruised around in a Ford Granada Coupé, singing their hymn to the mundane. 'I feed the pigeons, I sometimes feed the sparras too.'

And, even though just about everything else in North Greenwich has changed in the thirty years since, there is some 'parklife' here with a patch of grass decorated with lines of trees that have grown big enough not to be blown away by the next gust of wind. On this Sunday afternoon the park is sparsely populated but there is a boy kicking a ball about. His dad watches on and swiftly dismisses the idea there is no sense of community on this peninsula, describing how he is friendly with his neighbours and chats to them online. Pointing at the pub across the road, he smiles and adds: 'Sometimes, we'll meet up to have a few beers in the Pilot.'

The Rev. Jane Petrie is the local Church of England vicar, even though she doesn't have a church. Instead, she tends to spiritual needs partly by 'wandering around on foot'. Sometimes, the vicar also pops in to the Pilot to see her parishioners and maybe she even 'feeds the sparras too'. She says: 'In some ways I have more space to do my work without worrying about a church roof restoration fund. Like any community, this one is about people rather than a particular building and this is a good place to meet them.' Her small Anglican congregation has collected for vulnerable people living in Woolwich, as well as for a group of Afghan refugees. She holds Easter Sunday services out on the Thames foreshore at a spot covered with a mixture of sand, bricks and mud that is sometimes called a beach. And she conducts regular services in the new St Mary Magdalene Church of England School built for local children on the edge of the park.

The school's motto 'family, faith and fellowship' might have surprised some of the ceaselessly modern and outward-looking minds behind the Millennium Dome. So, too, might the enthusiasm with which Elizabeth II's Platinum Jubilee was celebrated by pupils being educated there in 2022. Some of the children came to school dressed as kings and queens, others enjoyed a 'Royal Tea Party' with iced biscuits and Union Jacks, while other pupils learned about different countries in the Commonwealth.

Many of those children live in Greenwich Millennium Village, a development on the eastern side of the peninsula, built at the same time as the Dome. It now has what it calls a 'village square' with a smattering of essential shops including a chemist, dry cleaners and hairdressers, as well as a health spa and the estate agent marketing suites that proliferate across the peninsula. But it has matured enough to have football coaching for children and a chess club that plays every Saturday afternoon at the Jetty close to the Pilot Inn. The people living here have even formed their own residents' association which organises an annual 'summer fayre' with live music and stalls, a community garden and litter picking. Long-running everyday problems discussed in its meetings or on its Facebook forum include noisy neighbours, bus services and the time it takes to fix the hot water. When baby birds in the nearby ecology park were attacked, the community organised a rota to keep an eye on them.

Sitting on a bench by the park are a group of bored-looking teenagers blasting music out of a portable speaker. Like others, they are quite defensive about place they live, even though most of them have to travel to school about twenty minutes away because there aren't enough places locally. 'We like it here,' says a girl who says her name is Marmalade, 'it's got everything we need.'

Perhaps the most traditional sight of all is the 6th Greenwich Park Brownies who meet regularly at Mary Magdalene school. They do all the things that Brownies have always done, like go on camps, earn badges and make the Brownie Promise: 'I will do my best: To be true to myself and develop my beliefs; To serve the King and my community; To help other people; and to keep the Brownie Guide Law.'

A pint and Sunday roast in a pub, a kickabout with your son in the park, an Anglican vicar, children celebrating a Royal Jubilee, a summer fête, some concerned residents complaining about the plumbing, a girl called Marmalade and a pack of Brownies – what could be more conventionally 'English' than that?

But take another look and you can see that the once-longed-for global modernity is never far away. The Pilot Inn is owned by Fullers, a chain of almost 400 pubs, restaurants and hotels across southern England which itself has been bought out by Asahi, a gigantic Japanese drinks corporation with revenues worth billions of pounds annually. The man kicking a football around the park with his son turns out to be Jorge Ortega, who is from Bilbao and works for a bank in the City of London. He explains the reason he chose to live in one of the modern apartment blocks nearby is that neither he, nor his Thai wife, want to be 'overwhelmed' by England. 'You can find that England – if you want to – in Old Greenwich where there's lots of historical buildings. This does not feel too English to me. Here, we've got every kind of nationality in the world. No one is imposing anything on us.'

The park itself, as well as the new Church of England school, was built with money from the Hong Kong Chinese developer Knight Dragon as part of efforts to provide some community infrastructure to go alongside all its faceless apartment blocks. The chair of the residents' association is Sten André Rigedahl, a Swedish national who arrived in London via Germany and Paris in 2004.

At the multi-faith prayer space – crammed between gyms, a nursery and an Asian noodle bar – that exists instead of a church in the peninsula's Aperture Building, the Anglican Jane Petrie attends meetings with Sheikh Ali Barakat, Balbir Singh Bakshi and Rabbi Ephraim Carlebach to foster understanding with local Muslims, Sikhs and Jewish people. Sitting next to Marmalade on the park bench is a boy named Diaz. His parents come from Argentina and he is keen to talk about how gangs are becoming active in the area. 'You can tell who they are because they have gold chains and Nike tracksuits,' he says. 'They used to drive their motorbikes right across here,' he adds, pointing at a now broken wooden bridge in the ecology park. The 'state-of-the-art' golf driving range is, at least when we visited, dominated by diverse young people on dates, falling over and laughing when they fail to hit the ball. It's all so much more human than the pictures in the brochure suggest.

This is, of course, a particularly cosmopolitan corner of a particularly cosmopolitan London. But it serves to illustrate how modernity and tradition have to rub along with each other in the real England of today, in a way that has not always been obvious in the strident talk of 'forces of conservatism', 'global futures' and 'threats to our way of life' or 'erasing history'. It has the same flavour of London that was captured in Michaela Coel's celebrated BBC drama series, *I May Destroy You*. She explored immediately recognisable and intense everyday relationships which are grounded in family and community, hope and desire. Her work is in many ways a counterpoint to a secular popular culture today that presents an image of perfect lives or flawless bodies – think of all those Instagram influencers with their filtered photos – and ignores the beauty found in difference just as much as the hardest-faced religious zealot ever did. Like other artists, Coel has shown how messy new realities can continue to grow and adapt at a time when young people are confronted with the kind of challenges – over their identity and climate or the economic prospects and dealing with new technology – which earlier generations could never have imagined.

Back in Greenwich, the local vicar Petrie acknowledges that 'this is a place that will take time to become what it's going to be', before adding: 'There are lots of people who want to make a connection. There are families putting down roots who intend to stay for a while. It's easy to see the tower blocks and miss all the ways in which community exists.'

The peninsula's Brownie Pack is a good example of what she means. At the start of the millennium, few would have expected Brownies, Cubs, Guides and Scouts to survive long as organisations. It was fashionable to sneer at their toggles, scarves and vows that originated with Robert Baden-Powell, the cricket-playing imperial hero from the Boer War's Siege of Mafeking. But they remain the biggest and most successful youth organisation in the country, one which has bent itself to fit the times. The Brownie Promise no longer includes a vow 'to serve my country' and 'love my God' because, as Julie Arkwright, the leader of 6th Greenwich Park Brownies, acknowledges, 'some of the girls have different gods – or maybe no god – and come from different countries'. The Brownie motto used to be 'lend a hand' but that was dropped for the more empowering message for young girls. They can now earn badges with names like 'My Rights', 'Make Change' and 'Speaking Out'. Arkwright says: 'Everybody knows the Brownies. It's a safe thing, isn't it? Parents remember it from their childhoods. Sometimes a girl brings in something her grandma had made when she was a Brownie. But girls don't join because it's traditional. They join because it's fun and interesting. If we don't adapt to modern life, we don't exist.'

In similar fashion, the popularity of writers like Robert Macfarlane with books like *The Old Ways* or *The Lost Words* suggests a desire to rediscover an Englishness that does not have to be the kind of exclusionary pastoralism examined in the previous chapter.[99] It has even begun to seep through into politics. A lot of what happened on St George's Day in 2024 was fairly predictable: the former Tory MP Nadine Dorries wrote in the *Daily Mail* that anyone who is loyal and patriotic gets 'mocked, belittled or openly scorned'; the *Sun* interviewed some cab drivers about the "bonkers ban" on flying the flag; while there were a handful of arrests outside a Whitehall pub following a nationalist rally attended by the GB News personality Laurence Fox. More interesting was a video from Keir Starmer where he talked about service and respect before listing the moments in his life when he had felt most patriotic: becoming the first person in his family to go to university; climbing Scafell Pike with his severely disabled mother; 'belting out the *Three Lions*' at Wembley during Euro '96; fighting the death penalty in countries that 'look up to this country's rule of law'; meeting voters "who all seem to share the same stoic wit and decency". A couple of months later, a Labour leader who is more comfortable than any of his predecessors with this subject became only the fourth leader from his party to win a general election with a campaign that began with a speech in Lancing, Sussex. He spoke about how his character had been shaped by growing up in Oxted, 'a small town not a million miles away from here' with its mix of 'Victorian redbricks … pebble-dashed semis [and] rolling pastures'. Surrounded by the kind of flag bunting more usually found at village fêtes, he once again described his everyday patriotism and added: 'Look – this England has always felt fairly removed from Westminster. Politics has always been something that happens far away.'[100]

For all that, the North Greenwich peninsula, which will perhaps for-ever by associated with Tony Blair, the previous Labour leader to win a general election, remains a place of huge flux and change without much scrutiny of how distant power over people's lives is wielded. Even the council seems far away in 'Old Greenwich' and the most widely available newspaper appears to be something called *The Peninsulist*, a cor-porate production from the developer Knight Dragon that consists of public relations puffery for exhibitions and restaurants or features reflecting on 'the joy of living' in 'New London'. Anyone wanting to catch up on off-brand news, like a lethal battle between 'machete and hammer-wielding' men on Barge Walk in the summer of 2021, must rely on the *News Shopper* series which does its best with a reporter covering multiple London boroughs from a base far away in the suburbs.[101]

Darryl Chamberlain, a former BBC journalist who lives nearby in Charlton and whose grandfather used to work at the gasworks on the Greenwich peninsula, has tried to fill this democratic void with a public-service news website called 853. It began after he attended a council meeting and was shocked by the treatment of a member of the public who was trying to raise an issue. For a time, he was the only journalist covering such politics but now his work is sometimes supplemented by material from a service paid for by the BBC. 'Our part of London has been going through this huge change all the time a complete vacuum in local news has been growing. That has made it so much harder for people to understand what's going on with the result they often feel disconnected from the area and from each other,' he says. 'It's a place dominated by this huge and unaccountable foreign developer. I just try to even up the score a little by writing about what's happening, what's planned, how people can take part in it. I go to council meetings, read documents, and talk to people – the stuff local newspapers used to do.'

When we go to see the man in charge of this one-company town, however, he is not a white-cat-stroking villain in some fortified penthouse atop the highest tower. Instead, Richard Margree is sitting in a café, eating a bowl of mulligatawny soup and ready to embark on a conversation that veers across art and philosophy as well as his favourite rock band, Rush. 'First you need endurance/First you've got to last,' he says, quoting from their song 'Marathon'.

Far from being able to do whatever he wants, he says, the development has endured delays from the drop-off in trade since Brexit, the Covid lockdowns and never-ending negotiations over myriad council planning rules. Barely an eighth of it has been built so far and he is desperate to see more people, more creative start-ups and independent shops bring the plan to life.

The chief executive of Knight Dragon describes how a project of such scale is both daunting and exciting. 'No one gets the chance to build an entire new district of London any more. But we don't want this to be the bastard son of Canary Wharf,' he says pointing at the opposite bank of the Thames, 'but something with its own sense of place – our big sky, our big Dome – of which all the different people who live here will feel proud.'

Rather than trying to 'make everything perfect', he wants a community to grow organically. Margree recalls seeing staff putting up a plastic fence in a public garden the developer had created. 'They told me people were taking shortcuts and making a mess by not sticking to the path. I told them to take the fence down. People will find their own way.'

Will what eventually emerges be recognisably England? 'Like the Dome in 1999, we don't know how all this will be seen in ten, twenty or thirty years' time,' he replies, carefully. 'I don't believe England is a single thing, but I think what we're doing here has the capacity to be another part of it.'

This development on the North Greenwich peninsula is certainly grandiose enough to be part of the New Britain myth but, if Margree is to be believed, it wants to leave a bit of space for Old England, too. There are plans to build more schools, as well as a theatre, a swimming pool and a new bus station. Knight Dragon has a community fund that subsidises sewing and gardening clubs. You can go for nice walks along the foreshore of the Thames with lots of places to sit and reflect on the passing river craft or the proliferating art sculptures.

The developer has also sought to pump some life into the area by opening a 'Design District' that offers independent businesses and creative organisations affordable space for rent. Many of the early tenants appear to be offering the kind of modernity that would make a certain type of traditionalist choke on their full English breakfasts. There is Queercircle, an LGBTQ+ charity 'working at the intersection of arts, culture and social action' with financial support from the Greater London Authority.[102] Wizard Works makes the 'cutest bags for urban and adventure cyclists ... with an aesthetic that lies somewhere between timeless classic and 80's rave'. Its co-owner, Veronica Lowe, is there when we visit and instantly disarms any sneering at the door. Not only does she seem committed to making her business succeed but she also has nothing but praise for her landlords. 'It's such a contrast to the last place we were in,' she says. 'It's like they understand us. They want to create this creative community and are constantly looking for feedback or ways to promote us.'

You bet they do. Ultimately the return on Knight Dragon's investment of £8.4 billion and 17,000 new homes will be a lot less if people don't want to live or work on the peninsula. Compared to the sterile commercial environment at the O2 Arena or the vacuous modernity that preceded it at the Millennium Dome, there is some real life and energy among those we met at the Design District. But both this strange new place – and England itself – could do with a few more pubs, parks and Brownie packs because it will not survive on modern art and inter-faith forums alone.

No one, no ideology and certainly no developer, has a monopoly on what it takes to make a successful community or a nation, but the story of North Greenwich in recent years can remind us what should have been obvious all along: the essence of this country is a messy muddle of tradition and global interconnection. It's always going to be both old and new.

6

Blackpool

England's Working Class: Red, White, Or Blue?

ARTIFICIAL SUNLIGHT

Blackpool was the future once. In 1879, this was the first place in the world to light up its streets with electricity. Soon, what had been just a small and relatively genteel Lancashire village had strung 'illuminations' along its shore and begun to measure its visitors in their millions.

The town doubled in size every decade to the First World War with the busiest railway station, the fastest trams and the highest tower in the country. People could dance to the most popular tunes, play the newest amusements, or take their pick of three piers that stretched out from the Golden Mile across the sands and into the sea. Blackpool – brash, brazen, dizzy, drunk, cheerful and cheap – was, for some at least, the best place in the world to be.

Working-class families who, for the first time in England's history, had some time and money to spare, flocked there from the industrial North and Midlands. Lancashire's cotton mill towns – the likes of Bury, Bolton, Blackburn and Burnley – took turns to have their 'wakes weeks' when they boarded trains to head exultantly for the seaside. It was where people's horizons lifted, the grinding reality of work was forgotten, or rigid rules about sex and class bent a little. *Hindle Wakes*, a 1912 play that was later turned into a film, tells the story of a mill girl who meets a factory owner's son in Blackpool and then resists parental pressure to marry him because she was entitled to enjoy 'a little fling' as much as anyone else.[1] Blackpool transported people like her to 'pleasure gardens' lit by the 'artificial sunlight' of hundreds upon hundreds of thousands of the brightest colours they had ever seen. When J. B. Priestley visited on his *English Journey* in the 1930s, he declared other destinations were 'merely playing at being popular seaside resorts' because 'Blackpool has them all licked'. Although he could not conceal his own distaste for its 'cheap restaurants and tea houses and shops piled and glittering with trash', Priestley declared it was 'a complete and essential product of industrial democracy' that offered a glimpse of a future that might, one day, be shared by all.[2]

In recent years, however, the future has seemed very far away. Blackpool's prosperity had always been the precarious kind based on seasonal tourism and part-time jobs. And, as England's biggest resort, it was left with the biggest problem when people began flying off to foreign destinations where there was no need for artificial sunlight and the wind off the ocean was a lot less bracing. After the mills, shipyards, pits and factories of northern England began to close, Blackpool found it was not really close to anything except the sea. If the Millennium Dome was meant to be the symbol of a confident new Britain looking forwards, Blackpool symbolised an older and more uncertain England looking backwards over its shoulder at the past.

It makes the town the setting for this book's sixth myth, one fixated on the allegedly homogenous views and apparent betrayal of the 'traditional' or, as it is often read, 'white' English working class. In the 'Brexit years', a long decade stretching from the financial crisis of 2008 to 2020 when abstract ideas of the future were being blown into their own thin air, political commentary became dominated by this earthier story of abandonment. Millions of white working-class voters in northern towns, it was said, had been left behind in the economy, looked down on by an out-of-touch elite, and seen their communities changed beyond all recognition by mass immigration. So, they 'took back control', voted to leave the European Union, and the 'red wall' of Labour-held seats in the North turned blue.

Along the way, this myth conflated economic and cultural grievance to twist England's politics into an ugly new shape. And in Blackpool it is not difficult to find reasons why it took hold.

A sense of loss and pain runs through the town like one of its proverbial sticks of seaside rock. More than a tenth of working-age inhabitants live on disability benefits. A place that is meant to be associated with happiness has one of the highest rates of anti-depressant prescriptions – more than two per person – of anywhere in the country while the local director of public health complains the town is a victim of 'shit life syndrome'. Out of 33,000 council wards across England, eight of the ten poorest are in Blackpool and, in some, life expectancy for men is more than twenty-five years lower than for those who live in London's richest boroughs.[3]

Whitehall labelled Blackpool such a 'cold spot' in the economy that at one point the English Tourist Board even stopped marketing it to foreign visitors. Of course, people do still come – millions of them every year – often for stag weekends, club nights and pub crawls. But families don't stay as long as they once did, leaving Blackpool with a lot of empty B&Bs and guest houses that have been turned into shoddy rented accommodation packed with housing benefit claimants.[4]

These poor, sick and vulnerable people get washed into the town on economic currents or memories of happy childhood holidays like the flotsam of every tide. Some get work during the summer but fall on hard times in the winter. Others have come straight out of prison with landlords buying up the cheapest accommodation in Blackpool specifically for ex-inmates including sex offenders, of which there are reported to be more than 800 in the town. At the same time, hundreds of England's most vulnerable young people have arrived after being placed in privately run children's homes by local authorities from across the country, with two-thirds of Blackpool's thirty-nine such institutions registered since 2016.[5]

Just a street or two back from the big rides at the Pleasure Beach and the weathered plastic of Sandcastle Waterpark are hotels that have been boarded up or turned into rented bedsits. There are busy food banks for people who cannot afford to eat, while other people are selling their bodies for sex. Large parts of the Golden Mile are now owned by the council after falling into financial difficulties, while even the newer attractions have a sort of gallows humour about them. At the Tower Dungeon there is a ride that 'simulates what it feels like to be publicly executed by hanging' with a fall of twenty-six feet as a noose appears and then the sound of a 'crowd cheering with excitement' as well as a 'cracking neck'.[6] The town's football club, Blackpool FC, known as the 'Tangerines' for their relentlessly cheerful bright orange kit, became infected by decay, too. For more than thirty years the club was owned by Owen Oyston, a convicted rapist, who stripped the club of millions as it briefly descended into football's fourth tier.[7]

Perhaps the best symbol of Blackpool's lost confidence is the fate of its 6,000 municipal deck chairs. These were sold off by the council in 2014 after an £80 million redevelopment of the beach that saw new 'sculpted spaces and the Spanish Steps leading down to the sea'. Publicity brochures claimed visitors preferred the new look because 'Blackpool's gone all continental'.[8] For some, this was just another example of the deracinated globalisation they felt had marginalised England's working class since the days of Margaret Thatcher and Tony Blair. But others saw it as a further commercial opportunity for cultural expropriation. The deck chairs were bought by the Stripes Company, a Cheshire-based business that supplied lawn furniture for the stately home TV drama *Downton Abbey*. The firm then refurbished Blackpool's old deck chairs, preserving 'the integrity of the original patina', before renting them out and selling them on as heritage items, either with their authentic worn plastic covers into which generations of bottoms had once sweated or with 'new luxury fabric'. The firm promised this would keep alive, if only in fancy gardens and corporate events far away from Blackpool, the 'enduring image of postcard humour, knotted handkerchiefs, fish and chips and seaside landladies [that] are the stuff of legend'.[9]

As a town that welcomed in the twentieth century by adopting a crest with the motto 'Progress' to go alongside its glittering electric lights, Blackpool was not meant to be about nostalgia. And, until quite recently, it wasn't. Nikolaus Pevsner, the foremost historian of England's architecture, noted with some bemusement in 1969 that Blackpool had not listed a single building for preservation.[10]

In the 1970s, Britain's great family entertainers – the likes of Ken Dodd, Russ Abbot, Cilla Black, Tommy Cooper, Les Dawson and Eric Morecambe and Ernie Wise – would still perform to capacity crowds at Blackpool's Grand Theatre or Opera House, often for two shows a night, six days a week through one of the town's long summer seasons. But those times have long gone and are now commemorated by an artwork called the Comedy Carpet, a vast 2,200-square-metre patchwork of granite spread out beneath the Tower into which all those legendary names have been carved along with catchphrases like that of Bruce Forsyth: 'Nice to see you – to see you ... nice!' Much to the dismay of Gordon Young, the artist who spent five years constructing this memorial to comedy, some sections of it have since been removed on the orders of health and safety officials who were worried, in suitably bleak fashion, that someone might 'step back off the very end of the carpet into the line of an oncoming tram'.[11]

In the 1980s Blackpool was still the biggest resort in Europe with more visitors than Greece and more hotel beds than Portugal. It had a successful pop group made up of six sisters, the Nolans. But Coleen, the youngest of them who has since become a presenter on the television talk show *Loose Women*, left the town in 2007 describing it as a 'binge-drinking hellhole'. She said: 'As much as I adored my childhood, I did not want my kids growing up there.'[12]

Blackpool was once very proud of the Arnold School that produced a series of show business stars ranging from Nicola Thorp of *Coronation Street* to Chris Lowe of the Pet Shop Boys. But this was closed down in 2013. The last old girl to make it big was Jenna Coleman, an actor who has starred in shows like *Emmerdale* and *Doctor Who* and played the title role in *Victoria*. Her grandfather ran a seaside amusement arcade and her father worked as a joiner fitting out the pubs. Coleman does not make too much noise about being from Blackpool now because she knows it is widely dismissed as 'stag-and-hen-do central' with 'willies made of seaside rock'. But she still thinks the town is worth defending. 'It has a charm you don't appreciate until you leave,' Coleman told one interviewer, 'something to do with faded 50s glamour and nostalgia.'[13]

This is why Blackpool's Tower Ballroom is still the highlight venue for *Strictly Come Dancing*. On the afternoon when we visit, the ballroom is filled with largely middle-aged or elderly couples waltzing around beneath dazzling chandeliers and the lavishly decorated gold ceiling modelled, apparently, on the ballrooms of the aristocracy. A woman in a sequined top plays old tunes on a Wurlitzer organ, while a special roped-off area has been set aside where visitors can sit with linen napkins to drink tea from blue and white china cups. Jane Brown, a sixty-year-old care worker who has come up to Blackpool with friends from Stoke-on-Trent, is one of them. 'This is so lovely,' she says. 'It's traditional English – a reminder of who we used to be before we lost our way a little.' When was that? 'I don't really know. It was after the 1950s, I think, when things really started to go wrong. That was because we didn't have enough pride in who we are as a country.'

A resort that was meant to be all about wonder and joy has now become synonymous with a myth of England's working class and a sense that things were better in the old days. What was once 'artificial sunlight' is now often sepia-tinted. And, even amid the illuminations of Blackpool's Promenade, what glitters is often not gold. Revelations about behind-the-scenes bullying has even taken the shine off *Strictly Come Dancing*.

AT THE END OF THE PIER

A short walk takes you a long way from the elegance of the Tower Ballroom, past restaurants pumping out the smells of deep-fried food and sound systems competing to make the most noise, to a cabaret theatre called Viva Blackpool. This is where a man billed as the 'King of Comedy' steps out into his audience armed with a camera for what he says is his 'favourite bit' of his show.

'I get to film women's tits,' explains Joey Blower, as the first cleavage he has picked on appears on the big screens behind him.

'Look at how they wobble when you laugh,' he says zooming in. 'How about these puppies!' he says of another, 'I bet all the wrinkles fall out of your face when you take your bra off.' He has a go at a few men, too, saying they look gay or fat before taking a close-up of a complicated 'comb-over' which he proceeds to ruffle up. The hair's unsmiling owner is swiftly reminded there is 'security in this room' and Blower goes off to find less risky targets. 'Let's have a look at your tits,' he says, before pointing the camera at a woman's knees to the hilarity of those sitting next to her. 'All right, love,' he says hovering a little uncertainly over an elderly woman. 'Give my best to Elvis because it won't be long now,' he says.

The most unsettling moment is when he goes over to a table where a young woman is sitting with her family. Blower sticks the camera in the face of the man she is sitting with and asks: 'Did you break her in?' Back comes the reply: 'Fucking right, I did!' She puts her hands over her eyes and shakes her head. Blower seizes on this as a revelation.

'How many here have shagged this one then?' he asks. 'See, even your dad's smiling!' A few minutes later, the same woman is brought up on stage. She is a student training to be a paramedic. But the King of Comedy is determined to get to the bottom of how old she was when she first had sex. 'Around fifteen,' she says eventually, defying the humiliation. 'Look at her mother's face!' he shouts pointing back at her table in triumph. And then he leans in towards his victim, who has folded her hands in front of her, to ask: 'Did it hurt?'

Even if this is a 'set-up' by a self-styled 'fat bastard' comedian who has been plying this trade for three decades in Blackpool, that doesn't make it fun. His performances are labelled as 'adult humour' with the clear warning that anyone 'easily shocked' shouldn't come. Much of the entirely white audience has dressed up for the occasion in jackets or sparkly tops, but the treat for which they are paying is not humour that cheers anybody up. He talks about masturbating on a bus or trying to drug a woman he had persuaded to come into his home, then does an offensive impression of his current wife who is from Thailand. Later, he puts up a video of their seven-year-old daughter on the same screen where he has shown his variety of breasts before asking everyone in the audience to wave at her and sing along to Dean Martin's 'Pretty Baby'.

Blower mentions more than once how he has recovered from prostate cancer and he is revered by some in this town for using his local celebrity to raise money for charity. But bitterness is never far from sentimentality. He says just 'because we take the piss out of someone who's a different colour' the liberal media executives he calls 'snowflakes' because they object to his act 'won't let us old ones on the telly'.

The previous night on the North Pier, Roy 'Chubby' Brown could also be found performing in Blackpool. Dressed in his trademark flying helmet and goggles, he is more famous than Blower, with fans buying upwards of £40 million worth of 'Chubby merchandise' and DVDs that have titles like *Thick as Shit* or *Fucked If I Know*.[14] But he was effectively barred from national television from 1989 until 2007 when Channel 4 made a documentary about 'Britain's rudest comedian' in which he admitted 'I can't change now'.[15] He has said the only way his audience of 'lorry drivers, road sweepers, fitters and welders' were going to be entertained these days 'is to be shocked'.[16]

As his audience is entering the theatre, a man and a woman who appear to be having sex in their seats are thrown out by four security guards. Within seconds of starting his act, Chubby Brown is ranting about how 'most of Britain is Black these days' and performing a song about the government's plan to send asylum seekers to Rwanda. He jokes about how his wife wanted to 'get physical' the other night, adding, 'she threw the first punch, I got her with an uppercut'. The audience laughed but most probably didn't know he had been convicted of hitting his ex-wife in the face so hard that he damaged her teeth, or that his autobiography opens with an account of dragging a man who had insulted him thirty feet along the same North Pier where they are sitting.[17] But much of his performance, as it rambles on pornographically about prostitutes, is more pathetic than anything else. Sometimes Chubby Brown messes up a joke or fails to reach his punchline. He says most of his old school mates are dead and makes endless references to Viagra pills. He seems thrilled to tell the audience about the man and woman who had been thrown out by security guards. 'She was giving him a blow job!' For him, it is proof that he still has a bit of edge. He didn't explain that they probably thought they could get away with having sex in the seats of his show because the theatre was only a third full.

Many councils around the country, including his hometown of Middlesbrough, have banned Chubby Brown from performing at their venues over recent years.[18] Like others who rage against 'cancel culture', he presents himself as standing up for 'freedom of speech' or giving voice to views that have been censored out by cosmopolitan, liberal society. 'I was on stage and I mentioned asylum seekers, the whole room stood up and clapped … I touched a nerve,' he said.[19] Some have tried to present both him and his audience as part of white working-class culture forced underground because it is deemed too vulgar to appear on TV stations they had paid for with their licence fees or the town halls they fund with their taxes.[20] For instance, an article in the *Spectator* about Chubby Brown, unintentionally written in the style of an aristocrat exploring the lower orders a century ago, attacks the 'progressive intellectuals' who ban such comedy shows even though they would not 'be seen dead' among the working-class audience for them. It adds: ' "Chubby" is just a low – if popular – comedian, most of whose *bons mots* you wouldn't be very surprised to hear at the end of a long evening in a lively pub in a down-at-heel area.'[21]

The resentment felt by such comedians is symptomatic of a deeper change whereby working-class people felt they were being marginalised not only in the economy but in every aspect of national life. The Labour Party, which had been created to represent working people in Parliament, was led by a succession of middle-class men for almost three decades from 1992. Over the same period, the number of MPs from manual working-class backgrounds has fallen from around a hundred to fewer than twenty.[22] And this was when other gateways through which working-class kids had once passed to find fame and fortune were also being crowded out by richer kids who spotted a slice of fun their parents did not already own. Although the proportion of rock and pop acts that went to private school has sometimes been exaggerated, those who have emerged since the millennium include the likes of Coldplay, Lily Allen, Florence Welch and Mumford & Sons.[23] Acting has similarly become dominated by the likes of Benedict Cumberbatch, Lily James and Eddie Redmayne, all of whom are from a distinctively privileged part of the English population. In sport, English rugby union has always been packed with the products of private schools but in cricket, which used to be a bit more mixed, the proportion of England players who were state-educated has fallen to less than a third.[24] Only football holds out, partly because its system usually prevents young players from fulfilling middle-class aspirations of a university education.

Stand-up comedians who had got their first break in working men's clubs or end-of-the-pier shows did not fit with the 'right-on' alternative comedy scene of people like Ben Elton and Jo Brand that was bursting out of university campuses onto TV screens in the 1980s and 1990s. There was still room – just about – for comedians such as Caroline Aherne who were part of a tradition of comedy being used to subvert class distinctions, such as the sketch she did for *The Fast Show* as a supermarket checkout assistant passing comment on every item. 'Ooh, Perrier Water. Just like water but, you know, fizzy ... Brown bread, very posh. Keeps you regular, doesn't it?'[25] Chubby Brown has even complained that he is the victim of double standards, saying that while he is never invited on TV, Jimmy Carr – whose live act has included jokes about rape, disabled people, Islam and the

Holocaust – is ubiquitous on comedy and panel shows. The difference between them might be that Carr points out the Holocaust is just about 'the worst thing that's ever happened in human history' – or it could be that with a first-class degree from Cambridge University he just knows how to play the Establishment game.[26]

This cultural conflict is core to the myth being examined here but it is far from straightforward. The likes of Blower and Chubby Brown are neither properly representative of Blackpool's comedy tradition nor of working-class culture, which has never been homogenous. Instead, these comedians are like the old 'hall of mirrors' – still found at Silcock's Fun Palace elsewhere on the Promenade – that twists reality into something mad and grotesque.

And most of the holidaymakers in Blackpool don't want to watch foul-mouthed 'fat bastard' comedians at all. Walking along the Promenade with her husband, Donna Perry explains she prefers to go to the karaoke 'for a giggle'. They often journey up to Blackpool from the Midlands for a break, usually staying at the same hotel they've been going to for years. 'We'll bring our granddaughter back for the illuminations later in the year,' she adds. No one is being rude or offensive on the South Pier on a bank holiday weekend as families wander around in the sunshine with their ice creams and lollies. A little girl wins a prize for 'hooking a duck' with a fishing rod. 'Everyone Wins A Prize' reads the sign above her head. 'What do you say to the man?' asks her mother. 'Thank you,' she replies, clutching her toy and smiling shyly. Even the Berkswell and Balsall rugby club, up for a weekend from Kenilworth, seem gentle as they nurse their hangovers. 'We only go to places beginning with the letter B,' explains one of them. 'We've been to Brighton and Bangor. Bournemouth is next.' Some of these heavily built men are squeezed into spangled dresses as part of a *Strictly Come Dancing* theme, but passers-by barely give them a second glance because such sights are not uncommon in this town. How are they finding Blackpool? 'It's lovely,' replies one of them, 'Everything is lovely!'

There is still much of this kind of joy to find in Blackpool. It is a democratic kind of place where people – most of them – treat everyone the same. And those who sneer at its enduring appeal usually fail to recognise that, by doing so, they show they have more in common with end-of-the-pier comedians than they would care to admit. Most of them would be justifiably outraged by what spews from the mouth of Blower or Chubby Brown, but they think nothing of indulging their own form of prejudice, an old one based on the class divisions that have always scarred England, and best described by an old-fashioned word: snobbery.

Blackpool has been jilted by a political elite with whom it once had a special relationship. For decades it had been a fixture of the annual party conferences when, at the end of September or the beginning of October, the country's most powerful people would pack out its hotels and the Empress Ballroom in the Winter Gardens. The Imperial Hotel still displays photographs of all the prime ministers through the years who have visited its 'Number 10' Bar.

And yet, as we write this, no major party has held its annual conference in Blackpool since 2007. In large part that is because, as politicians from all sides will privately admit, it is a bit too rough for them these days. It wasn't just Roy Chubby Brown and Joey Blower who were deemed beyond the pale, it was Blackpool itself.

A column by Mary Ann Sieghart for *The Times* in 2002 opened by describing how 'the biggest topic of conversation at the Labour Party conference this week' had been 'the aggressive ghastliness of Blackpool':

> While nearly all of the country has been transformed over the past 20 years, Blackpool has stayed stuck in a grotty, scruffy, low aspiration, poor-taste ghetto of its own. Newcastle and Gateshead are cool beyond belief. Liverpool and Manchester are urban phoenixes. Birmingham is a cultural magnet. Blackpool, by contrast, has no good shops, no good hotels, no artistic centres and only one good restaurant. Surely it is at least good at fun? Well, even though the town boasts a wonderfully smooth seafront promenade, there is nowhere here that can hire me a pair of in-line skates.[27]

The following week, she was back complaining about Blackpool's 'greasy spoon' cafés as she offered sympathy for anyone actually 'living in a town without any pretence at a decent cup of coffee or sandwich'.[28] Sieghart generally does not go out of her way to cause offence and her depiction of this town falling behind the big metropolitan centres can be borne out by all kinds of objective data. But the problems facing it went much deeper than her facile description implied and they were not going to be solved by the provision of a rollerblades rental shop or employing some skilled baristas, both of which can now be found quite easily on the seafront.

In some ways such cultural disdain for Blackpool was itself part of an older tradition. Just as Priestley found the town a little too trashy for him, there had been a battle in the Victorian era between those who wanted to maintain standards with local by-laws that prohibited spitting or protected the more refined areas of town from plebian incursions. As recently as the 1960s, there was a Blackpool Censorship Board that banned some of the 'sauciest' postcards from being sold by newsagents in the town.[29]

But such cultural and class divisions were thrown into ever sharper relief by economic decline across the North where old jobs continued to disappear, wages remained stagnant and the hours worked carried on increasing. Opportunities to own a home or build a decent life shrunk. Some young people headed off to university and those they left behind often felt cut off, even marooned. 'The economy of the oligarchs has been decoupled from that of the ordinary people,' concluded a leading economist at the time.[30] The towns of the North and the Midlands that had never recovered from the collapse of old industries examined in the previous chapter, got hammered again – first and worst – by the impact of financial crisis in 2008.

There was a widespread sense of decay with children's centres closing, libraries switching from professional to voluntary staff, social care services crumbling and schools unable to buy books. And Blackpool was hit harder than most northern towns by the austerity cuts of the 2010s because it had so many old, sick or poor people reliant on those services.[31]

Lack of money was not the only problem facing them; it was also the almost endless demands and stress of securing food, keeping children in school, staying safe from crime, filling in forms – endless forms – to get benefits, or finding a bus service that was still running. There were still daily triumphs, laughter and pride in defiance of poverty. But there was also raw despair, illustrated by countless anecdotes and confirmed by endless statistics, in which people caught up in this frenzy were giving up on the idea of progress. Despite the 'we're all in this together' slogan that slid from the lips of George Osborne and David Cameron during the austerity years after 2010, places like Blackpool were more 'in it' than others. It is still jaw-dropping to discover that schools in the poorest parts of England like this experienced a 60 per cent bigger cut in spending per pupil than the least deprived areas.[32]

This is why it became so easy to twist cultural grievances around economic and political ones. The result is a bitterly nostalgic story of earlier times, when comedians had accents as broad as the bums that filled deckchairs, and knotted hankies sat on top of balding pates that were – almost always – white.

'TWO ENGLANDS'

In 2019, a poll identified Blackpool South as being among the ten constituencies across the UK most opposed to the idea that 'immigrants should be free to move to Britain and work'.[33] It did not specify whether the immigrants in question were EU citizens, refugees from war zones like Syria and Afghanistan, or the Black and Asian arrivals from the Commonwealth who had been in Enoch Powell's crosshairs fifty years earlier.

But Blackpool is not a place that had been particularly affected by immigration of any sort. People generally come to England in search of steady, well-paid work and, as we have seen, that has been in short supply in this town. No less than 95 per cent of its 140,000 population is white, according to the latest census, compared to a national average of 81 per cent. And, though in the recent past Blackpool has attracted significant numbers of seasonal workers from Europe and has an established Polish community, the number of applications granted to EU citizens seeking to remain there after Brexit represented less than 2 per cent of the population.[34]

At face value, therefore, it seems bizarre that this issue should have got so much attention in Blackpool. But Nigel Farage, the politician who probably did most to meld anger over immigration into the myth of England's working class over these years, tells us: 'I don't think it's strange at all. People like the communities they live in and they're fearful. They can see what's happened in parts of east London or parts of Lancashire or Yorkshire just an hour's drive away from Blackpool. They don't want that.' While all that might make liberal metropolitan writers conclude 'these English are ghastly and beastly', he says we should realise working-class people objecting to immigration were being 'perfectly reasonable'.

Farage very deliberately chose this town as the venue for a UKIP party conference in 2015, and later launched the Brexit Party at a non-league football ground a few miles away. More recently, he has hosted his GB News television show from a bar in one of Blackpool's hotels. In between those events, this was the place that voted to leave the EU by the biggest margin in the whole of the North-west.[35]

Blackpool is not this politician's natural habitat. He is more likely to have been found over the years in London's TV studios or on the south-eastern coastlines which he sometimes patrols with binoculars to spot asylum seekers crossing the Channel. In recent years he has launched his own brand 'Farage Gin' which comes in red, white and blue varieties. The label shows him in waxed jacket and shooting cap, posing with a dog on a Cornish beach, above the legend pronouncing it is a 'Product of England'.[36] And yet he insists there is nothing incongruous about someone like him, a privately educated former City trader from the Home Counties, pitching for working-class votes in the North. 'Oh, I think I'm pretty classless actually, I certainly don't come from that Cameron–Osborne–Johnson-type background, I can get on with just about anybody,' he says. 'What northern people like about me is my directness.'

In his many incarnations as leader of UKIP, the Brexit party and Reform, Farage showed a talent for terrifying both Conservatives and Labour with this plain-speaking directness, especially over immigration. He complains about 'motorways that are not big enough' and 'kids having to go miles to go to primary school' because of the scale of immigration. Moving on to asylum seekers, he says they cause resentment among English people who see 'these young men getting housed for two years when our young people aren't – it's about fairness not racism'. Though he concedes that his hero, Enoch Powell, went too far with the 'Rivers of Blood' speech which we examined in Chapter 4, he says the 'rise of radical Islam makes people think he was right for the wrong reasons'.

Farage also – usually – coats himself in an old-fashioned style of the Englishman who doesn't like to make too much of a fuss. He famously described a journey on a commuter train a few years back when he couldn't 'hear English being audibly spoken in the carriage', saying: 'Does that make me feel slightly awkward? Yes, it does.'[37] And this is apparent, too, in his interview with us where he does his best to ensure nothing seems too hard-edged. Farage insists 'ethnicity' is 'too strong a word' to explain differences between people because 'the English themselves over the years have been an amalgamation of all kinds of different hordes'. He talks about 'how there are plenty of people from migrant backgrounds playing cricket for England and I am very happy for them to be doing so'. Does he think it is possible for an immigrant to become English? 'Yes, of course, it's about adopting a series of values like the rule of law,' he says, before he shifts his sights back to Islamist extremism, saying: 'That's where the threat lies.'

Like Brexit itself, which was always an abstract idea rather than a specific proposal, this vague hostility towards immigration and people of different ethnicity nonetheless had a big effect on politics in these years, particularly for a Labour Party that too often appeared to have taken working-class voters in northern towns for granted. Robert Ford, who was one of the first pollsters to spot UKIP's potential, has shown how a significant portion of voters in places like Blackpool preferred to blame falling living standards and status not on global capitalism or 'Tory austerity' but on asylum seekers and immigrants.[38]

In 2014, two unassuming academics from the University of Southampton, Will Jennings and Gerry Stoker, crystallised this into the idea that there were 'Two Englands'. Since the start of this century, they explained, growing economic inequality had opened up an ever-widening chasm in values and identity. 'In cosmopolitan areas we find an England that is global in outlook, liberal and more plural in its sense of identity,' they said. 'In provincial backwaters we find an England that is inward-looking, relatively illiberal, negative about the EU and immigration, nostalgic and more English in its identity.'[39]

Such a theory later found a blunter instrument in the form of David Goodhart. In 2017, he divided the people of England into two groups. The 'Anywheres', said Goodhart, are 'social and economic liberals, university-educated, with professional jobs, in the upper quartile of the income and class spectrum, comfortable with immigration, European integration and the spread of human rights legislation'. Whereas the 'Somewheres' are 'lower-to-middle incomes, not university-educated, older, living in small towns and suburbia, who value security and nostalgia'. Almost all you need to know about England today, Goodhart insisted, is found in his distinction. 'Somewheres' live in northern towns. In contrast, the 'Anywheres' are found in trendy urban places like north London even though he says their real home is 'nowhere'.[40]

Goodhart was criticised by many academics, including Jennings and Stoker, for making too 'crude' a distinction, one which underestimated the diversity of views in provincial towns and the strength of community in cosmopolitan cities.[41] His theory patronised 'Somewheres', caricaturing them as people so busy sharing solidarity with their neighbours that they do not care about global issues like refugees and climate change. It also insulted 'Anywheres' as being incapable of having an identity rooted in a sense of place or history. In fairness to him, he accepted there was another group he called 'Inbetweeners', one which he thought might include much of England's ethnic minority population, before conceding that most people don't neatly conform to any of his archetypes. Goodhart himself is an Eton-educated north Londoner who has spent his entire adult life within what he calls the 'liberal tribe' of media and politics which he thinks are the cause of so much harm. Like any skilled polemicist, however, he treats tens of millions of exceptions as proof of a rule that might be a bit snobbish itself.

Neil Kinnock, who came from a long line of miners, steelworkers and factory workers before leading the Labour Party through much of the 1980s and early 1990s, is perhaps better placed to judge this latest iteration of class politics. He suggests: 'I've noticed a lot of people these days inverted their privileges, often for kindly or sentimental reasons, so that they now believe being working class is the same thing as being blessed with infinite wisdom.' Although he says political leaders and their representatives should always listen so they can understand better the impact of unequal wealth and power, 'that does not mean we should patronise people by applying the lowest common denominator and just tell them what we think they want'. He tells us how his family 'weren't angels' but always knew who 'the true culprits' were for poverty. 'You have to cut through the bullshit,' he says. 'You have to recognise that sometimes, if not always, what people are saying has nothing to do with being "left out and left behind" – and everything to do with meanness and prejudice.'

Nonetheless, Goodhart succeeded in capturing the attention of his fellow chattering class members, not least because his categories seemed to map the divisions between Leavers and Remainers in the Brexit referendum of June 2016. For several years before and after that vote, camera crews descended on the high streets of northern towns to conduct vox pops with white working-class people who would confirm an analysis that might as well have been written on the train up from London. These reports often crackled with a racial charge as journalists nodded along encouragingly when their interviewees blamed immigrants for driving down wages or objected to them using public services.[42]

Of course, it was true that increasing numbers of people held such views during that time and they had a right to be heard. But it's wrong to claim they were being ignored. 'Somewhere' opinions were splattered daily over the front pages of most newspapers, as well as driving government policy on locking up criminals, benefit cheats and asylum seekers. Such coverage was always based on feelings not facts – or anecdotes rather than data – but it got to the point where anyone daring to challenge this narrative would be instantly dismissed for displaying dangerous, Metropolitan, out-of-touch tendencies. Only the bravest would point out the NHS or social care would collapse without the immigrants who were supposedly putting public services under such strain. An army of researchers was deployed to show immigrants had undercut the wages of the English who were already here, but no conclusive evidence was found. The best estimates appear to be that in the lowest paid sectors immigration had reduced wages by around one pence per hour.[43]

Perhaps privileged southerners like Goodhart or Farage were taken seriously as tribunes for the betrayed white working class because an unlikely political coalition was being built in England between supporters of the Countryside Alliance dressed in tweed jackets and ex-miners who used to wear donkey jackets. This was, after all, a time when Johnson could lay claim to a kind of authenticity even as he morphed from a liberal mayor of multicultural London into the figure-head of Brexit and then, perhaps most implausibly of all, a prime minister who purported to care deeply about the traditional working class.

Neither the official Leave campaign, which included Johnson, nor the separate one run by Farage, ever proposed a coherent set of policies on immigration. But few disputed that the issue was one of the main reasons they won, with the government announcing net annual immigration had reached a then record of 330,000 people just a month before the referendum. And in the years afterwards, when the net influx continued to rise, there was always something or someone new to hate. Once it was 'EU diktats', 'elf and safety' officials and Romanian crop pickers. Then it was 'wokeness', asylum seekers or Muslim women wearing burkas. When Boris Johnson provoked outrage, as he surely knew he would, by comparing the latter to 'letter boxes' and 'bank robbers', his supporters used the same response of comics like Roy Chubby Brown: 'Come on, it's just a joke.'[44]

A FOREIGN LAND AND A RED WALL

The blurred and inchoate arguments swirling around politics at this time were, at least partly, a function of how the practice of it was changing in those years before and after the referendum. Doorstep conversations were being replaced by the dehumanising algorithms that reduce the fears and hopes of tens of millions of individual people to rows upon rows of dots on a screen. The distance between Blackpool and Westminster is about 250 miles but it does not get any shorter when much campaigning is conducted through cyberspace.

Sometimes a glitch in the system reveals the source of a message that seems to be speaking so directly to a voter somewhere is, in fact, an algorithm which exists both nowhere and anywhere.

One such example was a targeted Facebook advert in the 2019 General Election that started well enough with a multicoloured panel appearing saying, 'It only takes 1,262 votes in Blackpool South to Get Brexit Done'. But then it went on to address people 100 miles away in North Wales. 'Your vote in Wrexham will be the difference between a majority government that will Get Brexit Done and another hung Parliament. It only takes 916 people to switch their vote in Wrexham to elect a Conservative MP that will Back Boris to Get Brexit Done,' it said.[45]

That message, 'Get Brexit Done', which was being hammered relentlessly into the heads of voters in Blackpool – and Wrexham – almost certainly began life in an over-lit conference room at a provincial hotel, the kind where everyone is given a choice of tea or coffee and asked to help themselves to a flavourless plastic-wrapped biscuit with a fancy foreign name. Such focus groups usually consist of maybe a dozen or so people who have been selected because they have characteristics – age, location, ethnicity, past voting behaviour or social class – that make them representative of those a campaign has decided to target. It's not always the most scientific of processes, with at least one regular participant telling us the agency who hires her will give prompts suggesting it would be helpful if she was, for instance, a fan of espresso coffee or a consumer of chicken burgers, even though she is vegetarian.

But those taking part in focus groups can have more influence on what governments and politicians eventually decide to do than they will ever get from voting, writing to their MP or protesting on the streets.

A sign that a new strategy or slogan has been inspired by one of these focus groups is when it contains a startling phrase presented as being 'in touch' with what people are really thinking. One such example was back in 2001, when the then Conservative leader William Hague warned that Britain would become a 'foreign land' if Labour won another election and promised he would 'give you back your country'.[46]

The phrase was almost completely devoid of substance. It was just a feeling, copied from focus group reports, from which slogans can be derived but never coherent policy. The speech was ridiculed by some, including a member of Hague's own shadow cabinet who said privately he would quite like to live in a 'foreign land' because the food and weather would be nicer. But Hague was ahead of his time because similar lines would appear regularly, not only in focus group reports over the next few years, but also in speeches by Nigel Farage and endless newspaper articles.[47]

On the morning of 24 June 2016, when a divided Britain woke up to find it had voted by 52 to 48 per cent for Brexit, it was the turn of Remainers to feel they were living in a 'foreign land'. Zadie Smith, whose novels had chronicled a forward-looking, modern and multi-ethnic nation in the New Labour years, tried to come to terms with the shock of this decision by phoning and emailing friends. ' "What have they done?" we said to each other, sometimes meaning the leaders, who we felt must have known what they were doing, and sometimes meaning the people, who, we implied, didn't ... We must have been living behind a kind of veil, unable to see our own country for what it has become.'[48]

Remainers who had not seen Brexit coming sometimes reacted with as much incoherent rage as those who had supported it. Many concluded that Leave supporters were simply 'ignoramuses'. Others suggested the result of the referendum should be revoked because people had been too easily influenced by 'false promises', 'tabloid urgings' or sinister psychometric digital adverts perhaps paid for by the Russian government.[49] Still more decided to start making the case for an open, outward-looking country in a way that pro-European politicians had not done – and perhaps should have been doing – for decades before.

The People's Vote campaign (for which one of the authors of this book once worked) demanded a fresh referendum on the specific terms of Britain's departure from the European Union, and in 2018 and 2019, organised three of the four biggest marches England had ever seen. Critics called those demonstrations 'the longest Waitrose queue in history' and infuriated Leavers decided they were another middle-class liberal ploy to deny them their democratic voice.

The paradox was that, in order to get heard in modern politics, a campaign that could have presented itself as a compromise for all those on both sides who had become frustrated with the Brexit process became part of the polarising problem it was trying to solve. Pro-Europeans found themselves mobilising an angry version of what was once regarded as the moderate centre ground. And, in doing so, they may have helped inflate further the myth of a betrayed white working class.[50]

The Conservative Party's landslide win at the December 2019 General Election saw it capture both seats in Blackpool for the first time in twenty-seven years. This was regarded as another brick broken in Labour's once-solid 'Red Wall' of constituencies across the North and the Midlands. And the new Tory MP for Blackpool South wasted no time in claiming his victory had been driven by working-class voters' loathing for 'woke and metropolitan values'.[51]

Scott Benton is a self-described socially conservative 'happy clappy' Christian who prays every day, says his favourite book is the

Old Testament Bible and didn't tell his parents he was gay until he got married at the age of thirty-three.[52] His first speech in the House of Commons tried to harness Blackpool's nostalgia for the past to the myth that had got him elected. He mentioned seaside rock, Margaret Thatcher, music-hall entertainer George Formby, the world's oldest electric tram line and the queen before saying his constituents, who 'are proud of our great country, our history and traditions', had voted for Brexit because they 'feel left behind by the pace of economic and social change in recent decades'.[53]

But Blackpool and its voters were never quite like the myth propagated by Benton. Like other seaside resorts, it has always had a get-rich-quick spirit of small enterprise, as well as those landladies behind whose net curtains and 'no vacancies' signs lurked a set of values that thoroughly disapproved of this town's more exuberant visitors.[54] Gordon Marsden, who clung on as a Labour MP through six General Elections before losing to Benton, says: 'Although people think of the town as a working-class playground, it has a lot of what might be called lower-middle class and working-class Tories.'

Across the North and the Midlands there were similar seams of such voters. They were noticed by Tory strategists like James Kanagasooriam, who is thought to have invented the term 'Red Wall'. He had foreseen how, in whole swathes of traditionally Labour territory, people's political allegiances were loosening as they developed 'a cultural sense of belonging that was more proximate to the Conservatives'. They were not always, or even mostly, the ex-miners or steel workers of those TV news vox pop caricatures. In Blackpool, they often live in houses with a couple of cars parked outside on new-build estates with names like Marples Grange where they are insulated from the poverty of the town centre. Far from voting for the Conservatives in 2019 as a revolt against economic change, they were often significantly more content with life over the past few decades than those who stayed loyal to Labour.[55]

An even bigger factor in the politics of Red Wall towns is that over a period of almost three decades a lot of people did not switch their support to other parties so much as stop voting entirely. Between 1992 and 2001 turnout in General Elections fell by a quarter as five million people stayed away from polling stations and they were disproportionately working class. Until the 1990s, there was little class difference in participation rates. But, by 2015, middle-class people had an 85 per cent likelihood of voting compared to just 48 per cent for the working class. In Blackpool South, turnout dropped from 77 per cent in 1992 to barely 52 per cent a decade later and it has not got back above 60 per cent since. One academic study concluded: 'The new party of the working class is no party at all.'[56]

Some of those non-voters will have participated in the 2016 referendum, others will have transitioned from Labour via other parties including UKIP on to the Conservatives, still more will have drifted off the electoral registers altogether. Marsden says he saw many of those who voted for him back in the 1990s slowly turning away from politics. 'London and Westminster seem a long way away,' he says. 'The institutions which kept our vote solid, where people discussed politics and were encouraged to vote, were slowly dying out. There used to be eight working men's clubs in Blackpool, now there is just one.'

These days those seeking a cheap drink in a traditional setting, if not a discussion of politics, might end up at the Ardwick pub on Foxhall Road in Blackpool where a pint of what it calls any of 'the big three' – Fosters, Strongbow or John Smiths – cost just £1.70 when we visited. Smoking a cigarette outside is a pensioner called Roy who, after a broken marriage, has washed up in Blackpool. 'I'm just living my life now,' he says. 'I've had three heart attacks, so I'm all knackered up. I'm fucked.' He stays in his flat and watches TV most days 'but once a fortnight I save up enough to come to the pub and have a binge, people are nice here – you can talk to them – and there are some real characters'. The main problem in Blackpool, he says, is that there are 'too many homeless people'. Does he vote? Roy narrows his eyes suspiciously before replying: 'I don't like to talk about politics. I used to be Labour, but I don't bother now. They're all the same.' How about Brexit? 'Nope, didn't vote. It makes no difference to me.'

James Graham grew up in another part of the Red Wall, Annesley, which was once part of the Nottinghamshire coalfields where all the pits closed after the bitterly divisive miners' strikes of the 1980s. Now one of the country's most successful playwrights and scriptwriters, he says: 'a village like mine is now known as a "former mining community in a post-industrial town". It is defined by what it once was and no longer will be again,' he says. 'What does it do to you if you're a thirteen- or fourteen-year-old kid and you're constantly told where you live is a former thing?' He tells us how he became 'obsessed about how England looks to its past', saying: 'In this country, we don't write new stories very well, but we do weaponise old ones. I just think England is in a constant state of grief. It keeps really testing to see if the person they have lost is there but they're not. And we don't know how to start a new relationship.'

Then he reaches for the metaphor of a reset button. 'Living in England for the past decade has felt like we were at the end of the TV series that just wouldn't get to the end,' says Graham. 'It was financial austerity and the financial crisis too. Then, through the Scottish referendum through to Brexit – every relentless, exhausting, unprecedented week we were having – it just felt like everyone was pushing the button and the country just would not reset. People would not stop recommissioning this awful drama. People are trying to press the punch button but it's just not resetting.'

A growing number of academics and pollsters have begun to acknowledge that there is more to the myth of the English white working class than its conventional telling allows. 'This is not a country that can be neatly divided between rooted and authentic "somewhere" communities and a rootless, self-centred "nowhere" ruling class who run things in their own interests,' says Robert Ford. 'The truth is messier.'[57]

Indeed, those who voted for Brexit in 2016 were not usually Labour or even particularly working class. 'The largest block of Leave voters were middle-class Conservatives, followed by working-class Conservatives,' says the veteran pollster Peter Kellner, the former president of YouGov which conducted a poll of 25,000 people into all this after the referendum. 'Out of 17.4 million Leave voters, just one in eight was a working-class Labour supporter. Of course, had even half of these 2.2 million voters backed Remain, the result of the referendum would be different. But to suggest that the Leave vote was dominated by working-class Labour supporters is simply untrue.'

None of which is to deny that Labour lost a lot of votes in Red Wall constituencies, and its stance on issues like immigration or Brexit, as well as the left-wing leadership of Jeremy Corbyn, played a big part. An influential book on the 2019 election, *Beyond the Red Wall*, written by Deborah Mattinson, who later became Labour's strategy director, analysed why they switched. Based on focus groups she conducted in traditionally Labour constituencies across the North and Midlands, she described how people saw the party as being for 'losers and scroungers' or filled with 'naïve and idealistic middle-class students – arrogant kids boasting degrees but lacking experience, young people who looked down on people like them'.[58] Political parties spend much of their time dissecting – or 'segmenting' – the component parts of the electorate, which was why Mattinson restricted membership of her focus groups to working-class people with a 'spread of ages from the late 30s up to the mid-70s', and 'asked for everyone to be past Labour voters who had switched to the Conservatives at the 2019 election'.[59]

And, inevitably in a political system where the MP for each constituency is determined through a first-past-the-post election, some voters matter more than others. But, as political strategists from every party admit, it's impossible to tell the full story of what is happening in the country as a whole through a very narrow slice of the electorate. There must be much more being said by all those people never invited to focus groups. How about those millions of young people and non-voters? What motives did millions more people have for switching from Labour to parties like the Greens and the Liberal Democrats? Why did some formerly loyal Conservatives hand their votes to other parties? Does anyone care about the views of people who always vote for the same party?

Just as Blackpool should not be defined by its end-of-the-pier comedians, the identity of the northern working class and England itself should not be determined either by a single group of voters or by caricatures of the places in which they live. People are more than identical bricks in a Red Wall that only moves when it is smashed down. All of them are part of an endlessly shifting electorate which is necessarily more of a muddle than those who run or write about politics would usually suggest.

By the same measure, towns like Blackpool should not pretend they are the only places where people have been suffering. Others have experienced the pain of austerity cuts to services and felt ignored. Once again, it was Zadie Smith who picked up on this when she returned to where she grew up in north London and described how so many of the ways 'England made me' were disappearing through austerity cuts:

My subsidized sports centre and my doctor's office, my school
music lessons paid for with pennies, my university fees. My NHS
glasses aged nine. My NHS baby aged thirty-three. And my local
library … Having one's own history so suddenly and abruptly made
unreal is an experience of a whole generation of British people, who
must now wander around like so many ancient mariners boring
foreigners about how they went to university for free and could
once find a National Health dentist on their high street.[60]

As she implied, it has often been the young who have been hit the
hardest, no matter where they live, what their ethnicity is, or the
social class to which they are deemed to belong. Technology and
global competition are disrupting the old paths into work, particularly for those who left school without going on to university, even as
those who did worry about their student debt. All of them will inherit
towering challenges such as climate change and inequality from their
parents. Many are already finding it impossible to dream of any kind
of economic security as they find themselves priced out of owning a
home and dependent on often exploitative private landlords. Those
who get well-paid work have to do longer hours and be monitored by
managers equipped with surveillance gadgets more sophisticated than
those dreamed up by the spy fiction of earlier generations.

Young people have voted in recent years by overwhelming margins
against Brexit and the Conservative Party. But, just as with marginalised
members of the working class, they do not vote very much. Turnout
among the under-twenty-fours fell from around two-thirds in 1992
to below half less than a decade later and has bumped along at similar
levels ever since. Even the so-called 'youth quake' in 2017, when it
was claimed lots of young people had flocked to the polling stations
inspired by Jeremy Corbyn, turned out to be a data error.

Discontent and disillusionment were not confined to any one group
in those Brexit years. In 2014, a poll asked whether the country had
changed for the worse in the past thirty years. Overall, 59 per cent of
people agreed, twice the proportion of those who disagreed. The figure
was marginally higher in the North and among the working class, but
not by much. Even in supposedly wealthy London, substantially more
people agreed with the statement than disagreed.[61] There was a grim
kind of national unity between different people in the Brexit years –

rich and poor, young and old, graduate and school-leaver, migrant and non-migrant, north and south – most were increasingly fed up, even if they sometimes disagreed about precisely why.

Philip Hensher, a writer whose novels revolve around the ordinary conflicts and muddle of English life, captured this widespread sense of the isolation and anxiety in his poignant audio short story 'Pressures, Residential', which is coincidentally read by Blackpool's Jenna Coleman. It is told in the form of the last email of a young woman who has nowhere to live after the break-up of her relationship and takes a job as a live-in 'guardian' of an opulent glass Thames-side tower in London. The apartments are empty, existing only to be bought and sold and bought again by non-residential foreign investors described as 'people a long, long way away that you will never see' who hold them as an accounting trick or to launder their money. There are only two people in the building. First, there is Kofi, the receptionist. He is an immigrant, nervous of his legal status and relieved to have the job even though he works crazy hours, commutes miles from home and is not even allowed to use the toilet on his tightly regulated breaks. And there is the narrator, Pippa, a young woman who has never quite found her way in life and settles for a job without purpose as the 'only way to afford anywhere to live in this, the city where I was born'. She would be an archetypal 'Anywhere' in David Goodhart's schema. But Pippa never comes close to doing well in England's twenty-first-century economy. Hensher's story ends with her accidentally locked out on the balcony of one of the flats hundreds of feet in the air, wearing nothing but a bikini and without any signal on her phone. Stuck on the outside of an empty building and gazing at the city at dusk, it is never clear if Pippa survives. But, 'nearly naked and quite isolated', she says: 'I had no idea what to do.' Just like the country itself.

Nostalgic or progressive, nationalist or multicultural, provincial or cosmopolitan, the pressure has been telling. In the years before Brexit, England was not run by ecstatically happy cosmopolitan city-dwellers – gripping the future in one hand and an expensive coffee in the other – whose sole aim in life was to make white working-class people miserable.

Nor, in the years since 2016, did successive pro-Brexit governments do much for those who might long for an imagined England where there were no immigrants and everyone ate tinned pilchards for tea.

There was little objective data to suggest life has got any better for such voters and growing polling evidence that showed many of them thought it had got even worse.[62]

Blackpool South's MP, Scott Benton, kept himself busy by being interviewed by Nigel Farage on GB News or getting ever more vocal about would-be refugees arriving in small boats hundreds of miles away on the south coast of England. He attacked his own government's decision to process a couple of hundred of them in an empty Blackpool hotel, saying, 'I fear the burden of housing these asylum seekers has fallen disproportionately on northern towns' like this. He got called out by fact-checking websites for making similarly false claims that some were being given the right to stay in Britain merely because they owned a pet. His voice only fell silent when he was filmed by reporters apparently offering to table parliamentary questions and lobby ministers on behalf of the gambling industry in exchange for money.[63] He was booted out of Parliament and Labour won both Blackpool seats in the 2024 general election, even though Farage finally got himself elected as an MP in another dilapidated seaside town at Clacton on the other side of the country. Places like Blackpool certainly don't have a monopoly on misery and powerlessness, nor do they have to own Brexit and its consequences. It's why the political myth of the white working class needs deflating because they deserve better MPs than the likes of Benton, or for that matter, Farage.

None of that was ever going to help the people of Blackpool and it's why the myth of England's working class needs deflating. Towns like this one do not have a monopoly on misery and powerlessness but nor do they have to own Brexit and its consequences. And they really do deserve better than to have MPs like him.

TAKING BACK CONTROL

The amusements and rides are shuttered tight against the mid-winter rain that arrives horizontally from the Irish Sea. Next to Blackpool's war memorial stands a hotel, the Metropole, that now looks so filthy it's hard to tell whether it ever had much elegance to fade. This is where the asylum seekers that have so upset the local MP are being 'processed'.

Unlike the hotel's previous occupants, however, there is not much joy for them in Blackpool. These asylum seekers are subject to a strict curfew, no rights to work and an allowance of just £40 a week to pay for food, clothing and everything else. Round a door at the back is a huddle of people trying to light cigarettes in the wind, including a Kurdish man called Mohammed who explains he fled war in his homeland and came to England by hiding on a truck. He says others came on boats and points out towards the sea. Does he like it in Blackpool? Mohammed begins to answer by smiling and tilting his head in embarrassed fashion before saying: 'I will be moved to somewhere else soon.' Then a woman who says she works 'for the government' shouts at him to come back inside.

A few hundred yards south, two homeless people are sitting on the ground in front of a plastic cup containing some coins. Peter Allcock has been in the town for almost all his life apart from when he has been sectioned for mental illness. He describes how they are sometimes attacked by 'blokes out on stag nights' and bad things happen all around. 'You go two streets that way and there are prostitutes – really young girls – that's not nice.' Sitting next to him is his girlfriend, who came to Blackpool to escape domestic violence. She describes how they got together when 'a car splashed us and we just both started laughing – and one thing led to another'. They now live together in a makeshift tent at the back of a nearby car park and, while they talk, occasionally take swigs from plastic bottles of white cider they have concealed under their sleeping bags. Neither has heard about 'culture wars' or cares about Brexit. But one political message has cut through. 'If I was Black and had some sob story behind me like those asylum seekers,' says Allcock, jabbing his thumb in the direction of the Metropole hotel and a group of people whose lives are as precarious as his own, 'I would be living in five-star luxury, wouldn't I?'

A little further down the Promenade, however, the sight of a giant and muddy hole being dug in the ground provides as much joy for sober-suited council officials as a trip to the Pleasure Beach would for ice cream-smeared children at the height of the summer season. This is the first phase in a £300 million project which we are told will result in new theme parks, luxury hotels, a thousand extra jobs and hundreds of thousands more visitors to the resort. It's all part of a much bigger programme described as a once-in-a-generation chance to 'turn around the decline of the late 20th century'.[64]

The bulldozers are not digging up just any old piece of land: it's where the fourteen platforms of what was once said to be the busiest railway station in the world used to welcome millions of holidaymakers to Blackpool. Central Station was closed in 1964 and later demolished because the local council had begun eyeing up these prime forty acres for a lucrative landmark development. But only some scruffy amusement arcades and an ugly concrete magistrates court were ever built.

In the half-century or so since there have been endless bold transformative plans for Blackpool that glowed as bright as the town's famous illuminations before fading away. The land where the old railway station had stood was going to be a £450 million 'Las Vegas-style super-casino' until Tony Blair's government decided Manchester might be a better bet and the idea ran aground on the granite of Gordon Brown's Presbyterian disapproval. Later, there was talk of turning it into an 'indoor rain forest', then a 'Snow Dome' leisure complex which was going to 'put Blackpool in the big league'. That also came to nothing as the town instead climbed to the top of different league tables for mental illness and sickness benefits, obesity and children in care, people on low wages or high on drugs. Those with long memories, therefore, might be forgiven for taking the latest helping of regenerative hyperbole with a little pinch of salt.[65]

We get a taste of it, too. On a visit to the Winter Gardens, one of its managers proudly shows off the refurbished Empress Ballroom where so many prime ministers have spoken in the past. Phil Jackson describes how it has retained a 'kind of magic', adding, 'we've had a lot of investment here and I really think the town is on the way back up'. Even as he is talking to us, however, he is interrupted by an anxious member of staff who tells him some homeless people are in the toilets and there have been complaints about them using needles. 'It's always the same when it rains,' says Jackson sadly, 'they come here to find somewhere dry.'

Even so, there is a risk of us becoming just the latest in a steady stream of writers over recent years who have stepped tentatively off the train from London in search of human misery to flesh out a predetermined narrative. Civic leaders in Blackpool often complain about the way deprivation in their town is portrayed in these articles. They say it not only deters investment and exacerbates a sense of powerlessness but also ignores signs of hope. Visitor numbers have grown in recent summers since the Covid lockdowns. The resort's appeal to ordinary families has been burnished as the council has banned new lap-dancing clubs, while new attractions for children like a Peter Rabbit adventure and a Harry Potter-themed mini-golf course called 'Hole in the Wand' have been opened. There are air shows, fireworks championships and laser displays to go along with the more traditional illuminations. The

Winter Gardens are these days likely to echo to crowds singing, 'Stand up if you love the darts,' because it has become one of the top venues for a sport which is so authentically for white working class men that middle class ones have started pretending they like it too. Such is the fashion for darts that Sky's viewing figures for a recent tournament will be bettered only by those for the football Premier League.[66]

For the same reason, it's not really true that Blackpool has been abandoned by Westminster politicians. Both Labour and Conservative governments have spent hundreds of millions of pounds in recent years improving the Promenade, strengthening sea defences and revamping its tramway system. Public funding, including from the European Union, was also used to rescue key attractions including Blackpool Tower and the Winter Gardens which were at risk of going bust. Blackpool was visited four times by three different prime ministers in 2022. On the same day as Rishi Sunak arrived in November that year, his government announced a multi-million-pound bailout for the redevelopment of the old railway station which had stalled because of a lack of funding.[67] In recent years, much of this has been done under the name of 'levelling up', a slogan for a set of policies which aim to make the poorest parts of England as prosperous as the richest.

Whether or not such gifts are merely a function of this town containing a key marginal Conservative constituency, the Labour leader of Blackpool Council, Lynn Williams, is grateful for what she can get. 'When I hear a minister is coming, I fix my face, put a big smile on and say "thank you". Then I tell them that they will never get true levelling up without properly funded public services.'

She's surely right to point out how headline-grabbing redevelopment projects do not, on their own, bring back the good times when vast sums of money have been cut from essential services. The council tells us it has had £1.4 billion sliced from budgets between 2010 and 2022 largely because of reduced central government funding and the escalating costs of the deprivation that resulted.[68]

In similar fashion, a plan to move thousands of Work and Pensions civil servants to a new office block in Blackpool might inject some life into the local economy, but it is tinged with a bitter irony given that this town has suffered so much from a decade-long squeeze on the benefits administered by that department. One piece of academic research conducted during the Brexit years calculated that welfare cuts were costing every adult of working age in Blackpool almost £1,000 a year.[69]

Local authorities like this one have little headroom to do much else for the most vulnerable people than fulfil their statutory duties. Any extra is more often than not found by bidding for pots of money from hundreds of different Whitehall programmes. 'They make funding available for one thing and leave us with less for everything else,' says Williams. 'Then the minister in question moves on and the money runs out again.'

Some of the grains of truth in the 'left-out-and-left-behind' myth of England's working class are sourced in such relationships between Westminster's government and its distant regional outposts. In 2020, for instance, a superfast broadband cable connection was installed under the Fylde coast stretching across the Atlantic to the United States that meant data could travel quicker to New York than from anywhere else in England. Blackpool's local plan talked excitedly about how it could become a 'Silicon Sands' digital business hub, making this the 'smartest and best connected town in the UK'.[70] But firms struggle to recruit IT specialists to Blackpool, while schools complain they are hamstrung from giving pupils the skills needed. Frank Norris, the chair of Blackpool's Education Improvement Board, says it's hard to adapt teaching for the jobs that might be created because of 'the straitjacket of the National Curriculum' that sets a high bar in maths to study computer science, together with what he calls 'the sausage-making machine of the exam system'.[71]

There are plenty of people who would blame those strictures and much else besides on the Conservative politician Michael Gove who, as education secretary for four years until 2014, was regularly in conflict with local authorities over the structure of schools, their finances and what should be taught.

When we spoke to him before the 2024 general election, he was still the government's levelling-up secretary and in reflective mood. 'One area on which I have changed my mind is local government,' he said, acknowledging that past rows meant he has never had an 'easy relationship' with many councils. 'The more I've thought about how you strengthen our democracy, how you make power accountable, how you get the right economic leadership, how you transform geographical inequalities, the more I've become convinced strengthening local government – embracing devolution – is critical.'

There is always a lot of talk about devolution, usually centred around the creation of more city mayors in places such as Manchester to build 'powerful engines of growth' and possibly new regional identities, too. But there are signs that national politicians from all sides are beginning to recognise this too often forgets towns like Blackpool. Gove's multiple visits to the resort over the last few years probably qualify him for some sort of travel discount. In 2023, he was back in Blackpool again with another multi-million-pound cheque to pay for a new higher education institution called a 'Multiversity' to help address the town's historic shortage of skills.

In contrast to Nigel Farage, it was also very noticeable how reluctant Gove was to reheat populist fury about immigrants and asylum seekers. 'I can't police others' language,' he said. In the years after the 2016 referendum in which both he and the issue of immigration played such key parts, the net influx of people into Britain continued to rise and reached 606,000 in 2022, largely because of a dramatic increase in non-EU migration. It is unlikely that those who voted for Brexit did so in the hope of replacing Polish plumbers with even greater numbers of immigrants from Asia and Africa.

For what it's worth, Gove said he thinks the issue has reduced in salience because ending the EU's free movement of people has given the UK control – at least nominally – over immigration numbers. But the public is more confused than ever with a majority of people continuing to believe overall levels are too high, while saying more are needed to work in the NHS, harvest England's crops and study in its universities.[72]

After more than a decade in government, Gove would much prefer to talk about Blackpool and the messier, slower – even publicity denying – process of adapting programmes to particular local circumstances or needs. He eschews the simplicity of the myth by recognising there is neither a single problem nor a one-size-fits-all solution for working-class towns which have 'their own set of particular reasons for suffering'. While other parts of the country desperately need to build more affordable homes to help young people get on the housing ladder, Blackpool has a vast surplus of scarcely inhabitable rented housing in this town which either needs to be improved or demolished altogether.

Keir Starmer, as leader of the opposition, also found himself on the well-trodden path to Blackpool. During a three-day 'listening tour' there in the summer of 2021, he ate fish and chips on the Promenade, ice cream on the North Pier and talked to panels of Tory-leaning Brexit voters in the Tower Ballroom. What appears to have had the deepest effect on him was a visit to a local school, St Mary's Academy, away from the cameras. He met a bunch of sixth formers who were obviously proud of their town. Then he asked how many of them thought they would have to leave Blackpool to fulfil their ambitions. 'They all put their hands up,' he said.[73]

Since then, Starmer has spoken a lot about recreating 'the basic, ordinary hope we used to take for granted' which he contrasted with the 'grandiose, utopian visions' that usually result only in more despair. He has promised to introduce a 'Take Back Control' Bill – a deliberate echo of the Vote Leave campaign slogan – so that towns like Blackpool can 'prosper by standing on their own feet'. When in opposition, he set out a series of 'missions' for a new Labour government that resemble some of those once trumpeted by Gove for levelling up. He was back again for a May Bank Holiday in 2023 buying another portion of vanilla ice-cream and promising extra neighbourhood police officers to sort out 'incidents in the local chippy'.[74]

Such policies ultimately stand or fall by whether they narrow the inequality between England's regions and improve real lives. The evidence is that since 'levelling up' briefly became the guiding purpose of the government in 2019, the gap has grown wider. One piece of analysis in 2023 suggested that on a dozen socio-economic indicators used by Whitehall, Blackpool was worse – or no better – off on every single one.[75]

There is a case for focusing less on redistribution of resources than on 'growing the cake'. But creating well-paid jobs or new sources of wealth in places like Blackpool is eye-wateringly expensive and the challenge presented by those sixth formers who told Starmer they needed to get out if they were to get on remains a big one. Too often, periodic spending announcements are just short-term cover for long-term austerity. A coherent strategy of building transport and digital connections, technology clusters and skills so that towns like Blackpool can prosper within 'regional hubs' may yet prove to be beyond any minister and every government, as the debacle over building a high-speed rail service from London to the north of England shows.

And, no matter how fast the wheels of regional economies turn, there will always be important jobs dealing with the needs of Blackpool that will never leave the town. And this is where a smaller, more everyday story about the community spirit among England's northern working class still offers some ordinary hope.

National problems like hospitals overflowing with patients that cannot be discharged might be expected to be worse in Blackpool. The reason that's not always the case is largely because of a team of people led by Karen Smith who work to integrate social care with Blackpool's Victoria Hospital. 'It's frantic and we're coming at this from every direction, but we don't fall out with each other,' she says. 'Everyone is a bit different. If someone can't be discharged because their fridge is broken or heating needs fixing, we get on with it. We can either do a direct payment or make sure their landlord gets the electrician and plumbers in.' They have set up a discharge ward at the hospital so that all the patients ready to leave are in one place. 'It makes them visible to us,' says Smith. 'We go in there and ask them directly "what can we do to get you home?" The government has started integrating care like this across the country and we're now responsible for other patients across Lancashire too, but I reckon it's quickest – usually – to get people back home if they live in Blackpool because we've been doing this here for ages and we know how to make it happen.'

So much of this kind of work is overlooked. Blackpool gets headlines for being a town where the most deprived school pupils are two years behind the national average and there are some of the highest rates of truancy or children disappearing out of education altogether. But they are getting better partly because Blackpool has teachers who go out in the evenings delivering meals to get families to feel more positive about children going to school – then turn up on their doorstep again the next morning to make sure they do. Head teachers have worked together to reduce the number of children being excluded or expelled, rather than compete as the Ofsted inspection regime incentivises them to do.[76]

None of this is to pretend that Blackpool's public services are perfect. On one day there is a story about hospital patients dying in corridors splashed across the local newspaper with a traumatised ambulance driver saying, 'nurses and doctors were in tears and relatives were screaming at us'. On others, there are reports on the 'chronic neglect' of children in care or inadequate standards at some privately run nursing homes.[77] The writer and campaigner James Bloodworth worked undercover as a home carer on a zero-hours contract in Blackpool for his book, *Hired*. He described how visits to lonely and vulnerable people who he was told to call 'customers' were limited to fifteen- or twenty-minute windows. 'Almost every carer had at least one story of an elderly person being left unfed or uncovered in a cold house,' he wrote. 'If you were late – and sometimes you were through no fault of your own – a customer could be left sitting in a urine-soaked pad for hours at a time.'[78] Significantly, however, Bloodworth didn't think the staff were heartless, just that the system itself lacked humanity.

The council points out how it has since raised carers' wages and paid them for the time it takes to travel between visits, as well as making clear no home visit should be for less than 30 minutes. Although underfunded Blackpool probably cannot afford to do much more, it's worth pointing out how most carers and council officials probably have reserves of patience or a sense of public service that the highest-paid executives of firms far away will never find within themselves. Imaginative welfare reformers like Hilary Cottam have begun to argue that the whole care sector should be rethought, so care is no longer treated as a tradable commodity from which firms can make fortunes from council contracts, nor assumed to 'operate in a social vacuum' irrespective of the poverty around it. There are other radical – or, in the view of critics, 'protectionist' – ideas coming out of neighbouring towns like Preston, which seeks to ensure money spent on everything from construction to catering by its own institutions like hospitals, housing associations – the council itself – goes to local people.[79]

Some of these ideas may be the outline of a more hopeful future and Blackpool, where so much care needs to be given so much better, could even be in the vanguard of bigger change. But, for now, there are thousands of people getting on with these so-called 'foundational' jobs, which are too tough, for whom the angry myth of abandonment does nothing.

Indeed, the beauty of what works in Blackpool is that it directly contradicts those that tell people that nothing works. At the Blackpool Pride in Place partnership, set up with funding from the Prince's Trust, Andy Clarke describes how businesses, charities, public services and local residents themselves have come together to improve Claremont, one of the poorest wards in the town. 'The Magic Club on Sherbourne Road has been the first safe place for young people to go for years,' he says. 'It gives kids the chance to learn stuff like digital skills, go on trips and do Duke of Edinburgh awards or just have some fun.' A community centre has been operating in an old Methodist church on Dickson Road where, for the past twenty years, it has been providing lunch for the lonely, exercise classes for the unhealthy and lessons on how to use the internet for the unconnected. Improving a community like Claremont can be as simple as organising the 'rubbish amnesties' so residents don't fly-tip old mattresses or other junk out onto the streets. 'None of this is a silver bullet,' says Clarke, 'but there are lots of people here who care about their town and they want to do something, working from the ground up. That's not "taking back control" or any of the slogans politicians use; it's just about taking responsibility for ourselves.'

And when you look for this kind of bottom-up hope, you begin to find it everywhere. The power of thousands of Blackpool football fans who boycotted games for five years – even when their team got to Wembley – forced Owen Oyston to relinquish ownership a few years ago. As soon as he was gone, volunteers turned up at Bloomfield Road to wipe down the seats and scrape seagull excrement from a stadium in which legends like Stanley Matthews, Stan Mortensen and Alan Ball once played.[80]

Even when attention focused on the big new theme parks where the railway station once stood, a more interesting development was taking shape next door. This is a museum, the first proper one this town has ever had, which is being built inside the new five-star Sands Hotel. 'Showtown' is being run in collaboration with London's Victoria and Albert Museum, which is lending it such entertainment crown jewels as the post-war entertainer Tommy Cooper's magic box and the undersized red fez he wore on stage, as well as the glasses of comedian Eric Morecambe and the clogs once filled by the feet of music hall legend Gracie Fields.

This is the very opposite of the ugly caricature of working-class culture offered by the likes of Roy Chubby Brown and Joey Blower at their end-of-the-pier shows, who have been mistakenly raised up by some as martyrs to a 'cancel culture'. Instead, the new museum is meant to celebrate the popular acts as part of Blackpool's offer to a new generation of tourists. 'Showtown is neither a mausoleum to, nor a parody of, the past,' says Tristram Hunt, the V&A director. 'It's about using this amazing technicolour heritage to help pay Blackpool's way again and the people who live there feel proud of their town.' Hunt has also begun a teaching programme to share the V&A's design expertise with secondary school pupils in Blackpool, Blackburn, Sunderland, Bradford, Sheffield, Coventry and Stoke, the last of which he previously represented as a Labour MP. 'It means we reach very different people to those who visit our museum in Kensington,' he says. 'I also think it refutes some of the sillier claims made after Brexit that London's cultural institutions were somehow not "real England" – whatever that is – or even part of another country entirely.'

The Showtown museum also encountered a problem that no one had anticipated: it received so many artefacts donated by people living in the area that curators could not cope. Instead of simply relying on gifts and loans from London, hundreds of people had started donating their own showbiz memorabilia. The museum, which suddenly had thousands of objects and records on its hands, was eventually forced to issue an apologetic notice asking people to stop giving them material for the next year.

Too often, England's supposedly homogenous working class are treated as an object to be spoken of – or spoken to – rather than as people who can speak for themselves.

We have already explored, in an earlier chapter and different context, the dissonance found in Hull. And on the opposite coast of England, Blackpool is its own place, too. It shares some, but not all, of the problems of towns like Bury or Burnley, while barely resembling great cities like Manchester or Leeds, even though they all get lumped together as England's 'North'.

The people of Blackpool don't need to be told who they are or what they should do by the likes of Nigel Farage and Michael Gove, or, for that matter, Boris Johnson and Keir Starmer.

In this chapter, we have sought to deflate an overstretched myth of the traditional working class. In doing so, the self-respect, decency and energy of real people has become more apparent. Those qualities may yet turn out to be worth more than any big redevelopment fund for Blackpool, not to mention the English working class and England itself, in the years ahead.

In the cold months of the winter at the end of 2022, a new illumination went up on the roof of the Grundy Art Gallery in the town that seemed to sum up all this pride. Spelled out in a defiant orange neon were words first said about this resort during its heyday a century ago, but which still have meaning today: 'BLACKPOOL STANDS BETWEEN US AND REVOLUTION'.

7

Oxford

England's Establishment: Still Standing, Still

Ten minutes into an open-top bus tour of Oxford and a tourist might well be wondering what the fuss is about. After setting off from the city's functionally dull railway station, the first building of any note is the corporate tinted glass and yellow brick of the Business School named after Wafic Saïd, a Syrian-born billionaire famed for fixing a massive weapons deal with Saudi Arabia. Far from being a centuries-old seat of learning beneath one of the city's 'dreaming spires', this is topped by a Middle Eastern ziggurat, opened in 2001 thanks to Saïd's then £70 million donation.[1]

The bus takes you past a couple of unremarkable hotels before doubling back around the city's one-way system. There, you can feast your eyes on the 1950s tower of Nuffield College 'capped by a copper-covered spike', all paid for by William Morris, Lord Nuffield, whose car works industrialised the eastern half of the city.[2] Then you go past a grassy mound that used to be a castle, an old prison next to a Wetherspoons pub, the reinforced concrete of the 1970s council offices, before the Westgate Shopping Centre looms into view, recently refurbished with every retail chain store, from Primark to John Lewis.

The heritage quotient begins to pick up outside Christ Church, the grandest college in Oxford, founded six centuries ago by Cardinal Thomas Wolsey with the proceeds from looting some local priories.

Then, at last, the bus turns right and the guide suggests that as the passengers' gaze glides down the gently curving line of honeyed stone colleges, chapels and churches towards the River Cherwell they might like to take photos of what she says is 'the most beautiful High Street in the world'.

This provides the setting to explore our seventh and final myth of England, which is all about the 'Establishment'. Exactly what that is, who belongs to it and where the boundaries lie is always a matter of dispute. Most would agree, though, that the Establishment is a collection of sometimes British but mostly English institutions, stretching out of great universities into the highest levels of politics, church and state, as well as culture and finance. These organisations are often very old, usually a little old-fashioned and almost always carry a dead weight of self-importance. The myth of the Establishment unites its most ardent admirers and its harshest critics. The Establishment's admirers say it has acted as a crucial shock absorber for centuries, enabling England to ride out the bumps in history, and is the reason this country exhibits remarkable continuity across the ages and generally avoids revolutions. Critics complain it is more like a roadblock to any kind of progress, one that frustrates 'the will of the people'. To both sides, these institutions are unchanging, immovable and, as the word 'Establishment' implies, fixed.

But, as with the other myths examined in previous chapters, if this was ever true it is not any more. The Establishment is still, just about, standing, but it is not standing still. The over-inflation of this myth, which has been brought about by those who want to maintain it and by those who want to destroy it, has been getting in the way of institutions performing vital roles at a time when they are needed most. Not only does the story of institutions being set in stone prevent them changing to meet the challenges of the time, it has also made them a target for the aggressively polarised arguments about national identity that have been unleashed in England.

All of which probably explains why, back on the top deck of the tour bus, the guide pointedly ignores a chunky and assertive-looking building on the High Street.

When it was first built, a hundred years or so ago, local people were upset that a useful row of shops – a milliner, a cutler, a cricket outfitter and an optician – had been razed to the ground to make way. Others complained the architecture was too ugly for this famous street.[3] More recently there has been a monumental row over a statue placed high on one of the building's walls of a casually dressed and moustachioed man, carrying a cap in one hand, with his left foot poised as if ready to stride purposefully forward into the world.

This flattering representation of Cecil Rhodes takes pride of place outside one of the university's colleges, Oriel, not because his studies there in the 1870s ever amounted to very much. It is there for the simple reason that he was an imperial adventurer who was able to pay for the entire building with a fraction of a fortune made from the extraction of African gold and diamonds.

Beneath the statue is a stone inscription saying in Latin:

E LARGA MVNIFICENTIA CAECILII RHODES

This translates as 'by means of the generous munificence of Cecil Rhodes', but also turns out to be a chronogram giving the date of construction and precisely the kind of conceit, carved in stone, that irritates so many people about this university. If you can be bothered to treat the enlarged letters as Roman numerals and then rearrange them in descending order of value (yes, really), you apparently get MDCCCLLVIIIIII. Of course, those responsible could have saved the stonemason a lot of trouble if they had asked for 'MCMXI' or just '1911' to be carved into the memorial instead. But that would have spoiled their attempt to express their deep gratitude to Cecil Rhodes by being too-clever-by-half.

The bulk of Rhodes' legacy paid for more than 8,000 international Rhodes Scholars who helped globalise Oxford as a brand of educational excellence. He stipulated these scholars should only come from what he termed 'the colonies' or the United States and – perhaps in a hint of his views about the superiority of Anglo-Saxon men – Germany. Notably, there were no Black Rhodes Scholars from South Africa, or women from anywhere, until the 1970s.[4]

By then, however, nobody seemed to mind that much about an image of a dead benefactor stuck high on a wall. For a long time, the only living creatures paying much attention to the Rhodes statue were the pigeons defecating copiously on its head. Then, in 2015, at another university in Cape Town and in front of another Rhodes memorial, Chumani Maxwele picked up a bucket of excrement – this time human – and hurled it at the sculpture.⁵ Within days, there were demonstrations in Oxford, too, where people chanted the same words heard in South Africa: 'Rhodes Must Fall!'

These protests were not only about the imperial past; they also challenged racism at the university in the present, new examples of which were emerging with depressing regularity. For instance, when a Black graduate returned to visit a friend at the university, CCTV images of him were issued to all students at that college along with a warning to 'remain vigilant' as he might be a danger to their 'wonderful and safe environment'.⁶ The Oxford Union, the university's debating society, advertised an event on the legacy of empire with a flyer featuring a pair of Black hands in manacles that offered a cut-price cocktail called 'the Colonial Comeback'.⁷ And, in the midst of all this, it was revealed that Oriel College had admitted just one Black British student in the previous six years.⁸

In the summer of 2020, the Black Lives Matter movement across the world reignited Oxford's campaign. Protesters declared a 'Freedom Summer', with no fewer than six sit-in demonstrations outside Oriel. Simukai Chigudu, a Zimbabwean-born professor teaching at Oxford, explained that the statue represented a nineteenth-century colonialism that was still infecting England's identity. 'It exists in the present as a kind of nostalgia for the country's hegemony on the world stage, while fuelling nationalism, buttressing white supremacy and generating anxieties about immigration and cultural change,' he wrote. 'The statue perfectly distils this imperial nostalgia into a concrete object.'⁹

Even though the head of Rhodes House had published a thoughtful response to the issue of historic injustice sveral years before, many fair-minded people did not know how to respond and tied themselves up in verbal knots to avoid taking too clear a position. 'Just leaving it there, as it is, is not helpful,' said the party's Oxford East Labour MP, Anneliese Dodds, before adding quickly that she didn't want to say anything more because she didn't think that would be 'helpful' either.¹⁰ Others, though, had no such problems. The former Conservative leader, Iain Duncan Smith, compared the prospect of the Rhodes statue being taken down to George Orwell's nightmare vision. 'I feel like we are on the edge of *1984*,' he said, 'where we are trying to expunge our history.'[11] For him and others, this played directly into their chosen narrative about a country divided between those who saw the past as a source of pride and a baying mob hell-bent on destroying it. The *Daily Mail* described how 'an angry crowd descended on Oxford University' demanding the 'marble sculpture be torn down'. It asked: 'So what next? Ban all books mentioning Rhodes? Burn them?'[12]

Back in Oxford itself, the debate turned into a characteristically self-conscious display of intellectualism that, far from being terrifying, was a bit annoying. The last event of Oxford's Freedom Summer comprised around forty students listening to calls for 'reading groups against racism'. Their stated aim was to 'destabilise the socio-political consequences of white settler colonialism'. A Facebook video of the event shows them joined by a lecturer wearing a pair of shorts who offered what he called 'brief comments' of a 'very modest and tentative' nature, constituting a 'preliminary exploration' of the different ways we can 'imagine and assemble the city as a form of collective living'. Almost twenty minutes later, his speech was still going, until he noticed the audience's attention wandering and decided to call it a day.[13] Oriel College's process to consider what to do in response to all of this was notably long-winded.

When both its undergraduate and graduate students voted in favour of removing the statue, the governing body embarked on what it described as a 'thoughtful period of debate and reflection'. Eventually, an announcement was made that the statue would be removed but, before doing anything too rash, it would wait for the verdict of an independent nine-person commission established to look into 'wider issues'.[14] Those commissioners considered why the college had such low numbers of Black students and heard from one who said the presence of the statue made her feel she did not 'really belong here'.[15] They sought out the views of local councillors and schoolchildren living in this diverse city, most of whom also said they wanted the statue gone.[16] They conducted a rigorous academic assessment which concluded that Rhodes had 'intensified racial segregation' in the Cape Colony, as well as using extreme violence in the invasion of what is now Zimbabwe where men, women and children 'sheltering in caves were blown up with dynamite'.[17] The commission examined almost 1,500 submissions, including an inspired suggestion from the artist Antony Gormley to turn the monument around to face the wall so that it would look as if Rhodes was being punished. The whole process went on for so long that one of the commissioners died. Finally, in May 2021, the independent report was published with the verdict that the college's decision to remove the statue had been correct.

Then Oriel College changed its mind. Citing 'regulatory and financial challenges', it announced that the Rhodes statue would stay exactly where it was. Instead, another task force was set up to decide on a 'visible contextualisation of the Rhodes legacy' and examine ways to improve diversity. The most obvious reason for this about-turn seemed to be simply money, just as the '£££' signs in Oxford's eyes had persuaded it to accept gifts from the likes of Cecil Rhodes in the first place. Unsourced reports in newspapers suggested that Oriel had already missed out on a seven-figure sum in donations because of the row and claims that a bequest worth as much as £100 million would be cancelled if the statue came down and that removing it would be subjected to legal challenges costing hundreds of thousands of pounds that could be spent elsewhere. But there were also suggestions from sceptics that other factors came into play, too.[18]

The head of Oriel's governing body – known as the Provost – entered this row as plain Neil Mendoza. He is now Baron Mendoza of King's Reach, having been awarded a seat in the House of Lords as a Conservative peer by Boris Johnson just a few months before the college decided to keep the statue. He was also handed a new role by the Culture Department dishing out £1.6 billion in arts grants. The ennobled Provost himself says there was 'no trade-off' involved and claims that these appointments had anything to do with the decision are 'completely untrue'. He abstained in votes by the college's 45-member governing body because his role in the government and as chair of Historic England meant 'Rhodes was bit of a minefield for me'. Although Mendoza supports government policy to 'retain and explain' statues, he denies discussing the issue with Johnson or his advisers and says the only time he called Downing Street during the dispute was to ask for better security at the college 'because the police weren't taking my concerns very seriously'. Instead, Mendoza suggests that he doesn't much like the way culture warriors on both sides have 'bashed our institutions,' adding: 'My instinct is usually to defend them'.[19]

The 'practical actions' Oriel has taken to defuse this controversy include a small metal sign that has appeared beneath the statue outside the building to which it is fastened with a padlock and chain. 'Rhodes, a committed British colonialist, obtained his fortune through exploitation of minerals, land and peoples of southern Africa,' it says. 'Some of his activities led to great loss of life and attracted criticism in his day and ever since.'

In the meantime, anyone stopping to look at his statue may notice pigeon-proof netting has been put up so that Rhodes is now even protected from the only opponents to have ever really left their mark.

ENGLAND'S ODDLY SHAPED ESTABLISHMENT

By maintaining the status quo, Oriel College could claim to have done what England's Establishment always does in the face of demands for change. Concessions are promised and sometimes even implemented – a bit – before peace returns. The final shape emerging out of clouds of vented steam rarely has clean lines. But, in its irregularity, it is recognisably what existed before.

After the best part of an hour on a bus tour going around Oxford, tourists arrive back at the railway station without it being entirely clear when, or even if, they went past the university. They have seen some beautiful old colleges, chapels and churches, but where exactly was this world-famous institution? The answer is that only a fraction of it can be seen from the outside and it has no centre. Much of Oxford's treasure is hidden behind the high walls and gates of thirty-nine individual colleges or buried deep in the underground libraries. It is a haphazard medieval system which defies any modern, logical notion of a campus.

One of the secrets of Oxford University is its ability to fashion a peculiar identity through similar blurred lines or even distortions. As far back as the fourteenth century, one of the colleges was trying to reinforce its importance in the national story by forging documents to prove it had been founded in 872 by King Alfred. This university is an institution of learning that prides itself on 'rigour' and 'evidence', but indulges make-believe and magic, too. It is no coincidence that this is where the parallel world of 'Wonderland' was invented by Lewis Carroll; where 'Narnia' was imagined by C. S. Lewis; and 'Middle

Earth' mapped out by J. R. R. Tolkien. When the film comedians Laurel and Hardy visited in the 1930s for *A Chump at Oxford*, the usually nervous and diminutive Laurel was magically transformed into a sporting and academic legend called Lord Paddington, able to beat a hundred men in a boxing match and go intellectually toe to toe with Albert Einstein, only to return to his normal self when hit on the head with a bottle.

Such contradictions are at the heart of the myth of the Establishment. Oxford was so Royalist in the English Civil War that it hosted the Court of King Charles I, but then refused to let him borrow a book from the Bodleian Library. The place is still riddled with confusions. It is a university that proclaims the values of meritocratic excellence while providing a stage for the worst excesses of privilege, or where avowedly left-leaning professors carrying plastic bags of stale biscuits stolen from their common room spend endless hours helping yet another generation of Old Etonians replicate the wealth of their parents.

Of all those who have tried to distil the essence of Oxford's myth, few have come as close as the playwright Tom Stoppard. He arrived in London's East End as Tomáš Sträussler, a Jewish child refugee from pre-war Czechoslovakia, and said he has spent much of his life since trying to be an 'honorary Englishman'. He never went to university, but his play *The Invention of Love* portrays Oxford in the latter half of the nineteenth century as a home to mawkish nostalgia and radical reform, ferocious religious faith and atheistic free-thinking, sexual repression and glorious liberation.

The central character is A. E. Housman, who in real life would go on to become an austere English academic and a role model for Enoch Powell. For Stoppard, Housman is a young Oxford student struggling with his repressed homosexuality who listens on in agony to a conversation between the Victorian Oxford scholars who thought of themselves as radicals, John Ruskin and Benjamin Jowett:

Jowett: The modern university exists by consent of the world outside. We must send out men fitted for that world. What better example can we show them than classical antiquity? Nowhere was the ideal of morality, art and social order realized more harmoniously than in Greece in the age of the great philosophers.

Ruskin: Buggery apart.
Jowett: Buggery apart.[20]

Stoppard shows the fictional Housman looking back on his life and realising that, despite such prejudice, this environment had allowed him to be himself precisely because it was comfortable with absurd hypocrisy. In much the same way as the university has no centre, the English Establishment lets a thousand contradictions bloom. As Housman says at the end: 'Oxford in the Golden Age! The hairshirts versus the Aesthetes; the neo-Christians versus the neo-Pagans; the study of classics for advancement in the fair of the world versus the study of classics for the advancement of classical studies – what emotional storms, and oh what a tiny teacup.'[21]

As an island of inclusion and tolerance in a sea of prejudice and ignorance, or a point of stability in a turbulent world, such an imaginary Oxford had real value. For the same reasons it is filled with myth, the university was where people with sharply varying views have been able to live, argue and sometimes fall in love with each other. Various other Establishment institutions that underpin this country are all supposed to work in this fashion, too. Their purpose is not to find absolutes where one side overcomes the other. Instead, they are meant to mediate disputes with fair rules, as well as paper over the cracks with layers of tradition bound together with strange ceremonies or little dollops of fantasy. In other words, these institutions are neither about keeping people forcibly apart nor about dragging them into conformity; at their best, they allow England to exist in a muddle and an irregular shape.

As ever, there is some truth in this myth. The best evidence for it can be found in the history of the 1930s and 1940s. Across the world at that time, the goose-stepping ideologies of Fascism and Communism longed to crush anyone who stood in their way or was different. Oxford University was one of the places in England that provided a sanctuary for those who disagreed.

Isaiah Berlin had arrived as a child refugee from Bolshevik Russia and went on to become one of the greatest liberal philosophers of the twentieth century. The university led the world in accepting Jewish refugee scholars from Nazi Germany including, briefly, Albert Einstein. At first, they sometimes rubbed some of their colleagues up the wrong way, with one complaining: 'That was the trouble with these new chaps: they didn't seem to care about British gentlemanly conventions.'[22]

Fractious senior common rooms in Oxford, as well as democracy itself, turned out to be much more resilient than many had expected. In England's muddled fashion, its Establishment helped create mechanisms that enabled people to disagree or dislike each other while still living, working and fighting together to defeat the straight lines of totalitarianism in the Second World War and the Cold War that followed.

For much of the last century, the institution of the BBC was an integral part of almost everyone's daily life with its mission to 'inform, educate and entertain' every citizen of the country. In 1940, Winston Churchill rallied a demoralised nation with his radio broadcasts on the BBC. In 1953, people from every class and region crowded around tiny black and white television sets to see the Coronation. England's victory over Germany in the 1966 World Cup Final still holds the record for this country's highest TV audience.

But it was the BBC's comedy that best demonstrated how people can come together despite all the differences in background, taste and politics. The *Morecambe & Wise Show* Christmas special in 1977 was watched by almost half the entire population. Often their humour was built around gently mocking guest stars like orchestra conductors or newsreaders who were part of a cultural elite. It was both democratic and inclusive enough for different kinds of people to laugh along at the same time, with each other or at themselves, in a shared moment. Situation comedies have even managed to turn the process of embracing reform, but not reforming, into the status of an instantly recognisable joke. The 1980s series *Yes, Minister* was about the obstruction of politicians by the permanent Civil Service. More recently – and daringly – the BBC made *W1A*, a comedy series about the fumblingly ineffective efforts of its executive 'Head of Values' to 'reimagine' the broadcaster for the future.

Underpinning the BBC's role in national life has been a reputation for fairness between rival interests. In similar fashion, people have generally believed that other institutions like England's judiciary or the British Civil Service are both ridiculous and incorruptible. The most ridiculous institution of them all, on the face of it, is the monarchy. Together with the rest of the United Kingdom, England enjoys a hereditary head of state of German descent who signs off every new law voted on by Parliament and the date of each General Election while owning £28 billion in assets and crown jewels, many of which were dubiously acquired from the empire. But Queen Elizabeth II succeeded in making the monarchy a space of calm and constancy that held the English Establishment together with other parts of the UK through a combination of dutiful hard work, charity and fastidious political neutrality. Her reign was the longest in history and she became so much part of everyday Englishness that, when a *Daily Mirror* reporter claimed that she had Cornflakes for breakfast from a plastic Tupperware box that she used to 'keep the cereal fresh', no one was really very surprised.[23] Her funeral was attended by elected heads of state from around the world who delayed an important United Nations summit so that they could pay respect to a woman who had always perhaps been keener to spend time with her corgis or horses than with them.

The seamless succession from her to her eldest son, which impressed so many as a masterclass in continuity, also meant King Charles III became the Supreme Governor of the Church of England. As we saw in Chapter 3, this is a religious denomination sometimes regarded as another example of this country's ungainly talent for meandering middle ways. The original 'broad church' produced a seventeenth-century edition of its Book of Common Prayer that was specific in its intent 'to keep the mean between two extremes'.[24]

Such institutional religious compromise is, however, not the result of standing still. It is the scar tissue of the most violent kind of action, much of which seems to have taken place through the centuries in the now tranquil streets of Oxford. Thomas Cranmer, the Archbishop of Canterbury and the original author of the Common Prayer liturgy, was burned at the stake in Oxford in 1556 for heresy. A few years later, Oxford's townsfolk watched as Catholic priests were hanged, drawn and quartered – a practice which involved their genitals being cut off and their intestines pulled out before their body was chopped into four pieces – the standard punishment for a treasonous Catholic under Elizabeth I, the 'Good Queen Bess'. Nor were the Rhodes Must Fall protests outside Oriel College on Oxford's High Street the first to gather there because people were feeling angry about a statue. In 1642, when another crowd stood in exactly the same spot, their focus was on the opposite side of the road. Puritan soldiers fighting for Parliament in the civil war denounced the 'idolatrous' statue that decorated the front of the University Church. They started firing their muskets at it, decapitating the images of both the Virgin Mary and the infant Jesus.

In the next century when the Wesley brothers, John and Charles, were founding 'low church' Methodism as students at Oxford, Protestants mobs were still killing hundreds of Catholics in London's Gordon Riots. When the Oxford Movement began their campaign in the nineteenth century to restore the Anglican 'high church' traditions, these divisions were at last beginning to be expressed through doughty speeches and stone monuments even as their religion helped destroy existing societies through the empire.

Political rights in England have been established through a similarly painful route. The monarchy was forced through civil war, or the threat of its return, to cede royal prerogative power to Parliament in the sixteenth and seventeenth centuries. What was once an entirely Protestant Parliament eventually removed discrimination against Catholics, Nonconformists, Jews and atheists. Whenever the system has shown signs of cracking, as it did under pressure from marching Chartists or hunger-striking and sometimes letter-bombing Suffragettes, more people have been allowed to vote: middle-class men in 1832; 'respectable' working men in 1867; any adult man with property in 1884; every adult man and some women in 1918; every adult woman in 1928; and every eighteen-year-old in 1969.

More recently, power has been devolved from Westminster in uneven lumps across the semi-autonomous smaller nations of the UK and a few regional mayors in England. Once again, because the road to democracy has been a long, winding and often bloodstained one in this country, it has never been set in stone. It remains riddled not just with contradictions but also with unfairness. The peculiarities of this country's system mean there is a vast disparity in the power of each vote depending on whether it is cast in a marginal constituency. Millions of people are not registered on the Electoral Roll or have given up on politics. The House of Lords still has a few dozen seats reserved for hereditary members, some of whom owe their position to ancestral robber barons from the Middle Ages, as well as many more for life peers appointed for their fawning loyalty or political donations that in other circumstances might be regarded as outright bribes.

Some think all this irregularity is the secret of the Establishment's survival. That was certainly the view of Sir Geoffrey Elton, Cambridge University's Regius Professor of History, in his final book, *The English*, published shortly before his death in 1994. He defended this haphazard constitution as providing a space in which to contain the political extremes found in Europe, which had therefore fostered a 'non-revolutionary' English working class. He extolled the virtues of institutions like the House of Lords, writing: 'Other countries, afflicted by revolutions, abolished noble titles and had to find other means of rewarding merit and satisfying blackmail ... that did far more harm to their nations.' It is tempting to dismiss such remarks as the late work of an elderly conservative Englishman. But then, in his preface, Elton reminded readers that – just like Tom Stoppard – he was a wartime Jewish refugee from the Nazis, who arrived in England at the age of seventeen as Gottfried Ehrenberg. 'Within a few months it dawned on me that I had arrived in the country in which I should have been born,' he wrote. 'In a way, this book tries to pay a debt of gratitude.'[25]

Such stability, the paradoxical result of nothing being too fixed, has always provoked fury as much as it has inspired admiration. Those who can be called 'preservationists' celebrate it all, arguing that the great institutions of England are what holds the nation together. On the other side are 'iconoclasts' who believe they simply allow the few to dominate the many and must be torn down to make way for their new England.

Among the latter group was the Marxist thinker Ralph Miliband, another Jewish refugee from the Nazis. He was grateful for the protection this country provided him and had fought for it by serving in the Royal Navy during the war. But he also believed the democratic power of the people was being frustrated by an Establishment run by an economic elite. 'It has remained a basic fact of life', he wrote, 'that the vast majority of men and women has been governed, represented, administered, judged, and commanded in war by people drawn from other, economically superior and relatively distant classes.'[26]

In making this argument, the iconoclastic Ralph Miliband ended up as much a propagator of the myth as any preservationist, because his case too depended on the idea of the Establishment's stubborn permanence. Like his fellow refugees Elton and Stoppard, Miliband believed the English Establishment acted as a block on revolution and brake on radical change. His real difference was that he thought this was a bad thing. The list of targets that Miliband raged against included the universities that employed him. He said the suppression of left-wing anti-war campus protests in the 1960s had shown that their governing bodies would always do the bidding of the powerful, while their intake of students was in any case utterly dominated by 'children of the middle and upper classes'.[27] Most of the time he also despaired of the Labour Party, which he regarded as far too attached to the unelected instruments of a capitalist state to deliver societal transformation through occasional parliamentary majorities.

In the acknowledgements of his final book in 1994, however, Miliband took paternal pride in thanking his two sons – David and Ed – for what he called their 'very helpful (and stringent) criticisms'. Back then both were recent graduates of Oxford University. Having grown up with a famous academic father and access to all kinds of networks, most people would have regarded them as among those middle-class students who do so well from elite universities. What's more, they had already embarked on a journey taking them from media and think-tank jobs into government as New Labour advisers and then ministers in the same cabinet. The two brothers famously ended up standing against each other for the Labour Party leadership as they pursued the parliamentary power their father had once dismissed as 'the most crippling of all illusions'.[28]

George Orwell wrote that 'England is a family with the wrong members in control,' and the Milibands have sometimes appeared to be a family arguing about precisely which of them should be in control. But one thing David and Ed had in common was in disagreeing with their father by believing it is possible to reform a system from within. This question about who gets to be inside the Establishment – whether or not having different hands on the levers of power makes much difference – has been at the heart of so many arguments in recent years. And it has meant England's old institutions, or, rather, the myth that says they never really change, has begun to be challenged from every direction.

263

THE ELITE AND ITS UNCIVIL CULTURE WAR

Even in the supposed 'Golden Age' of Oxford there was a lot wrong with this university. The privilege of being a student at one of its colleges was only available to a very few. There was never much room for the people of England to indulge their 'emotional storms' in what Stoppard had described as such a 'tiny teacup'.

Recent decades have witnessed a great expansion in higher education. The proportion of young people going to university has risen from less than 1 per cent in 1920 to almost 50 per cent a century later.[29] Oxford itself now has two universities with the newer one, a former polytechnic, Oxford Brookes, educating more undergraduates than its more famous neighbour.

But the grip of Oxford and Cambridge – 'Oxbridge' – on the upper echelons of just about everything has, by some measures, tightened. At the time of writing, of the fifty-seven prime ministers in the history of this country, thirty of them went to Oxford. That includes all of the last five and no fewer than fourteen out of the eighteen since the Second World War. More than a dozen prime ministers studied at Cambridge, while the rest include a few who were students in Scotland, one in eighteenth-century Netherlands, and a handful who did not go to university at all. There is only one prime minister ever to have gone to an English university which was not Oxbridge: Neville Chamberlain, who studied metallurgy at Birmingham. Even Keir Starmer, who, refreshingly, did his first degree at Leeds, went to Oxford for his second.

And, though the Establishment is more than just a list of prime ministers, so is Oxbridge's presence within it. As we write this, Cambridge educated the Archbishop of Canterbury, the governor of the Bank of England, the director-general of the BBC, the cabinet secretary, the chair of the Arts Council, the Master of the Rolls and the editor of the *Sun*. Oxford can claim the head of MI6, the chief executive of the NHS, the chair of the BBC, the owner of *The Times*, the editors of the *Daily Telegraph*, *Guardian*, *Independent*, *Daily Mail* and *Wall Street Journal* – the last of whom shared a house with the current editor of *The Economist* when they were students together. And, to the extent that the Establishment includes writers or academics, it should be acknowledged that those educated at Oxford include the authors of this book, too.

'Wherever you turn your eye,' remarked Cecil Rhodes before endowing the university with his tainted fortune, 'an Oxford man is at the top of the tree.'[30] And they have often crawled into this university across the canopy of branches connecting it to England's elite private schools.

Eton College is the most notorious example, having educated more than a quarter of British prime ministers, almost all of whom went on to Oxford, by being based on not just exclusivity but the active exclusion of the rest of England. A glance at Eton's list of sports fixtures, for instance, shows it only plays against other elite private schools.[31] The whole purpose is to ensure Old Etonians get a better chance of achieving wealth and power than everyone else. When it opened a new £18 million debating chamber in 2015, one teacher said the absence of microphones was designed 'to encourage boys to project their voices naturally and to command a chamber, as if it might be the House of Commons'.[32]

In fairness, access to Oxford University has widened in recent years with the proportion of places offered to products of private schools falling to below a third, much to the chagrin of parents who now complain their offspring face 'reverse discrimination'.[33] The ever-rising numbers of foreign students also enables the university to claim significantly higher levels of ethnic diversity.[34] And, in 2019, almost exactly a century after Oxford first allowed women undergraduates, it achieved parity between male and female students. But the young people who go there continue to be overwhelmingly middle or upper class. Surveys show four-fifths come from well-off professional families, and Oxbridge recruited more students from just eight elite schools, including two in the state sector, than from almost 3,000 comprehensive schools in poorer areas put together.[35]

When they leave university, Oxford's graduates largely pursue similar careers, live in similar places and breed with each other in a practice known by sociologists as 'assortative mating', which seems to fulfil the worst fears of a self-replicating elite. The journalist Adrian Wooldridge describes the depressing experience of opening the annual newsletter from the Oxford college he attended to read its 'self-satisfied litany of "all Balliol" marriages and "all Balliol babies" '.[36]

Of course, not everyone who studies or studied at Oxford is cut from the same cloth. For every David Cameron, George Osborne or Boris Johnson who dressed up in royal-blue tailcoats with ivory lapels as part of the Bullingdon Club dining society, there was a nerdier Jeremy Hunt or Ed Davey. They were followed by Liz Truss campaigning for the Liberal Democrats and against the monarchy and Rishi Sunak running a university-wide society for playing the stock market. There were the Miliband brothers – pick David or Ed – or an Andrew Adonis, donning Marks & Spencer jumpers to think serious thoughts. There was the very religious Ruth Kelly, who briefly dated the elder Miliband, and James Purnell, who was at the same college as Yvette Cooper who got married to Ed Balls, a Norwich City fan at a different college. They boycotted the 'elitist' Oxford Union debating society at a time when Johnson and then Michael Gove were its presidents. But Balls, Cooper, Adonis, Kelly and Purnell still all ended up together in the same cabinet with the Miliband brothers.

If regarding them all as being what the Oxford-educated journalist Simon Kuper has termed the 'Oxocracy' does not get us very far, the public still tends to regard them as a single homogeneous elite.[37] When Ed Miliband was Labour leader, people told focus groups that they thought this second-generation immigrant and product of an inner London comprehensive had gone to a private school just like the Eton-educated David Cameron. Similar research today apparently shows that some people think the prefix 'Sir' before Keir Starmer's name means the originally working-class Labour leader has some sort of hereditary title.

Part of the problem, as shown in the previous chapter, is that alternative routes into power have silted up in the past half-century. Peter Mair, an Irish political scientist, spent much of his life detailing how politicians who emerged out of organisations like trade unions, co-operatives and churches in the earlier twentieth century were better able to reflect the values, language and cultural reference points of ordinary citizens than those of today. In more recent years this connective tissue between politicians and communities has weakened, leaving an increasingly professionalised Establishment divorced from the everyday experiences of other people. Democracy, wrote Mair, 'is being steadily stripped of its popular component', as politicians develop their own specialised, technical language and reference points and networks from places like Oxford where those high college walls exclude everyone else.[38]

The *Guardian* columnist Owen Jones went to Oxford University himself before writing a book called *The Establishment* in which he worried people might think he was part of it. Jones cited the example of Danny Blanchflower, a dissident economist on the Bank of England's Monetary Policy Committee, who felt frozen out by the other members because he was the only one of them who didn't go to Oxbridge. But Jones was also at pains to avoid claiming the problems of this country were the result of a 'conscious, organised conspiracy' by such elites. Instead, he argued that the 'shared economic interests and common mentalities' created a built-in bias across politics, the media, the Civil Service and finance against change and in favour of a small state where the wealthy elite was lightly taxed while the poor were exploited.[39]

This stridently left-wing version of the myth has always reverberated across Labour politics. And yet in more recent years the iconoclasts wanting to smash the Establishment have not been coming only from the left because much of the right has begun battering some of England's most venerable institutions, too.

The catalyst for opening up this new flank against England's Establishment was, as for so much else besides, Brexit. As previous chapters have outlined, the reasons why people voted to leave the EU combined elements of different myths, and much of it was motivated by a desire to restore some gilt to various lost 'golden ages' in England. But the Leave campaign also developed a raw, anti-Establishment populism as it found itself up against a succession of prime ministers – both past and present – the Bank of England, the City of London, Britain's biggest businesses, all but the frumpiest celebrities, most of Whitehall and the overwhelming majority of economists.

Even after their victory in the 2016 referendum, many Brexit supporters became convinced they were being frustrated by a 'liberal left Remainer elite'. When High Court judges ruled that Parliament needed to approve any agreement to leave Europe, the *Daily Mail* branded them 'Enemies of the People'. That same newspaper responded to House of Lords foot-dragging on Brexit with a perhaps unconscious tribute to Lenin as it ran the headline 'Crush the Saboteurs'.[40] These Brexit supporters often used similar language to the left as they blew more hot air into this already over-inflated myth of an Establishment that frustrates the will of the people. To some, it was called 'the Blob', to others, like the political scientist Matthew Goodwin, it was a 'new elite' in thrall to a so-called 'woke ideology'. Oxford's own scourge of it, the economist Paul Collier, has described how 'meeting at university and developing a new shared identity' enables a group of professionals to bind themselves together to advance their own careers or interests. In turn, he says, they elevate 'characteristics such as minority ethnicity and sexual orientation into group identities' and claim 'moral superiority' over other people as a result. Together, these right-wing anti-Establishmentarians painted a picture of a ruling group puffed up by 'ethical self-justification', waving trans-friendly progressive rainbow flags, and threatening to cart off any white, non-university-educated, middle-aged men into 'diversity training' from which they will never return.[41]

In universities, there is at least some evidence to suggest that they have a point, as the intensifying argument about the impact of Equality, Diversity and Inclusion initiatives in Higer Education shows.[42]

It is probably no coincidence, therefore, that a series of right-wing iconoclasts have emerged from Oxford University in a state of furious rebellion against this orthodoxy. They included the Conservative Party strategists Steve Hilton and Dominic Cummings, who studied there only a few years apart and shared a desire to smash things up. When he was working for the conventionally Establishment prime minister David Cameron, Hilton proposed slashing the size of the Civil Service by as much as 90 per cent because he believed it was part of a 'deep state' conspiracy against the people or, possibly, just him.[43] Cummings, the director of the Leave campaign in 2016 and, for a time, Boris Johnson's closest adviser, made his name attacking Whitehall, universities, law courts and any other institution that got in his way. He became famous when Benedict Cumberbatch played him in Channel 4's *Brexit: The Uncivil War*, written by James Graham. Graham himself has no doubt about Cummings' destructive energy. 'I don't know where it comes from, but he just has so much resentment,' says Graham. 'He loathes the Westminster system, he loathes SW1 culture and thinks everyone around him is an idiot. He wants to burn it all down and start again.'

This was the backdrop to 'culture wars', a phrase that according to one analysis appeared in newspaper articles on just twenty-one

occasions the year before the EU referendum but nearly 1,500 times in
2021.[44] Not all of this has been an organic growth. A special Downing
Street unit was reportedly set up dedicated to 'weaponising woke'
which stuffs the boards of public regulators with Tory supporters,
plants stories in the media and places traps into which metropolitan
liberals can be relied upon to fall. Before the 2024 general election,
endless and largely fruitless efforts were made to prove that the deter-
minedly moderate Keir Starmer was secretly one of those 'lefty lawyers'
that certain newspapers think threaten a true Englishmen hold dear.[45]

The words 'cancel culture' did not appear in newspapers until
2018 but featured in no fewer than 3,670 articles just three years
later. One conservative think tank published polling showing a
large minority of students were now consistently opposed to free
speech while another drew up rankings that suggested that the
University of Oxford had become one of the most censorious anywhere in England.[46] This came to a climax – of sorts – in 2023, when
the critic of trans rights, Kathleen Stock, was invited to the Oxford
Union but found herself confronted by protesters who glued themselves to the stage to stop her speaking anywhere near their seat of
learning.

Yet, for all the heat being generated, reports of a 'cancel culture
crisis' in the Establishment have been endlessly exaggerated. The
government's own statistics have shown less than 0.1 per cent of
external speakers in English universities being been 'disinvited'.[47] It is
easy to throw around such phrases without recognising that the idea of
reasoned debate has already been distorted by the avalanche of information and imagery found on an under-regulated internet. To many
young people, the meaning of 'freedom of speech' has become less
about defending the rights of past heroes like Aleksandr Solzhenitsyn
and Nelson Mandela than about allowing Holocaust denial and torture porn.

In any case, the experience of another core part of the Establishment,
the National Trust, shows how these arguments can cut both ways.
This is an institution that has always seemed to exist for the preservation of old ideas as much as for the protection of England's architectural
heritage. In 2020, however, it drew up a list of ninety-three properties with links to either colonialism or slavery which included Francis
Drake's Buckland Abbey and Chartwell where Winston Churchill

had later lived.[48] Conservative MPs and newspaper columnists keen to burnish their new anti-Establishment reputations were predictably livid. And many of those who had been so keen to defend freedom of speech on campuses reserved their strongest venom for the only academic involved in writing the report, Corinne Fowler, a professor of Postcolonial Literature at Leicester University.

We went to meet her by driving north from Oxford, through the Cotswold countryside where so many members of the political–media Establishment like to relax on weekends, to one of the properties named in the report. If the National Trust has changed, the stately home of Charlecote Park looks pretty much the same as it ever did on days like this, with antlered deer gracefully decorating the grounds while homogenously white families chose treats at the tearoom which offers a full range of scones ready to be smeared in cream and jam.

Fowler sits in the sunshine and lists the statistics of the media bombardment she faced in the months that followed publication of the report: 'A hundred and twenty articles. One right of reply. Zero fact checks.' It led to police telling her not to go into work after she received online threats which included pictures of a noose, or messages like 'put her on the bonfire' and 'slap her 'til her teeth clatter'. When she was giving a lecture someone 'hacked into my power point presentation shouting the n-word'. Fowler says John Hayes, a former Tory minister who chairs the Common Sense Group of MPs, wrote not only to the *Daily Telegraph* to complain the report was 'coloured by cultural Marxist dogma', but also to her funders asking them to withdraw money from her academic research. 'They wanted me to fit some caricature of a lefty academic. They said it was an "error-strewn report". But there wasn't one mistake in that report. Not one. I thought we just had to stand our ground.'[49]

On a tour of the house she points out a large portrait of its seventeenth-century owner. In the painting's background is an enslaved African boy with an iron collar around his neck holding the reins of his master's horse. Further on there is a jewel-encrusted sword that was probably seized as a trophy from Indian rebels after the siege of Lucknow. 'We don't talk about this history enough and I think it's patriotic to want us to come to terms with it,' she says quietly. 'An organisation like the National Trust can't just celebrate the owners of houses like this. It is starting to talk about the servants who worked downstairs or the people and places who made all this wealth in the first place. I think that makes things more interesting.'

The backlash against her eventually petered out. A complaint to the Charity Commission that the Trust was pursuing a 'politically woke agenda' was rejected. A revolt at the annual general meeting led by a group called Restore Trust was defeated. And, despite people like the former *Spectator* editor Charles Moore threatening to rip up their membership cards, the National Trust – already the biggest supporter-based organisation in the UK – had a record increase in new recruits as its ranks swelled upwards towards six million.[50] The diversity of those members – on every measure from age and ethnicity to class and region – also improved, while polling in 2023 showed almost three-quarters of the public saw the National Trust as a 'force for good'.[51]

Even so, when Labour's leader Keir Starmer compared Conservative anti-woke campaigners attacking the institutions 'they once regarded with respect' to 'McCarthyist' paranoia about Communist influence on US culture in the 1950s, he was still able to provoke another remarkable spasm from a former Tory Cabinet minister. In the Daily Telegraph, Robert Jenrick wrote – contrary to most historical accounts - that the Cold War warrior who spearheaded the 'Red Scare', Joseph McCarthy, had been correct all along and, if anything, had 'underestimated the degree to which America's civic bodies and government departments had been compromised by Leftist intelligentsia.'[52]

The culture war has, however, been viciously fought across a range of other fronts, too. It has ranged across arts bodies, through museums, publishing houses and libraries. But nowhere has the barrage been more intense than at the BBC. In 2019, the broadcaster's adaptation of Charles Dickens' *A Christmas Carol*, featuring a mixed-race family and a plot line in which Tiny Tim's mother is blackmailed for sex by Scrooge who uses the word 'fuck' instead of 'humbug', was met with derision. By the time someone at the BBC suggested dropping 'Rule, Britannia!' from the annual singalong of *Last Night at the Proms*, ministerial condemnations of 'woke zealots' had developed flecks of foam around the mouth. When the BBC stuck to its long-term policy of describing Hamas as militants rather than terrorists after the murderous attacks on Israeli civilians in 2023, its director-general was hauled in to explain himself to Conservative MPs.[53]

Once again, this has not been an attack from just one side. The left has never really stopped regarding the same BBC as an agent of the 'security state' and, during Jeremy Corbyn's time as Labour leader, relations with the corporation became so poisonous that the BBC's first female political editor, Laura Kuenssberg, needed a bodyguard to attend the party's annual conference in 2017.[54] Even the centre joined in. The cerebral peer Andrew Adonis tweeted dozens of complaints in a single week that the 'Brexit Broadcasting Corporation' had 'largely created' Nigel Farage, who he said seemed to have got a season ticket for flagship BBC programmes like *Question Time*.[55]

In earlier decades, when the myth of the Establishment seemed more secure, the BBC would have dismissed such a multi-pronged assault as proof it was impartially upsetting all sides. But this is an era in which most people have shifted away from broadcast schedules to digital sub-scription platforms like Netflix and Amazon Prime and confidence about the future has drained away. The appointment of two Conservative supporters in Richard Sharp and Tim Davie to be the BBC's chair and its director-general in recent years, as well as an active former Conservative Downing Street spin doctor in the form of Robbie Gibb to act as an 'arbiter' of impartiality, prompted some of its leading journalists like Emily Maitlis to leave because they believe any remaining edge has been blunted in news coverage. BBC's topical comedy output was drastically cut back with much of the satire which so annoys ministers disappearing from screens. Gary Lineker, a former captain of the England football team, was briefly suspended from presenting *Match of the Day* after a tweet in which he compared the government's language around stopping asylum seekers to that of Germany in the 1930s.

The BBC lurched from one scandal, about failing to report evi-dence of Jimmy Savile's predatory paedophilia, to another, about how it tricked Princess Diana into her famous *Panorama* interview which rocked the royal family nearly thirty years ago. All of which has made the BBC an obvious target when ministers felt they needed to chuck some of what was called 'red meat' to their backbenchers in 2022. They announced plans to abolish the licence fee, which would strip the broadcaster of the funding that has long given it a measure of pol-itical independence.[56]

For three decades or more Boris Johnson roiled around this muddy cultural battlefield where his almost limitless capacity to undermine

Establishment institutions was matched by a talent that allowed him to slide away from any criticism. He had been sacked from *The Times* for making up a quote from his godfather, recorded promising to help get another journalist beaten up and dismissed from the Tory front bench in 2004 for lying about an affair with a woman who had an abortion as a result. For a long time, even when he reached cabinet rank, Johnson appeared unwilling – or possibly unable – to state accurately how many children he had fathered.[57] Nonetheless, his rise continued all the way up to Downing Street from where he illegally suspended Parliament during the Brexit debates, sought to rip up sections of an international treaty he had just signed, lied – repeatedly – to just about everyone, before undermining the rule of law by breaking the Covid lockdown rules his own government had introduced.

The cornerstone of this country's muddled and uncodified constitution is the assumption that those in a position of power are 'good chaps'. It is why, for instance, the rules of the House of Commons mean they are all called 'Honourable Members' and they get thrown out of the chamber if they call each other liars. It mattered, therefore, that the most important person in British politics was in every sense of the word dishonourable as he continued routinely telling half-truths and untruths in Parliament, while ignoring regulators and his own ethics advisers. By the start of 2022, research showed that fewer than half of voters in England thought that democracy was working. And only a fifth of the English public trusted either MPs or the government to improve their lives – with a similar proportion saying they believed what they were told by the media.[58]

Some observers remain puzzled why Johnson would do such reckless damage to the Establishment when he was so obviously part of it. The left say that he is simply the product of an entitled elitism, nurtured in school at Eton and at university in Oxford, by which people like him believe they can always do whatever they want. A more interesting explanation comes from conservative-minded preservationists who believe he never valued anything except in so much as it had value to him. His Eton teacher Martin Hammond wrote a school report expressing concern that the seventeen-year-old Johnson believed he was 'free of the network of obligation which binds everyone else'. Max Hastings, his former editor at the *Daily Telegraph*, warned before Johnson entered Downing Street, 'he is unfit for national office because it seems he cares for no interest save his own fame and gratification'. There are many other people whose dealings with him before and since led them to reach similar conclusions.[59]

But Johnson's peculiar political genius was to simultaneously attack the Establishment while wrapping himself tightly in a mythical version of it. This meant too many people excused him as a fun-loving eccentric who seemed more authentic than other politicians. Rather than softening his vowels a little or pretending he was a football fan, he showed every sign of relishing privilege. Some of those who know Johnson best, however, suggest the whole elaborate performance was an effort to conceal his own insecurity. Born in New York, to parents whose ancestry can be traced through Turkey, Germany, France, Switzerland and Lithuania, he spent large chunks of his childhood in Brussels before being packed off to boarding school where he was initially bullied 'for being a foreigner'. At Eton, Johnson is said to have developed a protective shell of a bumbling and dishevelled English character, forming friendships with people like Princess Diana's brother while perfecting 'upmarket laddish banter' based on a prep school vocabulary mixed with bits of Latin.[60]

Although at Oxford he instantly became a university-wide celebrity, his later confession that he had been among the members of the Bullingdon Club who were notoriously arrested for smashing up a restaurant in 1987 is said to have been another lie. According to at least one former member, Johnson was not one of those caught by the police that night. His account, given to a newspaper two decades later, of spending a night in the cells may have been invented because he wanted to be more like the posh English boys he admired so much.[61]

Ultimately, Johnson's antics in this uncivil culture war served only as a gigantic technicoloured distraction from the very real challenges facing both Establishment institutions and the country itself.

LIFTED OFF ITS MOORINGS

The early decades of the twenty-first century have often been described as an era of 'polycrisis'. After terror attacks in the United States at the start of this century came the war in Iraq, then there was the financial crash which in turn was followed by austerity, the Covid pandemic, the Russian invasion of Ukraine and renewed crisis in the Middle East. Like the tremors before an earthquake, the period of calm between each of these crises is getting ominously shorter. They have all been global in scale and the response in England, as elsewhere, has been to turn inwards, away from the world, and backwards to the myths of the past. If many people have been raging against the myth of an unchanging Establishment, it may be because they feel so impotent in the face of such deep change elsewhere.

Seen this way, the key question actually facing England's creaking institutions at this time is not how they deal with the past but whether they can help us all face up to a very uncertain future. What can one medium-sized country do to limit climate change, rein in supranational technology corporations or regulate international finance? How does it solve poverty in Africa, protect the earth's oceans and stand up to China? The problem is this country is too large to hide away from the world, but also too small to change that world.

Once again, the experience of Oxford University over recent years sheds light on what is happening to the rest of the Establishment and England as a whole. The reason why this old academic institution attracts such global admiration is not only because of the mythical idea of Englishness it represents but also because the university scores highly on international measures of excellence. And these days such a reputation can be monetised.

First, there is a steadily increasing flow of international students who pay significantly higher fees and represent 45 per cent of the total number studying at Oxford if you include graduates. Next, there are endless summer conferences where business delegates pay a fortune to stay in all those new student accommodation blocks. Then, perhaps most of all, there are ever-larger donations from very wealthy individuals.[62]

For a decade or more, Wafic Saïd held the record for the biggest single gift. Initially, his money was controversial among those academics who felt uncomfortable with his arms-dealing origins. There was resistance to building the Business School too close to their famous colleges, which is why it ended up on the site of the old railway station. But the eventual success of Saïd's beneficence has encouraged more. In 2010 came a £75 million donation from Leonard Blavatnik, a man who grew up in Ukraine and made much of his fortune investing in aluminium and oil during the chaotic days of Russia's cowboy capitalism, before donating to both the Conservative Party and Donald Trump's inauguration committee, then getting knighted for his philanthropy. Critics have pointed out that this multi-billionaire was remarkably silent when Vladimir Putin invaded the country of his birth, but the new 'Blavatnik School of Government' that has sprung up on Oxford's Walton Street is intended to 'educate leaders' and has since largely been filled by fee-paying overseas graduate students.[63]

He was followed by David and Simon Reuben, brothers who went from scrap-metal dealing in London to making their own billions in Russia after the collapse of Communism. Their £80 million donation is paying for a new addition to Oxford University called 'Reuben College'.[64] That gift was topped by £100 million for a vast new 'Life and Mind Building' from the chemical company Ineos, created by the Monaco tax exile and leading supporter of Brexit Jim Radcliffe. He was delighted to spend 2.5 per cent of the estimated £4 billion Ineos had saved through its new tax status on such a worthy project.[65]

Then came Stephen Schwarzman, the chair and CEO of the American investment company Blackstone, as well as a close friend, sometime adviser and donor to Donald Trump. The £150 million given by Schwarzman will pay for yet another new building in Oxford to be called the 'Stephen A. Schwarzman Centre for Humanities'.[66] His record looked set to be broken, too, following a decision by Linacre College to accept £155 million from an Asian consortium apparently on condition it changed its name to 'Thao College' in honour of Nguyen Thi Phuong Thao, the president and chief executive of Vietnam's biggest budget airline.[67] Back came Schwarzman to up his gift to £175 million even as there were reports that the Vietnamese investment for Linacre had fallen through.

None of this is to deny that the university requires sustained investment, and its vice-chancellor has complained that the endowment pot is 'woefully small' compared to competitors in the US. But it's still worth asking what many these recent donors have in common other than being humongously rich. The answer is that, unlike earlier generations of benefactors, none of them had studied at the university or had any significant connection with it before. Their gifts, therefore, cannot have been motivated by happy memories of punting down the Cherwell or rowing up the Isis. One explanation is that they all wanted to improve an already excellent university for entirely philantropic motivations. A more cynical view is they were seeking to polish – or protect – their reputations by associating themselves with a prestigious international brand. Those who argued against removing the Rhodes statue on the grounds that it is part of a sacrosanct heritage have generally been very quiet about all the modern buildings, named after these billionaire donors, transforming Oxford's architecture.

The globalisation of Oxford's brand may also be beginning to change the nature of the place. Competition to remain at the top of international rankings, the measures of which often include the number of citations each university researcher gets or the amount of grant income they can raise, can reduce academia to the kind of stifling blandness more often associated with algorithmic news aggregators or irradiated food. One Fellow of All Souls College, for instance, reminisces about how 'there was a certain sort of creativity and diversity around which, provided you were kept out of the way of more impressionable students, was probably a good thing'. He adds: 'Now you have to conform to some bureaucratic ideal of behaviour and meet performance indicators which don't indicate to me anyone is adding very much to the sum of human knowledge.'

At the same time some have articulated concern that the dependence on foreign income – especially from the estimated 140,000 Chinese students at UK universities in 2022 – could choke off criticism of troubling regimes overseas. On this question, the University of Oxford has rightly been more robust. It has refused a demand from the Chinese Embassy that its chancellor, Lord Patten, cancel a visit to Hong Kong where he had been Britain's last governor. The university has also told students from China they are permitted to submit some essays anonymously and has banned anyone filming them in seminar discussions so that they are protected against possible retribution when they return home. But other academic institutions have not necessarily got pockets deep enough to fund such principles. And controversy rages nonetheless. In 2021, Oxford renamed one of its physics professorships after the Chinese software firm Tencent, which has links to the Communist government and works with that country's security agencies on artificial intelligence. The price that time was an endowment worth the comparatively paltry sum of £700,000.[68]

When this university's supposedly core functions of research and teaching undergraduates from the UK have to be subsidised by donor income, foreign students and staging business conferences, there is a danger this tide of cash lifts Oxford even further off the moorings that once connected it to the country and the very qualities that made it attractive in the first place.

And universities are far from being the only English institutions that risk a passionless embrace with foreign money. The financial crisis of 2008 revealed to everyone just how much more the big financial institutions of England cared about global transactions than they did about investing in the mundane, day-to-day industry of the country. In the battles being fought over the future of the BBC, those who want the licence fee scrapped sometimes suggest the broadcaster should compete directly with the likes of Netflix for subscriptions in the worldwide entertainment market. But trying to do so would wreak huge damage on the cultural sector of the economy by reducing the proportion of 'British content' the BBC commissions. And the alternative option, of catering to niche markets that are willing to pay, would ensure that the cultural elitist caricature of the BBC propagated by its fiercest critics would at last become real.

Becoming too cosmopolitan or feeding off global wealth has caused trouble for the monarchy, too. In the final year of Queen Elizabeth II's reign, her grandson was attempting to live away from the media spotlight in Los Angeles where Netflix has made a fortune from its semi-fictional *The Crown*. It was there that Prince Harry and his wife Meghan, an African American actor who once starred in the legal drama *Suits*, launched their own mini-culture war by recording an interview with Oprah Winfrey and writing a book to accuse the royal family of institutional racism.[69]

At the same time in New York, Prince Andrew was hotly denying claims from an alleged victim of sex trafficking, Virginia Giuffre. She said the Duke had sexually assaulted her, first in London, then at a Manhattan mansion and on a private Caribbean island owned by the disgraced American financier Jeffrey Epstein. After much embarrassment, the Queen is said to have subsidised an out-of-court settlement in which Andrew admitted no liability but paid Giuffre millions of dollars shortly before the case was due to go to jury trial.[70] A few days later, back in England, it emerged that the Prince's Foundation, a charity set up by Charles, the then heir to the throne, was under police investigation for allegedly offering honours in return for donations from a Saudi Arabian businessman. The case was later dropped without any charges after the prince became king.[71]

In the same way that England's universities, banks, culture, football clubs and royal family are coveted by the global rich, so too are its judiciary and courts. Wealthy litigants flock to London from around the world with high-profile cases, such as that between the exiled Boris Berezovsky and Roman Abramovich, only the tip of the iceberg of a legal services export market worth upwards of £7 billion. In 2020, half of litigants in commercial cases were from outside the UK, with Russia and Kazakhstan providing more than anywhere else.[72] Some of those litigious oligarchs and tycoons were already based in London because it had become their 'laundromat' to clean up hundreds of billions of pounds of dirty cash every year. Others used England's courts to confer on their foreign dealings a veneer of respectability because, for decades, almost anyone bringing big money into this country has known they will be welcomed here with no questions asked. A few of them use libel actions in English courts to deploy a form of what is known as 'lawfare' or a 'Slapp' – Strategic Litigation Against Public Participation – to silence journalists working either in England or abroad. A Foreign Policy Centre survey of investigative journalists around the world has shown that London is where they receive the bulk of their legal threats from, in part because libel laws in England put the burden of proof on the defendant rather than the plaintiff and are tilted towards protecting rich VIPs because costs rapidly escalate, and you don't even have to be resident in England to bring a case.[73]

There is not much point in having a judicial system globally recognised for its fairness if access to it effectively depends on the size of your bank balance. The Law Society has warned justice now exists 'only for the wealthy' because a £1 billion cut in the budget for legal aid since 2010, combined with the closure of half the courts in the country and an acute shortage of staff, means that even if someone can initially afford a lawyer their cases take so long to reach trial or become so expensive that they often give up.[74] The backlog has got so bad in criminal cases that in 2021 there were more than 1,500 people who have been held on remand in jail without a trial for more than a year, a contravention of the kind of rights that some still like to think were guaranteed for the 'freeborn' English in Magna Carta.[75]

The countervailing forces described in this chapter – iconoclasts and preservationists from both the left and the right, national populists and desiccating globalisation – have thrown up so much dust there is a danger of missing the bigger point. An Establishment celebrated for an ability to hold different people together no longer appears to be doing so very successfully or is often not working for ordinary citizens at all.

And if the institutions that comprise it are to withstand the next set of approaching storms, they cannot afford to drift off into a global stratosphere reserved only for a few while ignoring the towering challenges that exist beyond its walls.

Oxford University, for instance, could do a lot worse than start engaging with the people on its own doorstep, for whom this city is not somewhere just to be passed through for a few years on the way to bigger things, but the place in which they live. Too often, the colleges have kept the rest of Oxford at arm's length, intervening only to keep any trace of industrial development well away from its spires. They have been reluctant to sell even a portion of the vast tracts of land they own for the affordable homes desperately needed in a city where average house prices are sixteen times more than local wages, a ratio larger even than London. Locals wanting to look inside one of the historic buildings that dominate space in the heart of their city would usually be asked to pay an entrance fee.[76] When the commission established by Oriel College into the future of its Rhodes statue surveyed the city schoolchildren to find out what they thought, half of them said they had never set foot inside any of the university's colleges.[77]

Entitled students have, of course, been causing resentment among Oxford's other inhabitants for almost eight centuries. The St Scholastica Day Riot in 1355 was sparked by some of them boorishly complaining about the quality of wine at Swindlestock Tavern and then throwing a pot of it in the face of the innkeeper. That resulted in a three-day orgy of death and destruction for which Oxford's citizenry was punished with an annual act of ritual humiliation in which dozens of them had to walk through the streets barefoot before swearing an oath promising to 'observe the university's privileges'. This tradition only came to an end in 1857 when the city's mayor, a plain-speaking Baptist baker called Isaac Grubb, said he had 'nothing for which to thank any member' of the university and refused point-blank to take part.[78]

In the years since, the city of Oxford has often seen more dramatic change than the university. William Morris's car works in Cowley brought generations of migrants from all over the world into a city where almost a quarter of the population is now from an ethnic minority. Poorer families priced out of the city centre moved to housing estates including one in Cutteslowe that once had a nine-foot wall topped with spikes across the middle of a road to separate private from council homes.[79] Next to the car works is Blackbird Leys, a housing estate which became infamous in the 1990s for its gangs of joyriders who would steal cars to race them around the streets.

Over the centuries there have been spasmodic attempts to close this gap between 'town and gown'. One was led by the Victorian reformer and Oxford's Professor of Fine Art, John Ruskin, who featured in fictional form discussing buggery in Stoppard's play; this scheme made real-life students, including a young Oscar Wilde, dig drainage ditches for poor local villagers. Most of their work was apparently so incompetent it never did anyone much good.[80] But for a long time there was an echo of that well-meant idealism in the form of the college named after Ruskin which was set up to provide a step-ladder for people who did not have the right qualifications for higher education.

In more recent years Ruskin College, perhaps in a sign of the priority given to such efforts, has had funding problems that have led it to sever links with the university and move out of the city's centre. But it has left behind a legacy in people like Josie Calvert, who came from what she describes as a pretty poor single-parent family living in a part of Oxford where some of the richest students would rent accommodation. She gave up on school before her GCSEs to work in a local burger bar and then have a baby at the age of sixteen. 'Students in those days,' she says, 'might as well have been aliens to me. They were just not part of the world I was in.'

When she got back into education through Ruskin, some of that separation continued to exist. Calvert would go to university economics lectures still in her work clothes but be the only one stopped on her way in and asked to show her pass. 'People there didn't think someone who looked like me could be a student,' she says. 'But

I decided not to care or be intimidated. And when I got to know some of them, I found out that some of them were really decent people who never pretended to be better than me – and sometimes worried they might be worse.' She later earned a first-class degree at Sussex and went on to a masters. In the years that followed, Calvert worked with international relief agencies and helped people across the world including in Zimbabwe – the very same country where Cecil Rhodes had wreaked such mayhem a century before.

So, what did she think about the Rhodes Must Fall protests on her city's High Street? 'I heard about them vaguely and, yeah, they should have taken that statue down,' she says. 'But I didn't get involved. There's so much else wrong with the times we live in now, including the mess people like Rhodes created for Africa today, I reckoned there might be more important fights to have. Especially for people like me.'

OXFORD, UNITED?

Oxford is covered in a cold mist on the morning we arrive in search of one last way of deflating England's myths. Outside the museum, building works are hidden behind hoardings showing Photoshopped inclusivity, accessibility and world-class everything. Inside, the most famous exhibit – shrunken human heads with lips sewn up and hair cascading – has been removed from public view as part of the museum's 'decolonisation plan'.

Later, walking up the High Street, we take a sharp right turn, round the back of the college where David Cameron studied politics and the front of one where Rishi Sunak did the same, then emerge on to Broad Street. This is where the college that educated Boris Johnson has, we are told, taken down its portrait of one old prime minister so it can avoid having to put one up of him, too.

We go past a giant Victorian spire which rises up to remind anyone interested that this was where a Church of England archbishop was burned at the stake four and a half centuries ago for beliefs these days shared by barely one in eight of England's people. Then on to Jericho, once an industrial working-class district, but where this old university has been expanding in this new global era. Here can be found the sparkling new Blavatnik School of Government, which is largely made of glass to symbolise 'transparency'. But the windows are tinted to stop anyone looking in, and, when we try, the men on the door waste no time in telling us, 'You're not coming in.'

Nearby, a 'social action fair' is taking place in a small chapel, arranged by an organisation called the Oxford Hub that was set up to coordinate charities and campaigns. Sitting behind their desks on one side of the room is a long line of representatives of the Students' Union with signs saying they are campaigning for feminist justice and disability rights, against homophobia and transphobia, or supporting international students. 'No,' says one of them, 'we don't have much to do with the city, we're here for students.' Another points out that 'we go on protests if local people ask us to', but a student who is fighting period poverty on behalf of women who cannot afford menstrual products, acknowledges she can't do much to help someone living out on the estates. 'My remit is really working in the colleges and university,' she says apologetically.

None of this would be a surprise to Martha Crawford, who grew up in Oxford and, unlike most of the people who live there, had a direct connection with the university because her mother was the day-to-day manager, or 'domestic bursar', at one of the colleges. Along with her three siblings, she worked there as a waitress in the dining hall and then as one of its 'scouts', the old-fashioned system of doing housekeeping for students or, as she puts it, 'cleaning some other teenager's bedroom'.

When she returned to the city as a community organiser, she struggled to build an alliance between the university and the townsfolk. 'One college did outreach to the Blackbird Leys estate and told them why they should care about things like Brexit,' she says. 'But they did not start with what people there wanted to talk about. They were then surprised when no one turned up.' She says the university does not engage well with issues that appear only local in scale, while many young people in the city are more concerned about 'the racism they experience every day' than about fighting over an old monument like the one outside Oriel College. 'No one ever mentioned the Rhodes statue to me without being prompted,' says Crawford. 'Maybe that's because it's outside a building from which they're generally excluded and certainly isn't part of their life.'

There are other identities to this city which go beyond the university and a car factory. It has a hugely successful music scene that has produced bands such as Radiohead, Supergrass, Foals, Ride and Glass Animals. For most, however, it is once again probably expressed through a football club.

Oxford United, which briefly hit the heights of the old First Division in the 1980s, has tried to foster a deeper connection with the famous university. The annual team picture is now taken beside one of those famous old buildings, while recent owners from Thailand and Indonesia have put a silhouette of the university's skyline on to kit worn by players in the hope that it might improve Far Eastern sales. But there is still a sense that any effort to cash in on a global brand in the same way the university itself has done will encounter sniffy disapproval. And, despite being the biggest landowners in the city, the colleges have never tried to help the club find a site for a new stadium to replace the current three-sided breeze-block construction next to a sewage works.

Only the harshest critic would ignore the enormous contribution Oxford University makes to a city where it employs an estimated 17,000 people and injects £750 million into the local economy each year. Even more wrong-headed would be to dismiss what it does for the national economy and the world. The university's academic research is said to have won more than seventy Nobel prizes, adding whole new layers to human understanding of everything from disease and hunger to literature and love.[81]

But, as one of its most senior leaders later tells us over lunch, 'this is a place that seems to have lost its confidence'. He describes how the failure of successive Oxford-educated politicians had shrouded the university in 'self-doubt' even as the resulting cultural conflicts had portrayed all those dreaming spires as no more than 'ivory towers'.

A few days earlier he was one of those who gathered with the great and the good to watch Chris Patten, the chancellor of Oxford University, speak in the seventeenth-century splendour of the Sheldonian Theatre. Baron Patten of Barnes to give him his full title - a member of the Most Noble Order of the Garter, a Companion of Honour, and a Privy Counsellor – ticks almost every Establishment box. He has been a cabinet minister, the last British governor of Hong Kong and a European commissioner. He chaired both the BBC and the Conservative Party when both were more certain of their place in the national story than they are now.

His speech, delivered a year before he announced his retirement in 2024, lamented everything from Brexit and political interference with 'un-corrupt' elite institutions and the 'de-platforming' shadow hanging over the cherished principle of free speech. Insisting the university was still very much a 'going concern' despite facing some 'headwinds', the chancellor wheeled out a quotation from *The Leopard* – a novel about a disintegrating kingdom – that has become the well-worn maxim of England's Establishment over the years: 'Things have to change in order to remain the same.'[82]

The occasion was the inauguration of Irene Tracey as Oxford's 273rd vice-chancellor, effectively the chief executive of the university. She is unusual in being only the second woman to hold the post and the first to have gone to a local comprehensive school near the city. And, when she rose to speak, Tracey politely rebutted Patten by giving what she called an 'update' on his quote from *The Leopard*. The task was 'more subtle' than changing merely to stay the same, she said. 'One evolves to be competitive for current circumstances. Evolving to remain the same might not cut it in today's climes.'

Tracey described how the messily devolved structure of the university had made it a 'very free place' for her to work without ever feeling too 'shackled by tradition'. She outlined her determination to extend the reach of the university's teaching, knowledge and discoveries with a huge innovation campus being built on the outskirts of the city that is sponsored by the insurance giant Legal & General. But she also emphasised the university must be a part of a community which cannot 'abstract itself from geography entirely, as some multi-national corporations have done'. Tracey, who had grown up in Oxford as 'town' rather than 'gown', added she was 'acutely conscious of the tensions' that exist with the rest of the city over housing shortages and much more besides.[83]

Whether or not such a prescription for deepening local, as well as global, engagement is enough to 'cut it in today's climes' and restore shaken confidence remains to be seen. But Tracey who, appropriately enough, is a professor in Anaesthetic Neuroscience – pain relief – has sought to salve some of the more recent wounds by condemning abuse of transgender students while also defending free speech within the 'bounds of civility'. In one interview she has said: 'We're only going to progress our thinking around issues, evolve what it is that we think is acceptable or not, or change people's minds if we discuss and debate. If we don't have that, we actually end up in a very, very dark place.'[84]

It can be argued that the Establishment has succeeded in restoring a measure of stability to chaos. A humiliated Jeremy Corbyn quit the Labour leadership in 2020 with his supporters still railing against a deep-state conspiracy against him. Johnson was ousted from Downing Street two years later in what some of his die-hard fans described as the 'Revenge of the Blob'. His preferred successor, Liz Truss, was forced to resign after just forty-four days after losing the confidence of the markets, or what she later called 'a very powerful economic establishment'.[85]

For a period afterwards, with Keir Starmer as Labour leader and Rishi Sunak as prime minister, it appeared there might even be a reasoned debate about the country's future. Unusually, both had successful careers outside Parliament, one as a barrister, the other as a banker. Starmer talked of restoring certainty for investors and relations with Europe, while Sunak – initially at least – seemed more sensible than either of his immediate predecessors[86]

But, at a time when everything from the economy and technology to the climate itself is being transformed at speed, this was always only going to be a temporary lull in hostilities. At the 2024 General Election, though, Sunak fumbled the loading mechanisms but still tried to fire some of those culture war artillery shells at Labour. And less than a month after Starmer became prime minister that summer, he had his mettle tested by far right riots in many towns and cities where angry white men had been whipped up into a racist fury by false information on social media. Later, as the new government stumbled over routine appointments and declarations of donations, even mainstream parts of the media appeared to be in a hurry to draw false equivalence with Boris Johnson's Downing Street - or stampede towards a conclusion that all politicians are as bad as each other and that government can never be a force for good. Such attitudes are, as we've seen, fertile ground for polarising populism of both the left and the right. It remains to be seen whether Starmer's pragmatic style of radicalism that seeks to adapt institutions to the challenges of this time will prevail, but the early signs were not encouraging.[87]

At this point, it is worth seeking the views of three people, though they would not always see it like this themselves, are all part of the

Establishment and know each other through the myriad connections that mark them out as part of it. Each of them is also aware that something is up. The first is the former Conservative politician Michael Gove who re-emerged after holding cabinet rank for a dozen years to be editor of the ultra-establishment Spectator magazine. We last met him in Chapter 6, trying to make sense of a levelling-up agenda for the northern working class, having felt looked down upon by the likes of David Cameron and most famously declaring during the Brexit campaign that the 'people of this country have had enough of experts'. When we went to see him, however, Gove mentions early on 'a desire for greater civility in politics'. Describing himself as 'both an economic migrant and an asylum seeker' from Scotland, he emphasised that England has a relatively 'gentle' or 'self-effacing' nationalism. 'I've generally thought of Englishness as an inclusive and polite form of national identity,' said Gove. For instance, he describes the BBC as 'an amazing national and international asset', and wonders aloud whether the current controversies are just another in a long series of 'bumps in the road'. There is always the sense with Gove that he has to fight a conflict in himself when strapping on his culture warrior armour. For example, a flash briefly appears in his eyes as he describes how the BBC's latest director-general used to share a flat with one of his junior ministers when they were both young Tory activists. Such appointments are important, he says, because 'just as Camberley Heath Golf Club will have a slightly higher proportion of Conservative voters in it, so in the BBC the number of people who think of themselves as Conservatives is probably in a minority'. But then Gove battens down his hatches and is serious again as he states firmly that 'the BBC's reputation for impartiality is important... and needs to be – what's the word?' Nurtured? 'Yes!'

The second is Tristram Hunt, an historian of the British Empire and a former Labour MP from one of those so-called Red Wall constituencies, who went on to become as the director of the Victoria & Albert Museum. He, too, had a walk-on part in the last chapter on Blackpool as he tried to develop its Showtown exhibition. Hunt says the V&A is determined to curate 'different ideas of who we are' from a vast collection of art and design, some of which was stolen from colonies while other parts represent the craft of English hands. 'People on both sides want to politicise this with the right branding us a liberal metropolitan conspiracy and the left saying we're a patriarchal,

Western privileged one. We have fought really hard to keep this civic space open to everyone.'

Museums like his have also come under relentless pressure either to repatriate artefacts taken from other countries or to refuse point-blank. His own view is that decisions should be taken on a case-by-case basis, understanding where each object has most cultural significance, adding: 'A lot of these artefacts help us realise our real place in, and responsibility to, the world so there is a good case for them staying here.' He takes us to see Tipu's tiger, an eighteenth-century mechanical toy created for the Muslim ruler of Mysore, which shows a red-coated British officer being eaten alive while his arm flaps away and a wailing sound is emitted. Hunt acknowledges this artefact was looted when Tipu Sultan's palace was ransacked, but thinks it should remain at his museum, as it tells an important story of India-British relations which also connects to modern audiences. 'After all, it's an English soldier getting eaten,' he adds.

The capacity of relics from the past to reignite England's myth was illustrated further by a row in 2023 over the 'Elgin Marbles', or 'Parthenon Sculptures', as they are known in Greece where they prefer to locate them in the temple where they stood for 2,300 years before being shipped off to England by the 7th Earl of Elgin at the start of the nineteenth century. Rishi Sunak, presumably in an effort to appease nationalist sentiments in the Conservative Party, refused to meet the Greek Prime Minister when he visited London because he objected to public calls to let the country where the sculptures were made 'borrow' them from the British Museum.

Finally, we went to see James Purnell, who has had as good a view as anyone of the recent battles fought over Establishment institutions. He studied at Oxford, worked for Tony Blair, became a Labour MP and the culture secretary in the cabinet, before quitting politics and moving to a senior post in the BBC and later running the University of the Arts London. As we speak, Purnell runs the University of the Arts London. 'One of the precious things with both universities and the BBC is they are places where everybody meets,' he says. 'Our rapidly changing society makes it more difficult to remain universal institutions which serve everyone – and I suppose that's what we're all grappling with right now – but it's hard to see how you find a solution without the universities or the BBC.' He suggests institutions like these should 'recommit to their original purpose in quite a conservative way and then be quite radical in how they deliver it … But they need to be a place where everybody gets the chance to express their opinion – and everybody gets challenged too.' This is important because the myth of the Establishment's permanence can make its proponents forget that what is left of its open spaces can only thrive if there is real debate and challenge, openness and argument.

The necessity of this was exemplified in the acclaimed *Small Axe* TV drama series in 2020 which chronicled England's Black communities' struggles and triumphs in the face of horrific racism in the late twentieth century. The director, Steve McQueen, was determined it would be shown on the BBC because this was not a niche drama about African-Caribbean culture but 'the untold stories of our nation'. He said: 'We changed it. Everything. What you wear. Everything. Mods and Rockers. Everything. These are British stories. Great British stories, that have been swept under the carpet … That's why I wanted it on the BBC … I wanted my mum to see it. I wanted these stories to go through the bloodstream of the country.'

This does not mean, however, that McQueen thinks the BBC is anything like as diverse or responsive as it should be. 'You see a film crew in London and they're predominantly white,' he said. 'Look around London and [the people] aren't.' He adds that only 'when we get crappy Black films' will he know progress has been made. Yet it is still important McQueen sees the BBC as an organisation that can prevent a confused and divided country coming apart at the seams. In contrast both to those iconoclasts who want to smash the system and to the preservationists who want to keep everything the same for ever, McQueen says, 'I don't want to break anything.' He believes that the best motto for reformers should be 'Handle things with care and make change possible.'[88]

Too often, when an institution comes under attack, there is a temptation to revert to a defence of the status quo. It is as ridiculous to pretend the BBC is incapable of bias or the Civil Service of obstruction as to hold fast to a notion of the infallibility of kings or believe that private schools are engines of mobility.

At the same time those advocating change are too often likely to fixate on a single big idea they believe will solve every problem, just like Brexit was supposed to do. Lots of fully paid-up members of the Establishment believe wholesale constitutional reform would revive democracy. Some, like the former Labour cabinet minister John Denham, have suggested dividing England up into a series of regions governed by their own elected assemblies, or that creating an English Parliament is the logical consequence of devolving so much power to other parts of the UK. Still more, especially on the centre-left, see proportional representation as a panacea.[89]

But breaking up England to save the Union with Scotland or giving it a new Parliament is more likely to inflame, rather than calm, nationalist urges across the UK. Although some form of voting reform may well be overdue, even talking about it – the 'D'Hondt formula', anyone? – usually triggers a stampede to the exit by much of the public. Constitutional reformers might be better off following the lead of their nineteenth- and twentieth-century predecessors who focused on widening participation in the democracy, possibly by widening the franchise to sixteen-year-olds or making it compulsory to vote as an act of citizenship, like filling in a census form or paying tax.

None of these ideas on their own, however, are going to tackle a more fundamental democratic blight. Access to England's Establishment – whether that is in universities like Oxford, the top jobs at the BBC or those in government – still seems confined to a narrow, self-replicating elite. There are sporadic efforts going on to widen the gateway. The London rapper AJ Tracey, for instance, has set up a fund to support Black students at Oxford because 'that kind of upper echelon is blocked for them'. He says: 'I don't want to be on the outside, trying to tell people what to do with their Establishment. I need to be inside trying to make a difference.' The Grime artist Stormzy has launched a similar scheme at Cambridge.[90]

But a more optimistic story comes from a young campaigner who came to regard the Establishment, and the people within it, more as an opportunity than as a barrier to be overcome.

Chrisann Jarrett arrived in this country with her parents as a child from Jamaica, went to school in the London borough of Hackney and was excited when she earned a place to study law at the LSE. Only then did she discover that she had neither citizenship nor a permanent resident visa. It meant she would have to pay tens of thousands of pounds in extra fees without being eligible for student loans. For a time, it looked like she wasn't going to university at all. 'I'd never felt hopeless before,' she says, 'it was a new kind of feeling.'

Initially she sought help from migrant and refugee groups who treated her as a new immigrant seeking a right to stay in a foreign country. 'That didn't seem right – I had been here since I was eight,' she says. Instead of railing against the unfairness of the system, however, she drew strength from her deep sense of belonging. Jarrett found dozens of other young people in her position and together they used national institutions – universities, the BBC, newspapers, Parliament and the courts – to make their case. She deployed stereotypically English symbols when lobbying the government such as asking the then Conservative immigration minister Caroline Nokes to a meeting by sending her an invitation printed on a gigantic cutout image of a cup of tea. When Nokes eventually agreed, the campaigners turned up with a home-made lemon drizzle cake like those usually seen at village fêtes.

'The system can be horrible,' says Jarrett, 'but you can't engage with it unless you know the terms of their engagement. We weren't going out and protesting. We were saying, "Meet with me one-to-one. Let me tell you why this is wrong and let's work out how we can work together."' She and her fellow campaigners ended up being supported by a cross-party group of MPs, including Nokes, as they fought their case all the way through the arteries of the legal system into the heart of the Establishment at the Supreme Court – and won.

Since then, Jarrett has gone on to be awarded an MBE and create an organisation pointedly called 'We Belong' that not only campaigns against exclusion of people but also finds connections between them. 'I've experienced the brilliance of this country,' she says. 'Every time I'd actually meet with someone, they understood what I was asking for and why this was justice. I experienced kindness from them. What makes this country great is the people.'

The way forward should be neither to replace what exists with the clean, straight lines favoured by global brands and authoritarian regimes, nor to make the most minimal adjustments needed for everything to stay the same. This is surely a time when England needs more spaces for debating different ideas, resolving disputes and living with disagreement, not fewer.

The idea of a privileged elite, out of touch and far removed from the experience of most people, is part of the myth that people tell about the Establishment – and institutions like Oxford University sometimes tell about themselves – as it wobbles in the face of scorn and the prospect of irrelevance.

But there is another sliver of hope to be found in perhaps the most famous story to have come out of Oxford in recent years. Within two weeks of the Covid virus beginning to make its deadly way around the world in 2020, Professor Sarah Gilbert and a team of scientists at Oxford University's Jenner Institute initiated development of a vaccine.

In record time, without any corners being unduly cut, a manufacturing deal was done with AstraZeneca, clinical trials were completed and regulatory approval granted. Since then, billions of doses of the Oxford-AstraZeneca vaccine have been produced worldwide. It led to Gilbert getting a standing ovation when she turned up at Wimbledon in 2023, being awarded scientific medals and receiving a damehood from Princess Anne, as well as having a tribute Barbie doll modelled on her red hair and square-rimmed glasses that now sits on her desk.

But this success was often in spite, rather than because, of the grandiose mythology of Oxford. When we talk to Gilbert, it is clear from the outset she does not see herself as part of anyone's Establishment. Her experience of the university is a long way from Hogwarts dining halls, punts and mortar boards. 'I don't have much to do with dining on the "high table" at the colleges and such things,' she tells us. A state-educated daughter of a teacher and a shoemaking firm's manager in Kettering, she did her first degree at the University of East Anglia, her PhD at Hull, and spent a year working at a brewing research centre before getting an academic job at Oxford.

The Oxford-AstraZeneca vaccine was developed in a suburb of the city, up a hill and far from any old colleges. Gilbert's laboratories are in the kind of modern office building that is surrounded by car parks, trees still attached with bits of plastic to stakes and the kind of landscaping where it looks like the bulldozers have only just left. The guided-tour buses for tourists do not come near. 'We're not in the centre of Oxford,' says Gilbert firmly, 'we're a research site on a modern campus in Headington.'

Bringing knowledge together with enquiring minds in a place where they can exchange ideas and find solutions is what universities are meant to do. But, at least in Gilbert's experience, there wasn't anything particularly magical about this one that might explain its elevated position in the English Establishment. 'Look, there are lots of specialities in Oxford. I can't speak for all of them and I know lots of politicians were educated here, but the reason I stayed is simply because we have got our facilities onsite together with a lot of people together working collaboratively on vaccine research,' she says. 'It was the best place in the country to do this only because over the last twenty-five years we've built all that up. None of it necessarily needed to happen at Oxford.'

Although Gilbert's work has had extraordinary impact, she emphasises how mundane much of her life has been. 'We're not some other part of society, we're ordinary people,' she says. 'We're scientists that have expertise in certain areas. We don't live a life that is different to other people in this country.' In *Vaxxers*, a book she co-wrote with her colleague Catherine Green, Gilbert described simultaneously battling a wasp infestation in her house, worrying about how to get her mother-in-law into the car for Christmas and remembering to buy food for dinner – even as newspaper paparazzi were appearing outside her offices and politicians queued up to be photographed with her.[91]

Gilbert talks about the pandemic as a shared experience. 'People stuck to the rules, helped their neighbours with their shopping, stayed at home.' So, what did she think about Downing Street having all those parties? Gilbert pauses, before picking her words very carefully: 'We didn't do that. We didn't have parties. We were working hard, too. But it was possible to do so within the rules. We didn't see any reason to break them.' She was similarly unimpressed by any effort to co-opt her project into some form of vaccine nationalism.[92] 'We didn't get caught up with that,' she tells us. 'We weren't competing or using soundbites. For the most part people recognised the need to work together. We never said we needed to be the first or the best. What we said is that the world is going to need a lot of vaccines and we didn't know which would work best.'

Perhaps attaching the name 'Oxford' to this vaccine spread some Establishment gilt over it. But many people in this country felt affinity with, and pride about, the 'Oxford jab' for different reasons. If it didn't quite match the efficacy rates of more expensive foreign vaccines provided by the likes of Pfizer or Moderna, this one was good enough. There was no need for the vaccine to be kept frozen at some ridiculously low temperature so it was seen as the 'workhorse' in a global effort and could more easily be shipped around the world or manufactured in other countries. And nor was it making some giant pharmaceutical firm even richer because AstraZeneca had been persuaded to forgo any profits for the duration of the pandemic.

This was a time when the fragility of the once seemingly immovable institutions of government in the face of an iconoclastic philosophy of moving fast and smashing things was being laid. Evidence to the public inquiry into their handling of Covid has shown that Dominic Cummings who was briefly the most powerful adviser in the land, dismissed the Cabinet as "largely irrelevant" and 'not a place for serious discussion". The Cabinet Office, which is supposed run government machinery was variously described as "a bomb site" and "a dumpster fire", while a myriad of health bodies, local or devolved government was portrayed merely as obstacles to his will. At the same time, Whitehall's two most senior civil servants were exchanging text messages describing those running Downing Street as 'poisonous', 'mad' and unfit for office. 'I've never seen a bunch of people less well-equipped to run a country," Simon Case, then head official in the Cabinet Office, wrote in July 2020 to Mark Sedwill, the cabinet secretary.

In similar fashion, when the Covid vaccine programme was rolled out across England, it was neither outsourced to the private sector nor promoted as some sort of futuristic technology. Instead, it was provided through familiarly reassuring, widely trusted and – most importantly – already existing institutions. The jabs were delivered in GP surgeries, community centres or even at football grounds, including that of Oxford United where people arriving were greeted by members of the Royal Voluntary Service. Most seemed content to wait their turn and no one – not even with the most expensive private doctor – could jump the queue or purchase preferential access.

It is that sense of shared experience and common interests which is the source of the stability of this country's democracy more than the unseen hand of a shadowy elite. The NHS itself is an example of a national institution held in the deepest affection by the public because it is recognisably fair. There are lots of problems with the healthcare system in this country but, with the exception perhaps of a certain kind of resistance to reform, these are not the same as those that afflict the Establishment.

Gilbert says the biggest one she has faced has often been over funding, with much of her time over the past twenty-five years devoted to filling in forms for grants and, as she puts it, 'raising the money for my own salary'. Although Oxford University has combined assets estimated at upwards of £9 billion, it has not trickled down into some crucial areas of research. Until Covid came along, a laboratory at the wrong end of town was not a priority for the big donations rolling in to build grand new pieces of architecture among all those medieval colleges.[93]

Since then, working on vaccines has become significantly more fashionable and a donor has come forward with £3 million to endow a new Professor of Vaccinology which bears the same name as Oxford's Business School. That's right, the money was from Wafic Saïd. The announcement that the 'Oxford vaccine hero' scientist was being funded by a man who brokered possibly the biggest arms deal in history – to sell deadly weapons to an authoritarian Saudi regime – generated no controversy. Saïd, whose first job in England was selling kebabs, has long since been given full membership of the Establishment as 'one of this country's most munificent philanthropists'.[94]

For all the mythology of places like Oxford, these institutions neither stand still nor stay the same. If they are sealed in varnish now as heritage items to adorn the reputations of the very rich, their meaning will be lost just as surely as if they are pulled down by an angry mob. But these misshapen English institutions, with their odd nooks and crannies clawed out of power by the bare, bleeding hands of previous generations, can still serve a purpose for the future if we recognise that, like the NHS, they do not belong to anyone in particular.

The ground occupied by the Establishment is a vital space that must be made more open and used by different groups. These institutions should be forced to widen their relevance to ordinary English life, as well as their access for ordinary English people. And those who have been left outside for so long need to know that the treasure inside belongs to them, too.

8

England
Ordinary Hope

This journey through England has plotted a path around the over-sized myths that act as roadblocks to any kind of progress. The winding road we have taken has shown us a very different landscape, one littered with ambiguity. But it also offers us a route map towards new possibilities.

If those writing about England are usually drawn to the brightest vision, the hottest issue or just the loudest noise, this book has taught us that real hope is found in ordinary life and has been obscured from view for too long.

The historical myths that are usually used to puff up this country that is not quite a country, like those of Francis Drake and William Wilberforce, are filled with paradox and far more interesting than the storybook versions allow. Similarly, the political figures that we have interviewed are often far less monstrous and preposterous than their caricatures would suggest. There is complexity everywhere. That even goes for Nigel Farage, who has spent much of his life pouring oil on the cultural fire, but told us that his favourite place in England was London, because the multicultural melting pot of 'our global capital city' gets 'faster and more trendy every year that comes'.

Restoring the nuance to these stories is not just about correcting the historical and political record. This myth-puncturing process is also necessary for the future. Each chapter of our book has explored solutions that grow out of the muddle of everyday life in this peculiar country. None of them pretend to fix everything, but they can all help fix something.

At Runnymede, we saw that liberty is best conceived not in terms of English exceptionality as some sort of Anglo-Saxon birthright sealed with the blood of dead kings. We suggested that it is everyday freedom – the mundanity of a quiet life that many take for granted – which has most meaning in England now, not least because it is still such a revelation for people fleeing from terror and tyranny.

In Plymouth, the aggressively macho nationalist idea that Brexit can restore this country's global reach is already being exposed as irrelevant and ridiculous in equal measure. But we also saw that England's long relationship with the sea is being adapted there once again to harness the wind that blows across it. Provided that ideas of becoming a green energy 'superpower' do not themselves become overblown, this technology can help England find a place in the world more suited to the challenges of this time.

When we went to Hull, we explored the many reasons why no one in England should believe they have a mission to civilise either the world or each other. When the English escape the moral straitjacket imposed in the past and reject any sense of feeling superior to others, however, there is a deeper lesson to be learned. This shows the unexpected beauty and love to be found in the complex corners of life, especially those aspects of it which are too often dismissed as dissonant.

Of course, dissonance can cause problems itself, not least in the hate-filled English myth of racial insularity which once poisoned much of Wolverhampton. But the antidote is found not by abandoning difference, but by working with it. Genuinely diverse groups can come together not when they are told they must but when they realise what they already have in common in the places where they live. Such ground might still be disputed, as we saw in an arcane planning dispute over car parking for a Sikh temple, or shared, through support for the city's football club which has sought to open itself out to the whole community rather than merely parts of it.

All of that is better than the Teflon-coated vision of a future emptied of the past that was once symbolised by the Millennium Dome. Indeed, what was once modern is now itself growing old, a process of ageing and maturing that offers new ways of imagining what it means to be English as each generation adapts old stories to their time.

Similarly, the backward-looking, retro-fitted and over-politicised myth of a left-behind white English working class has done nothing to address the towering social challenges facing a town like Blackpool. But at this seaside resort we found real hope in the multiple ways people are just getting on with the job of caring for each other. Chipping away at seemingly immovable problems in towns like these is more deserving of investment than the endless big headline-grabbing initiatives that achieve little change before being washed away like so many sandcastles on Blackpool's beach.

And, finally, we saw how the honeyed-stone heritage of Oxford that is so attractive to the global rich flitting in from their airport lounges to their business conferences can obscure the reality of a city that has overpriced housing and factories, too. If the often complacent institutions that make up England's Establishment are to provide stability to a country that is being lifted off its moorings, they must anchor themselves to the lives and experiences of the people who live in it.

This has been a book which deflates the myths of England. And we know there is a danger that when those blown-up ideas of England crumple, as they surely will, their failure may add to a sense of bewilderment or doubt about the future.

There will always be those like the politician Robert Jenrick who seek to exploit that. He wrote an article for the *Daily Mail* in 2024 - filled with the usual hot air about a country that 'invented parliamentary democracy, pioneered the Industrial Revolution, ended the slave trade, and stood alone against Hitler in Europe's darkest hour' - should now proudly unite behind this overstretched mythological identity and put its 'own citizens first'.[1] There will also be others, like the former leader of the Green Party, Caroline Lucas, who try to replace the dangerous myths of the past with equally unreal alternatives, aspirations for a more noble England which, although well-intenioned, are just as likely to fail.[2] We believe, instead, that even in people's disengaged disenchantment there is a source of hope, one which is all the better because it's so very ordinary.

The experience for many over the last decade or so has been not so much like falling off a cliff as slipping down a slide. For all the noise and the chaos in our politics, people are busy going to school, falling in and out of love, maybe having children of their own, working and growing old. In between all that, they argue, fight, laugh, eat curry, swear, drink too much, can't believe their gas bill, then switch channels when the news comes on because it is all a bit depressing.

The England found in endless variations of people's everyday existence is too often bypassed and overlooked because most people do not fit a single national story. What we have tried to show here is that for all the half-truths and outright lies, the real source of energy and renewal in England is found in its subtle imperfection.

Other cultures celebrate imperfection. There are Punjabi rugs which have flaws deliberately woven into their designs and the deliberate asymmetry found in Islamic architecture or Japanese art – but England's overblown myths squeeze all of that out.

The best of this, or probably any country, emerges from its muddled complexity rather than from straight lines. There is real power in everyday lives and everyone's hands. England has harnessed some of that before.

We believe the people who live in it can do so again.

Notes

1 RUNNYMEDE

1 Dan Jones, *In the Reign of King John*, London, Head of Zeus, 2015, p. 191.
2 'Egham Races', Charlotte Young, accessed at http://eghammuseum.org/egham-races/
3 C. R. L. Fletcher and Rudyard Kipling, 'The Reeds of Runnymede', in *A School History of England*, Oxford, Clarendon Press, 1911.
4 Nicholas Watt, 'David Cameron Fluffs Citizenship Test', *Guardian*, 27 September 2012.
5 'Magna Carta Teacher's Resources', https://www.nationalarchives.gov.uk/education/resources/magna-carta-teachers-resources/
6 See http://liberteas.co.uk/
7 Jill Lepore, 'The Rule of History', *New Yorker*, 13 April 2015.
8 See https://magnacarta800th.com/projects/round-5-grants/scotland-link-to-magna-carta/
9 Eleanor Davis, 'The Queen and Prince William at Runnymede', *Surrey Advertiser*, 16 June 2015.
10 David Cameron, 'Magna Carta 800th anniversary: PM's speech', accessed at https://bit.ly/3MQ5Gsq
11 Editorial, 'The Sun Says', *Sun*, 16 June 2015.
12 Eleanor Davis, 'Magna Carta Queen statue', *Surrey Advertiser*, 9 March 2015.
13 Eleanor Davis, 'Magna Carta Queen statue', *Surrey Advertiser*, 22 April 2015.

14 Amani Hughes, Paul Harper and Eleanor Davis, 'Magna Carta', *Surrey Advertiser*, 14 June 2015.

15 Simon Schama, *History of Britain*, vol. 1, London, BBC Books, 2000.

16 See https://blogs.bl.uk/digitisedmanuscripts/2015/05/the-first-edit ion-and-translation-of-magna-carta.html

17 Tom Bingham, *The Rule of Law*, London, Penguin, 2011, p. 10.

18 J. C. Holt, *Magna Carta*, Cambridge, Cambridge University Press, 1992, p. 5.

19 Susan Reynolds, 'Magna Carta in its European Context', *History, Journal of the Historical Association*, 2016.

20 Ibid.

21 Bingham, *Rule of Law*, pp. 106–9.

22 Jones, *Reign of King John*, pp. 155–68.

23 Bingham, *Rule of Law*, pp. 16–17.

24 Sir Edward Coke MP quoted in William Cobbett, *Cobbett's Parliamentary History of England*, vol. II, London, R. Bagshaw, 1806, p. 357.

25 Hannah Ellis-Peterson, 'Sculpture at Runnymede', *Guardian*, 15 July 2015.

26 Ingrid von Rosenberg, 'Transformations of Western Icons', *Journal for the Study of British Culture* 15.1 (2008): 59–74.

27 See https://www.law.berkeley.edu/wp-content/uploads/2019/02/Civil-liberty-and-fundamental-rights-a-Neo-Roman-approach.pdf

28 John Milton, *The Tenure of Kings and Magistrates*, London, Matthew Simmons, 1649.

29 Sir Thomas Rainborough quoted in Bingham, *The Rule of Law*, p. 55; Christopher Hill, *The World Turned Upside Down*, London, Viking, 1972, p. 312.

30 Christopher Hill (ed.), *Winstanley: 'The Law of Freedom' and other Writings*, Cambridge, Cambridge University Press, 1983, p. 113.

31 Christopher Hill, *Intellectual Origins of the English Revolution – Revisited*, Oxford, Oxford University Press, 1997, p. 211.

32 David Allen Green, 'The Myth of Magna Carta', *Financial Times*, 16 June 2015.

33 See Rogers Smith, *Civic Ideals*, New Haven, Yale University Press, 1999.

34 George van Cleve, '"Somerset's Case" and Its Antecedents in Imperial Perspective', *Law and History Review* 24.3 (2006).

35 Robert Tombs, *The English & Their History*, London, Penguin, 2015, pp. 33–6.

36 Thomas Milton Kemnitz and Fleurange Jacques, 'J. R. Stephens and the Chartist Movement', *International Review of Social History* 19 (1974): 219.

37 Alfred, Lord Tennyson, 'You Ask Me Why, Tho' Ill At Ease ...', in *Poems* I, London, Edward Moxon, 1842, pp. 175–6.

38 Henrietta E. Marshall, *Our Island Story*, London, Weidenfeld & Nicolson, 2007, p. 157.

39 Ibid., pp. xv–xvi.

40 Edward Jenks, 'The Myth of the Magna Carta', *Independent Review* (1904): 260–74.

41 Charlotte Higgins, 'Sanctuary for human rights', *Guardian*, 15 June 2018.

42 See https://winstonchurchill.org/publications/finest-hour-extras/churchill-to-gift-magna-carta/

43 House of Commons, 3 December 1953, vol. 521, col. 1297–8.

44 Tony Benn, *Arguments for Democracy*, London, Penguin, 1982, p. 175.

45 Tony Benn, 'Left supports right', *Daily Telegraph*, 29 June 2008.

46 See https://magnacarta800th.com/lectures/the-assault-on-liberty/

47 Dominic Raab, *The Assault on Liberty*, London, Fourth Estate, 2009, pp. 3, 23.

48 Sam Knight, 'The man who brought you Brexit', *Guardian*, 29 September 2015.

49 Daniel Hannan, *How We Invented Freedom*, London, Head of Zeus, 2013, p. 109.

50 Daniel Hannan, 'Magna Carta', *Wall Street Journal*, 30 May 2015.

51 Priti Patel, 'Let's go', *Daily Mail*, 21 February 2016.

52 House of Commons, 22 September 2020, vol. 680, col. 814.

53 See https://www.gov.uk/government/consultations/human-rights-act-reform-a-modern-bill-of-rights

54 Tom Baldwin, *Keir Starmer: The Biography* (London: William Collins, 2024), 76.

55 Prime Minister's remarks at the opening plenary session of the European Political Community: July 18, 2024. https://www.gov.uk/government/speeches/pms-remarks-at-the-opening-plenary-session-of-the-european-political-community-18-july-2024

56 Simon Hooper, 'Magna Carta', Aljazeera, 15 June 2015; https://www.occupy.com/article/freer-ive-ever-been-squatted-eco-village-overshadows-royals-magna-carta-celebrations

57 See https://daddydragon.co.uk/2020/08/10/english-petition-on-american-soil/

58 See https://thesecretbarrister.com/2020/11/28/can-magna-carta-and-common-law-give-you-immunity-from-covid-regulations/

59 https://unherd.com/2021/04/how-the-left-gave-up-on-freedom/

60 'Educated, young and wealthy', *Daily Telegraph*, 2 December 2021.

61 'Britain's newest immigrant group', *The Economist*, 25 September 2022.

62 Calum Macleod, 'Magna Carta hits great wall', *The Times*, 14 October 2015.

63 See https://www.gov.uk/government/publications/survey-of-hong-kong-british-national-overseas-visa-holders-2021/hong-kong-bno-survey-results-accessible-version

64 Daniel Hannan, 'Let's build a self-governing Hong Kong in Britain', *Sunday Telegraph*, 6 June 2020.

2 PLYMOUTH

1 Robert Saunders, 'Myths from a small island', *New Statesman*, 9 October 2019.

2 Charlotte Edwards and Nicholas Cecil, 'David Davis', *Evening Standard*, 28 September 2018.

3 Giles Sheldrick, 'Farage revolution revealed', *Daily Express*, 4 May 2019.

4 Jacob Rees-Mogg, 'Unreformed Marxist Corbyn', *Daily Express*, 4 November 2019.

5 Jacob Rees-Mogg, 'My Vision', *Brexit Central*, 21 June 2018.

6 Jonathan Beale, 'HMS Queen Elizabeth', BBC News, 21 May 2020; Greg Heffer, 'Boris Johnson vows to make UK "foremost naval power in Europe"', Sky News, 19 November 2020.

7 See //www.gov.uk/government/speeches/pm-speech-in-greenwich-3-february-2020

8 Harry Kelsey, *Sir John Hawkins*, New Haven, Yale University Press, 2003.

9 Lorenzo Morotti, 'Drake sculpture', *Marin Independent Journal*, 29 July 2020.

10 David Reynolds, *Island Stories*, London, William Collins, 2019, p. 7.

11 Walter Raleigh, 'A Discourse of the Invention of Ships', in *The Works of Sir Walter Raleigh* 8 (reprinted 1965), p. 325.

12 John Sugden, *Sir Francis Drake*, London, Pimlico, 1996, pp. 7, 100.

13 N. A. M. Rodger, 'Queen Elizabeth and the Myth of Sea-Power in English History', *Transactions of the Royal Historical Society* 14 (2004): 153–74.

14 Cheryl A. Fury, *Tides in the Affairs of Men*, Westport, Conn.; London, Greenwood Press, 2002, p. 122.

15 Hugh F. Rankin, *The Golden Age of Piracy*, New York, Holt, Rinehart & Winston, 1969, p. 17.

16 Kenneth R. Andrews, *Drake's Voyages*, New York, Charles Scribner's Sons, 1967, pp. 33–4.

17 N. A. M. Rodger, *The Safeguard of the Sea*, London, Penguin, 2004, p. 346.

18 Ibid., p. 19.

19 Sugden, *Sir Francis Drake*, pp. 27–31.

20 Open letter by Elizabeth I to the mayors of England, 11 July 1596, *National Archives* (PC 2/21 f.304).

21 Philip Nichols quoted in Sugden, *Sir Francis Drake*, p. 70.

22 Sugden, *Sir Francis Drake*, p. 141.

23 William Camden quoted by Nikki Marmery, *On Wilder Seas*, London, Legend Press, 2020.

24 Herman A. Harper, *To Rule the Waves*, New York, HarperCollins, 2004, p. 94.

25 Rodger, *Safeguard of the Sea*, pp. 244–5.

26 A poem, said to be by Drake, published in Sir George Peckham, *A True Reporte, of the Late Discoveries, and Possession, Taken in the Right of the Crowne of Englande, of the New-Found Landes*, London, 1583.

27 The first purportedly factual reference is found in William Oldys, *The Life of Sir Walter Ralegh*, Oxford, Oxford University Press, 1829.

28 Sugden, *Sir Francis Drake*, p. 235; Kelsey, *Sir John Hawkins*, pp. 321–2.

29 Willard Farnham, *The Medieval Heritage of Elizabethan Tragedy*, Oxford, Blackwell, 1963, p. 431.

30 Rodger, *Safeguard of the Sea*, p. 206; Sugden, *Sir Francis Drake*, pp. 243–5.

31 Kenneth R. Andrews, *Trade, Plunder and Settlement*, Cambridge, Cambridge University Press, 1984, pp. 252–3.

32 These accounts include Richard Hakluyt's *The Principall Navigations, Voiages, and Discoveries of the English Nation*, London, George Bishop and Ralph Newberie, 1589. See also Claire Jowitt, *The Culture of Piracy, 1580–1630*, Surrey, Ashgate, 2010, pp. 8–9, 54, 56.

33 Reynolds, *Island Stories*, pp. 66–7.

34 Peter Earle, *The Pirate Wars*, New York, St Martin's Press, 2003, p. xi.

35 See https://saveourstatues.org.uk/

36 Carl Eve, 'City entrepreneur sends more than 2000 emails', *Plymouth Herald*, 19 December 2021.

37 Edward Oldfield, 'Rusty Reg tombstoners', *Plymouth Herald*, 12 May 2021; Senjay Boztas and Vanessa Thorpe, 'Antony Gormley', *Observer*, 4 June 2022.

38 James Tully, *Public Philosophy in a New Key* II, Cambridge, Cambridge University Press, pp. 223–56.

39 Sheryl Julian, 'History is served', *Chicago Tribune*, 20 November 1996.

40 Virginia DeJohn Anderson, 'New England in the Seventeenth Century', in *The Oxford History of the British Empire* I, ed. Nicholas Canny, Oxford, Oxford University Press, 1998.

41 Niall Ferguson, *Empire*, London, Penguin, 2004, pp. 68–9.

42 See http://www1.somerset.gov.uk/archives/ASH/Bloodyassize.htm

43 Ian K. Steele, *The English Atlantic, 1675–1740*, Oxford, Oxford University Press, 1986.

44 J. R. Seeley, *The Expansion of England*, London, MacMillan and Co., 1883, p. 8.

45 Ibid., pp. 12–13.

46 Ibid., p. 296.

47 Elizabeth Abbott, *Sugar*, London and New York, Duckworth Overlook, 2009, pp. 56–70.

48 John Darwin, *Unfinished Empire: The Global Expansion of Britain*, London, Penguin, 2012, p. 39.

49 Alvin O. Thompson, 'Race and Colour Prejudices and the Origin of the Trans-Atlantic Slave Trade', *Caribbean Studies* 16.3 (1977): 29–59.

50 Hillary Beckles, 'Black Female Slaves and White Households in Barbados', in *More Than Chattel*, ed. David Barry Gasper and Darlene Clark Hine, Bloomington, Ind., Indiana University Press, 1996, pp. 111–25.

51 Ibid., p. 40.

52 Douglas Hall, *In Miserable Slavery*, London, Macmillan, 1989, pp. 70–3.

53 Simon Schama, *The History of Britain* II, London, BBC Books, 2001, p. 442.

54 Trevor Burnard, *Mastery, Tyranny, and Desire*, Chapel Hill, NC, University of North Carolina Press, 2004, pp. 5, 156.

55 See https://www.gresham.ac.uk/watch-now/how-place-slavery-british-identity

56 Joseph E. Inikori, *Africans and the Industrial Revolution in England*, Cambridge, Cambridge University Press, 2002, pp. 227–8, 237.

57 Daniel Defoe, *A Brief Account of The Present State Of The African Trade*, London, J. Baker, 1713, p. 55.

58 Padraic X. Scanlan, *Slave Empire: How Slavery Built Modern Britain*, London, Robinson, 2020, pp. 49–54.

59 'Defining Britain's Post-Brexit Role In The World', *Centre for Brexit Policy*, June 2022: 39.

60 Celina Fox, *The Ingenious Mr Dummer*, London, British Library 2007, p. 26.

61 Alfred, Lord Tennyson, 'The Fleet', first published in *The Times*, April 1885.

62 Richard Dawkins, *The Selfish Gene*, Oxford, Oxford University Press, 1989, p. 324.

63 N. A. M. Rodger, *The Command of the Ocean*, London, Penguin, 2004, pp. 270–352.

64 William Dalrymple, 'The East India Company', *Guardian*, 4 March 2015.

65 Robert Tombs, *The English & Their History*, London, Penguin, 2015, pp. 404, 541–4.

66 Rodger, *The Command of the Ocean*, pp. 408–88.

67 Rodger, 'Queen Elizabeth and the Myth of Sea-Power', 168–72.

68 Tombs, *The English*, p. 373.

69 Stephen J. Thorne, 'The Royal Navy's War on Trees', *Legion Magazine*, 15 February 2022.

70 Ibid., 307.

71 Constantin Frantz, quoted in Reynolds, *Island Stories*, p. 41.

72 Bernard Porter, *Britain Before Brexit*, London, Bloomsbury, 2021, p. 15.

73 Darwin, *Unfinished Empire*, p. 11.

74 See https://www.liverpoolmuseums.org.uk/ports-of-transatlantic-slave-trade

75 House of Commons, 13 March 1812, vol. 21, col. 1262.

76 R. N. Worth, *History of Plymouth from the Earliest Period to the Present Time*, Plymouth, William Brendon and Son, 1871, p. 322.

77 Eric Black, 'Damnation Alley', *Plymouth Herald*, 21 September 2019.

78 G. H. Bennett, *Dockyard, Naval Base and Town*, Plymouth, University of Plymouth, 2017. See also Metropolitan Police: 'Contagious Diseases Act, Plymouth and Devonport, 1872', The National Archives, TNA: WO33/24.

79 Charles Kingsley, *Westward Ho!*, New York, Ticknor & Fields, 1855, p. 228.

80 See https://www.kiplingsociety.co.uk/poem/poems_englishflag.htm

81 See https://www.kiplingsociety.co.uk/poem/poems_burden.htm

82 Joseph Chamberlain, quoted in Julian Amery, *The Life of Joseph Chamberlain* V, London, Macmillan, 1969, p. 31.

83 See, for instance, https://www.historic-uk.com/CultureUK/Legend-Of-Drakes-Drum/

84 See John Grindrod, *Concretopia*, London, Old Street, 2014; Jeremy Gould, *Plymouth: Vision for a Modern City*, Swindon, English Heritage, 2010.

85 See https://new.plymouth.gov.uk/plymouth-report

86 See https://www.plymouth.gov.uk/sites/default/files/VAWG_Report.pdf

87 Karl McDonald, 'How David Davis promised the earth', *The i*, 18 July 2016.
88 See https://www.npr.org/2019/09/23/763452863/transcript-greta-thunbergs-speech-at-the-u-n-climate-action-summit
89 'Greta Thunberg', BBC News, 14 August 2019.
90 Mattha Busby, 'Arron Banks jokes about Greta Thunberg', *Guardian*, 15 August 2019.
91 See https://www.weforum.org/agenda/2019/04/these-3-countries-are-global-offshore-wind-powerhouses/, and https://www.gov.uk/gov ernment/news/major-acceleration-of-homegrown-power-in-brita ins-plan-for-greater-energy-independence
92 'Parts of Plymouth which could vanish', *Plymouth Herald*, 15 June 2021.
93 Sally Guyoncourt, 'A young woman wears Walkers crisps', *The i*, 18 September 2019; 'Walkers launches recycling scheme', BBC News, 10 December 2018.
94 'Nancy Astor', BBC News, 28 November 2019.
95 See https://www.chathamhouse.org/2020/11/examining-impacts-uk-foreign-aid-budget-cut
96 'What Impact Will the Covid-19 Crisis Have?', *New Culture Forum*, 21 June 2020; 'The address where Eurosceptics and climate change sceptics rub shoulders', *Independent*, 10 February 2016; 'Sir John Hawkins Square signs', *Plymouth Herald*, 23 March 2022.
97 Philip Churm, 'Another female Tory councillor in Plymouth quits', *Plymouth Herald*, 24 January 2023; 'Plymouth council leader quits after approving cutting down of 110 trees', *Guardian*, 23 March 2023.

3 HULL

1 Philip Larkin, 'Here', *Collected Poems*, ed. Anthony Thwaite, London, Faber & Faber, 1988, pp. 136–7.
2 Dan Kemp, 'Anger as Philip Larkin statue reduced to looking "like a demented fool"', *Hull Daily Mail*, 18 April 2019.
3 Philip Larkin, 'Letter to Robert Conquest', *The Selected Letters of Philip Larkin*, ed. Anthony Thwaite, London, Faber & Faber, 1992, p. 584.
4 Philip Larkin, quoted in Stephen Walsh, 'What a Hole', *Guardian*, 30 May 2017.
5 Dan Kemp, 'Greatest Hullensian of all time crowned', *Hull Daily Mail*, 7 March 2021.

6　House of Commons, 18 April 1791.

7　Adam Hochschild, 'English Abolition', *New York Review of Books*, 14 June 2007.

8　Linda Colley, *Britons*, New Haven, Conn., Yale University Press, 1992, p. 359.

9　Eric Williams, *Capitalism and Slavery*, Chapel Hill, NC, University of North Carolina Press, 1944, p. 181.

10　See http://factsabouthull.blogspot.com/2017/01/fact-87-citys-son-on-pedestal.html.

11　'Archbishops lead slave trade walk', BBC News, 24 March 2007.

12　David Smith, 'You, the Queen, should be ashamed!', *Guardian*, 27 March 2007.

13　'Tony Blair's statement', *The Times*, 27 November 2006.

14　Andrew Roberts, 'Recolonise Africa!', *Daily Mail*, 8 January 2005.

15　Boris Johnson, 'Africa is a mess, but we can't blame colonialism', *Spectator*, 2 February 2002.

16　Niall Ferguson, *Empire: How Britain Made the Modern World*, London, Penguin, 2003, p. 115.

17　See https://twitter.com/nfergus/status/888086778732728320?lang=en

18　Keith Thomas, *In Pursuit of Civility*, Waltham, Mass., Brandeis University Press, 2018, p. 223.

19　David Ewing Duncan, 'The Black Legend', *Atlantic*, August 1991.

20　Darwin, *Unfinished Empire*, pp. 30–2.

21　Tristram Hunt, *Cities of Empire*, London, Penguin, 2014, pp. 194–5, 207.

22　William Hague, *William Wilberforce*, London, Harper Perennial, 2008, p. 3.

23　Ibid., p. 8.

24　Robert Isaac Wilberforce and Samuel Wilberforce, *The Life of William Wilberforce* I, London, John Murray, 1838, p. 8.

25　Hague, *Wilberforce*, pp. 27–36.

26　Hochschild, 'English Abolition'.

27　Lord Nelson to Simon Taylor in *The Naval Miscellany* I, ed. John Knox Laughton, London, Navy Records Society, 1902, pp. 438–9.

28　Adam Hochschild, *Bury the Chains*, London, Macmillan, 2005, p. 245.

29　Tristram Hunt, *The Radical Potter*, London, Allen Lane, 2021, pp. 221–31.

30　William Wilberforce quoted in Anne Stott, *Wilberforce: Family and Friends*, Oxford, Oxford University Press, 2012, p. 226.

31 Olaudah Equiano, *The Interesting Narrative of the Life of Olaudah Equiano or Gustavus Vassa, the African*, London, Cradock and Joy, 1814, pp. 63–6.

32 Hochschild, *Bury the Chains*, p. 127.

33 Akala, *Natives*, London, Hodder & Stoughton, 2018, pp. 96–7; Andrew Jack, 'Monumental struggle', *Financial Times*, 16 June 2020.

34 See Sudhir Hazareesingh, *Black Spartacus*, London, Penguin, 2021.

35 Laurent Dubois, *Avengers of the New World*, Cambridge, Mass., Harvard University Press, 2005, pp. 167–216.

36 House of Commons, 16 March 1824, vol. 10, col. 1134.

37 Quoted in Hochschild, *Bury the Chains*, p. 324.

38 Scanlan, *Slave Empire*, pp. 281–3; Reynolds, *Island Stories*, p. 181.

39 Accessed 10 May 2022, https://www.ucl.ac.uk/lbs/project/context/

40 Scanlan, *Slave Empire*, pp. 299–331.

41 Hugh Thomas, *The Slave Trade*, London, Picador, 1997, p. 784.

42 See http://www.sierraleoneheritage.org/sites/monuments/kingsyard

43 Michael J. Turner, 'The Limits of Abolition: Government, Saints and the African Question', *The English Historical Review* 112 (1997): 319–57; Stephen Tomkins, 'William Wilberforce was complicit in slavery', *Guardian*, 3 August 2010.

44 T. P. Thompson quoted in Turner, *Limits of Abolition*, p. 348.

45 Afua Hirsch, *Brit(ish)*, London, Vintage, 2018, pp. 55–6.

46 Marika Sherwood, *After Abolition*, London, I.B. Tauris, 2007, pp. 58–83.

47 David Olusoga, *Black and British*, London, Pan Macmillan, 2016, pp. 345–6.

48 Reynolds, *Island Stories*, p. 175; James J. Hammond, *Selections from the Letters and speeches of the Hon James H. Hammond*, New York, John F. Trow & Co., 1866, p. 317.

49 Sven Beckert, *Empire of Cotton*, London Vintage, 2016, pp. 294–6, 337; Reynolds, *Island Stories*, p. 358.

50 P. Colquhoun quoted in Hague, *Wilberforce*, pp. 106–7.

51 Robert J. Hind, 'William Wilberforce and the Perceptions of the British People', *Historical Research* 60 (1987): 325; Hague, *Wilberforce*, p. 108; E. P. Thompson, *The Making of the English Working Class*, London, Victor Gollancz, 1963, p. 412.

52 See Ford K. Brown, *Fathers of the Victorians*, Cambridge, Cambridge University Press, 1961; House of Commons, 16 December 1819, vol. 41, col. 1214.

53 William Hazlitt, *The Spirit of the Age*, London, Henry Colburn, 1825, p. 359.

54 William Wilberforce, Bodleian Papers c.4.15–16, Nov 30, 1786; 16 December 1786.
55 Ibid.; 'Press Gang Riot', Hull History Centre blog, 12 May 2022.
56 Hind, 'William Wilberforce and the Perceptions of the British People', p. 323.
57 William Roberts, *Memoirs and Correspondence of Mrs Hannah More* II, London, R. B. Seeley and W. Burnside, 1834, p. 455.
58 William Wilberforce, *A Practical View of the Prevailing Religious System of Professed Christians*, Ireland, T. Cadell, jun. and W. Davies, 1797, p. 274.
59 'Mike Pence, Pro-Life Champion', *Daily Citizen*, 1 February 2019.
60 'Church apologises for slave trade', BBC News, 8 February 2006.
61 Hind, *William Wilberforce and the Perceptions of the British People*, p. 326.
62 Hochschild, *Bury the Chains*, p. 329.
63 Scanlan, *Slave Empire*, pp. 266–70.
64 Eliza Ann Foster, *Mrs Eliza Ann Foster*, London, John Mason, 1844, p. 65.
65 Ibid., pp. 69, 8; Catherine Hall, 'Of Gender and Empire', in *Gender and Empire*, ed. P. Levine, Oxford, Oxford University Press, 2004, p. 60.
66 Foster, *Mrs Eliza Ann Foster*, p. 182.
67 Ibid., pp. 199–201.
68 Ibid., p. 224.
69 Hague, *Wilberforce*, pp. 424–5.
70 Owen Bread, *Bread's New Guide and Hand-Book to Worthing and its Vicinity*, London, Hamilton Adams & Co., 1859.
71 K. J. Allison, 'Protestant Nonconformity', in *A History of the County of York East Riding* I, London, Victoria County History, 1969, pp. 311–30.
72 See https://www.workhouses.org.uk/Hull/; K. J. Allison, 'Hull, 1700–1835', pp. 174–214; Henry Schroeder, *The Annals of Yorkshire from the Earliest Period to the Present Time*, Leeds, Crosby & Co., 1851, p. 399.
73 Charles Dickens, *Oliver Twist*, London, Richard Bentley, 1838, pp. 9–10.
74 Charles Dickens, Letter to Theodore Compton, 26 January 1844, in *The Letters of Charles Dickens* IV, pp. 30–1.
75 Thompson, *Making of the English Working Class*, pp. 355, 370, 377–8.
76 Samuel Smiles, *Self Help*, London, John Murray, 1859, pp. 21–6.
77 See https://etheses.whiterose.ac.uk/11050/
78 Peter Stubley, *Serious Religion and the Improvement of Public Manners*, Durham, Durham University, 1991, p. 165.

79 James Sibree, *Fifty Years' Recollections of Hull*, Hull, A. Brown & Sons, 1884, p. 21.

80 Ibid., pp. 87–97.

81 Ibid., pp. 32–9, 54.

82 Kate Fox, *Watching the English: The Hidden Rules of English Behaviour*, London, Hodder & Stoughton, 2004, pp. 436–7.

83 Michel Antony Bull, 'Mariners, the Media, and Middle Class Morality', University of Hull, 2019, pp. 49–50; Erika Rappaport, 'The Temperance Tea Party', *Journal of British Studies* 52 (October 2013): 990–1016; Angus Young, 'The forgotten Hull pub chain that never sold a drop of beer', *Hull Daily Mail*, 23 August 2020.

84 K. J. Allison, 'Protestant Nonconformity', pp. 311–30; Brian Harrison, *Drink and the Victorians*, London, Faber & Faber, 1971, 2nd edn, 1994, pp. 290–335.

85 Hague, *Wilberforce*, pp. 161–2.

86 Lord Palmerston to Sir George Bonham, 29 September 1850, F.O. 17/173.

87 Cobden Papers (BL Add. MSS 436350), Cobden to Bright, 17 October 1858; Lord Palmerston, 3 March 1857, *Hansard*, vol. 144.

88 Charles Dickens, *Bleak House*, London, Bradbury & Evans, 1853, p. 58.

89 Charles Dickens, *The Posthumous Papers of the Pickwick Club*, London, Chapman & Hall, 1837, pp. 176–7.

90 Jenny Hartlet (ed.), *The Selected Letters of Charles Dickens*, Oxford, Oxford University Press, 2012, p. 328.

91 Priya Satia, *Time's Monster*, London, Penguin, 2020, pp. 75–81; T. B. Macaulay quoted in Henry Sharp (ed.), *Selections from the Educational Records* I, Calcutta, Government Printing, 1920, p. 107.

92 *The Morning Journal* (Kingston, Jamaica), 23 October 1865.

93 Catherine Hall, 'The Economy of Intellectual Prestige', *Cultural Critique* 12 (1989): 190–1.

94 Catherine Hall, *Civilising Subjects*, Cambridge, Polity, 2002; Benjamin Disraeli, *Sybil or, The Two Nations*, London, Henry Colburn, 1845, p. 85.

95 Bernard Porter, *The Absent-Minded Imperialists*, Oxford, Oxford University Press, 2004, p. 21.

96 Anandi Ramamurthy, *Imperial Persuaders*, Manchester, Manchester University Press, 2003, pp. 24–62.

97 John McKenzie, 'Comfort and Conviction', *Journal of Imperial and Commonwealth History* 36 (2008): 659–68.

98 George Combe, 'On the Coincidence Between the Natural Talents and Dispositions of Nations and the Development of Their Brains', *Phrenological Journal and Miscellany*, 2 (1824): 1–19.

99 Robert Louis Stevenson, *The Strange Case of Dr Jekyll and Mr Hyde*, Harlow, Longman, Green & Co., 1886; H. G. Wells, *The Time Machine*, London, William Heinemann, 1895.

100 Charles Darwin, *Descent of Man, and Selection in Relation to Sex* I, London, John Murray, 1871, pp. 200–1.

101 A. F. R. Wollaston, *Life of Alfred Newton*, New York, Dutton, 1921, pp. 118–120.

102 Burkhard Conrad, 'The Politics of a Conversion', *International Journal for the Study of the Christian Church*, 16 (2016): 182–96.

103 Anthony Trollope, *The Clergymen of the Church of England*, London, Chapman & Hall, 1866, pp. 55–66.

104 Sheldon Hall, 'The untold story of the film Zulu', *Independent on Sunday*, 19 January 2014.

105 Christian Wolmar, *Railways & The Raj*, London, Atlantic Books, 2017.

106 Cynthia Behrman, 'The After-Life of General Gordon', *Albion*, 1971, p. 50.

107 Yann Beliard, 'Imperial Internationalism?', *Labour History Review*, 74 (2003): 319–29.

108 Alessandro Saluppo, 'Strikebreaking and Anti-Unionism on the Waterfront', *European History Quarterly* 49 (2014): 570–96.

109 Margaret MacMillan, *The War That Ended Peace*, London, Profile Books, 2013, pp. 159–60.

110 R. G. Burnett, *The Life of Joseph Rank*, London, Epworth Press, 1945, p. 107.

111 Andrew Motion, *Philip Larkin*, London, Faber & Faber, 1993, pp. 276–8.

112 Ibid., p. 446; Larkin, 'Aubade', *Collected Poems*, pp. 208–9; Hague, *Wilberforce*, p. 502.

113 Philip Larkin, *Further Requirements*, ed. Anthony Thwaite, London, Faber & Faber, 2001, p. 128.

114 Larkin, 'Here', *Collected Poems*, pp. 136–7.

115 Ibid., 'Homage to a government', 'Going, Going'.

116 'Religion, England and Wales: Census 2021'; Church of England, *Statistics for Mission*, London, The Church of England Research and Statistics, 2020.

117 'Religion in England and Wales', Office of National Statistics, 2011.

118 Matt Woodcock, *Being Reverend*, London, Church House, 2020, pp. 149–50, 159, 224.

119 See https://biblicalstudies.org.uk/pdf/churchman/113-03_254.pdf

120 Melvin Tinker, 'It seemed good to the Holy Spirit and to us?', *Churchman*, Autumn 1994.

121 Ibid., pp. 242–6; Joseph McCormick, 'Petition calls for sacking of vicar', *Pink News*, 23 June 2015; 'Hull CofE minister criticised for homosexual pride service', *The Christian Institute*, 1 August 2017.

122 YouGov/Jayne Ozanne survey 22–27 February 2022, https://docs.goo gle.com/spreadsheets/d/15BPQCrqio-DwXaossjIsO2Zwdw1_S94y/ edit#gid=1274331876

123 "We are deeply deeply deeply sorry," - Archbishop Justin Welby, Anglican Communion News Service, July 23, 2024; Madeline Davies, 'New churches are dropping the word "church", report finds,' *Church Times*, August 13, 2024

124 Alice Thomson and Rachel Sylvester, 'The suggestion that I, as arch-bishop, should not be political is a nonsense', *The Times*, 22 May 2022.

125 'Health in Coastal Communities', Chief Medical Officer's Annual Report 2021.

126 Neil T. Gavin, 'Below the Radar', *British Journal of Sociology* 72 (2021): 707–24.

127 Mark Duell, 'Judge's fury as he jails shameless benefits cheat mother', *Daily Mail*, 4 January 2017.

128 See John Milbank, *The Future of Love*, London, SCM Press, 2009.

129 William Temple, *Christianity and Social Order*, Harmondsworth, Penguin, 1942, p. 74.

130 Andew Rumsey, *Parish*, London, SCM Press, 2017; Andrew Rumsey, *English Grounds*, London, SCM Press, 2021.

131 See https://cmis.hullcc.gov.uk/cmis/Portals/0/Corporate%20Plan/ Hull%20City%20Council%20Corporate%20Plan%202018-2022. pdf?ver=2019-02-12-110026-997

132 'Sketches, Stories of Art and People', BBC Radio 4, 17 August 2022.

133 Lottie Brazier, 'Genesis P-Orridge', *Guardian*, 18 December 2018.

134 Ed West, 'What is the point of having a "city of culture"?' *Spectator*, 20 November 2013; Paul Sims, 'Scrapital of culture', *Sun*, 1 January 2017.

135 'Cultural Transformations', Culture, Place and Policy Institute, University of Hull, November 2019 (revised April 2021). See also Alan Johnson, *This Boy*, London, Bantam Press, 2013.

136 Jack Bowman, 'The history of Hull's Dead Bod', *Hull Live*, 16 April 2023.

4 WOLVERHAMPTON

1 'Sir Jack Hayward', *The Times*, 15 January 2015.

2 Peter Madeley, 'Enoch Powell', *Express & Star*, 12 February 2018.

3 See https://anth1001.files.wordpress.com/2014/04/enoch-powell_spe ech.pdf

4 House of Commons, 21 January 1971, *Hansard*: 809, 1377.

5 Bagehot Column, 'The shadow of Enoch Powell', *The Economist*, 6 April 2017.

6 Amol Rajan and Ian McDiarmid, '50 Years On', BBC Radio 4, 14 April 2018.

7 Rupert Jones, 'My grandparents, Enoch Powell and the day they fell out', *Guardian*, 22 October 2016.

8 Keith Kyle, 'Impressions of Nietzsche', *London Review of Books*, 11.14, 27 July 1989.

9 See https://www.enochpowell.net/fr-80.html

10 'The Woman Who Never Was?', *Document*, BBC Radio 4, 22 January 2007; 'Was Powell speech just a river of lies?', *Express & Star*, 16 March 2008.

11 Simon Heffer, *Like the Roman*, London, Weidenfeld & Nicolson, 1998, pp. 463–7.

12 'Hostile but no-one hurt', *Express & Star*, 29 April 1968.

13 'Powell's place in history', *Daily Telegraph*, 9 February 1998.

14 'UK Independence Party leader names Enoch Powell', *Glasgow Herald*, 23 October 2008.

15 BBC2, *Newsnight*, 12 August 2011.

16 Camilla Schofield, *Enoch Powell and the Making of Postcolonial Britain*, Cambridge, Cambridge University Press, 2013, p. 324.

17 See http://enochpowell.info/wp-content/uploads/Speeches/1957-1961.pdf

18 Powell, St George's Day speech, available at https://www.peterlilley.co.uk/858-enoch-powell-memorial-speech-delivered-st-georges-day-1999/

19 Ibid.

20 See http://enochpowell.info/wp-content/uploads/Speeches/Oct-Dec%201968.pdf.

21 Ibid.

22 'Odd Man Out: A Film Portrait of Enoch Powell', BBC News and Current Affairs, 1995; see also Heffer, *Like the Roman*, pp. 267, 745.

23 Caroline Davies, 'The coal was painted white', *Daily Telegraph*, 4 May 2002.

24 Stuart Jeffries, 'Mordor, he wrote', *Guardian,* 19 September 2014.

25 Cathy Spencer, '20 years of unlocking town past', *Express & Star*, 27 August 2007.

26 Disraeli, *Sybil*, Book 3, Ch 4.

27 House of Commons, *Census of England and Wales*, vol. b1, *Administrative Areas*, London, HMSO, 1911, p. xv; John Bateman quoted in Guy Shrubsole, *Who Owns England?*, London, William Collins, 2019, p. 30; Lucy Lethbridge, *Servants*, London, W. W. Norton, 2013.

28 Ernest Rhys (ed.), *The Old Country: A Book of Love and Praise of England*, London, J. M. Dent, 1917.

29 See http://www.historywebsite.co.uk/articles/ww1/war.htm

30 See http://www.ukwarmemorials.org/

31 Peter Firchow, 'The Land of Lost Content', in Evelyn S. Firchow and Bernfried Nugel (eds), *Reluctant Modernists*, London, Lit Verlag, 2002, p. 13.

32 Scott Pettitt, 'Housman and the Unattainable', *The Housman Journal* 40 (2014): 39–40.

33 Heffer, *Like the Roman*, pp. 17–19.

34 Cited in Schofield, *Enoch Powell*, p. 52.

35 Heffer, *Like the Roman*, pp. 33–4. See also https://www.westminster-abbey.org/abbey-commemorations/commemorations/a-e-housman.

36 Toby Neal, 'Enoch Powell's Family Links and Childhood Memories of Shropshire', *Shropshire Star*, 15 April 2021.

37 George Orwell, *Inside the Whale and Other Essays*, London, Victor Gollancz, 1940.

38 Peter Madeley, '"A fit country for heroes"', *Express & Star*, 23 November 2018.

39 Tombs, *The English*, p. 632; Ann Dummett and Andrew Nicol, *Subjects, Citizens, Aliens and Others*, London, Weidenfeld & Nicolson, 1990, p. 112; Lethbridge, *Servants*, pp. 150–2.

40 Raphael Samuel, *Island Stories: Unravelling Britain*, London, Verso, 1999, p. 88.

41 The line is spoken by Frank Gibbons in *This Happy Breed*, directed by David Lean (Universal-International, 1943), at 1 hr 55 mins.

42 See https://spinnet.humanities.uva.nl/images/2013-05/baldwin1924.pdf

43 Alexandra Harris, *Romantic Moderns*, London, Thames & Hudson, 2010, p. 142; see also David Matless, *Landscape and Englishness*, London, Reaktion Books, 1998; Angus Calder, *The Myth of the Blitz*, London, Pimlico, 1992, pp. 180–208.

44 Jed Esty, *A Shrinking Island*, Princeton, Conn., Princeton University Press, 2004, p. 39.

45 Evelyn Waugh, *Brideshead Revisited*, London, Chapman & Hall, 1945, p. 139.

46 H. V. Morton, *In Search of England*, New York, Dodd, Mead, 1927, p. 180.

47 Max Hastings, 'A very English hypocrite', *Daily Telegraph*, 4 May 2004.

48 Thomas Sharp quoted in David Matless, *Landscape and Englishness*, London, Reaktion Books, 2016, p. 33; Harris, *Romantic Moderns*, pp. 184–5.

49 Samuel, *Island Stories*, pp. 132–53.

50 J. B. Priestley, *English Journey*, Bradford, Great Northern Books, 2012, pp. 319–22.

51 Ibid., pp. 107–8.

52 Ibid., p. 203.

53 Gill Saunders, *Recording Britain*, London, Victoria & Albert, 2011, pp. 7–51.

54 Ibid.

55 Bradleygirl, 'WW2 People's War', BBC, 5 May 2005.

56 George Orwell, 'The Lion and the Unicorn', in *Collected Essays*, London, Secker & Warburg, 1961, p. 57.

57 J. B. Priestley, *Postscripts*, London and Toronto, William Heinemann, 1940, p. 68.

58 Ibid., p. 74.

59 Robert Mackay, *Half the Battle*, Manchester, Manchester University Press, 2002, p. 62.

60 Ibid., p. 86.

61 David Low, 'Very well, alone', *Evening Standard*, 18 June 1940.

62 Connelly, *We Can Take It!*, pp. 135–43.

63 Phil Piratin, *Our Flag Stays Red*, London, Lawrence & Wishart, 2006, pp. 73–4.

64 Marc Stears, *Out of the Ordinary*, Cambridge, Mass., Harvard University Press, 2021, pp. 68–82, 97–104.

65 See https://www.lse.ac.uk/Events/Events-Assets/PDF/2017/2017-MT03/20171129-MinoucheShafik-Transcript.pdf.

66 Joshua Levine, *The Secret History of the Blitz*, London, Simon & Schuster, 2015, p. 86.

67 Ibid., p. 200.

68 Orwell, *Lion and the Unicorn*, p. 65.

69 Reynolds, *Island Stories*, p. 89.

70 Stears, *Out of the Ordinary*, pp. 133–58.

71 Jeff Farrell, 'Ex-SAS soldier claims no deal Brexit would be a "blessing"', *The i*, 16 December 2018.

72 Toby Neal, 'Party like it's 1945', *Express & Star*, 8 May 2020.

73 *Desert Island Discs*, BBC Radio 4, 19 February 1989.

74 Heffer, *Like the Roman*, p. 99.

75 Nicholas Owen, 'The Conservative Party and Indian Independence, 1945–1947', *Historical Journal* 46 (2013): 414; Schofield, *Enoch Powell*, p. 66; Peter Brooke, 'India, Post-Imperialism and the Origins of Enoch Powell's "Rivers of Blood" Speech', *Historical Journal* 50 (2007): 669–87.

76 Richard Austen Butler, *The Art of the Possible*, London, Hamish Hamilton, 1971, p. 141.

77 Heffer, *Like the Roman*, p. 115.

78 Enoch Powell, 'Circulated Letter from Enoch J. Powell to Ian Macleod', 15 February 1957, POLL 3.2.1.2, File 4.

79 Schofield, *Enoch Powell*, pp. 132–4.

80 Heffer, *Like the Roman*, pp. 398, 422, 843. See also Philip Stephens, *Britain Alone*, London, Faber & Faber, 2021, pp. 123–30.

81 David Edgerton, *The Rise And Fall of the British Nation*, London, Allen Lane, 2018, pp. 281–309, 313–18.

82 Mark Andrews, 'Age of affluence forged in the Black Country', *Express and Star*, 21 July 2021.

83 Harold Macmillan, speech at Bedford Football Club, 20 July 1957.

84 R. A. Butler, 'Commonwealth Migrants', 6 October 1961, C(61) 153, CAB 129/107.

85 Stuart Jeffries, 'Britain's most racist election: the story of Smethwick, 50 years on', *Guardian*, 15 October 2014.

86 Shirin Hirsch, *In the Shadow of Enoch Powell*, Manchester, Manchester University Press, 2018, pp. 43–4.

87 Sathnam Sanghera, 'The Turban Bus Dispute,' BBC Radio 4, 16 April 2018.

88 Roy Lewis, *Enoch Powell: Principle in Politics*, London, Cassell, 1979, pp. 115–17.

89 See https://www.enochpowell.net/fr-80.html; 'An Anti-Immigration Speech Divided Britain 50 Years Ago', *Morning Edition*, NPR, 20 April 2018.

90 Leo Benedictus, 'How the British fell out of love with drugs', *Guardian*, 24 February 2011.

91 'Paul McCartney', *Playboy*, December 1984.

92 Alex Sayf Cummings, '"No Pakistanis"', *Salon*, 14 April 2013.

93 Mary Whitehouse, *Who Does She Think She Is?*, London, New English Library, 1971, p. 29. See also Ben Thompson, *Ban This Filth!*, London, Faber & Faber, 2012.

94 Alan Bennett, 'An Englishman Abroad', BBC, 1983, 60 mins.

95 Helen Weathers, 'My mother was a snob', *Daily Mail*, 28 May 2008.

96 Schofield, *Enoch Powell*, pp. 120–1.

97 Rob Waters, 'Black Power on the Telly', *Journal of British Studies* 54 (2015): 947–70.

98 'Coloured family attacked', *The Times*, 1 May 1968.

99 'Town that has lost its reason', *Observer*, 14 July 1968; 'Coloureds not joining the police', *Express & Star*, 22 April 1968.

100 Ibid.

101 Maurice Toaland, quoted in Hirsch, *Shadow of Enoch Powell*, pp. 85–7.

102 Diana Spearman, 'Enoch Powell's postbag', *New Society*, 9 May 1968; Amy Whipple, 'Revisiting the "Rivers of Blood" controversy', *Journal of British Studies* 48 (2009): 717–35.

103 S. Zaidi and H. Waqar, 'The Janus-face of Techno-nationalism', *Technology and Culture* 49 (2008): 62–88.

104 See http://enochpowell.info/wp-content/uploads/Speeches/Oct%201 967-Feb%201968.pdf

105 Enoch Powell, quoted in Schofield, *Enoch Powell*, p. 277, and Robert Saunders, *Yes to Europe! The 1975 Referendum and Seventies Britain*, Cambridge, Cambridge University Press, 2018, p. 266.

106 Paul Gilroy, *There Ain't No Black in the Union Jack*, London, Routledge, 1992, pp. 49–50.

107 Enoch Powell, *Wrestling with the Angel*, London, Sheldon, 1977, pp. 14–19; Enoch Powell, 'How the Church Militant is fighting the wrong fight', *The Times*, 25 November 1970.

108 Powell, *Wrestling with the Angel*, p. 3.

109 Lenny Henry, *Who Am I Again?*, London, Faber & Faber, 2019, p. 169.

110 Ibid., p. 139.

111 Ibid., p. 187.

112 See https://anth1001.files.wordpress.com/2014/04/enoch-powell_spe ech.pdf

113 'Caparo in administration', *Express & Star*, 20 October 2015; West Midlands Regional Economic Development Institute Partnership, 'West Midlands Combined Authority State of the Region Report', July (2020).

114 https://jimmysirrelslovechild.co.uk/fans/exeter-v-wolves-1978; Sanghera, *Empireland*, p. 5.

115 'John Barnes interview', *Independent*, 31 May 2013.

116 'Meet Punjabi Wolves', *Guardian*, 15 December 2015.

117 'Priti Patel says fans have right to boo', *Independent*, 14 June 2021. Gareth Southgate, 'Dear England', *Football Tribune*, 8 June 2021.

118 ITV News, 'Pensioner admits sending racist and threatening emails to MPs,' ITV News, 4 June 2018, https://www.itv.com/news/2018-06-04/ pensioner-admits-sending-racist-and-threatening-emails-to-mps

119 David Lammy, *Tribes, A Search for Belonging in a Divided Society*, (Constable, 2020) p. 158.

120 Marion Brennan, 'Wolves fans buy part of club's history from landmark city church', *Express & Star*, 17 November 2017, https://www.expressands tar.com/news/2017/11/17/take-a-pew---and-a-slice-of-wolves-history/

121 Krishan Kumar, *The Making of English National Identity*, Cambridge, Cambridge University Press, 2003, p. 272.

5 GREENWICH

1 Imogen West-Knights, 'Was the Millennium Dome really so bad?', *Guardian*, 12 March 2020.

2 Adam Nicolson, *Regeneration*, London, HarperCollins 1999, p. 1.

3 Francis Fukuyama, *The End of History and the Last Man*, New York, Free Press, 1992.

4 'Oasis star Noel Gallagher's shocking revelation', *Daily Mail*, 24 September 2008.

5 'Britain's 20 favourite meals', *Daily Mirror*, 11 December 2018.

6 *Arsène Wenger*, directed by Gabriel Clarke and Christian Jeanpierre, Amazon Prime, 2021, 1 hr 35 mins.

7 Mark Leonard, *Britain^TM*, London, Demos, 1999, pp. 4–5.

8 Simon Partridge, *The British Union State*, London, Catalyst Press, 1999.

9 Norman Davies, *The Isles: A History*, New York, Oxford University Press, 1999, p. xxv; Linda Colley at https://webarchive.nationalarchives.gov.uk/ukgwa/20040809182858/http://www.pm.gov.uk/output/Page3049.asp

10 See http://enochpowell.info/wp-content/uploads/Speeches/Nov%201973-Feb%201974.pdf

11 Ibid., 241.

12 Barbara Castle, *The Castle Diaries, 1974–76*, London, Weidenfeld & Nicolson, 1980, p. 28.

13 See https://www.youtube.com/watch?v=d-EeiAZfFB0

14 See https://media.nationalarchives.gov.uk/index.php/rabies-outbreak/

15 Saunders, *Yes to Europe!*, pp. 233–4, 250–1.

16 Ibid., pp. 187–9.

17 Ibi., p. 20.

18 Ibid., pp. 383–5.

19 See https://www.margaretthatcher.org/document/102692

20 See https://www.margaretthatcher.org/document/103864

21 See https://www.youtube.com/watch?v=JdEVmIRlozM

22 See https://www.margaretthatcher.org/document/104989

23 See https://www.youtube.com/watch?v=UhpZ7vY8Lrg

24 See https://www.margaretthatcher.org/document/102990; see also https://www.margaretthatcher.org/document/107240

25 See Brian Harrison, *Finding a Role*, Oxford, Oxford University, 2012.

26 Duncan Weldon, *Two Hundred Years of Muddling Through*, London, Abacus, 2001, p. 260.

27 'The Good Old Days', quoted in Raphael Samuel, *Island Stories* II, New York, Verso, 1998, p. 334.

28 Samuel, *Island Stories*, p. 347.

29 See https://www.ons.gov.uk/employmentandlabourmarket/peopleinw ork/employmentandemployeetypes/articles/thehistoryofstrikesinth euk/2015-09-21.

30 Margaret Thatcher, quoted in Samuel, *Island Stories*, p. 337.

31 Matthew Parris, *Chance Witness*, London, Penguin, 2013, pp. 194, 198.

32 Quoted in Charles Moore, *Margaret Thatcher: The Authorized Biography* I, London, Penguin, 2014, p. 453.

33 Andrew Marr, *The Real Elizabeth*, New York, Holt, 2011, p. 248.

34 Letter from Robert Armstrong quoted in Dan Davies, *In Plain Sight*, London, Quercus, 2014, p. 416.

35 'Jimmy Savile', *Independent on Sunday*, 22 July 1990.

36 Davies, *In Plain Sight*, p. 47.

37 *The Report of the Investigation into Matters Relating to Savile*, Leeds, Leeds TH NHS Trust 2014, pp. 48, 143–62.

38 E. J. Hobsbawm, *Nations and Nationalism Since 1780*, Cambridge, Cambridge University Press, 1990, p. 143.

39 Owen Gibson, 'Margaret Thatcher era left mark on football', *Guardian*, 9 April 2013.

40 Martin Bagot, 'Bernard Ingham still refuses to say sorry', *Liverpool Echo*, 26 April 2016.

41 Lord Justice Taylor, *The Hillsborough Stadium Disaster: Final Report*, London, HM Stationery Office, 1990.

42 David Conn, *The Football Business: Fair Game in the '90s?*, Edinburgh, Mainstream, 1997, pp. 175–6.

43 'Toxteth Riots', BBC News, 30 December 2011.

44 Ibid.

45 Andy Beckett, *Promised You a Miracle*, London, Allen Lane, 2015, p. 303.

46 See https://www.margaretthatcher.org/document/107834.

47 See https://www.margaretthatcher.org/document/107332.

48 Ibid.

49 See https://johnmajorarchive.org.uk/1993/04/22/mr-majors-speech-to-conservative-group-for-europe-22-april-1993/

50 See John Harris, 'Marxism today: the forgotten visionaries', *Guardian*, 29 September 2015.

51 Francesca Klug, *Constitutional Reform*, London, Constitution Unit, 2020.

52 Dave Haslam, 'Strangeways Here We Come: Ecstasy', *London Review of Books*, 23 January 2003.

53   Tony Blair, *A Journey*, London, Arrow Books, 2011, p. 257.

54   Private conversation.

55   Tony Blair, speech at launch of Millennium Dome, 24 February 1998.

56   Nicolson, *Regeneration*, p. 240.

57   House of Commons Select Committee on Culture Media and Sport, 'The Millennium Dome, Minutes of Evidence', 2 December 1997.

58   Peter Oborne, *The Rise of Political Lying*, New York, Simon & Schuster, 2005, pp. 3–4.

59   Nicolson, *Regeneration*, pp. 260–1.

60   Blair, *A Journey*, p. 256.

61   Tony Blair, speech to Sedgefield Constituency Labour Party, see https://www.theguardian.com/politics/2007/may/10/labourleadership.labour2

62   Tony Blair, speech to the Labour Party conference, see https://www.theguardian.com/politics/2006/sep/26/labourconference.labour3

63   Tom Baldwin, *Ctrl Alt Delete*, London, Hurst & Co., 2018, pp. 45, 131–9.

64   Ibid., pp. 9–13.

65   Andrew Roberts, *The Aachen Memorandum*, London, Weidenfeld & Nicolson, 1995.

66   See https://www.city-journal.org/html/after-modernism-11801.html

67   Roger Scruton, *England: An Elegy*, London, Bloomsbury, 2000, pp. vii, 85.

68   See https://conservative-speeches.sayit.mysociety.org/speech/601112

69   'Thousands march for countryside', *Daily Telegraph*, 22 September 2002.

70   Paul Doyle, 'We don't need Kroenke's money', *Guardian*, 27 April 2007.

71   'Tales and wonder', *Observer*, 28 June 1998.

72   Nicholas Watt and Patrick Wintour, 'How immigration came to haunt Labour', *Guardian*, 24 March 2015.

73   See http://www.britishpoliticalspeech.org/speech-archive.htm?speech=279.

74   Blair, *A Journey*, p. 248.

75   Lawrence Freedman, 'Force and the International Community', *International Relations* 3 (2017): 107–24.

76   Tony Blair, 'Memo from Tony Blair to George W. Bush, July 28, 2002', cited in House of Commons, *The Report of the Iraq Inquiry Executive Summary*, London, House of Commons, 2016, p. 15.

77   See https://www.theguardian.com/uk/2005/sep/27/labourconference.speeches

78 See https://www.ukpol.co.uk/tony-blair-2001-speech-at-lord-mayors-banquet/

79 Andrew Porter, 'Brown targets Tory heartlands Tory values', *Daily Telegraph*, 25 September 2007.

80 See https://www.theguardian.com/politics/2007/feb/27/immigrationpolicy.race

81 Jez Butterworth, *Jerusalem*, London, Royal Court, 2009.

82 Simon Bowers, 'Libor-rigging scandal', *Guardian*, 4 July 2016.

83 Andrew Parker, 'Ten More Charged in KPMG Tax Shelter Case', *Financial Times*, 18 October 2005.

84 Martin Arnold, 'HSBC hopes to leave era of scandals behind', *Financial Times*, 18 February 2018.

85 'Boris Johnson: Ceremony left me "crying like a baby"', BBC News, 28 July 2012.

86 See https://general-election-2010.co.uk/2010-general-election-manifestos/Conservative-Party-Manifesto-2010.pdf, 21.

87 Andrew Hough, 'Revealed: David Cameron's favourite childhood book', *Daily Telegraph*, 29 October 2010.

88 See https://www.gov.uk/government/speeches/eu-speech-at-bloomberg.

89 Tim Ross and Tom McTague, *Betting the House*, London, Biteback, 2015, p. 173.

90 'Nigel Farage: "Labour hate concept of Englishness"', BBC News, 21 November 2014.

91 Philip Cowley and Denis Kavanagh, *The British General Election of 2015*, London, Palgrave Macmillan, 2016, p. 172.

92 See https://www.theguardian.com/politics/2006/oct/04/conservatives2006.conservatives

93 Stephens, *Britain Alone*, pp. 355–6.

94 Rowena Mason, Heather Steward and Jessica Elgot, 'David Cameron rejects charge of crying wolf', *Guardian*, 9 May 2016.

95 Oliver Wainwright, 'Bikes, buses and bridges: Boris Johnson's nine biggest design blunders', *Guardian*, 27 July 2016.

96 Accessed at https://www.greenwichsociety.org.uk/News/Knight-Dragon-Consultation/

97 Oliver Wainwright, 'Revealed: how developers exploit flawed planning system to minimise affordable housing', *Guardian*, 25 June 2015.

98 Robert Booth and Aamna Mohdin, 'Shared ownership households complain of housing segregation', *Guardian*, 1 April 2019.

99 Robert Macfarlane, *The Old Ways*, London, Penguin, 2012; Robert Macfarlane and Jackie Morris, *The Lost Words*, London, Penguin, 2017.

100 Tom Baldwin and Marc Stears, 'In Search of Englishness,' *The New European*, May 1, 2024, Tom Baldwin, *Keir Starmer: The Biography,* (William Collins 2024, 2nd edition) p. 399.

101 Jamie Bennett-Ness, 'Shocking moment men with machetes fight in Greenwich street', *News Shopper*, 3 June 2021.

102 See https://queercircle.org/about/

6 BLACKPOOL

1 Stanley Houghton, *Hindle Wakes*, Cornell University Press, 2009, first published 1912.

2 Priestley, *English Journey*, p. 215; Alan Brodie and Matthew Whitfield, *Blackpool's Seaside Heritage*, Swindon, English Heritage, 2014, pp. 51–93; Madeleine Bunting, *The Seaside: England's Love Affair*, London, Granta, 2023, pp. 275–7.

3 https://www.exasol.com/2017-04-13-over-64-million-prescriptions-of-antidepressants-dispensed-per-year-in-england/; Sarah O' Connor, 'Left behind', *Financial Times*, 16 November 2017; https://www.gov.uk/government/statistics/english-indices-of-deprivation-2019

4 Rosie Waites, 'Blackpool: Why isn't it marketed to foreign tourists?', BBC News, 14 October 2011.

5 'Why have so many children's homes opened in Blackpool?', BBC News, 11 August 2022.

6 Ibid.; https://www.thedungeons.com/blackpool/whats-inside/what-is-the-dungeon/drop-dead/

7 David Conn, 'Oystons ordered to buy out Blackpool shareholder', *Guardian*, 6 November 2017.

8 See https://www.visitblackpool.com/detail/blackpool-beach-275980/

9 See https://www.thestripescompany.com/shop/Blackpool-Heritage-Deckchairs

10 Nikolaus Pevsner, *The Buildings of England: Lancashire, the Rural North*, London, Penguin, 1969, p. 68.

11 Helen Nugent, 'Anger piles up over Blackpool comedy carpet destruction', *Guardian*, 20 March 2012.

12 Bunting, *The Seaside*, p. 278; Becky Pemberton, 'Loose Women's Coleen Nolan is blasted by Blackpool residents', MailOnline, 4 November 2015.

13 See https://www.greatbritishlife.co.uk/people/22615992.lancashire-school-helped-victoria-actress-jenna-coleman-road-stardom/

14 Alwyn Turner, *All In It Together*, London, Profile Books, 2021, p. 128.

15 *Roy Chubby Brown: Britain's Rudest Comedian*, directed by Will Yapp, Channel 4, 2007.

16 Zara Whelan, 'Roy Chubby Brown on Brexit, Jeremy Corbyn and being called racist', *Daily Post*, 27 September 2017.

17 Martin Emmerson, 'Chubby divorced by battered wife', *Daily Mirror*, 7 February 1998; Roy Chubby Brown, *Common As Muck*, London, Hachette, 2006.

18 See https://www.facebook.com/rcbshow/posts/386509332845102

19 Ibid.

20 Turner, *All In It Together*, p. 131.

21 Andrew Tetterborn, 'The snobbery of Roy Chubby Brown's critics', *Spectator*, 10 September 2021.

22 Richard Cracknell and Richard Tunnicliffe, *Social Background of MPs 1979–2019*, London, House of Commons Library, 2022.

23 Simon Price, 'How my research into pop's posh takeover was hijacked', *Guardian*, 24 February 2014.

24 https://www.thefulltoss.com/england-cricket-blog/white-posh-english-crickets-class-problem/

25 Brian Logan, 'When did comedians get so middle-class?', *Guardian*, 21 July 2010.

26 Katie Razzall, 'Jimmy Carr', BBC News, 7 February 2022.

27 'No female politician today', *The Times*, 2 October 2002.

28 Mary Ann Sieghart, 'Still in the greasy spoon era', *The Times*, 9 October 2002.

29 Bunting, *The Seaside*, p. 284; John Windsor, 'All up front, but now just a little behind', *Independent*, 22 January 1994.

30 Wolfgang Streeck, 'How Will Capitalism End?', *New Left Review* 87 (2014).

31 Centre for Local Economic Strategies, *A Summary of Austerity in the North West and a Case Study of Blackpool Council: Final Report*, Manchester, Centre for Local Economic Strategies, 2014.

32 See https://ifs.org.uk/publications/2021-annual-report-education-spending-england

33 See https://unherd.com/2019/11/who-cares-about-immigration/

34 https://www.blackpooljsna.org.uk/Blackpool-Profile/Ethnicity.aspx; Colin Ainscough, 'This is how many EU citizens in Blackpool have applied to stay in the UK after Brexit', *Blackpool Gazette*, 11 February 2020.

35 BBC News, 'EU Referendum: North West towns vote Leave as cities votes Remain', BBC News, 24 June 2016.

36 https://twitter.com/Nigel_Farage/status/1566471401153957888?ref_src=twsrc%5Etfw%7Ctwcamp%5Etweetembed%7Ctwterm%5E1566471401153957888%7Ctwgr%5Edc37d0dba4d20a87056f6a01a3aa43e55e4086f6%7Ctwcon%5Es1_&ref_url=https%3A%2F%2Fwww.theguardian.com%2Fpolitics%2F2022%2Fsep%2F05%2Fnigel-farage-gin-sparks-cornish-controversy

37 Andrew Sparrow, 'Nigel Farage: parts of Britain are "like a foreign land"', *Guardian*, 8 February 2014.

38 Maria Sobolewska and Robert Ford, *Brexitland: Identity, Diversity and the Reshaping of British Politics*, Cambridge, Cambridge University Press, 2020, pp. 89–214.

39 Will Jennings and Gerry Stoker, 'The Bifurcation of Politics', *Political Quarterly* 3.87 (2016): 372–82.

40 David Goodhart, *The Road to Somewhere*, London, Hurst & Co., 2017, p. 5.

41 Will Jennings and Gerry Stoker, 'Tilting Towards the Cosmopolitan Axis?', *Political Quarterly* 3.88 (2017): 359–69.

42 Maria Sobolewska and Ford, *Brexitland*, pp. 89–214.

43 Jonathan Portes, 'Immigration and Wages', *National Institute of Economic and Social Research*, 11 June 2016; 'The Labour Market Effects of Immigration', The Migration Observatory at the University of Oxford, 24 March 2023.

44 Boris Johnson, 'Denmark has got it wrong', *Daily Telegraph*, 5 August 2018; Greg Wilford, 'Bojo cleared', *Sun*, 20 November 2018.

45 See https://www.facebook.com/ads/library/?active_status=all&ad_type=political_and_issue_ads&country=GB&id=264312184485119&view_all_page_id=8807334278&search_type=page&media_type=all

46 See at https://www.theguardian.com/politics/2001/mar/04/conservatives.speeches

47 Sparrow, 'Nigel Farage'; Leo McInstry, 'For the sneering, posturing Labour the North is a foreign land', *Daily Express*, 14 December 2019.

48 Zadie Smith, 'Fences: A Brexit Diary', *New York Review of Books*, 18 August 2016.

49 See, for instance, Richard Dawkins, 'Ignoramuses should have no say on our EU membership – and that includes me', *Prospect*, 9 June 2016; 'Professor A. C. Grayling's Letter', *New College of the Humanities*, 1 July 2016.

50 See https://ukandeu.ac.uk/brexit-witness-archive/tom-baldwin/

51 See https://www.politics.co.uk/mp-comment/2022/01/10/we-cannot-balance-environmentalism-on-the-backs-of-the-poor-as-energy-costs-soar/

52 See https://www.youtube.com/watch?v=OrdBj-E9RUY

53 House of Commons, 23 January 2020, vol. 670, cols 468–471.

54 John K. Walton, *The Blackpool Landlady*, Manchester, Manchester University Press, 1978.

55 'The Red Wall reconsidered', *The Economist*, 31 March 2021; Deborah Mattinson, *Beyond the Red Wall*, London, Biteback, 2020, pp. 203–4.

56 Geoffrey Evans and James Tilley, *The New Politics of Class*, Oxford, Oxford University Press, 2017, pp. 175–88.

57 Sobolewska and Ford, *Brexitland*.

58 Mattinson, *Beyond the Red Wall*, p. 129.

59 Ibid., pp. 10–11.

60 Zadie Smith, 'North West London Blues', *New York Review of Books*, 12 July 2012.

61 YouGov/Prospect survey results, 26–29 January 2014.

62 Toby Helm, 'One year on, most voters say Brexit has gone badly', *Observer*, 25 December 2021.

63 'Blackpool hotel to house 220 asylum seekers', BBC News, 8 September 2021; Sarah Turnnidge, 'No evidence asylum seekers have used pets to argue against deportation', *Full Fact*, 13 December 2021.

64 'From humble beginnings to world's busiest train station', *Blackpool Gazette*, 10 December 2018.

65 'Plans revealed for Blackpool snow dome', *Blackpool Gazette*, 15 October 2009.

66 Josh Gorton, 'World Matchplay darts', *Blackpool Gazette*, July 20, 2023; Bagheot, 'Inside the Banter-Industrial Complex', *The Economist*, December 20, 2023.

67 'Blackpool's Landmark Attractions Set to Benefit from £38.9 million Investment', UK Government, 30 March 2010; Shelagh Parkinson, '10 years on', *Lancslive*, 4 April 2020; 'Levelling up investment unlocks £300 million Blackpool regeneration', UK Government, 11 November 2022.

68 Information from Blackpool Council.

69 'Hitting the poorest places hardest', Centre for Regional Economic and Social Research, Sheffield Hallam University, 2013, p. 14.

70 'Blackpool Town Prospectus: 2030 agenda for action', Blackpool Partnership Board, 2 February 2022, 29 f.

71 See Rachel Sylvester, 'The Times Education Commission', *The Times*, 15 June 2022, p. 24.

72 Heather Rolfe, Sunder Katwala and Steve Ballinger, 'Shifting Views: Tracking attitudes to immigration', British Future, October 2022.

73 Shelagh Parkinson, 'Keir Starmer says skilled jobs and a conference return are among his hopes for Blackpool', *Blackpool Gazette*, 15 July 2021.

74 Alice Suffield, 'Everything Keir Starmer told us ' LancsLive, May 1, 2023.

75 Joe Mayes, Andre Tartar and Demetrios Pogkas, 'UK's Poorer Regions Fall Further Behind', *Bloomberg*, 25 January 2023.

76 Blackpool Opportunity Area, 'Creating a Continuum of Provision to support high needs pupils', Evaluation Report, December 2021.

77 Amy Fenton, 'It was horrendous', *Lancslive*, 11 January 2023; Susan Newton, 'Blackpool care home where meds go missing and incidents hidden from loved ones', *Lancslive*, 11 May 2022.

78 James Bloodworth, *Hired*, London, Atlantic Books, 2019, p. 112.

79 Hilary Cottam, *Radical Help*, London, Verso, 2017; Matthew Brown and Rhian E. Jones, *Paint Your Town Red: How Preston Took Back Control and Your Town Can Too*, London, Repeater Books, 2021.

80 Tabby Kinder, 'Simon Sadler: Blackpool's block trade king', *Financial Times*, 1 June 2022.

7 OXFORD

1 Charles Moore, 'The Road from Damascus', *Spectator*, 14 January 2012.

2 Geoffrey Tyack, *Oxford*, Oxford, Oxford University Press, 1998, p. 301.

3 See http://www.oxfordhistory.org.uk/high/tour/south/095_101.html

4 Cecil John Rhodes, *Will and Codicils of the Rt. Hon. Cecil John Rhodes*, Oxford, Oxford University Press, 1929, p. 12.

5 Eve Fairbanks, 'The birth of Rhodes Must Fall', *Guardian*, 18 November 2015.

6 Tom Jenkins, 'Oxford College sends out security email', *Tab*, 6 February 2017.

7 Abby Young-Powell, 'Oxford Union accused of racism', *Guardian*, 29 May 2015.

8 Richard Adams and Helena Bengtsson, 'Oxford accused of "social apartheid"', *Guardian*, 19 October 2017.

9 Simukai Chigudu, 'More than just a statue', *Guardian*, 24 May 2021.

10 Fran Way, 'Oxford MP Anneliese Dodds on BBC about Cecil Rhodes statue', *Oxford Mail*, 8 June 2020.

11 Josh White, Daniel Martin and Jim Norton, 'Rhodes: now the backlash', *Daily Mail*, 19 June 2020.

12 Larisa Brown and Rebecca Camber, 'Toppling the past', *Daily Mail*, 10 June 2020.

13 See https://www.facebook.com/watch/live/?ref=watch_permalink&y+ 406443460315349

14 See https://www.oriel.ox.ac.uk/about-college/news-events/news/ statement-governing-body-oriel-college

15 *Report of a Commission of Inquiry Established by Oriel College, Oxford into Issues Associated with Memorials to Cecil Rhodes*, by the Commission of Inquiry Established by Oriel College, Oxford, April 2021, p. 53.

16 Ibid., p. 139.

17 Ibid., pp. 98–126.

18 Javier Espinoza and Gordon Rayner, 'Cecil Rhodes statue to remain', *The Telegraph*, 29 January 2016.

19 Camilla Turner, '"Common Sense" kept Rhodes standing, say Oriel insiders', *Sunday Telegraph*, 30 May 2021.

20 Tom Stoppard, *The Invention of Love*, New York, Grove Press, 1997, p. 17.

21 Ibid., p. 102.

22 Anthony Grenville, 'The refugee scholars', *Jewish Renaissance*, October 2019.

23 See https://www.royal.uk/coronation-day-speech-2-june-1953; Ryan Parry, 'I could have poisoned the Queen!', *Daily Mirror*, 19 November 2003.

24 *The Book of Common Prayer*, London, John Baskerville, 1662.

25 Geoffrey Elton, *The English*, London, Wiley-Blackwell, 1992, pp. xii, 222–4.

26 Ralph Miliband, *The State in Capitalist Society*, London, Weidenfeld & Nicolson, 1969, pp. 66–7.

27 Ibid., pp. 40, 246–8.

28 Ralph Miliband, *Socialism in a Sceptical Age*, London, Polity Press, 1994.

29 Paul Bolton, *Education: Historical Statistics*, standard note: SN/ SG/4252, London, House of Commons Library, 2012; Sean Coughlan, 'The symbolic target of 50% at university reached', BBC News, 26 September 2019.

30 Brian Roberts, *Cecil Rhodes*, London, Hamish Hamilton, 1987, p. 49.

31 https://sport.etoncollege.com/OpponentMaps.asp?Id=65

32 Clive Aslet and Greg Hurst, 'Eton's £18m hall', *The Times*, 9 June 2015.

33 Peter Hitchens, 'The Oxbridge war on private schools doesn't help the poor', *Mail on Sunday*, 6 November 2022.

34 Sean Coughlan, 'Thousand fewer UK students at Oxbridge', BBC News, 26 February 2019.

35 Alastair McCall, 'Top universities fall short', *Sunday Times*, 17 September 2021; Hannah Richardson, 'Oxbridge uncovered', BBC News, 20 October 2017; The Sutton Trust, 'Eight schools send as many pupils to Oxbridge as three-quarters of all schools', *Sutton Trust*, 7 December 2018.

36 Adrian Wooldridge, *The Aristocracy of Talent*, London, Allen Lane, 2021, p. 312.

37 Simon Kuper, *Chums*, London, Profile, 2022, p. 3.

38 Peter Mair, *Ruling the Void*, London, Verso, 2013, p. 2.

39 Owen Jones, *The Establishment*, London, Penguin, 2014, pp. xvii, 15, 256.

40 *Daily Mail*, 4 November 2016; *Daily Mail*, 18 April 2017.

41 See Matthew Goodwin, *The New Elite*, London, Penguin, 2023; Paul Collier, *The Future of Capitalism*, London, Penguin, 2019, pp. 3–4; and Alistair Heath, 'The blob is taking back control', *Daily Telegraph*, 24 November 2021.

42 See https://policyexchange.org.uk/publication/academic-free dom-in-the-uk-2/

43 Steve Hilton, 'Steve Hilton: Yes there is a Deep State', Fox News, 3 February 2018.

44 'Woke, Cancel Culture and White Privilege', Ipsos Mori/King's College, 12 May 2022.

45 Tim Shipman, 'How the Tories weaponised woke', *Sunday Times*, 13 June 2021; Rob Merrick, 'Tory insiders', *Independent*, 5 August 2020.

46 See: https://policyexchange.org.uk/publication/academic-free dom-in-the-uk/; https://www.civitas.org.uk/publications/academic-freedom-in-our-universities/

47 Anna Fazackerley, 'Gavin Williamson using "misleading" research', *Guardian*, 27 February 2021.

48 Sally-Anne Huxtable, Corinne Fowler, Christo Kefalas and Emma Slocombe (eds), *Interim Report on the Connections Between Colonialism and Properties now in the Care of the National Trust, Including Links with Historic Slavery*, Swindon, National Trust, 2020.

49 The Common Sense Group, 'Letters: Britain's heroes', *Daily Telegraph*, 9 November 2020.

50 Vanessa Thorpe and James Tapper, 'National Trust sees off culture war rebellion in an AGM of discontent', *Observer*, 30 October 2021; Jack Blackburn, 'National Trust is building its reputation, poll shows', *The Times*, 30 September 2023.

51 Jon Alexander and Ariane Conrad, *Citizens*, Kingston-upon-Thames, Canbury Press, 2022, pp. 180–6.

52 Robert Jenrick: 'Keir Starmer's Labour is complicit in the woke takeover of Britain's institutions,' *Daily Telegraph*, 26 January 2024.

53 James Delingpole, 'BBC's A Christmas Carol', *Spectator*, 26 December 2019; Kevin Schofield, 'BBC Director General Tim Davie to speak at private meeting of Tory MPs', *Huffington Post*, 20 October 2023.

54 Peter Walker, 'BBC Political Editor given bodyguard', *Guardian*, 24 September 2017.

55 Sky News, 'Lord Adonis: "BBC created Brexit and Farage"', YouTube, 8 April 2018.

56 Jim Waterson, 'Emily Maitlis says "active Tory party agent" shaping BBC news output', *Guardian*, 24 August 2022; Alex Farber, 'BBC cuts make Have I Got News for You the last satire standing', *The Times*, 31 March 2023; Jim Waterson, 'BBC licence fee to be abolished in 2027 and funding frozen', *Guardian*, 16 January 2022.

57 Gavin Cordon, 'Boris Johnson: three decades of scandals, blunders and rows', *Evening Standard*, 12 January 2022.

58 See https://www.carnegieuktrust.org.uk/blog-posts/loss-of-public-trust-in-government-is-the-biggest-threat-to-democracy-in-england/

59 James Grant, 'Letter Goes Viral', *Daily Mail*, 13 January 2022; Max Hastings, 'I Was Boris Johnson's Boss', *Guardian*, 24 June 2019.

60 Purnell, *Just Boris*, pp. 129–30.

61 Jin Pickard, 'David Cameron and the Bullingdon Night of the Broken Window', *Financial Times*, 4 April 2010.

62 See https://www.ox.ac.uk/about/facts-and-figures/student-numbers

63 Luke Harding, 'Oxford University criticised for accepting oligarch's £75m donation', *Guardian*, 3 November 2015; Henry Foy and Max Seddon, 'From Russian oil to rock'n'roll', *Financial Times*, 6 June 2019; Figures for proportion of students from outside the UK and Europe are taken from https://www.bsg.ox.ac.uk/2020-21-annual-report

64 Andrew Jack, 'Reuben brothers fund new Oxford college with £80m donation', *Financial Times*, 11 June 2020.

65 Catherine Bennett, 'Just what was it exactly that Oxford University saw in the billionaire boss of Ineos?', *Observer*, 24 January 2021.

66 Branwen Jeffreys, 'Oxford University accepts £150m from US private equity boss', BBC News, 19 June 2019.

67 Billy Kenber, 'Oxford's Linacre College to be renamed after £155m Vietnamese donation', *The Times*, 3 November 2021.

68 Richard Kirbaj and Sian Griffiths, 'Security services fear the march on universities of Beijing's spies', *Sunday Times*, 27 October 2019; Rory Sullivan, 'Oxford students told to submit work on China anonymously', *Independent*, 28 September 2020; Matt Dathan and Charlie Parker, 'Oxford renames 120-year-old Wykeham professorship', *The Times*, 9 February 2021.

69 Michael Holden and Guy Faulconbridge, 'Meghan accuses UK royals of racism', *Reuters*, 8 March 2021.

70 'What are the accusations against Prince Andrew?' BBC News, 4 January 2022; Victoria Ward and Josie Ensor, 'Queen to help pay for £12m Prince Andrew settlement', *Daily Telegraph*, 15 February 2022; Christine Emba, 'What Prince Andrew's settlement says about wealth and accountability', *Washington Post*, 15 February 2022.

71 Mary O'Connor, 'Police to investigate Prince Charles' charity', BBC News, 17 February 2022; 'King Charles charity: No further police action over Prince's Foundation honours probe', BBC News, 21 August 2023.

72 Ben Stockton, 'Justice for Sale', *The Bureau for Investigative Journalism*, 8 July 2021.

73 Susan Coughtrie, 'The UK as a key nexus for protecting media freedom and preventing corruption globally', Foreign Policy Centre, 9 December 2020.

74 Owen Bowcott, 'Justice "only for the wealthy"', *Guardian*, 20 September 2018.

75 Fair Trials, 'One in ten of the remand population in England and Wales have been in prison for more than a year', *Fair Trials*, 1 December 2021.

76 Richard Whiting, 'University and Locality', in *The History of the University of Oxford* III, ed. Brian Harrison, Oxford, Clarendon Press, 1994, pp. 561–4.

77 *Report of a Commission of Inquiry Established by Oriel College*, p. 139.

78 C. J. Day, 'The University and the City', in *The History of the University of Oxford* VI: *Nineteenth-Century Oxford, Part 1*, eds M. G. Brock and M. C. Curthoys, Oxford, Clarendon Press, 1997, p. 442.

79 Naomi Harring, 'Cutteslowe Walls', *Oxford Mail*, 6 September 2018.

80 Bernard Richards, 'Oscar Wilde and Ruskin's Road', *The Wildean* 40 (2012): 74–88.

81 https://www.ox.ac.uk/research/engage-with-us/local-community/part-of-oxford/economy

82 'Chancellor welcomes New VC of Oxford Irene Tracey', University of Oxford, 10 January 2023.

83 'New Vice-Chancellor ready to fire and wire', University of Oxford, 10 January 2023.

84 Nicola Woolcock, 'Oxford has let down transgender students, vice-chancellor says', *The Times*, 3 October 2023; Canqi Li, 'In conversation with Prof. Irene Tracey', *Oxford Student*, 12 June 2023.

85 Tim Ross, 'Revenge of the Blob', Politico, 9 July 2022; Camilla Turner, 'Liz Truss', *Sunday Telegraph*, 5 February 2023.

86 Henry Mance, 'Is Britain Tiring of the Culture Wars?', *Financial Times*, 15 July 2022 and https://doc.cdn.yougov.com/vf1ghxf7kh/YG%20 trackers%20-%20Trust.pdf

87 Keir Starmer, Speech in Buckinghamshire, 12 December 2023.

88 Steve McQueen interview with David Olusoga, 'These are the Untold Stories of our Nation', *Sight and Sound*, 13 November 2020.

89 Meg Russell and Jack Sheldon, *Options for an English Parliament*, London, Constitution Unit, 2018.

90 Shanti Das, 'Rapper AJ Tracey: why I'm launching fund to help Black students at Oxford', *Observer*, 16 October 2022.

91 Sarah Gilbert and Catherine Green, *Vaxxers*, London, Hodder & Stoughton 2021.

92 See https://www.huffingtonpost.co.uk/entry/oxford-university-astrazeneca-vaccine-uk-flag-union-jack_uk_5fbfdd14c5b68ca87f827a0e

93 'Oxford and Cambridge University colleges hold £21bn in riches', *Guardian*, 18 May 2018.

94 Sebastian Shakespeare, 'Wafic Said's £3.3m shot in the arm', *Daily Mail*, 11 November 2020.

8 ENGLAND: ORDINARY HOPE

1 Robert Jenrick, commentary, Daily Mail, September 21, 2024.

2 Caroline Lucas, *Another England* (London: Penguin, 2024).

Acknowledgements

We began writing this book during the pandemic, when one of us was stuck in Sydney, Australia, leaving the other to travel around England, talking to people at a time when we were all more nervous about the future than usual. As such, we have depended even more than usual on the help, kindness and goodwill of many people, including some whose names we will never know.

We are hugely grateful to the brilliant team at Bloomsbury, especially Jasmine Horsey, Alexis Kirschbaum, Richard Collins, Hayley Camis, Molly McCarthy, and Francisco Vilhena. We would also like to thank our agents Georgina Capel and Catherine Clarke. Each of these hugely talented individuals not only believed in the book at key stages but provided crucial advice which made what you have here immeasurably better than it otherwise would have been. Further invaluable research assistance and technical support was provided by Alexander Fitzpatrick, Jamie Ranger and Mark Riboldi.

We are also indebted to the scores of people who talked with us about England over the years we were working on developing this argument. Most of them appear somewhere else in this book, so readers can see the power of their insights there. But our thinking was also shaped by conversations over many years with friends and colleagues, including Tim Allan, Danielle Allen, James Baggaley, Matthew Baldwin, Torsten Bell, Bill Bush, Alastair Campbell, Michael Freeden, Bonnie Honig, Mathew Humphrey, Sunder Katwala, Rachel Kinnock, Ferdinand Mount, Andrew Palmer, Anand Menon, Jonathan Rutherford, Emily Spence, Jane Stears, Daniel Stilitz, Amanda Tattersall, Joanna Thom, Nick Timothy,

Alan Todd, Eloise Todd, Luke Tryl, Chris Williams, Dan Whitaker, Jon Wilson and Hughie Wong. We also give a particular thanks to Ed Miliband, who first asked us to write about England, even if he probably wasn't very sure about what we'd come up with. Among the most generous of friends was the historian, Kit Kowol, who read the entire manuscript and provided essential guidance even when he was moving to Australia. We also owe a big debt to our colleagues and collaborators on other projects who often had to carry the burden for us while we were working on this, including the amazing teams at the Sydney and UCL Policy Labs, and the inspiring people on the Ordinary Hope project group.

Finally, we want to thank our immediate families. Rebecca, Frankie and Arthur, and Lizzy and Freya. They have asked the hardest questions and been the most sceptical, but they've always supported us on every step of the way. That is why this book is dedicated to them.

Index

About the Type

The text of this book is set in Linotype Stempel Garamond, a version of Garamond adapted and first used by the Stempel foundry in 1924. It is one of several versions of Garamond based on the designs of Claude Garamond. It is thought that Garamond based his font on Bembo, cut in 1495 by Francesco Griffo in collaboration with the Italian printer Aldus Manutius. Garamond types were first used in books printed in Paris around 1532. Many of the present-day versions of this type are based on the *Typi Academiae* of Jean Jannon cut in Sedan in 1615.

Claude Garamond was born in Paris in 1480. He learned how to cut type from his father and by the age of fifteen he was able to fashion steel punches the size of a pica with great precision. At the age of sixty he was commissioned by King Francis I to design a Greek alphabet, and for this he was given the honourable title of royal type founder. He died in 1561.